COMPUTER ARCHITECTURE AND IMPLEMENTATION

This textbook provides a clear and concise introduction to computer architecture and implementation. Two important themes are interwoven throughout the book. The first is an overview of the major concepts and design philosophies of computer architecture and organization. The second is the early introduction and use of analytic modeling of computer performance.

The author begins by describing the classic von Neumann architecture and then presents in detail a number of performance models and evaluation techniques. He goes on to cover user instruction set design, including RISC architecture. A unique feature of the book is its memory-centric approach – memory systems are discussed before processor implementations. The author also deals with pipelined processors, input/output techniques, queuing modes, and extended instruction set architectures. Each topic is illustrated with reference to actual IBM and Intel architectures.

The book contains many worked examples and over 130 homework exercises. It is an ideal textbook for a one-semester undergraduate course in computer architecture and implementation.

Harvey Cragon holds the Ernest J. Cockrell, Jr., Centennial Chair Emeritus in Engineering at the University of Texas at Austin. He is a member of the U.S. National Academy of Engineering, a Life Fellow of the IEEE, and a Fellow of the Association for Computing Machinery. He has over 30 years' industrial experience, including 25 years with Texas Instruments. He has written over 50 technical papers and holds 9 patents in the field of computer engineering.

COMPUTER ARCHITECTURE AND IMPLEMENTATION

HARVEY G. CRAGON

University of Texas at Austin

CAMBRIDGE
UNIVERSITY PRESS

PUBLISHED BY THE PRESS SYNDICATE OF THE UNIVERSITY OF CAMBRIDGE
The Pitt Building, Trumpington Street, Cambridge, United Kingdom

CAMBRIDGE UNIVERSITY PRESS
The Edinburgh Building, Cambridge CB2 2RU, UK   http://www.cup.cam.ac.uk
40 West 20th Street, New York, NY 10011-4211, USA   http://www.cup.org
10 Stamford Road, Oakleigh, Melbourne 3166, Australia
Ruiz de Alarcón 13, 28014 Madrid, Spain

First published 2000

Printed in the United States of America

Typeface Stone Serif 9.25/13 pt.   *System* LaTeX 2_ε [TB]

A catalog record for this book is available from the British Library.

Library of Congress Cataloging-in-Publication Data

Cragon, Harvey G.
      Computer architecture and implementation / Harvey G. Cragon.
          p.   cm.
      ISBN 0-521-65168-9 (hard.)
      1. Computer architecture.   I. Title.
   QA76.9.A73C74   2000
   004.2′2–dc21   99-16243
                                                             CIP

ISBN 0 521 65168 9 hardback

CONTENTS

PREFACE

This textbook is intended for use in a one-semester, upper-division undergraduate course. It is expected that the students will have had courses in logic design with state machines and assembly language programming. A course in data structures as well as basic operating systems would be helpful.

There are two major themes running through this book. The first theme is an overview of the major ideas and design philosophies of computer architecture and implementation with some insight into their historical development. We are inclined to forget the work of our predecessors in computer design; the few pages devoted to this topic may help to rectify this neglect.

The second theme is the introduction and use of analytic modeling of computer performance. I believe that engineering students should take an engineering approach to the study of computer architecture and implementation. Various design trade-off issues will be examined with analytical models. What is an engineering approach? Consider the following two quotations.

> "What distinguished the engineer from the technician is largely the ability to formulate and carry out the detailed calculations of forces and deflections, concentrations and flows, voltages and currents, that are required to test a proposed design on paper with regard to failure criteria. The ability to calculate is the ability to predict the performance of a design before it is built and tested." (Petroske 1996).
> "... it is much easier to have some vague notion about any subject, no matter what, than to arrive at the real truth about a single question, however simple that may be." (Descartes 1629).

In addition to the two major themes, this book will introduce students to a new vocabulary. Whenever a new topic is approached, it is inevitable that one learns a new vocabulary. Therefore, whenever a new word or term is introduced, this book attempts to provide a definition along with common synonyms. We recommend that students obtain a copy of a computer dictionary to support their studies. Reference can also be made to an on-line dictionary of computer terms at ⟨http://wombat.doc.ic.ac.uk/foldoc/index.html⟩.

One of the problems in the computer field is the lack of a standard set of terms. For example, the Intel x86 architecture uses the term linear address whereas I prefer the term virtual address, as used with the IBM S370 and S390. The reason for the preference is that the IBM S370 predates the virtual-memory version of the Intel x86 and established precedence. Thus, in the text, wherever possible, the term with precedence is used.

The von Neumann architecture is used in Chapter 1 to introduce the basic principles of computer architecture. Students should know what von Neumann proposed with this architecture and what its limitations were. These limitations were overcome in subsequent architectures while the underlying design remained unchanged.

Two architecture families will be extensively used for illustrations: The IBM S360/370/390 and the Intel x86 up to the Pentium Pro with MMX extensions. These two families represent the two most widely used processors today. For mainframe applications, the IBM family is preeminent in the world. The Intel family is found in approximately 90% of all personal computers. These two families are the most likely to be encountered by students after they finish their studies.

The sequence of presentation in this book differs from that found in other texts. It starts with a computer overview in Chapter 1 that covers the von Neumann architecture and some of its precursors. Chapter 2 introduces analytical performance modeling, learning curves, and other related evaluation techniques. The modeling technique will be used throughout the balance of the book.

Chapter 3 describes the issues in user instruction set design. The instruction set architecture taxonomy of addresses, data types, and operations is introduced. This chapter also provides a basic treatment of computer arithmetic and the IEEE floating-point standard.

Because a memory-centric view of a computer is taken, the text turns to memory implementation in Chapter 4. I believe that students should be exposed to memory systems before processors, as the process state is held memory and is the focus of how problems are solved. Further, I approach the memory system by first looking at virtual memory that provides the functionality required of large programs and large data sets.

Performance follows functionality, from a designer's point of view; thus caches are covered after virtual memory. The gap between the cache and the disk is then covered by describing interleaved memory and DRAM organizations. Performance models for hierarchical memories are used throughout the chapter to illustrate design trade-offs.

Following the chapter on memory, the issues of processor implementation are addressed. First, hardwired and microprogrammed implementations are covered in Chapter 5. Then Chapter 6 addresses the ideas and issues of pipelining. The techniques of performance models are interwoven with the functional descriptions of processor implementation.

Chapter 7 covers input/output. In this chapter we look at requirements for various workloads and examine how these requirements are satisfied in contemporary systems. Bus design and serial communications are discussed along with clock recovery and clock synchronization. A brief introduction to queuing theory is included in this chapter.

The concluding chapter, Chapter 8, covers extensions to the user instruction set architecture that support operating systems, virtual memory, caches, and multiprocessors.

This chapter concludes with a description of the MMX extensions to the Intel Pentium Pro.

A final goal of this book is to enable students to read the current literature on computers with understanding and appreciation of the ideas presented. This is accomplished by exposing students to the basic principles of architecture and implementation, and by careful use of the nonstandard terminology of this field.

REFERENCES

Petroski, H. (1996). *Invention by Design,* Harvard U. Press, Cambridge, MA, pp. 89–90.

Descartes, R. (1692). *Rules for the Direction of the Mind.*

ONE

COMPUTER OVERVIEW

1.0 INTRODUCTION

The general-purpose computer has assumed a dominant role in our world-wide society. From controlling the ignition of automobiles to maintaining the records of Olympic Games, computers are truly everywhere. In this book a one-semester course is provided for undergraduates that introduces the basic concepts of computers without focusing on distinctions between particular implementations such as mainframe, server, workstation, PC, or embedded controller. Instead the interest lies in conveying principles, with illustrations from specific processors.

In the modern world, the role of computers is multifaceted. They can store information such as a personnel database, record and transform information as with a word processor system, and generate information as when preparing tax tables. Computers must also have the ability to search for information on the World Wide Web.

The all-pervasive use of computers today is due to the fact that they are general purpose. That is, the computer hardware can be transformed by means of a stored program to be a vast number of different machines. An example of this power to become a special machine is found in word processing. For many years, Wang Laboratories was the dominant supplier of word processing machines based on a special-purpose processor with wired-in commands. Unable to see the revolution that was coming with the PC, Wang held to a losing product strategy and eventually was forced out of the business.

Another example of the general-purpose nature of computers is found in the electronic control of the automobile ignition. When electronic control was forced on the auto industry because of pollution problems, Ford took a different direction from that of Chrysler and General Motors. Chrysler and General Motors were relatively well off financially and opted to design special-purpose electronic controls for their ignition systems. Ford on the other hand was in severe financial difficulties and decided to use a microprocessor that cost a little more in production but did not require the development costs of the special-purpose circuits. With a microprocessor, Ford could, at relatively low cost, customize the controller for various engine configurations by changing the read-only memory (ROM) holding the program. Chrysler and General Motors, however, found that they had to have a unique controller for each configuration of auto – a very expensive design burden. Microprocessor control, as first practiced by Ford, is now accepted by all and is the industry design standard.

A number of special-purpose computers were designed and built before the era of the general-purpose computer. These include the Babbage difference engine (circa 1835), the Anatasoff–Berry Computer (ABC) at Iowa State University in the late 1930s, and the Z3 of Konrad Zuse, also in the late 1930s. Other computers are the Colossus at Benchly Park (used for breaking German codes in World War II) and the ENIAC (which stands for electronic numerical integrater and computer, a plug-board-programmed machine at The University of Pennsylvania). These computers are discussed in Subsection 1.3.1.

Each of the early computers noted above was a one-of-a-kind machine. What was lacking was a design standard that would unify the basic architecture of a computer and allow the designers of future machines to simplify their designs around a common theme. This simplification is found in the von Neumann Model.

1.1 VON NEUMANN MODEL

The von Neumann model of computer architecture was first described in 1946 in the famous paper by Burks, Goldstein, and von Neumann (1946). A number of very early computers or computerlike devices had been built, starting with the work of Charles Babbage, but the simple structure of a stored-program computer was first described in this landmark paper. The authors pointed out that instructions and data consist of bits with no distinguishing characteristics. Thus a common memory can be used to store both instructions and data. The differentiation between these two is made by the accessing mechanism and context; the program counter accesses instructions while the effective address register accesses data. If by some chance, such as a programming error, instructions and data are exchanged in memory, the performance of the program is indeterminate. Before von Neumann posited the single address space architecture, a number of computers were built that had disjoint instruction and data memories. One of these machines was built by Howard Aiken at Harvard University, leading to this design style being called a Harvard architecture.[1]

A variation on the von Neumann architecture that is widely used for implementing calculators today is called a tagged architecture. With these machines, each data type in memory has an associated tag that describes the data type: instruction, floating-point value (engineering notation), integer, etc. When the calculator is commanded to add a floating-point number to an integer, the tags are compared; the integer is converted to floating point, the addition is performed, and the result is displayed in floating point. You can try this yourself with your scientific calculator.

All variations of the von Neumann that have been designed since 1946 confirm that the von Neumann architecture is classical and enduring. This architecture can be embellished but its underlying simplicity remains. In this section the von Neumann

---

[1] The von Neumann architecture is also known as a Princeton architecture, as compared with a Harvard architecture.

architecture is described in terms of a set of nested state machines. Subsection 1.2.1 explores the details of the von Neumann architecture.

We should not underestimate the impact of the von Neumann architecture, which has been the unifying concept in all computer designs since 1950. This design permits an orderly design methodology and interface to the programmer. One can look at the description of any modern computer or microprocessor and immediately identify the major components: memory, central processing unit (CPU), control, and input/output (I/O).

The programmer interface with the von Neumann architecture is orderly. The programmer knows that the instructions will be executed one at a time and will be completed in the order issued. For concurrent processors, discussed in Chapter 6, order is not preserved, but as far as the programmer is concerned order is preserved.

A number of computer architectures that differ from the von Neumann architecture have been proposed over the years. However, the simplicity and the order of the von Neumann architecture have prevented these proposals from taking hold; none of these proposed machines has been built commercially.

State Machine Equivalent

A computer is defined as the combination of the memory, the processor, and the I/O system. Because of the centrality of memory, Chapter 4 discusses memory before Chapters 5 and 6 discuss the processor.

The three components of a computer can be viewed as a set of nested state machines. Fundamentally, the memory holds instructions and data. The instructions and the data flow to the logic, then the data (and in some designs the instructions) are modified by the processor logic and returned to the memory. This flow is represented as a state machine, shown in Figure 1.1.

The information in memory is called the process state. Inputs into the computer are routed to memory and become part of the process state. Outputs from the computer are provided from the process state in the memory.

The next level of abstraction is illustrated in Figure 1.2. The logic block of Figure 1.1 is replaced with another state machine. This second state machine has for its memory the processor registers. These registers, discussed in Chapter 3, include the program counter, general-purpose registers, and various dedicated registers. The logic consists of the arithmetic and logic unit (ALU) plus the logic required to support the interpretation of instructions.

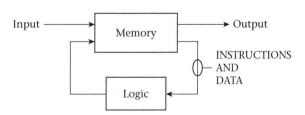

Figure 1.1 State machine

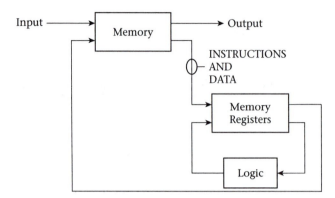

Figure 1.2 State machine II

The information contained in the registers is called the processor state. The processor state consists of (1) the information needed to interpret an instruction, and (2) information carried forward from instruction to instruction such as the program counter value and various tags and flags. When there is a processor context switch, it is the processor state that is saved, so the interrupted processor state can be restored.[2]

When microprogramming is discussed in Chapter 5, we will see that the logic block of Figure 1.2 can also be implemented as a state machine. For these implementations, there are three levels of state machine: process state, processor state, and micromachine processor state.

We now examine the major components of a computer, starting with the memory. As discussed in the preceding paragraphs, the memory is the space that holds the process state, consisting of instructions and data. The instruction space is not only for the program in execution but also for the operating system, compilers, interpreters, and other system software.

The processor reads instructions and data, processes the data, and returns results to memory, where the process state is updated. Thus a primary requirement for memory is that it be fast; that is, reads and writes must be accomplished with a small latency.

In addition, there are two conflicting requirements for memory: memory should be both very large and very fast. Memory cost is always a factor, with low cost being very desirable. These requirements lead to the concept of hierarchical memory. The memory closest to the processor is relatively small but is very fast and relatively expensive. The memory most distant from the processor is disk memory that is very slow but very low cost. Hierarchical memory systems have performance that approaches the fast memory while the cost approaches that of the low-cost disk memory. This characteristic is the result of the concept of locality, discussed in Chapter 4. Locality of programs and data results in a high probability that a request by the processor for either an instruction or a datum will be served in the memory closest to the processor.

The processor, sometimes called the CPU, is the realization of the logic and registers of Figure 1.2. This portion of the system fetches instructions, decodes these

---

[2] A context switch saves the processor state and restores a previously saved processor state.

instructions, finds operands, performs the operation, and returns the result to memory. The complexity of the CPU is determined by (1) the complexity of the instruction set, and (2) the amount of hardware concurrency provided for performance enhancement.

As shown in Figure 1.2, a computer must have some method of moving input data and instructions into the memory system and moving results from the memory to the outside world. This movement is the responsibility of the I/O system. Input and output devices can have differing bandwidths and latency. For example, keyboards are low-bandwidth devices whereas color display units have high bandwidth. In between we find such devices as disks, modems, and scanners.

The control of I/O can take a number of forms. At one extreme, each transfer can be performed by the CPU. Fully autonomous systems, such as direct memory access (DMA), however, provide high-bandwidth transfers with little CPU involvement. I/O systems are discussed in Chapter 7.

The formal specification of a processor, its interaction with memory, and its I/O capabilities are found in its instruction set architecture (ISA). The ISA is the programmer's view of the computer. The details of how the ISA is implemented in hardware, details that affect performance, are known as the implementation of the ISA.

1.2 THE VON NEUMANN ARCHITECTURE

The von Neumann ISA is described in this section. Except for the I/O, this architecture is complete and represents a starting point for the discussion in the following chapters. The features found in this architecture can be found in any of today's architectures; thus a thorough understanding of the von Neumann architecture is a good starting point for a general study of computer architecture. This architecture, of which a number were actually built, is used in this book for a simple example rather than the presentation of a contrived example of a simple architecture. When a von Neumann computer was actually completed at Princeton University in 1952, it was named the Institute for Advanced Studies (IAS) computer.

The von Neumann architecture consists of three major subsystems: instruction processing, arithmetic unit, and memory, as shown in Figure 1.3. A key feature of this architecture is that instructions and data share the same address space. Thus there is one source of addresses, the instruction processing unit, to the memory. The output of the memory is routed to either the Instruction Processing Unit or the Arithmetic Unit

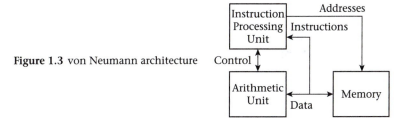

Figure 1.3 von Neumann architecture

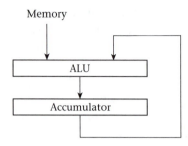

Memory

Figure 1.4 Accumulator local storage

depending upon whether an instruction or a datum is being fetched. A corollary to the key feature is that instructions can be processed as data. As will be discussed in later chapters, processing instructions as data can be viewed as either a blessing or a curse.

1.2.1 THE VON NEUMANN INSTRUCTION SET ARCHITECTURE

The von Neumann ISA is quite simple, having only 21 instructions. In fact, this ISA could be called an early reduced instruction set computer (RISC) processor.[3] As with any ISA, there are three components: addresses, data types, and operations. The taxonomy of these three components is developed further in Chapter 3; the three components of the von Neumann ISA are discussed below.

Addresses

The addresses of an ISA establish the architectural style – the organization of memory and how operands are referenced and results are stored. Being a simple ISA, there are only two memories addressed: the main memory and the accumulator.

The main memory of the von Neumann ISA is linear random access and is equivalent to the dynamic random-access memory (DRAM) found in today's processors. The technology of the 1940s restricted random-access memory (RAM) to very small sizes; thus the memory is addressed by a 12-bit direct address allocated to the 20-bit instructions.[4] There are no modifications to the address, such as base register relative or indexing. The formats of the instructions are described below in the subsection on data types.

Local storage in the processor is a single accumulator, as shown in Figure 1.4. An accumulator register receives results from the ALU that has two inputs, a datum from memory, and the datum held in the accumulator. Thus only a memory address is needed in the instruction as the accumulator is implicitly addressed.

Data Types

The von Neumann ISA has two data types: fractions and instructions. Instructions are considered to be a data type since the instructions can be operated on as data, a feature called self-modifying code. Today, the use of self-modifying code is considered

---

[3] An instruction set design posited by Van der Poel in 1956 has only one instruction.
[4] The Princeton IAS designers had so much difficulty with memory that only 1K words were installed with a 10-bit address.

to be poor programming practice. However, architectures such as the Intel x86 family must support this feature because of legacy software such as MSDOS.

Memory is organized with 4096 words with 40 bits per word; one fraction or two instructions are stored in one memory word.

FRACTIONS

The 40-bit word is typed as a 2's complement fraction; the range is $-1 \leq f < +1$:

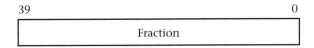

INSTRUCTIONS

Two 20-bit instructions are allocated to the 40-bit memory word. An 8-bit operation code, or op-code, and a 12-bit address are allocated to each of the instructions. Note that, with only 21 instructions, fewer op-code bits and more address bits could have been allocated. The direct memory address is allocated to the 12 most significant bits (MSBs) of each instruction. The address and the op-code pairs are referred to in terms of left and right:

39	28 27	20 19	8 7	0
Left Address	Left Op-Code	Right Address	Right Op-Code	

Registers

A block diagram of the von Neumann computer is shown in Figure 1.5. Note that I/O connections are not shown. Although only sketchily described in the original paper on this architecture, I/O was added to all implementations of this design.

The von Neumann processor has seven registers that support the interpretation of the instructions fetched from memory. These registers and their functions are listed in Table 1.1. Note that two of the registers are explicitly addressed by the instructions and defined in the ISA (called architected registers) while the other six are not defined

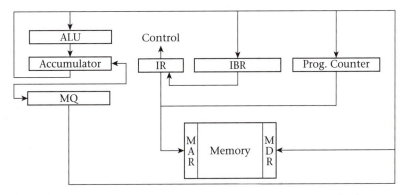

Figure 1.5 Block diagram of the von Neumann architecture: MQ, multiplier quotient register; IR, instruction register; IBR, instruction buffer register; MAR, memory address register; MDR, memory data register

TABLE 1.1   VON NEUMANN ISA REGISTERS

Name	Function
Architected Registers	
Accumulator, AC, 40 bits	Holds the output of the ALU after an arithmetic operation, a datum loaded from memory, the most-significant digits of a product, and the divisor for division.
Multiplier quotient register, MQ, 40 bits	Holds a temporary data value such as the multiplier, the least-significant bits of the product as multiplication proceeds, and the quotient from division.
Implemented Registers	
Program counter, PC, 12 bits *	Holds the pointer to memory. The PC contains the address of the instruction pair to be fetched next.
Instruction buffer register, IBR, 40 bits	Holds the instruction pair when fetched from the memory.
Instruction register, IR, 20 bits	Holds the active instruction while it is decoded in the control unit.
Memory address register, MAR, 12 bits	Holds the memory address while the memory is being cycled (read or write). The MAR receives input from the program counter for an instruction fetch and from the address field of an instruction for a datum read or write.
Memory data register, MDR, 40 bits	Holds the datum (instruction or data) for a memory read or write cycle.

* The program counter is a special case. The PC can be loaded with a value by a branch instruction, making it architected, but cannot be read and stored, making it implemented.

but are used by the control for moving bits during the execution of an instruction (called implemented registers).

Operations

The operations of the von Neumann ISA are of three types:

- moves between the accumulator, multiplier quotient register, and memory
- ALU operations such as add, subtract, multiply, and divide
- Unconditional and conditional branch instructions that redirect program flow.[5]

The von Neumann ISA consists of 21 instructions, shown in Table 1.2, which are sufficient to program any algorithm. However, the number of instructions that must

---

[5] Many computer historians credit the von Neumann ISA with the first use of conditional branching with a stored program computer. No prior computer possessed this feature and subprograms were incorporated as in-line code.

TABLE 1.2 THE VON NEUMANN ISA

Move Instructions

1.	$AC \leftarrow MQ$	Move the number held in the MQ into the accumulator.
2.	$M(x) \leftarrow AC$	Move the number in the accumulator to location x in memory. The memory address x is found in the 12 least-significant bits of the instruction.
3.*	$M(x,28:39) \leftarrow AC(28:39)$	Replace the left-hand 12 bits of the left-hand instruction located at position x in the memory with the left-hand 12 bits in the accumulator.[†]
4.*	$M(x,8:19) \leftarrow AC(28:39)$	Replace the left-hand 12 bits of the right-hand instruction in location x in the memory with the left-hand 12 bits in the accumulator.

ALU Instructions

5.	$AC_c \leftarrow M(x)$	Clear the accumulator and add the number from location x in the memory.
6.	$AC \leftarrow AC_c - M(x)$	Clear the accumulator and subtract the number at location x in the memory.
7.	$AC \leftarrow AC_c + |M(x)|$	Clear the accumulator and add the absolute value of the number at location x in the memory.
8.	$AC \leftarrow AC_c - |M(x)|$	Clear the accumulator and subtract the absolute value of the number at location x in the memory.
9.	$AC \leftarrow AC + M(x)$	Add the number at location x in the memory into the accumulator.
10.	$AC \leftarrow AC - M(x)$	Subtract the number at location x in the memory from the accumulator.
11.	$AC \leftarrow AC + |M(x)|$	Add the absolute value of the number at location x in the memory to the accumulator.
12.	$AC \leftarrow AC - |M(x)|$	Subtract the absolute value of the number at location position x in the memory into the accumulator.
13.	$MQ_c \leftarrow M(x)$	Clear the MQ register and add the number at location x in the memory into it.
14.	$AC_c, MQ \leftarrow M(x) \times MQ$	Clear the accumulator and multiply the number at location x in the memory by the number in the MQ, placing the most-significant 39 bits of the answer in the accumulator and the least-significant 39 bits of the answer in the MQ.
15.	$MQ_c, AC \leftarrow AC \div M(x)$	Clear the register and divide the number in the accumulator by the number at location x of the memory, leaving the remainder in the accumulator and placing the quotient in MQ.
16.	$AC \leftarrow AC \times 2$	Multiply the number in the accumulator by 2.
17.	$AC \leftarrow AC \div 2$	Divide the number in the accumulator by 2.

Control Instructions

18.	Go to $M(x,2\ 0:39)$	Shift the control to the left-hand instruction of the pair in $M(x)$.
19.	Go to $M(x,0:19)$	Shift the control to the right-hand instruction of the pair in $M(x)$.
20.	If $AC \geq 0$, then $PC \leftarrow M(x,0:19)$	If the number in the accumulator is ≥ 0, go to the right-hand instruction in $M(x)$.
21.	If $AC \geq 0$, then $PC \leftarrow M(x,20:39)$	If the number in the accumulator is ≥ 0, go to the left-hand instruction in $M(x)$.

* These instructions move the address portion of an instruction between memory and the accumulator. These instructions are required to support address modification. Indexing, common today in all computer's ISAs, had not yet been invented.
† The notation $M(x,0:19)$ means the right-hand 20 bits of location $M(x)$; $M(x,20:39)$ means the left-hand 20 bits, and so on.

be executed is considerably greater than that required by more modern ISAs. The instructions are grouped into three groups: move, ALU, and control. This grouping is typical of all computers based on the von Neumann architecture. A more modern terminology, not the terminology of von Neumann, is used in Table 1.2.

1.2.2 INSTRUCTION INTERPRETATION CYCLE

Interpretation of an instruction proceeds in three steps or cycles. The instruction is fetched, decoded, and executed. These three steps are discussed in the following subsections.

Instruction Fetch

A partial flow chart for the instruction fetch cycle is shown in Figure 1.6. Because two instructions are fetched at once, the first step is to determine if a fetch from memory is required. This test is made by testing the least-significant bit (LSB) of the program counter. Thus, an instruction fetch from memory occurs only on every other state of the PC or if the previous instruction is a taken branch. The fetch from memory places a left (L) and a right (R) instruction in the instruction buffer register (IBR).

Instructions are executed, except for the case of a branch instruction, left, right, left, right, etc. For example, consider that an R instruction has just been completed.

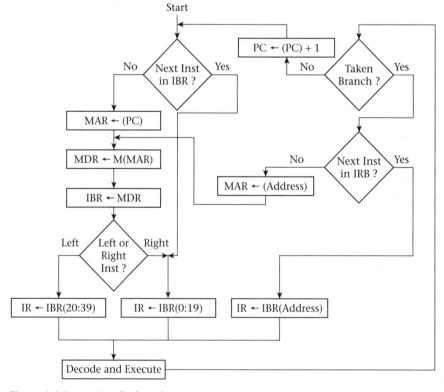

Figure 1.6 Instruction fetch cycle

There is no instruction in the IBR and a reference is made to memory to fetch an instruction pair.

Normally, the L instruction is then executed. The path follows to the left, placing the instruction into the instruction register (IR). The R instruction remains in the IBR for use on the next cycle, thereby saving a memory cycle to fetch the next instruction.

If the prior instruction had been a branch to the R instruction of the instruction pair, the L instruction is not required, and the R instruction is moved to the IR. In summary, the instruction sequence is as follows:

Sequence	*Action*
L followed by R	No memory access required
R followed by L	Increment PC, access memory, use L instruction
L branch to L	Memory access required and L instruction used
R branch to R	Memory access required and R instruction used
L branch to R	If in same computer word, memory access not required
R branch to L	If in same computer word, memory access not required

After the instruction is decoded and executed, the PC is incremented for the next instruction and control returns to the start point.

Decode and Execute

Instruction decode is only indicated in Figure 1.6. However, the instruction has been placed in the IR. As shown in Figure 1.7, combinatorial logic in the control unit decodes the op-code and decides which of the instructions will be executed. In other words, decoding is similar to the CASE statement of many programming languages. The flow charts for two instruction executions are shown in Figure 1.7: numbers 21 and 6. After an instruction is executed, control returns to the instruction fetch cycle, shown in Figure 1.6.

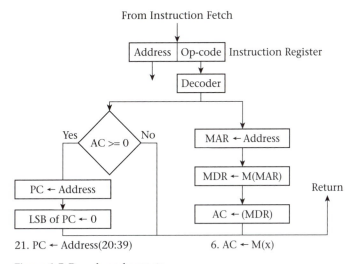

21. PC ← Address(20:39)   6. AC ← M(x)

Figure 1.7 Decode and execute

The sequencing of the instruction interpretation cycle is controlled by a hard-wired state machine, discussed in Chapter 5. Each of the states is identified in flow-chart form, flip flops are assigned to represent each state, and the logic is designed to sequence through the states. After the invention of microprogramming, the flow chart is reduced to a series of instructions that are executed on the micromachine. In other words, a second computer, rather than a hardwired state machine, provides the control.

Example Program

Without indexing, the complexity of programming the von Neumann ISA is illustrated with the following example shown in Table 1.3. We wish to compute the vector add of two vectors of length 1000:

$$Ci = Ai + Bi.$$

Vector **A** is stored in locations 1001–2000, vector **B** in locations 2001–3000, and vector **C** in locations 3001–4000. The first steps of the program initialize three memory

TABLE 1.3 VECTOR ADD PROGRAM

Location	Datum/Instruction	Comments
0	999	Count
1	1	Constant
2	1000	Constant
Inner Loop for Each Add		
3L	AC ← M(3000)	Load **B**i
3R	AC ← AC + M(2000)	**B**i + **A**i
4L	M(4000) ← AC	Store AC
Loop Test and Continue/Terminate		
4R	AC ← M(0)	Load count
5L	AC ← AC − M(1)	Decrement count
5R	If AC ≥ 0, go to M(6,0:19)	Test count
6L	Go to M(6,20:39)	Halt
6R	M(0) ← AC	Store count
Address Adjustment (Decrement)		
7L	AC ← AC + M(1)	Increment count
7R	AC ← AC + M(2)	Add constant
8L	M(3,8:19) ← AC(28:39)	Store modified address in 3R
8R	AC ← AC + M(2)	Add constant
9L	M(3,28:39) ← AC	Store modified address in 3L
9R	AC ← AC + M(2)	Add constant
10L	M(4,28:39) ← AC	Store modified address in 4L
10R	Go to M(3,20:39)	Unconditional branch to 3L

locations with the count 999, the constant 1000 (for testing the number of times the operation is performed), and the constant 1 (for a decrement value).

1.2.3 LIMITATIONS OF THE VON NEUMANN INSTRUCTION SET ARCHITECTURE

There are a number of major limitations of the von Neumann ISA highlighted by the vector add program of Table 1.3. The first limitation has been noted in Subsection 1.2.2: there are no facilities for automatic address modification as with modern processors. Thus the addresses in the instructions must be modified by other instructions to index through an array. This is the self-modifying code that is very prone to programming error.

In addition, modular programming was unknown at the time of the von Neumann ISA development. Thus the architecture provides no base register mode to assist in partitioning instructions and data.

Another major limitation can be found in the vector add program of Table 1.3. With this architecture, the program counter is an implemented register. All modern processors have an architected program counter; thus the PC can be stored and restored, thereby enabling the programming concepts of subroutines and procedure calls. These concepts cannot be used on the von Neumann ISA with its implemented program counter.

Finally, as mentioned in Subsection 1.2.1, the I/O was only briefly mentioned in the original paper on the von Neumann ISA. The implementation of the I/O on this and other computers will be discussed in Chapter 7.

1.3 HISTORICAL NOTES

Indexing: Apparently, the first incorporation of indexing to an ISA was with the Mark I, developed by Kilburn and Williams at The University of Manchester, 1946–1949, and produced by Ferranti Corp. The first Ferranti machine was installed in 1951. Although this machine is well known for the development and the use of virtual memory, the pioneering work regarding indexing is equally important. Indexing was provided as an adjunct function, called the B lines or B box.

The IBM 704, announced in 1954, has three index registers. These registers, along with floating point, provided the hardware support for the development of FORTRAN (Blaauw and Brooks 1997). It is interesting to note that the IBM 701, first installed in 1953, required program base address modification, as did the von Neumann ISA.

Subroutines: A subroutine is a program that executes only when called by the main program. After execution, the main program is then restarted. Because subroutines require a return to the main program, a necessary condition for subroutine support is that the program counter must be saved. As the von Neumann ISA had no provisions for saving the program counter, the ISA cannot execute subroutines.

This problem was first solved by Wheeler for the EDSAC at Cambridge University under the direction of Maurice Wilkes (Wilkes, Wheeler, and Gill 1951). The program counter became architected, permitting its contents to be saved and restored. A further discussion of subroutines is found in Chapter 3.

1.3.1 PRECURSORS TO THE VON NEUMANN INSTRUCTION SET ARCHITECTURE

There were a number of precursor computers to the von Neumann ISA. Noteworthy are the machines of Babbage, Atanasoff, Zuse, Aiken, and Eckert-Mauchly. Even before these machines there had been several centuries of study and design of calculating aids and mathematics, particularly the invention of logarithms and advances in numerical analysis. These topics are outside the scope of this textbook but reference can be made to the papers of Chase (1980) and de Solla Price (1984) for information. For additional information on the early computers, the reader is referred to Goldstein (1972) and Randell (1973). Extensive coverage can be found in the *IEEE Annals of the History of Computing*, now in its 21st volume. The reprint series of the Charles Babbage Institute (Cambell-Kelly and Williams 1985) provides insight into the writings of the early computer pioneers.

The early computers were designed to solve two types of problems. First, there was a problem in preparing tables of functions; the machines of Babbage, Aiken, and Eckert-Mauchly were designed for this purpose. The second problem class was the solution of systems of linear equations; the machines of Atanasoff and Zuse were designed for these problems. For both problem types, the amount of labor required for human solutions to anything but trivial cases was excessive, and, as the problem became larger, errors would be made even when mechanical calculators were used for the arithmetic. Thus very large problems were almost intractable; they took too long and were too full of errors.[6]

Charles Babbage (1792–1871) can be called the father of modern computers. At the beginning of the 19th century, a critical need existed for computationally reliable printed tables of functions. Babbage posited that a difference engine could meet this need. He built a small model during 1820–1822 of a difference engine having six significant digits for functions with a constant second difference; a replica is shown in Figure 1.8. The method of differences was adopted as it requires only addition and subtraction. The technology for these operations had been long demonstrated, starting with Blasé Pascal's mechanical adding machine, which used rotating decimal wheels.

In 1836, efforts to make a larger, 26-decimal-digit, sixth-difference version of the difference engine eventually failed because of the difficulty of manufacturing the parts and the withdrawal of British government financial aid. A reproduction of this larger machine, built to Babbage's drawings, was completed in 1991 and can be found in the London Science Museum. Even though Babbage never completed the difference

---

[6] During the 1930s, the Works Progress Administration hired young women to compute tables by hand. Calculators were not used, as one of the goals of the program was to put as many people to work as possible.

Figure 1.8 Replica of Babbage difference engine (courtesy International Business Machines Corporation)

engine, a machine based on his ideas was completed by Edvard Scheutz in 1843 in Stockholm, Sweden.

With the failure of the difference engine design effort, Babbage turned his attention to an "analytical engine." He attempted to design a machine that could perform any sequence of operations and that would not be a slave to the numerical analysis technique of differences. The analytical engine consisted of three parts: the store is the memory of a modern computer, the mill is the arithmetic unit of a modern computer, and the third part is the control. The store and the mill would be sequenced by punched cards, a technology perfected by the Jacquard loom. Thus Babbage spelled out the three major components of a modern computer.

John Atanasoff (1903–1995), Professor of Mathematics and Physics at Iowa State College, made the first machine that brought computer technology out of the mechanical and relay ages into the electronics age. Atanasoff saw the need for an apparatus for solving systems of linear algebraic equations. He estimated that the time in hours for using mechanical calculators to solve n simultaneous linear equations with n unknowns was

$$\frac{n^3}{64} \text{ h.}$$

Thus, large systems of equations, such as $n = 30$, would require over 50 8-h days, with the opportunity for many errors. In the spirit of physics researchers, he proceeded to design and construct an apparatus for the solution of these systems of equations. This apparatus is a special-purpose digital computer known as the Atanasoff–Berry Computer (ABC). Berry was a research assistant to Atanasoff. Unfortunately, Atanasoff's work did not become widely known until 1967–1969 when patent litigation over the ENIAC patent between Sperry-Rand and Honeywell revealed that John Mauchly

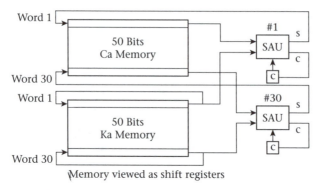

Figure 1.9 Organization of the ABC memory and SAUs

(one of the designers of ENIAC) visited with Atanasoff in 1940 or 1941 and received information on the ABC.

In addition to the decision to construct an electronic computer, Atanasoff made a number of other design decisions that are noteworthy. First, arithmetic would be performed by logical operations, not enumeration or counting as with Babbage. Second, the data type would be a 50-bit signed, binary integer that uses 1's complement (see Chapter 3 for a discussion of 1's complement arithmetic). Third, memory would be provided by a motor-driven drum of rotating capacitors: the first DRAM. The rotation time is 1s; the capacitors are refreshed each rotation.

The organization of the memory and the serial arithmetic units (SAUs) is shown in Figure 1.9. There are two memory banks, Ca and Ka. Each bank is 30 words of 50 bits. The coefficients and constant of one equation are loaded into Ca and the coefficients and constant of another are loaded into Ka. Thirty full adder/subtractors add or subtract the bits of Ka and Ca, saving the carry, and replacing Ca with the sum, bit by bit. With 30 words, the system limit is 29 equations with 29 unknowns.

The coefficients and the constant of one equation are read from the card reader into the Ca memory and the other equation into the Ka memory. By Gaussian elimination, one of the coefficients in Ca is reduced to zero. The technique iteratively subtracted the 30 coefficients in Ka from Ca, reducing one coefficient of Ca to zero (the coefficient to be eliminated). The process consists of successively dividing the coefficients by two in each cycle. When the coefficient becomes negative, subtraction is changed to addition; when the coefficient becomes positive, addition is changed to subtraction – a process akin to nonrestoring division (a topic discussed in Chapter 3). After one coefficient of Ca is reduced to zero, the results are punched into an output card and two new equations are introduced by the card reader; the problem has been reduced by one unknown. This process of input, compute, and output continues until all of the coefficients of the system are available.

Figure 1.10 (Atanasoff 1984) shows an artist's conception of the final version of the ABC tested in the spring of 1942. Atanasoff reported difficulty with reliable punching of the output cards. Because of wartime demands on Anatasoff and his students' leaving school for the military or war work, no further work was accomplished, and the machine was eventually scrapped. Today, elements of the machine can be seen at The

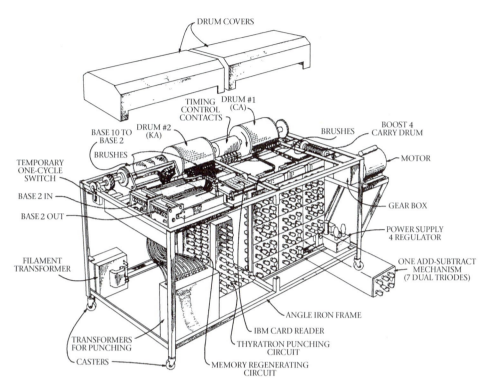

Figure 1.10 The Atanasoff–Berry computer (© 1984 IEEE)

Computer Museum in Boston. A working replica of the ABC has been constructed at Iowa State University and is on permanent display there.

Konrad Zuse (1910–1995) worked in Germany and designed and built a number of machines during the period 1934–1944: Z1, Z2, and Z3. The primary motivation for these machines was the solution of systems of linear equations. Because he had a degree in civil engineering, Zuse was interested in the problem of static engineering of load-bearing structures. This problem required the solution of a system of linear equations, one example requiring 30 equations with 30 unknowns. Several months were required for solving this problem with mechanical calculators (Ceruzzi 1981, Rojas 1997).

Zuse's work seems to have been supported by his family and occasional small grants from the Henschel Aircraft Company. Unfortunately, the Z3 was destroyed in a bombing raid on Berlin, but a reproduction was built in 1961–1963 from the original plans.

The Z3 is a relay machine, with approximately 2600 relays. A block diagram of the Z3 is shown in Figure 1.11 (Ceruzzi 1981). Note that the primary data type is floating point, base 2, and the program input is from previously used punched 35-mm movie film. The main memory (64 words of 22 bits plus sign) is directly addressed and implemented with relays. Output used lamp displays, and no provisions for printing results were provided. Input is by means of a keyboard. With disjoint program and data memories, the Z3 is classified as a Harvard architecture. The minimum provision

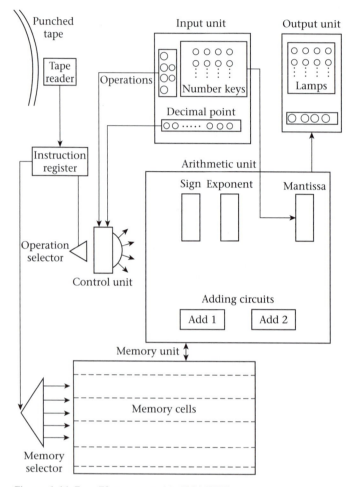

Figure 1.11 Zuse Z3 computer (© 1981 IEEE)

for input and output is not surprising, given that solving large systems of simultaneous linear equations is compute bound: few inputs, a lot of computing, and few outputs.

The internal architecture is a basic register file of two registers. Instructions were of the form

R2 ← R1 op R2.

The instruction set consisted of 11 operations–everything we expect in a modern computer except for conditional branching, the ability to use subroutines, and indexing. Looping could be provided when a loop was made of the punched film.

The instruction set and the number of cycles required per instruction are given in Table 1.4. The cycle time is estimated to be 5.33 Hz. Finally, a rudimentary form of pipelining and concurrency is used. The tape reader is two instructions ahead of the instruction in execution. This allows two instructions to be reversed in execution,

TABLE 1.4 Z3 INSTRUCTION SET AND EXECUTION TIME

Type	Description	Cycles	Time (s)
Arithmetic	Multiplication	16	3
	Division	18	3.4
	Square root	20	3.75
	Addition	3	0.56
	Subtraction	4–5	0.75–0.93
	Reciprocal		
	Square		
	Negation		
	Double		
	Halve		
	Times 10		
	Times 1/10		
Memory	Load	1	0.18
	Store	0–1	0–0.18
I/O	Read keyboard	9–41	1.68–7.7
	Display result	9–41	1.68–7.7

two memory operations can be performed ahead of the time to overcome the slow memory, and a temporary result can be saved in a register to be used on a subsequent instruction. These ideas will be appreciated when pipelining is described in Chapter 6.

Howard Aiken (1900–1973), Assistant Professor at Harvard University, in 1937 proposed the development of a machine for the production of tables of functions usually defined by infinite series. He was aware of the work of Babbage but apparently not aware of the work of Atanasoff and Zuse. Babbage's technique of differences was rejected as being too constrained for the problems envisioned by Aiken. In his proposal (Aiken 1937) he stated that the processes to be carried out are "evaluation of formulae and the tabulation of results, computation of series, solution of ordinary differential equations of the first and second order, numerical integration of empirical data, and numerical differentiation of empirical data." To achieve these ends, a programmable device with the normal arithmetic functions would be required.

Aiken took his ideas to IBM and received encouragement and, more important, financial and engineering support. As a result, the machine was designed and constructed by a group of skilled engineers at IBM. This is unlike the situation for many early machines that were designed and constructed by ad hoc teams of university faculty and students. IBM had extensive experience in tabulators, machines that used punched cards to perform some limited calculations under plug-board control.[7] Thus it was natural that this technology would be applied to what became known as the

---

[7] Much of the World War II code breaking work in the U.S. depended on tabulating machines for gathering statistical information on Japanese messages.

MECHANICAL DRIVE SYSTEM

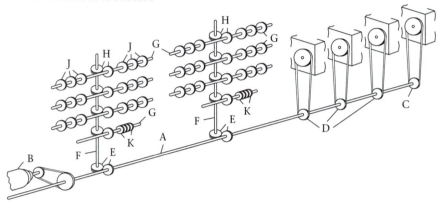

Figure 1.12 Harvard Mark I mechanical drive (courtesy Harvard University)

sequence-controlled automatic calculator (SCAC), later as the Harvard Mark I (The Staff of The Computation Laboratory 1946).[8]

Like the Babbage analytical engine and the Z3, the Harvard Mark I has disjoint instruction and data memories. The program is stored on a 24-channel punched paper tape: instructions are read into the processor in sequence with no looping capability. The memory is composed of 60 24-bit decimal registers. Each of these registers acts as an accumulator that distributes the arithmetic function (there is no centralized arithmetic unit as with the von Neumann ISA). Data input is by means of one of three punched paper tape readers identical in design to the program reader.

The registers are stepping switches J, driven from a motor B and rotating shafts, A, F, and G, as shown in Figure 1.12. The stepping switches are engaged to the shaft by electromechanical clutches. Addition is performed by the following scheme. Say, for example, a switch has the number 3 and another has the number 5 and the 3 is to be added to the 5. A cam-driven pulse generator would produce signals from the 3 switch that would engage the clutch of the 5 switch for three steps, then disengage the clutch, leaving 8 in the switch. Today, this scheme seems to be almost unworkable. Nevertheless, the IBM engineers produced a very reliable computer in 1943 that remained in service until 1959.[9]

Machine instructions include the usual add and subtract with multiplication and division. Other instructions with their execution times are shown in Table 1.5. The data type is 23-decimal digits in sign and magnitude representation. The decimal point is positioned by means of plug-board interconnections. However, because of the difficulty of programming the decimal point, the decimal point was set between the 15th and the 16th digits for most of the life of the machine. In Chapter 3, this data type, called mixed, will be discussed.

---

[8] In the early days a "computer" was a person who performed calculations. A "calculator" was a machine that performed calculations.

[9] When asked in later years why he used the IBM technology rather than some other, such as electronic, Aiken pointed out that IBM, not some other company with electronics experience, provided the money.

**TABLE 1.5 MARK I
INSTRUCTION EXECUTION
TIMES**

Instructions	Seconds	Cycles
Addition	0.3	1
Subtraction	0.3	1
Multiplication	6.0	20
Division	11.4	38
$Log_{10}(x)$	68.4	228
10^x	61.2	204
$\sin x$	60.0	199

J. Presper Eckert (1919–1995) and *John Mauchly* (1908–1980) developed the Electronic Numerical Integrator and Computer (ENIAC) at the Moore School of The University of Pennsylvania under contract from the U.S. Army. Development started in 1942, and the machine was operational in 1946 (Goldstine and Goldstine 1946).

The data type is 10-decimal digits with a sign. The organization is similar to that of the Mark I in that the basic memory and computing elements are accumulators. Implementation is with vacuum tubes and the add cycle is 1/5000th of a second–16 times faster than the Mark I. The purpose of this machine is to compute and print tables of functions and firing tables for artillery. Function switches provide tabular input of 104 words of 12-decimal digits plus sign.

The ENIAC has 20 accumulators that are plugged together by means of five buses to form a primitive data flow processor. Three of the accumulators are shown in Figure 1.13 along with the five buses (Goldstine and Goldstine 1996). Note that each bus and the plug cables that interconnect the accumulators to the buses have 11 conductors composed of 10 digits plus a sign. The overall view of this machine is that it is composed of 20 calculators with interconnections between them. A constant transmitter could broadcast constants to all the accumulators. Also shown in Figure 1.13 are the circuits for issuing timing pulses that synchronize the operation of the accumulator. Because the output of this machine consists of tables, a printer is included.

Programming is more constrained than with the Mark I. The accumulators were patched by means of cables into the buses that received timing pulses from a central source. The patching set the algorithm to be solved. As an example, consider the problem of computing a table of n, n^2, and n^3 for n, $n + 1$, $n + 2$, and so on, as shown in Table 1.6.

The calculation is seeded with the initial values of 2, 2^2, and 2^3 (2, 4, and 8) that are entered into accumulators 18, 19, and 20. With the list of operations shown, the next values are computed. Initial values of 1, 1^2, 1^3 could also have been used with the same results after more steps.

Thus we see that the initial values of 2, 4, and 8 are changed to 3, 9, and 27. At the end of each iteration, the results would be printed. Note the concurrency of steps 2

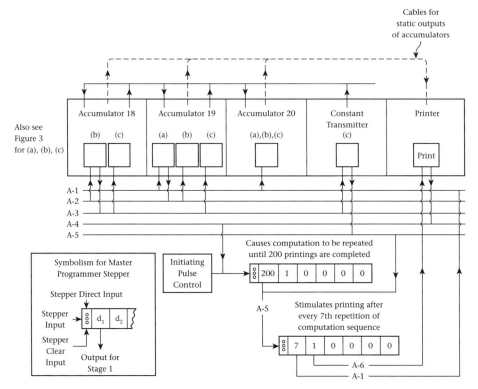

Figure 1.13 ENIAC, three accumulators (© 1996 IEEE)

and 3. As there are no dependencies (discussed at length in Chapter 6) these operations can be executed in parallel.

It is easy to imagine the difficulty of programming or setting up this machine. Debugging must have been a difficult job. Fortunately, reprogramming was infrequent since the computer time for a single job was extensive as only input constants were changed from run to run.

TABLE 1.6 COMPUTING n, n^2, AND n^3 ON THE ENIAC

Step	Operation Initial Value	Accumulator 18 $n = 2$	Accumulator 19 $n^2 = 4$	Accumulator 20 $n^3 = 8$
1	Add the contents of A19 three times to A20.	2	4	$8 + 12 = 20$
2	Add the contents of A18 two times to A19.	2	$4 + 4 = 8$	
	Add the contents of A18 three times to A20.			$20 + 6 = 26$
3	Add the constant 1 to A18, A19, and A20.	$2 + 1 = 3$	$8 + 1 = 9$	$26 + 1 = 27$

TABLE 1.7 EARLY COMPUTER FEATURES

Feature	ABC	Zuse Z3	ENIAC	Harvard Mark I
Motivation	Simultaneous linear equations	Simultaneous linear equations	Ballistic firing tables	Functions defined by infinite series
Primary data type	50-bit integer (base 2)	22-bit F.P. (base 2)	10-digit integer (base 10)	24-digit integer (base 10)
Memory	2, 30w × 50 Capacitor, refreshed every second	64w × 22, relay	20 words × 10 digits, vacuum tube	60 words × 24 digits, stepping switches
ALU	Centralized 30, one for each word	Centralized	Accumulators, distributed	Accumulators, distributed
Program input	Hardwired for one algorithm	Punched film	Plug wired	Punched paper tape
Data input	Punched cards	Keyboard	Switches, IBM card reader	Switches, punched paper tape
Data output	Punched cards	Display lights	Punched cards	Punched cards, printer
Logic	Vacuum tube, bit serial, word parallel	Relay, word parallel	Vacuum tube, word parallel	Electromechanical, word parallel
Clock rate (Hz)	60	5.3	100 K	300
Date first operational	1942	1941	1945	1944
Estimated cost (U.S. $)	7000	6500	486,804	450,000

* The rotating shaft drove and synchronized all of the stepping switches in the system and is analogous to the common clock of modern processors.

Summary. A brief summary of some of the salient features of the ABC, Z3, ENIAC, and the Mark I is given Table 1.7.

We conclude this brief discussion of early computers with a comment on wartime work in Great Britain. A significant vacuum tube machine was designed and built for the purpose of breaking high-grade enciphered German Army teleprinter messages. The first model of this computer, named Colossus, was installed in December 1943. By war's end, 10 of these machines were operational. However, the existence of Colossus remained under security wraps until 1975 (Randell 1976).

REFERENCES

Aiken, H. (1937). "Proposed Automatic Calculating Machine," *IEEE Spectrum*, August 1964. Also in (Randell 1973)

Atanasoff, J. V. (1984). "Advent of Electronic Computing," *IEEE Annals of the History of Computing*, **6**:3.

Blaauw, G. and Brooks, F. P. Jr. (1997). *Computer Architecture, Concepts and Evolution*, Addison-Wesley, Reading MA.

Burkes A. W., Goldstine, H. H., and von Neumann, J. (1946). "Preliminary Discussions of the Logical Design of an Electronic Computing Instrument," U.S. Army Ordnance Department Report.

Cambell-Kelly, and Williams, M. R., eds. (1985). *The Moore School Lectures, Theory and Techniques for Design of Electronic Digital Computers*, reprinted in the Reprint Series for the History of Computing, Vol. 9, Charles Babbage Institute, MIT Press, Cambridge, MA, Tomash Publishers, Los Angeles.

Ceruzzi, P. E. (1981). "The Early Computers of Konrad Zuse, 1935 to 1945," *IEEE Annals of the History of Computing*, **3**:3.

Chase, G. C. (1980). "History of Mechanical Computing Machinery," *IEEE Annals of the History of Computing*, **2**:3.

de Solla Price, D. (1984). "A History of Calculating Machines," *IEEE Micro.* **4**:1, pp. 22–52.

Goldstine, H. H. and Goldstine, A. (1996). *The Electronic Numerical Integrator and Computer (ENIAC)*, M.T.A.C. 2, No. 15, 97–110 (1946). Reprinted in (Randell 1973) and in *IEEE Annals of the History of Computing*, **18**:1.

Goldstein, H. H. (1972). *The Computer from Pascal to von Neumann*, Princeton U. Press, Princeton, New Jersey.

Randell, B., ed. (1973). *The Origins of Digital Computer: Selected Papers*, Springer-Verlag, New York.

Randell, B. (1976). "The Colossus," Technical Report series No. 90, Computing Laboratory, University of Newcastle upon Tyme, U.K.

Rojas, R. (1997). "Konrad Zuse's Legacy: The Architecture of the Z1 and Z3," *IEEE Annals of the History of Computing*, **19**:2.

The Staff of The Computation Laboratory. (1946). *A Manual of Operation For The Automatic Sequence Controlled Calculator*, reprinted in the Reprint Series for the History of Computing, Vol. 8, Charles Babbage Institute, Tomash Publishers, Los Angeles.

Wilkes, M., Wheeler, D., and Gill, S. (1951). *The Preparation of Programs for an Electronic Digital Computer*, Addison-Wesley, Cambridge, MA. Reprinted in the Reprint Series for the History of Computing, Vol. 1, Charles Babbage Institute, Publishers, Los Angeles.

EXERCISES

1.1   Write the program for vector addition by using the ISAs of the IBM PowerPC and the Intel Pentium.

1.2   Rewrite the von Neumann ISA vector add program for vectors of length 300.

1.3   Is there a reason why the vector add program is written so that the vectors are added starting with the large address working back to the small address?

1.4   Babbage was interested in the solution to the expression $n^2 + n + 41$ for increasing integer values of n. Show how this problem is solved on the difference engine for $n = 1, 2, \ldots, 10$.

1.5   Obtain the first terms of sin by using a well-known series expansion. Then compute the first 10 terms of the sin function by using the methods of differences.

1.6   Use the ENIAC and the format of Table 1.6 to compute n, n^2, and n^3 for $n = 1$, $n = 2$, and $n = 3$.

1.7 Expand the program of Table 1.6 to compute n^4 with the ENIAC. Hint: $(n+1)^4 = (n+1)(n+1)(n+1)(n+1)$.

1.8 Write a program to evaluate a 3×3 determinant for the Z3. Assume that the nine inputs are keyed in by means of the keyboard.

1.9 Show the method by which the ABC solves the following simultaneous equations. Use decimal values and plot the convergence of the first coefficient to zero:

$$2x + 5y = 9,$$
$$3x + 2y = 8.$$

1.10 Compare the characteristics of each of the four machines described in Table 1.7 with modern machines or current research.

1.11 Figure 1.10 shows a rotating drum with brushes used to make conversions between base 10 and base 2. Suggest how this device performs this function.

1.12 Show the execution steps for Instructions 1 and 3 in Table 1.2 in the flow-chart form used in Figure 1.7.

TWO

PERFORMANCE MODELS
AND EVALUATION

2.0 INTRODUCTION

Designers evaluate the performance of computers and the effect of design changes to a computer or subsystem. In general, there are two common techniques for performing these evaluations: simulation and analytic models.

Simulation has a major disadvantage of hiding the effects of workload or architectural parameters that are the input to the simulator. The simulation produces some single measure of performance but the underlying basis for the number is obscure. On the other hand, analytic models must explicitly comprehend each of the workload and architectural parameters. Because of the small time required for obtaining a solution as parameters vary, the effect of these parameters can be evaluated and understood. However, these models do not generally comprehend concurrency and are subject to significant error. Nevertheless, analytic models are used throughout this book for evaluating workloads and architectural parameters because of the insight into design options provided. Note that some of the parameters of an analytic model have been obtained by simulation of a small portion of a system. Memory behavior parameters are examples.

2.1 PERFORMANCE MODELS

For a computer or a computer subsystem, what measures of performance can be used by a designer when making design choices? In the domain of computers, we are generally interested in two things: the time to do tasks and the rate at which given tasks are performed. For example,

Task A executes in 3 μs per task,
Task A executes at a rate of 3.33×10^5 executions per second.

Note that for a common work load (Task A), time and rate have a reciprocal relationship. Because a computer has a clock that controls all of its functions, the number of clocks is frequently used as a measure of time. If the clock period of the processor is 50 ns,

300 clocks per execution of Task A,
Task A executes at a rate of 0.0033 tasks per clock.

CPI Model

A basic time model that is widely used in evaluating processors is clocks per instruction (CPI). The metric measures the time, in clocks, a processor takes to execute an average instruction:

$$CPI = \frac{\text{number of clocks}}{\text{number of instructions executed}}.$$

The reciprocal of CPI is instructions per clock (IPC). IPC is a measure of processing rate and is a useful measure of performance in some situations.

CPI is illustrated with the following example: A task that takes 1×10^6 clocks to execute 5×10^5 instructions has a CPI of 2.0. Small values of CPI indicate higher performance than large values of CPI. For many processors, different instructions require a different number of clocks for execution; thus CPI is an average value for all instructions executed. Further, different programs use instructions in different mixes. CPI combines the weighted use of each instruction class (the fraction of the total instructions) with the number of clocks per instruction class to give a weighted mean, a topic discussed further in this section.

Speedup

Designers are faced with the question of evaluating the effect of modifying a design, called design A, to design B. Is the modified design, design B, better than design A? The answer is found by using the concept of speedup. Note that speedup is a dimensionless ratio:

$$\text{Speedup} = \frac{\text{Time A}}{\text{Time B}} = \frac{\text{CPI A}}{\text{CPI B}} = \frac{\text{Rate B}}{\text{Rate A}} = \frac{\text{IPC B}}{\text{IPC A}}.$$

If design B is an improvement, then the speedup will be greater than 1. If design B hurts performance, the speedup will be less than 1. If speedup is equal to 1, there is no performance change. This relationship recognizes that reducing CPIs is associated with improved performance because the number of clocks is a measure of time and an instruction is a measure of the work performed.

Percent Difference and Change

We are also interested in the percent difference in the performance between two systems, A and B. For the following derivations, assume that Rate A > Rate B and that Time A is < Time B:

$$A \text{ is } x\% \text{ faster than B (Rate)} = 100\left(\frac{\text{Rate A} - \text{Rate B}}{\text{Rate B}}\right)$$

$$= 100\left(\frac{\text{Rate A}}{\text{Rate B}} - 1\right)$$

$$= 100(\text{Speedup} - 1).$$

$$A \text{ is } x\% \text{ faster than B (Time)} = 100\left(\frac{\text{Time B} - \text{Time A}}{\text{Time B}}\right)$$

$$= 100\left(1 - \frac{\text{Time A}}{\text{Time B}}\right)$$

$$= 100\left(1 - \frac{1}{\text{Speedup}}\right).$$

EXAMPLES

1. Processor A performs a given task in 1 s while processor B requires 2 s for the same task. By what percentage is A faster than B?

    Solution

    The speedup of A over B is $2/1 = 2$. Thus A is $100(1 - 1/2) = 50\%$ faster than B.

2. Processor A performs the same task at the rate of 1 task per second while B performs the same task at 0.5 tasks per second. By what percentage is A faster than B?

    Solution

    The speedup is $1/0.5 = 2$. Thus A is $100(2 - 1) = 100\%$ faster than B.

    Comment

    Note that the same change in performance of processor A compared with processor B gives a 100% improvement in rate and a 50% improvement in time.

3. What is the maximum percentage of difference in rate and time that can exist between two processors?

    Solution

    If the rate of processor A is infinite, the maximum percentage of difference in rate between the two processors is ∞ %. With an infinite rate, the time for processor A is reduced to zero and the maximum percentage of difference in time is limited to 100%.

4. A processor executes 100M instructions per second (where M indicates 10^6). With an improved memory, the execution rate increases to 125M instructions per second. What is the percentage of change in performance?

    Solution

    The speedup resulting from the memory change is $125M/100M = 1.25$. Thus the percentage of change in performance is $100(1.25 - 1) = 25\%$.

5. The same processor requires 1×10^{-8} s per instruction. This rate increases to 8×10^{-9} s per instruction with the change. What is the percentage of change in performance?

    Solution

    The speedup is $1 \times 10^{-8}/8 \times 10^{-9} = 1.25$. The percentage of change in execution rate is $100(1.25 - 1) = 25\%$.

Means and Weighted Means

We now turn to the important topic of means and weighted means. There is a natural desire to characterize some performance measure of a computer with a single number that can be compared with the comparable number of another computer or used to evaluate a design modification. We find a single number by evaluating a number of measurements or observations and mathematically determining the central tendency or the mean of the observations. With computers, we can make three types of measurements or observations: (1) the time needed to perform a task, (2) the rate at which a task is performed, and (3) the ratio of times or rates called speedup in the preceding subsection.

There are three types of means used to find the central tendency of the measurements: arithmetic mean for time, harmonic mean for rates, and geometric mean for ratios. The observations for these three means may have equal weights or be weighted. If the name of the mean does not use the word weighted, it is assumed that the observations have equal weight. The selection of the correct mean is determined by the type of observed data and by the desired evaluation of the data (Croxton, Cowden, and Klein 1967).

In many of the subsequent discussions of weighted means, the term weight will be used to refer to the fractional occurrence of an event, in which the fraction is $x/100$, or to the frequency of an event, in which the frequency is also given as $x/100$. There will be cases in which the context of the model implies the use of the terms frequency of use or fraction of time rather than weight. In general, these three terms are synonymous and the sum of weights, fractions, or frequencies is equal to one.

Time-Based Means

Smith (Smith 1988) states that "the time required to perform a specific amount of computation is the ultimate measure of computer performance." Thus time measurements are usually fundamental measurements in the field of computer performance modeling. When other measures are used, the validity of these measures can usually be checked by converting to time. In later chapters we consider and model such measures as latency time, access time, wait time, and response time.

Arithmetic Mean. The arithmetic mean is used to find the central tendency for equal weight time measurements. The arithmetic mean of the time per event is determined by

$$\text{arithmetic mean} = \frac{1}{n} \sum_{i=1}^{n} T_i.$$

An arithmetic mean requires that the data points have equal weights, and the result is frequently called the average. For example, the average grade, x', in a class is the sum of the observed grades divided by the number of students:

$$x' = \frac{1}{n} \sum_{i+1}^{n} x_i.$$

EXAMPLE

A particular job is run on a corporate mainframe on the first of each month. The times required for running this job over a 4-month period are 2 h, 2.2 h, 1.9 h, and 2.3 h. What is the mean or average time to run this job?

Solution

The data points have equal weight as the same job is run each month. Thus the arithmetic mean or average is used to find the central tendency. The mean or average time to run a job over the 4-month period is

$$\frac{2.0 + 2.2 + 1.9 + 2.3}{4} = \frac{8.4}{4} = 2.1 \text{ h per job.}$$

Weighted Arithmetic Mean. For many cases, computing an equal-weight arithmetic mean will give misleading results. Care must be taken when events occur at different fractions of the total events and each event requires a different amount of time. The weighted time per event is the weighted arithmetic mean, defined as

$$\text{weighted arithmetic mean} = \sum_{i=1}^{n} W_i T_i.$$

The weighted arithmetic mean is the central tendency of time per unit of work. W_i is the fraction that operation i is of the total operations, and T_i is the time consumed by each use. Note that $W_1 + W_2 + \cdots + W_n = 1$ and that W_i is not the fraction of time that the operation is in use.

EXAMPLE

A processor has two classes of instructions: class A instructions take two clocks to execute whereas class B instructions take three clocks to execute. Of all the instructions executed, 75% are class A instructions and 25% are class B instructions. What is the CPI of this processor?

Solution

The observations are in time and are weighted. Thus the CPI of the processor is determined by the weighted arithmetic mean:

$$CPI = W_A \, CPI_A + W_B \, CPI_B,$$
$$CPI = (0.75 \times 2) + (0.25 \times 3) = 1.5 + 0.75 = 2.25 \text{ clocks per instruction}$$

Comment

When solving a problem such as this one, add the event probabilities together and verify that the sum is one; if the sum is not equal to one, there is some error in the solution. A good practice is to use a table, as shown in Table 2.1, for the solution of these problems rather than attempt to bind variables to an equation.

Rate-Based Means

Performance is sometimes measured as rates. For example, my car goes 25 MPH or my computer performs 100 million instructions per second. Likewise, a computer may execute 0.5 IPC, the reciprocal of CPI. Thus, instead of time, we can also consider rates for evaluating performance or design changes. When rates are the observed events, the harmonic mean and the weighted harmonic mean will provide the central tendency of the observations.

TABLE 2.1 WEIGHTED ARITHMETIC MEAN (WAM)

Instruction Type	Weights	Clocks	Product
A	0.75	2	1.50
B	0.25	3	0.75
	SUM = 1.0		WAM = 2.25 clocks per instruction

Harmonic Mean. The harmonic mean is the central tendency of the observations expressed as rates having equal weights and the result is the mean events per unit of time:

$$\text{harmonic mean} = \frac{1}{\frac{1}{n}\sum_{i=1}^{n}\frac{1}{R_i}} = \frac{n}{\sum_{i=1}^{n}\frac{1}{R_i}}.$$

The harmonic mean is defined as the reciprocal of the arithmetic mean of the reciprocals of the values and is the central tendency of units of work per units of time.

EXAMPLE

Consider the example in the subsection on arithmetic means of jobs being run on the corporate computer. We express the observations in a rate measure of jobs per hour. These data are 0.5, 0.45, 0.53, and 0.43 jobs per hour. What is the central tendency of these measurements in jobs per hour?

Solution

The central tendency is found by using the harmonic mean:

$$\text{Jobs per hour} = \frac{4}{\frac{1}{0.5} + \frac{1}{0.45} + \frac{1}{0.53} + \frac{1}{0.43}} = \frac{4}{2 + 2.2 + 1.9 + 2.3}$$

$$= \frac{4}{8.4} = 0.476.$$

Comment

Note that 0.476 jobs per hour is the reciprocal of 2.1 h per job found previously with the arithmetic mean.

Weighted Harmonic Mean. When the observed rate data are weighted, the mean becomes

$$\text{weighted harmonic mean} = \frac{1}{\sum_{i=1}^{n}\frac{W_i}{R_i}},$$

where W_i is the fraction of the total task, not time, that is performed at R_i. The result is the central tendency in weighted events per units of time.

TABLE 2.2 SOLUTION WITH WEIGHTED HARMONIC MEAN (WHM)

Weight	Rate	Quotient
0.4	10 million/s	$0.4/10 = 0.04$
0.6	5 million/s	$0.6/5 = 0.12$
SUM $= 1.0$		WHM $= 1/(0.04 + 0.12) = 1/0.16 = 6.25$ million instructions per second

EXAMPLES

1. A program executes in two modes: 40% of the program instructions execute at the rate of 10 million instructions per second and 60% execute at the rate of 5 million instructions per second. What is the weighted execution rate in millions of instructions per second?

   Solution

   Because the observations are rates and the executions are weighted, use the weighted harmonic mean to find the central tendency, shown in Table 2.2.

2. Solve the same problem by using times in seconds per instruction, rather than rates.

   Solution

   Because the data are in time and the executions are weighted, use the weighted arithmetic mean as shown in Table 2.3.

   Comment

   The two results have a reciprocal relationship, as expected:

   $$\frac{1}{1.6 \times 10^{-7}} = 6.25 \times 10^6.$$

   We can derive the weighted harmonic mean from the weighted arithmetic mean by taking the reciprocal of time, which is rate, and then the reciprocal of the summation.

TABLE 2.3 SOLUTION WITH WEIGHTED ARITHMETIC MEAN (WAM)

Weight	Time	Product
0.4	1×10^{-7} seconds per instruction	0.4×10^{-7}
0.6	2×10^{-7} seconds per instruction	1.2×10^{-7}
SUM $= 1.0$		WAM $= 1.6 \times 10^{-7}$ seconds per instruction

Ratio-Based Means

Some data observations are the ratios of either times or rates. For example, we may execute a number of benchmarks on two computers and find the time ratio for each of the benchmarks. For these cases, we find the measure of central tendency of the ratios by computing the geometric mean or the weighted geometric mean.

Geometric Mean. The geometric mean is used for evaluating performance when the observations have equal weights and are the ratios of times, rates, or the result of normalization. The geometric mean is the central tendency of ratios; it is not an overall performance measure such as total system speedup:

$$\text{geometric mean} = \sqrt[n]{\prod_{i=1}^{n} \text{ratio}_i}.$$

The proper use of the geometric mean is illustrated with the following examples.

EXAMPLES

1. An amplifier has three stages with gains of 2, 3, and 6 for a total gain of 36. The gains of the stages are increased to 3, 4, and 7 for a total gain of 84. What is the central tendency of the gain improvement per stage?

    Solution
    Because we are dealing with ratios and the observations have equal weight (because the amplifier stages are in cascade), the central tendency of the increase in stage gain is found with the geometric mean:

    $$\text{mean increase per stage} = \sqrt[3]{\frac{3}{2} \times \frac{4}{3} \times \frac{7}{6}}$$

    $$= \sqrt[3]{2.333} = 1.326.$$

    Comment
    The mean increase per stage is the ratio 1.326 or 32.6%. Note that the geometric mean is *not* the overall increase of the amplifi er gain, which is $84/36 = 2.333$. However, because the gains of the stages multiply, the total increase of the amplifi er's gain is the mean increase per stage raised to the power of the number of stages. That is, the total increase in amplifi er gain is $1.3263^3 = 2.333$, which is the product of the individual stage increases.

2. The designers of a processor can reduce the clock period by 50% (a ratio of 0.5) and reduce the CPI by 25% (a ratio of 0.75). The time to execute an instruction is the product of the CPI and the clock period. What is the mean improvement for these two design changes in percent?

    Solution
    This problem deals with ratios of equal weight. Thus the solution is found with the geometric mean:

    $$\text{mean reduction per change} = \sqrt{0.5 \times 0.75}$$

    $$= \sqrt{0.375} = 0.612 = 38.7\%.$$

TABLE 2.4 LOOP EXECUTION TIME (CLOCKS)

Loop	Computer A	Computer B	Speedup
1	39	20	1.95
2	53	27	1.96
3	27	13	2.08
4	31	13	2.38

Comment

Note that the overall improvement in the processor's performance is $100(1 - 0.375) = 62.5\%$. The mean reduction per change is not the average of the two reductions; $(50\% + 25\%)/2 = 37.5\%$. Remember that problems such as this can be checked by use of time. Before the change, the normalized CPI is 1. After the change, the normalized CPI is $0.5 \times 0.75 = 0.375$ and the percent improvement is $100(1 - 0.375) = 62.5\%$.

3. Two computers execute four loops of a scientific program in the number of clocks shown in Table 2.4. What is the central tendency of the speedup for the loops?

Solution

The observations are clocks, a measure of time, and the events are of equal weight; thus the central tendency of the speedup for the four loops is found by the geometric mean. Remember that speedup is a dimensionless ratio:

$$\text{Mean loop speedup} = \sqrt[4]{1.95 \times 1.96 \times 2.08 \times 2.38} = \sqrt[4]{18.9} = 2.08.$$

Comment

There is a temptation to average the speedups for the four loops to find an average speedup. This calculation is $8.37/4 = 2.09$. Although close to the geometric mean, this result is not correct.

The geometric mean is frequently and incorrectly used to summarize computer performance by a single number, as noted in the comment above. Consider the following example. Two computers, A and B, execute three programs in the time shown in Table 2.5.

TABLE 2.5 PROGRAM EXECUTION TIME (S)

Program	Computer A	Computer B	Ratio A/B
1	1500	150	10
2	2300	200	11.5
3	24,000	2500	9.6
TOTAL TIME	27,800	2850	

The geometric mean of the ratios is $\sqrt[3]{10 \times 11.5 \times 9.6} = \sqrt[3]{1104} = 10.33$. Does this number represent a valid measure of the speedup of computer B over computer A for these three programs? The answer is no; 10.33 is the central tendency of the ratios.

Recall that the ultimate measure of performance is time. The total time for computer A is 27,800 s and for computer B is 2850 s with a speedup of $27,800/2850 = 9.75$. It is tempting to find the speedup by taking the arithmetic mean of the three ratios. The result of this operation is $10 + 11.5 + 9.6 = 31.1/3 = 10.37$. Again, this result is close to the speedup found from total time but incorrect insofar as finding a single number that represents the relative performance of the two processors.

Weighted Geometric Mean. For cases in which the observed ratios are weighted by the fraction of use, the weighted geometric mean is used to find the central tendency:

$$\text{weighted geometric mean} = \prod_{i=1}^{n} \text{ratio}^{w_i}.$$

EXAMPLE

For the example above, assume that for a particular benchmark, loop 1 is executed 20 times, loop 2 is executed 30 times, loop 3 is executed 50 times, and loop 4 is executed 100 times. What is the mean speedup of the four loops?

Solution

The weight for loop 1 is $20/200 = 0.1$, loop 2 is 0.15, loop 3 is 0.25, and loop 4 is 0.5. The weighted geometric mean provides the weighted mean speedup of the four loops:

$$\text{mean loop speedup} = 1.95^{0.1} \times 1.96^{0.15} \times 2.08^{0.25} \times 2.38^{0.5}$$
$$= 1.069 \times 1.106 \times 1.201 \times 1.543 = 2.19.$$

Comment

The weighted mean loop speedup is biased to loop 4, which has both the greatest speedup (2.38) and the highest use (50%). As with other problems, the speedup of the processor executing the weighted loops is found with the weighted total times for computers A and B.

$$\text{speedup} = \frac{\text{Weighted time A}}{\text{Weighted time B}}$$
$$= \frac{(0.1 \times 39) + (0.15 \times 53) + (0.25 \times 27) + (0.5 \times 31)}{(0.1 \times 20) + (0.15 \times 27) + (0.25 \times 13) + (0.5 \times 13)}$$
$$= \frac{3.9 + 7.95 + 6.75 + 15.5}{2 + 4.05 + 3.25 + 6.5} = \frac{34.1}{15.8} = 2.16.$$

Means Summary

The six means are summarized in Table 2.6. We select the proper mean equation for solving a problem by determining the units (times, rates, or ratios) and determining if the observations are of equal weight or weighted. Remember that the mean, however determined, is the central tendency of times, rates, or ratios. Only arithmetic and harmonic means give an indication of overall performance.

> **TABLE 2.6 ARITHMETIC, HARMONIC, AND GEOMETRIC MEANS**
>
> | Mean | Equal Weights | Weighted | Units |
> |------|---------------|----------|-------|
> | Arithmetic | $AM = \dfrac{1}{n}\sum_{i=1}^{n} T_i$ | $WAM = \dfrac{1}{n}\sum_{i=1}^{n} W_i T_i$ | $\dfrac{time}{unit\ of\ work}$ |
> | Harmonic | $HM = \dfrac{n}{\sum_{i=1}^{n}\frac{1}{R_i}}$ | $WHM = \dfrac{1}{\sum_{i=1}^{n}\frac{W_i}{R_i}}$ | $\dfrac{units\ of\ work}{time}$ |
> | Geometric | $GM = \sqrt[n]{\prod_{i=1}^{n} r_i}$ | $WGM = \prod_{i=1}^{n} ratio^{w_i}$ | Ratio |

EXAMPLES

1. You are processing 200 jobs on a computer. The first 100 jobs are processed at 50 jobs per hour, and the second 100 jobs are processed at 100 jobs per hour. What is the mean rate of processing the 200 jobs?

Solution

The correct solution is found by use of the harmonic mean with equal weights. The reasons are that this problem is stated in rates (jobs per hour) and the work performed is the same (100 jobs); thus the weights are the same:

$$\text{mean rate} = \frac{2}{\frac{1}{50} + \frac{1}{100}} = \frac{2}{0.02 + 0.01} = \frac{2}{0.03} = 66.7 \text{ jobs per hour.}$$

Comment

This problem can also be solved in time. The first 100 jobs required 2 h whereas the second 100 jobs required 1 h. Thus the average time to process the 200 jobs is 3 h, giving a rate of $200/3 = 66.7$ jobs per hour.

2. A computer executes task A in 1 s and task B in 10 s. For each execution of task B, task A is executed nine times. What is the processing rate of the computer in tasks per second?

Solution

The observations are units of time and the number of executions is weighted. However, the question asks for processing rate. Thus the weighted arithmetic mean is used to find the central tendency of the time, which is then converted to rate. The weight for task A is $9/10 = 0.9$ and for task B is $1/10 = 0.1$. The weighed arithmetic mean execution time $= 0.9 \times 1 + 0.1 \times 10 = 1.9$ s, and the weighted execution rate is $1/1.9 = 0.526$ tasks per second.

Comment

Another way of solving this problem is to convert the observations to rates and find the central tendency with the weighted harmonic mean:

$$\text{weighted execution rate} = \frac{1}{\frac{0.9}{1} + \frac{0.1}{0.1}} = \frac{1}{0.9 + 1} = \frac{1}{1.9} = 0.526$$

Compound Growth Rate

Another concept of interest to computer engineers is compound growth rate. If each year we can have a processor that is twice as fast as last year's processor, the compound growth rate of performance is 100% per year. A doubling in performance every 2 years results from a compound growth rate of 41% per year. Compound growth rate is identical to compound interest earned on money. Each year the interest rate is computed on the principle plus the prior year's interest.

The formula for compound growth rate is

$$\text{last value} = \text{starting value} \left(1 + \frac{\text{growth rate}}{100}\right)^{\text{number of time intervals}}$$

$$\text{growth rate} = 100 \left(\sqrt[\text{number of time intervals}]{\frac{\text{last value}}{\text{starting value}}} - 1\right).$$

A growth rate of 10% per year and a starting value of 1 will have a value of 1.464 after 4 years. Note that the interval can be any unit of time that is consistent with the definition of the growth rate.

EXAMPLES

1. In 1995, a transaction server performed at the rate of 100 transactions per second. The server is upgraded over the years and in 2000 performs at the rate of 700 transactions per second. If the transactions are identical, what is the compound growth rate of the transactions per second over this 5-year period?

   Solution
   The speedup in processing rate is $700/100 = 7$. The compound growth rate is $100(\sqrt[5]{7} - 1) = 47.5\%$ per year.

2. What would be the performance in transactions per second for a similar server in the year 2005 assuming that the compound growth rate remains the same?

   Solution
   The transaction per second rate of this server will be $700 \times 1.475^5 = 4887$ transactions per second.

2.2 AMDAHL'S LAW

This law models the speedup of a computer when it is processing two classes of tasks; one class can be speeded up whereas the other class cannot (Amdhal 1967). This situation is frequently encountered in computer system design. The solution of Amdahl's law model is normalized to the execution time of the system before any speedup is applied.

Assume that a program has two components, $t1$ and $t2$. The component $t2$ can be speeded up. What is the overall speedup of the system?

$$\text{speedup} = \frac{t1 + t2}{t1 + (t2/n)}$$

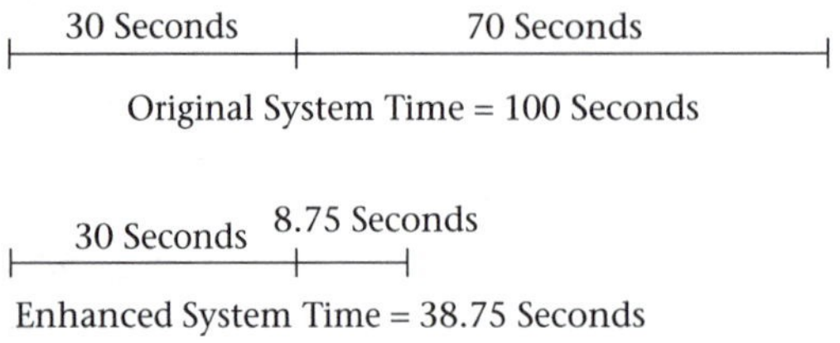

```
 |————————————+————————————————————————————————————|
    30 Seconds                    70 Seconds
             Original System Time = 100 Seconds
```

Figure 2.1 Amdahl's law

```
                  8.75 Seconds
 |————————————+————————|
    30 Seconds
 Enhanced System Time = 38.75 Seconds
```

For some problems, we may not know the values of $t1$ and $t2$. However, we do know the fraction of time that can or cannot be speeded up. We define a to be the fraction of time[10] that cannot be speeded up and $1 - a$ as the fraction of time that can be speeded up by a factor n:

$$t1 + t2 = 1,$$

$$a = \frac{t1}{t1 + t2} = t1,$$

$$1 - a = \frac{t2}{t1 + t2} = t2.$$

Thus the normalized speedup is

$$\frac{1}{a + \frac{1-a}{n}}.$$

Consider these limits. As $a \rightarrow 0$ (in other words, the complete program can be speeded up), speedup $\rightarrow n$ and as $n \rightarrow \infty$ (in other words, $t2$ is reduced to zero), speedup $\rightarrow 1/a$. This second limit tells us that if 10% of the time of the original system cannot be speeded up, then the greatest speedup possible for the system is 10.

Problems that can be solved by Amdahl's law may be easier to visualize graphically rather than by attempting to bind values to the equation. This is illustrated by the following example.

EXAMPLE

An executing program is timed, and it is found that the serial portion (that portion that cannot be speeded up) consumes 30 s whereas the other portion that can be speeded up consumes 70 s of the time. You believe that by using parallel processors, you can speed up this later portion by a factor of 8. What is the speedup of the system?

Solution

A graphical solution to this Amdahl's law problem is shown in Figure 2.1. The 70-s portion of the time is decreased by a factor of 8 to 8.75 s. The speedup of the system is found by dividing the original time (100 s) by the enhanced time (38.75 s). Thus speedup is 2.58. The same result can be found by binding the

---

[10] The variable a is not a weight of work as used in finding the arithmetic mean.

arguments to Amdahl's law. For the original system, $a = 0.3$, the enhancement is $n = 8$. Thus the speedup is calculated as

$$\text{speedup} = \frac{1}{0.3 + (0.7/8)} = \frac{1}{0.3 + 0.0875} = \frac{1}{0.3875} = 2.58.$$

EXAMPLE

Derive Amdahl's law for the case in which a is the fraction of time that can be speeded up.

Solution

The solution is found by substituting a for $(1 - a)$ and $(1 - a)$ for a:

$$\text{speedup} = \frac{t1 + t2}{(1 - a) + (a/n)}$$

$$= \frac{1}{(1 - a) + (a/n)}.$$

2.3 MOORE'S LAW

In 1965 Gordon Moore (Moore 1965), at the time head of research at Fairchild Semiconductor, observed that the number of circuits per die had doubled every year since 1959. In a later paper (Moore 1979) he extended the data and restated his case by pointing out that the number of circuits per die is still doubling every year, as shown in Figure 2.2. Moore said, "I expect a change in the slope to occur at about the present time. From a doubling of the slope of the curve annually for the first 15 years or so, the slope droops to about one-half its previous value to a doubling once every two years." This observation came to be known as Moore's law and is a useful tool for making projections on the circuit density of chips.

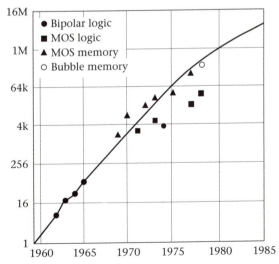

Figure 2.2 Moore's law (©1979 IEEE): MOS, metal-oxide semiconductor

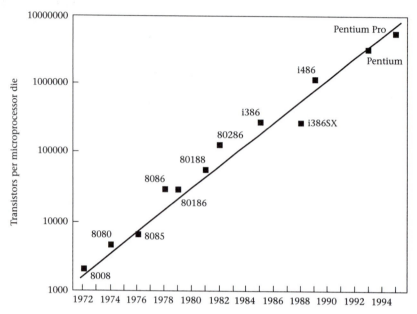

Figure 2.3 Transistors per microprocessor

Recent data taken from various sources, shown in Figure 2.3, confirm the slope to be approximately 1.4 or doubling the number of transistors per microprocessor every 2 years.[11] Moore's law indicates the largest possible number of transistors per die that can be produced. However, smaller dies can and will be produced as well. Note that the law has been restated from transistors per die to transistors per microprocessor.

The design cycle of an integrated circuit can be as short as a few months for a standard cell design to as long as several years for a complex microprocessor. In the latter case, the designers must be able to project ahead so as to forecast accurately the manufacturability of a proposed design. Moore's law is a useful tool for the designer to ensure that a new design will not be "behind the curve" when it is completed.

There are two major reasons why Moore's law holds. First, the die area is increasing because of the ability to image over a larger area; second, the size of the features that can be processed is decreasing, making it possible to place more devices on a given area. Increased area times decreased geometry results in more devices per die. These improvements are the result of improved lithography, clean rooms, and overall process control. Improvements do not "just happen"; they take large investments on the part of the semiconductor manufacturers and the research community in new design techniques, materials, and manufacturing technology. A modern chip factory costs in excess of $1 billion today.

Moore's law is now observed to hold true in hard disks as well as semiconductors. Figure 2.4 shows that the increase in the disk bit density of 2.5-in. disks is even greater than that of chips. The forecast is made that, by the year 2030, 10^9 megabytes per

---

[11] Another example of compound growth.

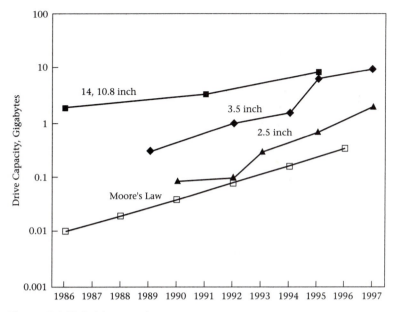

Figure 2.4 Disk-drive capacity

square inch will be achieved. With the expected growth in software size, this capacity will be needed.

These remarkable increases in disk bit density are the result of massive research and development (R&D) investments in disk technology. Some of the results of this R&D are smaller read and write heads that are closer to the disk surface and changed aspect ratios of the bit from 20×1 to 1×1 or square. In addition, improved electronics are able to read smaller- and higher-frequency signals.

EXAMPLES

1. In 1970 wafers had a diameter of 2 in. By 1997 12-in. wafers were entering production. What is the compound rate of increase in wafer area per year?

   Solution

   The wafer area in 1970 was 3.14 sq. in., whereas in 1997 the wafer area was 113 sq. in. The area increase is $113/3.14 = 36$. Over the period of 27 years, the compound rate of increase is 14% per year. We check this result by observing that $1.14^{27} = 36$.

2. In 1970 the geometry size was 10 μm,[12] whereas in 1997 the geometry was 0.6 μm. What is the compound rate of increase in devices per unit area?

   Solution

   The decrease in geometry size is $10/0.6 = 16.66$ and the number of devices increases as the square of the geometry size. This increase is $16.66^2 = 278$ per unit of area. A 278-fold increase over 27 years is a compound growth rate of

---

[12] A micrometer (μm) is one millionth of a meter or approximately 1/25,000 of an inch.

23.2% per year. We check this result by observing that $1.232^{27} = 280$; the difference is due to rounding.

3. Do the results of examples 1 and 2 above support Moore's law?

Solution

Not directly; wafer area is not a direct indicator of die area. However, investigation will show that the number of dies per wafer has held relatively constant over many generations of the x86 architecture at approximately 80 dies/wafer. Thus the wafer area is a good surrogate for die area.

The increase in die area times the devices per die is $36 \times 278 = 10,008$. This is a compound rate of increase over the 27 years of 41%. A 41% per year compound growth rate will give 99% growth in 2 years; $1.41^2 = 1.99$. This is very close to doubling every 2 years, as forecasted by Moore's law.

2.4 LEARNING CURVE

There are dramatic examples all around us that show that the cost of computing (processors and memory) is decreasing rapidly. The reason for these decreases is that the manufacturers make large investments in processes and manufacturing equipment that will result in a reduction in manufacturing costs. For many products in which these investments have been made, researchers have observed an effect called the learning curve.[13]

Figure 2.5 shows the price of integrated circuits during 1964–1966 (Conley 1970). These integrated circuits were small scale integration (SSI) devices of one to three gates each. For each doubling of the volume, the price was reduced by approximately 25%. For example, the price was $10.50 at the 5-million point and $3 at the 80-million point.

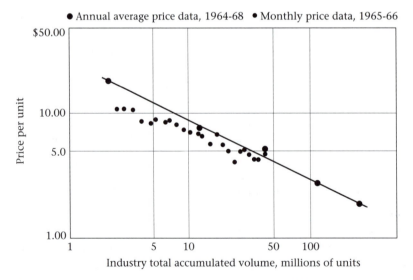

Figure 2.5 Learning curve for integrated circuits (©1970 IEEE)

---

[13] Also known as an experience curve.

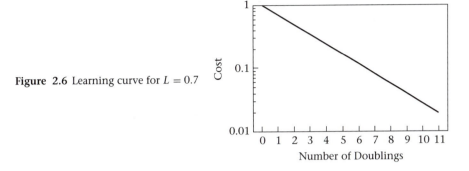

Figure 2.6 Learning curve for $L = 0.7$

The learning curve law states that costs go down by a fixed percentage each time the number of units produced doubles. Figure 2.6 shows the curve in cleaned-up form. The learning curve factor L is defined as the fraction of cost remaining after the volume doubling. In other words, if cost is reduced 30% with each doubling of volume, the learning curve factor is 0.7. Note that cost is in terms of constant dollars to remove inflation or deflation from the model.

Based on Figure 2.6, if 1 million devices have been produced at a cost of $1 per device, the second million devices will cost only $0.70; the cumulative volume is now 2 million devices. When another 2 million devices are produced, the second 2 million will cost $0.49, and if another four million devices are produced, these devices will cost $0.329.

The learning curve is stated mathematically as

$$\text{present cost} = \text{base cost} \times L^{\text{number of doublings}}.$$

If a product has a base cost of $1000 for the first unit and the volume produced is 1024, there have been $\log_2 1024$ or 10 doublings of cumulative volume. If $L = 0.9$, then the cost of the last units produced is $1000 \times 0.9^{10} = \$348$.

Learning curve theory requires that the units being produced must remain the same over the period of interest. Example constant units are bits of DRAM, gates, and M&M chocolates. Learning curve theory is difficult to apply to products such as automobiles and personal computers because there is no normalizing unit. In general, we do not buy the same PC today we bought 2 years ago. However, the under-$1000 PC is an example of the learning curve at work.

Unfortunately, a number of authors have incorrectly reported that learning curve theory projects costs are reduced by a fixed percentage every year. This is a phenomena observed with DRAMs, but there is no theory to support this conjecture. It has also been observed that the cumulative volume of DRAM bits has approximately doubled every year for the past decade, leading to the erroneous conclusion that learning curve theory is time based.

EXAMPLE

In 1990, 4M-bit DRAMs sold for approximately $40. Assume that (1) the selling price is a function of manufacturing cost, (2) the cumulative volume of DRAM bits doubles every year after 1990, and (3) the learning curve factor is 0.75. What would you expect a 4M-bit DRAM to sell for in 1999, 2005?

Solution

The estimated price of a 4M-bit DRAM in 1999 is $40 \times 0.75^9 = \$3.00$. In 2005 the estimated price will be $40 \times 0.75^{15} = \$0.53$.

Keep in mind that learning curve theory applies to manufacturing costs. From time to time the selling prices of DRAMs will be higher or lower than the price forecasts by learning curve theory. The reason for this is supply and demand. When supplies are tight, the devices will be priced high with resulting high profits, as in 1995. However, when supplies are plentiful, selling prices will be lower, as in 1996–1999. Also remember that the learning curve reduction in costs does not occur by magic. There must be a substantial investment in R&D, process development, and new manufacturing equipment.

2.5 GROSCH'S LAW

In 1953 Herb Grosch formalized an observation that has been widely misapplied in recent years (Grosch 1953). He observed that "...giving added economy only as the square root of the increase in speedup – that is, to do a calculation ten times as cheaply you must do it one hundred times as fast." In other words, $C = K\sqrt{P}$, where P is the computing power, K is a constant, and C is the system cost.

This observation has been turned around to state that computing power increases as the square of the cost of the computer, or $P = KC^2$. This means that for twice the money one obtains four times the computing power.

Figure 2.7 shows the price of three Pentium II processors equally configured but with 300-, 333-, and 350-MHz clocks. Assume that the clock frequency is a surrogate for computing power. Also shown for comparison is Grosch's law, starting at $1200.

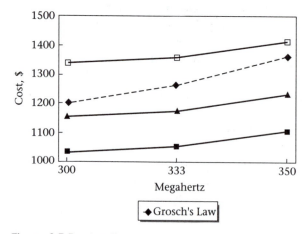

Figure 2.7 Pentium II system prices

The conclusion that can be drawn from these data is that there is only a rough correlation between real market prices and Grosch's law for PCs. However, if one needs to make a price forecast for a faster PC, Grosch's law provides a good rule of thumb.

EXAMPLE

The consumer price of a 350-MHz Pentium II PC is $1699. Estimate the price of a 500-MHz version of equal configuration that will be sold in 2 years.

Solution

There are two effects at work here. Grosch's law indicates that the price will be

$$\$1699 \sqrt{\frac{500}{350}} = \$1699 \times 1.19 = \$2021.$$

However, as production volume has to increase, PCs have experienced a learning curve of $L = 0.7$ per year for many years. Thus the expected price of the faster PC in 2 years will be

$$\$2021 \times 0.7^2 = \$2021 \times 0.49 = \$990.$$

Comment

With the combination of Grosch's law and the learning curve, we can forecast that the price of this faster computer in 2 years will cost approximately $709 less than the base model. This estimate assumes that the memory, disk, and I/O complement remain the same.

2.6 STEADY-STATE PERFORMANCE

There are a number of ways by which the steady-state performance may be measured. One of the more common measures is millions of instructions per second (MIPS). This measure is the result of observing how many instructions are executed by a processor in a time period. From this, the MIPS measure can be computed.

EXAMPLE

A given processor executes 2-million instructions in 3 s. What is the MIPS measure of performance?

Solution

$$\text{MIPS} = \frac{\#\ \text{instructions executed}}{\text{Seconds} \times 10^6}$$

$$= \frac{2 \times 10^6}{3 \times 10^6} = 0.66\ \text{MIPS}.$$

The MIPS measure of processor performance is best used when comparing the performance of two processors with the same instruction set (an Intel Pentium and a Pentium Pro, for example) executing the same program. If the instruction sets are different, the MIPS measure can be misleading. For example, if one of the processors has a multiply instruction and the other performs multiplication by a subroutine, the MIPS rating is ambiguous as the same instructions are not being executed. This deficiency leads to another method for measuring performance.

We find this other measure of processor performance by computing the time to execute a task. This performance model is

$$\text{task time} = \text{number of instructions executed} \times \text{CPI} \times \text{time per clock}$$
$$= \frac{\text{number of instructions executed} \times \text{CPI}}{\text{clock frequency}}.$$

This model can be modified for various situations. For example, assume you want to know the performance impact if you are modifying the execution unit of a given processor, say an Intel Pentium, and are not changing the clock frequency. Knowledge of the change in CPI is all that is required because the number of instructions as well as the time per clock are unchanged. The determination of CPI for a processor is described in Chapter 5 for hardwired processors and in Chapter 6 for pipelined processors.

A measure of processor performance used with scientific calculations is millions of floating-point operations per second (MFLOPS). This measure considers only the floating-point instructions executed; it does not consider instructions such as loads, stores, and branches. The reason they are not considered is that they are overhead instructions and do not contribute directly to the operational performance of the processor.

EXAMPLE

A processor executes 10-million floating-point and 1-million overhead instructions in 50 ms. What is the MFLOPS rating of this processor?

Solution

$$\text{MFLOPS} = \frac{10 \times 10^6}{50 \times 10^{-3} \times 10^6} = 200$$

Comment

The 1-million overhead instructions do not contribute to the MFLOPS rating. The MIPS rating is 220 when the overhead instructions are counted.

2.7 TRANSIENT PERFORMANCE

Section 2.5 discussed two measures of computer performance, the time to perform a task and the rate of performing tasks. Time is a useful measure for tasks such as performing a large SPICE evaluation of a die design. Rate measures are useful from mainframe and server applications that are receiving a job stream. Note that these measures of time and rate are the average performance in steady-state operation.

However, steady-state performance measures are relatively useless for many computer uses today. PCs and the clients attached to servers require another performance measure: response time or the transient performance. With a PC, when users click on a new task icon, they would like to see the results immediately, or at least with negligible delay. The same is true with a request presented to a server.

Chapter 7 discusses a queuing theory model that is useful for modeling the performance of I/O devices when the system is under a steady-state condition. This model is the so-called open-system model. For closed systems, such as are found with a collection of terminals attached to a server, the closed-system model is also described.

For systems for which there is a single user of a resource, such as a PC, executing only one task, the transient performance measure of response time becomes simply the sum of the times required for performing each task in satisfaction of the request. For example,

response time = operating system time + disk access time + data transfer time.

Because the disk access time is usually much greater than the other two times, disk access time is a good estimate of the transient response time of a request that uses the disk. For this reason, the disks used on single-user workstations and PCs need the smallest access time consistent with the cost of the system.

We see similar transient response time considerations with systems such as the World Wide Web (WWW). When a heavily loaded server is accessed, the server response time constitutes a major portion of the total response time, regardless of the bandwidth of the modems and network. At other times, such as at 2:00 A.M., when the servers are lightly loaded, the bandwidth of the network assumes the dominant role in determining response time. WWW response time can be modeled by means of the open-queuing theory model, as discussed in Section 7.6. Thus response time is a function not only of the hardware but also of the environment at the time of the request.

REFERENCES

Amdahl, G. M. (1967). "Validity of the Single Processor Approach to Achieving Large Scale Computing Capabilities," *Proceedings AFIPS Spring Joint Computer Conference.*

Conley, P. (1970). "Experience Curves as a Planning Tool," *IEEE Spectrum,* **7**:6, pp. 63–68.

Croxton, F. E., Cowden, D. J., and Klein, S. K. (1967). *Applied General Statistics,* 3rd ed., Prentice-Hall, Englewood Cliffs, NJ.

Grosch, H. R. J. (1953). "High Speed Arithmetic: The Digital Computer as a Research Tool," *Journal of the Optical Society of America,* **43**:4, pp. 306–310.

Moore, G. (1965). "Cramming More Components onto Integrated Circuits," *Electronics,* April 19, 1965, pp. 114–117.

Moore, G. (1979). "VLSI: Some Fundamental Challenges," *IEEE Spectrum,* **16**:4, pp. 30–37.

Smith, J. E. (1988). "Characterizing Computer Performance with a Single Number," *Communications of the ACM,* **31**:10, pp. 1202–1206.

EXERCISES

2.1 Go to a library and check your local newspapers. Find the advertised prices for disks and DRAMs used in PCs. The prices are user prices and are usually found in the business sections. Tabulate these prices for the past five years (old newspapers will be found on microfilm) and compute the learning curve factor, assuming that volume doubled every year. Make sure that you adjust for inflation.

TABLE 2.7 NETWORK PROTOCOL LAYER IMPROVEMENTS

Protocol Layer	Performance Improvement (%)
7	18
6	13
5	11
4	8
3	10
2	28
1	5

2.2 The performance improvements (in time reduction) in the latest version of seven layers of a new networking protocol were measured separately for each layer, as shown in Table 2.7. What is the mean or average improvement per layer? What is the overall speedup of the protocol?

2.3 Two benchmarks are run on a computer. BM 1 executes at 10 MIPS, and BM 2 executes at 15 MIPS. What single number should be used to represent the performance of this processor?

2.4 Three computers execute two benchmarks in the times shown in Table 2.8 (Smith 1988).

Answer the following questions, showing the calculations:

> A is x% faster than B for BM 1.
> A is x% faster than C for BM 1.
> B is x% faster than C for BM 1.
> B is x% faster than A for BM 2.
> C is x% faster than A for BM 2.
> C is x% faster than B for BM 2.
> B is x% faster than A for the two benchmarks.
> C is x% faster than B for the two benchmarks.
> C is x% faster than A for the two benchmarks.

2.5 An enhanced computer system executes two programs in 40 s with 80% of the time devoted to the nonenhanced program. When the two programs are

TABLE 2.8 BENCHMARKS (BMs) ON THREE COMPUTERS

BM	Computer A	Computer B	Computer C
1 (s)	1	10	20
2 (s)	1000	100	20
TOTAL TIME (s)	1001	110	40

executed on the nonenhanced system, the execution time is 200 s. What is the speedup of the enhanced portion?

2.6   Your company is able to produce twice as many of a product each year as during the year before. At what rate is the cumulative volume of this product increasing per year? Explain your answer.

2.7   Two microprocessors have been designed. One processor has an initial manufacturing cost of $1000 and the other has an initial manufacturing cost of $512. The learning curve for both processors is 0.80. What is the ratio of the cumulative volume of the two processors at which their manufacturing costs are equal?

2.8   A formula for determining the MIPS of a processor is

$$MIPS = \frac{\text{clock frequency}}{CPI \times 10^6}.$$

Derive this formula from

task time = number of instructions executed $\times$ CPI $\times$ time per clock.

2.9   Explain the origin of the names arithmetic mean, harmonic mean, and geometric mean.

2.10   One of the most frequently used applications of the geometric mean is to calculate compound growth rate. Derive the compound growth formula, given in Section 2.1, from the geometric mean.

THREE

USER INSTRUCTION SET DESIGN

3.0 INTRODUCTION

Over the past four decades of computer design and development, significant attention has been paid to the design of the processor instruction sets or the instruction set architecture (ISA), also known as the machine language. During the early period, starting with von Neumann, designers focused primarily on the design of instructions that supported the user or application program. Three developments then expanded this focus to the instruction support of operating systems, virtual memory systems, and multiprocessors, covered in Chapter 8. Each of these expanded capabilities has been considered to be invisible to the user programmer. For efficient and logically correct implementations and use, these support instructions usually operate in a protected mode not available to the user.

Because computers are general-purpose machines, functions can be provided by programming that are not available in the ISA. An example is the use of a subroutine to provide floating-point operations and data types. Functions and data types that are provided in the ISA are called architected, and functions and data types provided by programming are called programmed.

Instruction sets of early computers were designed in an environment of few resources. The memory was small, requiring that the instructions be as dense as possible. The resources for performing operations were likewise limited, leading to primitive instruction sets that would be recognized today as reduced instruction set computers. The von Neumann ISA contained only 21 instructions. All addresses are direct with address arithmetic, indexing for example, being performed by instructions operating on the program itself (called self-modifying code).

Blaauw and Brooks note that the fundamental difference between a machine language and a natural language is that a machine language is costly. They cite four aspects of cost that influence ISA design:

1. One wants interpretation to be swift and the interpreter simple, so machine languages are rigidly constrained, using few constructs.
2. Cost with respect to space and time requires compactness of representation expressed in the bit budget of the representation and the bit traffic of the use of this representation.

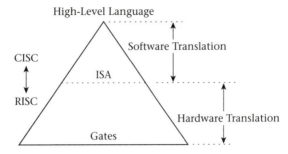

Figure 3.1 ISA lexical level

3. Fundamental technological reasons make it simplest to represent information by two-state devices, so most machine languages employ only two symbols, 0 and 1.
4. To simplify interpretation, statements are constrained to be parseable without dependence or context, and even semantic interpretation has at most a limited context-dependence (Blaauw and Brooks 1997).

3.1   LEXICAL LEVEL

A primary consideration in the design of an ISA is establishing the lexical level of the machine language. ISAs with a high lexical level are usually called complex instruction set computers (CISCs) and those with a lower lexical level are called reduced instruction set computers (RISCs). This concept is illustrated in Figure 3.1.

A program written in a high-level language, C for example, is compiled into the language of the target machine's ISA. The program in the ISA is then interpreted by hardware to turn the gates of the processor and memory on and off. A few lines of C code can result in controls being exercised on millions of gates – a significant increase in the information content of the program.

CISC machines move the ISA upward, thereby reducing the semantic gap that must be spanned by the compiler and increasing the semantic gap spanned by the hardware. Experimental computers have been built that execute a program in a high-level language directly without software support. On the other hand, RISC architectures increase the software semantic gap and decrease the hardware semantic gap. The argument for RISC is that a faster system will result because of the simpler instructions. This argument has not proven to be completely true with modern microprocessors. The ultimate RISC is found in the work of van der Poll, who devised an ISA with only one instruction! Further discussion of the RISC and CISC architectural styles is found in Section 3.3.

3.2   INSTRUCTION SET ARCHITECTURE

An ISA specifies three things: operations, data types, and addresses. Figure 3.2 shows these components and the bindings that exist between them. Bindings are the specification relationships between the components. For example, if the ISA has floating-point data types, there must be floating-point operations and vice versa. If the ISA

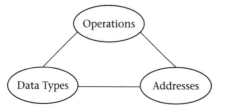

Figure 3.2 ISA components

has single- and double-precision integers, the addresses must be bound to the data types so that alignment in memory is enforced. When operations look for operands in memory and/or registers, the proper address must be provided in the address field(s) of the instruction.

In some designs, binding is enforced in the hardware whereas in other designs binding is enforced in the software. For example, some processors have instructions such as AddFloat and AddInteger. In this case, the operands in memory must be bound to the operation by the address in the instruction. In other words, floating-point and integer operands are stored in different regions of memory and are identified by their address. In other cases, operations such as add and subtract are generic. By tagging the operands or binding by addresses, the proper data type is identified. Establishing the binding between the three components is a task that must be carefully established by the ISA designer.

The components of an ISA shown in Figure 3.2 are allocated into instructions consisting of bit fields in the instruction word. In general, the instruction has two types of fields: operation field or op-code and address field or fields.

Op-Code	Address(es)

In many ISAs, the number of bits in the op-code field is $\geq \log_2$ (number of operations). For example, 8 bits can uniquely specify up to 256 operations or operation/data types, depending on how the operations are bound to the data types. Addresses are discussed in detail in Subsection 3.2.1, but the number of fields and their lengths are functions of how operands are addressed in either memory and/or registers.

All instructions have direct effects that are specified by the instruction and may have side effects. A side effect is a consistent result of an instruction that is in addition to the direct effect. An example of a side effect is found in incrementing the program counter during the execution of an instruction. Another example is found with instructions that, after an ADD, say, set an indicator bit if the result is equal to zero or is negative.[14] In general, side effects are used to carry information forward from one instruction to subsequent instructions. A side effect result may become an explicit operand of a subsequent instruction. Side effects must be defined in the ISA so there is no misunderstanding between the ISA designer and the programmer.

To understand how a stored programmed computer works, one must understand the function of the program counter illustrated in Figure 3.3. This counter provides

---

[14] Indicator bits, or flags, record the result of a comparison. Indicators are discussed further in Section 3.2.3.2.

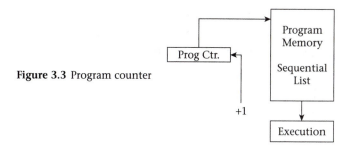

Figure 3.3 Program counter

the mechanism for indexing through a program stored in the program memory as a sequential list of instructions. The program counter, also called location counter or instruction pointer in some ISAs, points to the first instruction in the list to be executed. During the execution of the first instruction, the program counter is incremented by one so that it then points to the second instruction, then the third, and so on. The linear accessing of instructions from the sequential list can be redirected by means of branch and jump instructions.

Not all computers use a program counter, as some early computers stored the program as a linked list. With these computers, each instruction held the address of the next instruction. This technique was used because memory was sequentially accessed, not random as with modern memory technology.

EXAMPLE

Is the program counter a portion of the process state or the processor state?

Solution

There are a number of reasons why the program counter is a portion of the processor state: (1) The program counter is not explicitly described in a high-level language program, (2) the program counter carries information forward from one instruction to the next, and (3) the content of the program counter is saved on a context switch with the other processor state information.

3.2.1 ADDRESSES

We begin the discussion of the three components of an ISA by considering addresses. The organization of memory and the procedures by which the processor acquires operands and disposes of results is a paramount ISA design consideration. ISAs support one or both of the following operation types, shown in Table 3.1.

TABLE 3.1 REQUIRED ADDRESSES			
Type	Sources	Destination	Example
Dyadic	2	1	Add, subtract, multiply
Monadic	1	1	square root

Thus the instruction must provide two or three addresses as required by the operation. Keep in mind, however, that the addresses may be implicit or explicit. An operand may also be encoded in the instruction, called an immediate operand or literal, and does not require an address but must be bound in some way to the op-code.

EXAMPLE

Consider the operation left shift applied to an integer. Is this operation dyadic or monadic?

Solution

It all depends on your point of view. As a left shift is a multiplication by 2, the operation is dyadic. One operand is explicitly addressed while the second operand is implied in the op-code. The destination is the same as the source; thus only one address is required in the instruction.

On the other hand, the operation can be considered as monadic with one source and one destination. The destination is the same as the source, so only one address is required.

The memory of a modern processor is a hierarchy. That is, there are two levels of memory defined at the ISA level. The first level is composed of registers with various organizations and the second level is called main memory.[15] The register level is implemented in the logic of the processor whereas main memory is implemented with a slower and less costly technology, such as metal-oxide semiconductor (MOS) DRAMs. Hierarchical memory was first described by von Neumann (von Neumann 1945).

The following are the basic memory organizations for the sources or operands and the destination of the result:

1. The sources and the destinations are stored in main memory and the addresses in the instructions point to main memory. This organization is called memory to memory.
2. The sources and the destinations are stored in a local register file and the addresses point to this register file. This organization is called load/store or register file. Special load and store instructions are required for moving data between memory and the register file.
3. One source and the destination are available in a single register, called an accumulator. The other source is in memory; see Figure 1.4.
4. The sources and destinations are stored in a local push-down stack, called an evaluation stack. Special load and store instructions, usually called push and pop, are used to move data between main memory and the evaluation stack.

We now discuss these register and memory addressing options in more detail. The following discussion describes the memory organization with addresses and shows symbolically what operation is performed. A diagram of the instruction format is shown for each memory organization and its op-code. Ai is a direct memory address field and Ri is a direct register address field.

---

[15] Main memory will be referred to as real memory starting in Chapter 4.

- Three-address, memory to memory:

Op-Code	A1	A2	A3

Each instruction has three addresses, two for sources and one for the destination. The addresses point to memory and can be either a full memory address or a shortened base displacement that is added to a word-length base register:

$M(A3) \leftarrow (M(A1)) \text{ op } (M(A2))$.[16]

- Two-address, memory to memory:

Op-Code	A1	A2

Each instruction has two addresses for the two sources. The destination is one of the sources. Thus the result overwrites one of the source operands. The addresses point to memory and can be either a full memory address or a shortened base displacement that is added to a word-length base register:

$M(A1) \leftarrow (M(A1)) \text{ op } (M(A2))$.

- Three-address, register to register:

Op-Code	R1	R2	R3

For load/store register file architectures, the sources and the destination are in the register file. The addresses point to the register file and have as many bits as needed to address the registers (usually 4, 5, or 6 bits):

$R(R3) \leftarrow (R(R1)) \text{ op } (R(R2))$.

Because the operation instructions address only the register file, this architecture must have load and store instructions to move operands and results to and from memory:

Op-Code	A	R

Load: $R(R) \leftarrow (M(A))$,
Store: $M(A) \leftarrow (R(R))$.

Note that the load and store instructions have two addresses, the memory address and the register address.

- Two-address, register to register:

Op-Code	R1	R2

For load/store register file architectures, the sources and the destination are in the register file. The destination is written into the location of one of the source operands.

---

[16] When the name of a field is in ( ) such as (A1), the meaning is "the contents of field A1." Thus, (M(A1)) means the contents of the memory location addressed by the contents of the field A1.

The addresses point to the register file and need as many bits as there are registers (usually 4, 5, or 6 bits):

R(R1) ← (R(R1)) op (R(R2)).

Because the operation instructions address only the register file, this architecture must have load and store instructions to move operands and results to/from memory:

Op-Code	A	R

Load: R(R) ← (M(A)),
Store: M(A) ← (R(R)).

• One-address accumulator:

Op-Code	A

The number of addresses can be further reduced by having one of the operands addressed implicitly with the result returned to the same location. The implicitly addressed register is called the accumulator:

Acc ← (Acc) op (M(A))

An operand in memory is fetched; the operation is performed with the other operand in the accumulator, and the result is returned to the accumulator, as shown in Figure 1.4. The accumulator can be cleared with a Clear Acc instruction or by a special instruction that clears the accumulator and loads an operand from memory.

• Zero address or stack:

Op-Code

Addresses can be further reduced with an evaluation stack as the internal register organization. All addresses are implied. For a dyadic operation, the two source operands are taken from the top of stack (TOS) and the top of stack-1 (TOS-1), also known as the next top of stack, and the result is returned to the TOS. The instruction contains only an op-code, op. The operation performed is

TOS ← (TOS) op (TOS-1).

Depending on the ISA design, the TOS-1 may or may not be vacated. As with a register file architecture, load and store instructions must be provided to move data to and from the stack. The load is called push and the store is called pop. Only the memory address is explicit; the TOS address is implied in the op-code:

Op-Code	A

push: TOS ← (M(A)) (the stack is pushed down to vacate TOS),
pop: M(A) ← (TOS) (The stack is popped to fill TOS from TOS-1).

TABLE 3.2 INSTRUCTION FORMAT BITS

Architecture Type	Bits
Three address, memory to memory	$P + 3A$
Two address, memory to memory	$P + 2A$
Three address, register to register	$P + 3R$
Load/store	$P + A + R$
Two address, register to register	$P + 2R$
Load/store	$P + A + R$
One address, accumulator	$P + A$
Zero address, stack	P
Push/pop	$P + A$
Multiple accumulator	$P + A + R$

- Multiple accumulator:

Op-Code	A	R

$R(R) \leftarrow (R(R))$ op $(M(A))$.

The multiple accumulator architecture selects a register from the register file to be an accumulator. Because both a memory and a register address are available, special load and store instructions are not required.

The various instruction compositions (and local storage) are never found as "pure" architectures except in RISC designs. CISC ISAs are composed of several of these design options. The Intel Pentium supports load/store register file for integers, accumulator for integers, and an evaluation stack for floating point. A combination of the accumulator, register-to-register, and multiple accumulator architectures are used with the IBM S360.[17]

Bit Budget

Observe that each of these register organizations has differing numbers of bits in their instruction formats. A major consideration in ISA design in the early decades of the computer industry was the minimization of the bits required to represent a program. The number of bits is known as the bit budget.[18] To illustrate how the bit budget is computed, assume that an op-code has P bits, a memory address has A bits, and a register address has R bits. Table 3.2 tabulates the number of bits required for each instruction format.

---

[17] The designation S360 is used in this text to identify all members of this ISA family: S360, S370, S390. The specific designation will be used when the feature being discussed applies to one of the family members.

[18] Bit budget may be measured in bits, bytes, words, or instructions. Any consistent metric will suffice.

TABLE 3.3 INSTRUCTION BIT BUDGET FOR A = B + C

ISA	Program	Bit Budget
Three address Memory to memory	Add: M(A) ← M(B) + M(C)	$P + 3A$
Two address Memory to memory	Move: M(Temp1) ← M(C) Add: M(Temp1) ← M(Temp1) + M(B) Move: M(A) ← M(Temp1)	$3P + 6A$
Three address Register to register	Load: R(1) ← M(B) Load: R(2) ← M(C) Add: R(3) ← R(1) + R(2) Store: M(A) ← R(3)	$4P + 6R + 3A$
Two address Register to register	Load: R(1) ← M(B) Load: R(2) ← M(C) Add: R(1) ← R(1) + R(2) Store: M(A) ← R(1)	$4P + 5R + 3A$
One address Accumulator	ClrAdd: Acc ← M(B) Add: Acc ← Acc + M(C) Store: M(A) ← Acc	$3P + 3A$
Zero address Stack	Push: TOS ← M(B) Push: TOS ← M(C) Add: TOS ← TOS + TOS-1 Pop: M(A) ← TOS	$4P + 3A$

The memory and the register organizations with the instruction format influence the bit budget required for a program. Consider the simple assignment statement

$$A = B + C.$$

The values B and C are in memory, and result A will be returned to memory. Neither of the sources will be overwritten. The results of this analysis are shown in Table 3.3.

Before we consider addresses further, we need to look at another aspect of memory organization. Memory is a linear array of addressable units (AUs). Some memories are organized with byte AUs whereas others are organized with word AUs. If the word is 4 bytes, then a four-times larger memory can be addressed with the same number of address bits.

The processor registers, on the other hand, are usually addressed to the primary data type. In other words, if the integer primary data type is a word, the register file is word organized. If the processor has disjoint floating-point registers, such as the IBM S360, the Intel x86, and the PowerPC, the floating-point registers are usually allocated to 8 bytes.

Variable-length instructions lead to the issue of instruction alignment in memory. Consider a byte-organized memory. Data types of 2 bytes are constrained to start on even-numbered bytes (0, 2, 4, . . . ,). Data types of 4 bytes must start on every fourth

								AU Type
MSB				Address Bits			LSB	
								Byte
							x	1/2 Word
						x	x	Word
					x	x	x	Double Word
				x	x	x	x	Quad Word

Figure 3.4 Byte address to AU-type binding

even byte (0, 4, 8, 12, . . . ,), and so on. Alignment must be bound to the data type expected by the op-code. For example, a double-precision floating-point operation will ignore the three least-significant bits (LSBs) of the address. The relationship between the size of the data-type AU and the address LSBs that are ignored (indicated by x) is shown in Figure 3.4.

Byte Order

I must now introduce an unfortunate and messy problem with processors that have byte-organized memory. When a multibyte word is transferred to or from the processor and the memory or to the I/O, which byte is transferred first, the most-significant byte (MS Byte) or the least-significant byte (LS Byte)? Various manufacturers have, over time, introduced different standards for allocation position and numbers to bytes in multibyte integer and floating-point data types. Allocation itself is not a major problem; only when there are transfers between registers (either in the same computer or different computers) does it become a problem. Which byte is transferred first and how are the MS Bytes and the LS Bytes addressed in memory? This problem is called the Endian problem (Cohen 1981, Kirrmann 1983). There are two allocations, as shown in Figure 3.5, for 16-bit (2-byte) signed integers.

Little Endian: The LS Byte is allocated to lowest address in memory. The LS Byte is read from memory first.
Big Endian: The MS Byte is allocated to the lowest address in memory. The MS Byte is read from memory first.

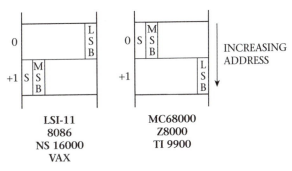

Figure 3.5 Big and Little Endian integer allocations (© 1983 IEEE)

In addition to the byte locations, for 2-byte integers, the Little Endian assigns the Byte number B0 to the LS Byte and B15 to the sign of the MS Byte. The Big Endian does just the opposite, with B0 the sign or MS Byte and B15 the LS Byte. A further complication arises with manufacturers who designate bits as B1–B16 rather than B0–B15.

With the Little Endian, when a 2-byte word is loaded from memory into a register, the first byte is placed in the right-hand byte position of the register, and the second byte is placed in the left-hand byte position. The opposite is true for the Big Endian. Examples of the use of Little and Big Endian assignments in memory are

Little Endian: PDP-11, VAX, x86, PowerPC (supports).
Big Endian: IBM S360, MC680 x0, PowerPC (default).

Memory Addressing Modes

The von Neumann architecture had one memory addressing mode: the address in the instruction pointed directly to a memory location. This primitive addressing was quickly found to be inadequate because of the need to index into complex data structures, such as an array. Without hardware support for addressing, too many processor resources were needed to form the address. A subroutine, 8 of the 16 instructions shown in Table 1.6, had to be executed (with self-modifying code) to compose the addresses.

The address that results from the various operations on an address is called the effective address (EA). The IBM S370 and S390 use the term logical storage address or logical address and the Intel Pentium Pro uses the term offset.

Indexing was recognized as being a necessary additional addressing mode. At Manchester University in the early 1950s, a register was attached to the address bus that holds an integer to be added to the address. The value in this register was incremented after each use. Other addressing modes have been added to ISAs over the years. Some of these are shown in Table 3.4.

The Sun Microsystems SPARC has an interesting addressing mode: $EA = A \times B + C$. This effective address mode is used for indexing into an array or matrix. Consider the $n \times m$ matrix of Figure 3.6, with $m = 4$ and $n = 5$. The matrix is stored column major with the memory addresses shown. Memory location 1 holds the first $(1, 1)$ element of the matrix in Figure 3.6. When the program needs to address the i, j element of the matrix, the EA of the desired element is found by

$$\begin{aligned}
EA(i, j) &= \text{address}(1, 1) + (i - 1)n + j - 1 \\
&= \text{address}(1, 1) + in - n + j - 1 \\
&= \text{address}(1, 1) - n - 1 + in + j.
\end{aligned}$$

$$\begin{matrix}
& \longrightarrow i \\
\downarrow & \begin{bmatrix} 1 & 6 & 11 & 16 \\ 2 & 7 & 12 & 17 \\ 3 & 8 & 13 & 18 \\ 4 & 9 & 14 & 19 \\ 5 & 10 & 15 & 20 \end{bmatrix} n \\
j & \quad\quad m
\end{matrix}$$

Figure 3.6 Matrix addressing

TABLE 3.4 ADDRESSING MODES

Mode	Operand Effective Address
Direct	The address in the instruction is the effective address.
Indexed	An index value is added to the direct address.
Base + displacement	The address in the instruction is a displacement that is added to a full-length base register.
Base + displacement + index	The address in the instruction is a displacement that is added to a full-length base register and a full-length index register.
Autoincrement–decrement	The index register(s) may be a special register or in the general-purpose register file. This register is automatically adjusted in one of four modes: preincrement (before the operation is performed), postincrement (after the operation is performed), predecrement (before the operation is performed), postdecrement (after the operation is performed).
Indirect	An effective address is determined by any mode, the operand is fetched, and the operand is the effective address. This addressing mode may be one level or multilevel.
Immediate or literal	The operands are in the instruction; no address is required.
Register	The operands are found in the register file.
Register deferred	The value in the addressed general-purpose register is the effective address to memory.

The EA formula is divided into two parts. The $[\text{address}(1, 1) - n - 1]$ part is computed by the compiler, which knows the value of n and the address of the first element. The result of this operation is placed in a base register. The second part, $in + j$, is a run-time calculation that uses the addressing mode $\text{EA} = \text{A} \times \text{B} + \text{C}$. Two instructions are now needed to form the effective address of i, j. Assume that the compiler-generated portion of the EA has been computed and is stored in a base register:

Compiler: $\text{base} = \text{address}(1, 1) - n - 1,$

1st instruction: $\text{base}' = \text{base} + j,$

2nd instruction: $\text{EA} = i \times n + \text{base}'.$

EXAMPLE

A matrix, $m = 4$ and $n = 5$, is stored in memory starting at location 100. What is the effective address of $i = 3$ and $j = 3$?

Solution

The compiler computes the value: $100 - 5 - 1 = 94$, and places it in a base register. At run time the effective address is computed with the following two instructions:

1. $94 + 3 = 97,$
2. $3 \times 5 + 97 = 112.$

3.2.2 OPERATIONS

Operations, as specified in the op-code of the instruction set, define what is to be accomplished. For user code, there are three general groups of operations:

- arithmetic and logical
- moves of data between memory locations and/or registers
- control instructions such as branches, jumps, subroutine calls, and returns

The arithmetic and logical instructions and control instructions perform the operations that are the major purpose of the processor; these instructions do the work whereas the move instructions are overhead. A program written in a high-level language does not have explicit moves; moves are added by the compiler to accommodate the memory organization of the processor.

A prime consideration in the selection of operations to be included in the ISA is their frequencies of use. If an operation is deemed to be unnecessary because of its low frequency of use or its being too costly to implement, there must be primitive operations that permit the synthesis of the compound operation. If, for example, multiply is not selected as an operation, then the primitives of shift and test must be included. The ISA designer must be sure that complex functions, such as transcendental functions, can be programmed with reasonable execution efficiency.

Arithmetic and Logical Instructions

These instructions constitute the core of the instruction set as seen by the user. The arithmetic operations of add, subtract, multiply, and divide are usually architected. With addition and multiplication, results can sometimes exceed the range of representation. The designer must make explicit provisions for this occurrence. For example, two 16-bit integers multiplied together will produce a 32-bit result. If the integer data type is fractional, the least-significant 16 bits are dropped. If the data type is whole number, the most-significant 16 bits are dropped. Adjusting the result of an operation to fit the expressible size requires an operation called the domain function.

With logical operation, although there are 16 functions of two Boolean variables, the function NAND can be used to create all of the other 15 functions by repetitive application. The two functions NOT and AND can also be used.

EXAMPLE

Show a sequence of instructions that program the bitwise Exclusive OR function of two words by using only the NAND instruction.

Solution

Assume that the processor is a stack architecture. The NAND operations NANDs the TOS with the TOS-1 and places the result in the TOS. The TOS, TOS-1, and other stack locations are shown (separated by commas) in the following program:

Instruction	*TOS, TOS-1, ..., TOS-n*
Push A	A, x
Push A	A , A, x
NAND	A′, x
Push B	B, A′, x
NAND	(BA′)′, x
Push B	B, (BA′)′, x
Push B	B, B, (BA′)′, x
NAND	B′,(BA′)′, x
Push A	A, B′, (BA′)′, x
NAND	(AB′)′, (BA′)′, x
NAND	((BA′)′(AB′)′)′, x
Pop C	x

Comment

The Exclusive OR function required 12 instructions. As this operation is frequently used, it is included in the ISA of most processors. A duplicate instruction can be used in place of the second of the pair of pushes of A and B to eliminate the memory bandwidth required for fetching the second operand.

Move Instructions

Move instructions are not explicit in a high-level language. Various types of moves are added by the compiler to match the program to the memory system design of the specific ISA. In addition, moves are needed to (1) move operands around in memory space to simplify addressing, (2) move operands between memory and a register file for load/store register file architectures, and (3) move for loading and storing the contents of special registers. This third class of moves can be explicit or as side effects, as in the case of storing and loading the contents of the program counter after a context switch. Explicit moves are of the following types:

memory to memory,
memory to/from general-purpose register(s),
memory to/from dedicated register(s).

In some ISAs, move instructions are bound to a number of data types: byte, 2 byte, etc. We also find move instructions that move a block of operands for such tasks as loading or storing the complete register file in one instruction.

An example of an implicit move is found in the subroutine call and return instructions. These instructions move the program counter to and from a temporary memory space. A call instruction places the contents of the program counter in either a memory location or a dedicated register such as the TOS. A return instruction reads the previously saved program counter value and places it into the program counter:

call: Temporary location ← (PC),

return: PC ← (temporary location).

Control Instructions

The normal sequence of instruction execution is provided when the program counter is incremented. The next instruction is found in the next memory location following the location of the present instruction.[19] Control instructions permit this linear sequence of instructions to be changed and program control transferred to another nonsequential memory location. A taxonomy for these instructions is

- branches
    conditional
    unconditional
- calls and returns to/from subroutines or procedures
- interrupts and exceptions

Branches assume that the change in the flow of the program is permanent, that is, the state of the branched-from program fragment is not retained. On the other hand, calls assume that the change in flow is not permanent and the program control will return to the calling program. This means that the state of the calling program must be retained. Interrupts are like calls in that most interrupted programs will be reinstated after the interrupt is serviced.

Branches. There are two forms of branch instructions: conditional and unconditional. The conditional branch operation allows a program to be redirected based on the result of an operation or when the limit of an iteration is reached.[20] Two forms of conditional branch instructions are architected in various processors:

1. A pair of orthogonal instructions. The first instruction performs the test and sets an indicator bit (discussed further in Subsection 3.2.3.2). The second instruction tests the indicator bit and either continues sequential execution or places a target address in the program counter and branches. The second instruction does not need to be the immediate successor to the first instruction: there can be intervening instructions. Examples of this type of branch are found with the IBM S360 ISA and the x86 ISA.

2. A single instruction that performs the test and continues or does not continue the sequential execution based on the result of the test. This type of branch instruction is called test and branch. Examples of this type of branch are found in most early ISAs such as the von Neumann ISA and with the MIPS R2000 architecture.[21] This form of branch does not use indicator bits; thus information cannot be passed

---

[19] The program counter is incremented by the length of the current instruction modulo, the AU. If memory is organized by bytes and the current instruction is 2 bytes, the program counter is incremented by 2.

[20] Believed to be first used on the Bell Labs Mark V.

[21] The R2000 processor was the first implementation of the MIPS architecture. Since that time, the MIPS architecture has evolved through five generations and a large number of implementations of the architecture. The description of the R2000 implementation and the MIPS architecture that it implements should be interpreted in the appropriate historical context and not as a representation of the MIPS architecture as it exists today.

to subsequent instructions. The R2000 instruction compares the contents of one register with zero:

BGEZ: Branch on greater than or equal to zero.

In addition to the conditional branch operation, an unconditional branch, or jump, is found in most ISAs. This class of instruction permits explicit transfer of control and is used for such things as returning from subroutines. Another type of unconditional branch is called a trap. Traps are instructions that unconditionally change the value of the program counter when a side effect event occurs, such as an arithmetic error.

Unconditional branches do not have to be explicitly architected. A reserved register or memory location can hold zero, and a conditional branch can test for zero, giving the equivalent of an unconditional branch.

Calls and Returns to/from Subroutines.   Subroutines fall into two general categories: open and closed. Open subroutines are a set of sequential instructions that are incorporated into the main program during the assembly process. In other words, they appear as in-line code. Closed subroutines, on the other hand, can be called from any point in the main program and return control to the main program. Closed subroutines are designed to be reusable; that is, they can be used again. If the subroutine changes itself during execution, as can be done with a self-modifying program, the changes must be undone before the return. Subroutines can be reusable in one of the following ways:

Serially reusable: can have only one activation at a time,
Re-entrant: can have two or more activations at a time,
Recursive: re-entrant and can call itself.

The type of reusability supported has a direct impact on the architecture as each activation requires the allocation of storage space. The design issue is whether storage space is provided by the system software or by hardware. The usual design answer is that space is allocated by the system software. The Intel 432, no longer produced, provides an example of a processor that used hardware space allocation.

The minimum architectural requirements for closed subroutines were posited by J. P. Eckert (Eckert 1946), as follows:

1. instruction to return to the main routine
2. the numbers required in the subroutine computation
3. instructions telling it where the result of the computation is to be stored.

We can see that the von Neumann ISA falls short of providing these facilities, especially the third. The program counter cannot be saved because it is implemented; thus there is no way that a return can be made to the main program. In the discussion that follows, the program that calls the subroutine is named the caller, and the called program is named the called.

REQUIREMENT 1

A major issue in the design of call instructions is the storage of the return address. The return address is usually the value in the program counter plus 1. This value can be stored in either (1) a process state location or (2) a processor state location (a special register or a stack).

Store in Process State: With early processors that supported self-modifying programs, the call instruction stored the return program counter value in a register or memory location. Instructions in the called subroutine loaded this value into the address portion of an unconditional branch, which is the last instruction of the subroutine.

The first implementation of subroutines was with the EDSAC at Cambridge University, developed under the direction of Maurice Wilkes. Wilkes, Wheeler, and Gill wrote the seminal work on subroutines for the EDSAC (Wilkes, Wheeler, and Gill 1951). The EDSAC technique worked as follows:

The call instruction performed two steps

accumulator ← (PC) + 1,
PC ← subroutine address.

Knowing the subroutine's length, the first instruction in the called subroutine placed the contents of the accumulator into the address field of the last instruction; an unconditional branch.

address, last instruction ← (accumulator)

This subroutine calling technique became known as branch and link and was favored by many early computer designers. When the subroutine reaches its end, the unconditional branch returns control to the caller. Note that this technique requires self-modifying programs that are not supported on some modern processors.

Another early instance of an architected PC, providing for subroutine calls and returns, is found on the Atlas I, renamed the MU1. This machine had an instruction STA that stores the address of the next instruction to be executed, (PC) + 1. This address is later loaded into an index register, providing a subroutine return as all addresses, even instruction addresses, are indexed (Blaauw and Brooks 1997).

Store In Processor State, Special Register: For processors that do not support self-modifying programs, it is necessary to store the program counter value in an architected register. For example, the IBM S360 branch-and-link instruction places the incremented program counter value into one of its general-purpose registers along with an instruction length code, the condition code bits,[22] and the program mask. The address of the first instruction of the subroutine is either the normal effective address for the 16-bit RX format or the address is taken from the register file in the 32-bit RR format. IBM S360 instruction formats are shown in Chapter 8 in Figure 8.3. Subroutine returns use the branch-on-condition instruction that loads the program counter with the previously stored value in the register.

Nesting of subroutines is accomplished by use of an unassigned register for each level of nesting. Obviously, if nesting is too deep, the processor will soon run out of registers for normal usage. Using registers this way is one of the penalties of a limited-size, completely general-purpose register file.

---

[22] Indicators encoded into a 2-bit condition code.

The MIPS R2000 uses another version of branch and link named jump register and link (JALR). This instruction places the value of the next instruction to be executed (PC + 1) into register 31. As branch instructions find the target address in register 31, any branch instruction can be used for the return. Because this processor does not use indicators for determining a conditional subroutine call, there is one instruction that combines the test and the call. The other instruction is unconditional. These instructions are

1. link and branch on greater than or equal to zero,
2. link.

Because a dedicated register, R31, is the link register, nesting of subroutines is possible only with the expenditure of overhead in the form of context switches. The context switch parks the value in R31 before the subroutine call. Another context switch is required to unwind the first one.

Store in Processor State, Stack: Another form of processor state storage is the stack. With the execution of a call instruction, the value in the program counter is pushed on the stack and the program counter is loaded with the address of the first instruction of the subroutine.

A return from the subroutine requires only that the top of the stack be popped into the program counter. As described above, the saved program counter value is the address of the call instruction. Thus the program counter must be incremented before the next instruction after the return. For processor implementations that increment the program counter at the end of an instruction, this scheme also works.

An advantage of using a stack for saving the program counter is that nesting of subroutines (a subroutine calls a subroutine) is automatic. As each subroutine is called, the program counter value is pushed on the stack. At each return, the stack is popped, returning to the calling subroutine. Some low-cost microcomputers have a fixed-depth stack, 4–6 levels, that requires an enforcement of the depth of subroutine stacking.

The Intel Pentium Pro procedure stack is shown in Figure 3.7. Parameters passed to the called procedure, and local variables for the calling procedure are pushed onto the stack. The return instruction pointer is the value of the calling program counter plus one instruction. The ESP (stack pointer) and EBP (pointer to data in the stack) registers are allocated to the general-purpose register file, shown in Figure 3.8.

The Intel Pentium Pro, because of the segmentation organization of memory and the protection mechanism, provides four types of calls with their returns. These are

near call: a call within the current code segment
far call: a call to another code segment
interprivilege-level far call: a call to a different segment at a different privilege level
task switch: a call to a different task.

REQUIREMENTS 2 AND 3

These requirements call for the transfer of information between the caller and the called. For very simple ISAs, the responsibility for meeting these requirements is

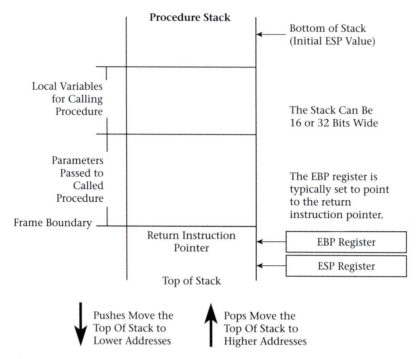

Figure 3.7 Intel Pentium Pro procedure stack (courtesy of Intel Corporation)

delegated to the subroutine itself, and no special hardware other than the ability to load and store the program counter is required. However, modern processors meet these requirements with hardware support.

Parameter Passing: Parameters are passed by the caller to the subroutine by storing the parameters in memory locations set by convention. In other words, an agreed-on region of memory is reserved for parameter passing. The results of the subroutine are also deposited into locations agreed on by convention.

For ISAs with stacks, such as the Pentium Pro, the caller pushes the parameters onto the stack. This is convenient because with nested subroutines the parameters for a second or third call will also be pushed. Thus the active subroutine will find its

General-Purpose Registers

31	16 15	8 7	0	16-bit	32-bit
		AH	AL	AX	EAX
		BH	BL	BX	EBX
		CH	CL	CX	ECX
		DH	DL	DX	EDX
		BP			EBP
		SI			ESI
		DI			EDI
		SP			ESP

Figure 3.8 Pentium Pro general registers (courtesy of Intel Corporation)

parameters on the top locations of the stack. One of two conventions must be adopted: a fixed number of parameters will be pushed, or a count of parameters must be pushed with the parameters.

Another technique for parameter passing is to designate, by convention, one or more of the general-purpose registers for parameters. This convention has the advantage of eliminating the time required for passing parameters, but for computers with small register files, the number of registers that can be allocated is small and reduces the number of parameters that can be passed.

Parameters can also be stored by the caller in memory, and the address of the space passed as a parameter in one word of the register file. The locations in memory are named the argument list, and the pointer is named the argument pointer. This technique eliminates the need for prior allocation of parameter space in memory. The ISA must, however, support the use of addresses from the register file.

The Intel Pentium Pro provides an example of the design of parameter passing facilities. This processor provides three methods: by means of the general-purpose registers, by means of the stack shown in Figure 3.7, or by means of an argument list.

A call instruction saves only the value of the program counter on the stack; it does not save the register file values. Thus up to six of the registers can be used for passing parameters to/from a called subroutine. Parameters can be passed by pushing onto a stack in the stack frame. The stack frame base pointer is used as a frame boundary for the parameter stack. When an argument list is used, the argument pointer is passed to the called subroutine in an agreed-on register of the register file.

Saving the Processor State: When a subroutine is called, the state of the processor must be saved so the subroutine can use the resources such as the register file, stack pointers, indicator bits, and the like. The design issues are how and where the processor state is saved.

There are two choices for the how-to-design issue. The caller or called program can be given the responsibility. It is possible for the caller to copy all of the processor state into a designated space before the subroutine is called. The called subroutine must then initialize the processor state before subroutine execution begins. When control is returned to the caller, the processor state must be retrieved to reestablish the process state that existed before the call. This technique requires presenting a uniform interface to all subroutines.

On the other hand, the called subroutine can be given the task of storing and restoring the processor state. There is an advantage to this technique in that all of the processor resources may not be needed by the subroutine, resulting in a reduced time for saving and restoring the processor state. For example, if only one register is needed by the subroutine, why save and restore all the other registers? Also, if the indicator bits will not be used, why save and restore them?

Interrupts and Exceptions. Sequential flow of program control can be changed by branches or jumps that are an integral part of the executing program. There are other processor- and system-related events that can require a change in program flow, frequently for an extended period of time. These events are called interrupts. Interrupts are of three types:

- Internal: events that are requested by the program. Operating system calls and program trace traps are examples.
- Synchronous: events from inside the processor. Arithmetic exceptions and page faults are examples.
- Asynchronous: events usually from outside the processor. I/O requests and time out signals are examples.

Internal and synchronous interrupts will occur at the same place in the program when run with identical programs and data. Asynchronous interrupts can occur at any time and the program is unable to anticipate their occurrence. Internal hardware failures are considered to be asynchronous events.

Interrupt design has some of the characteristics of subroutine call design. A major difference is that none of the subroutine call techniques discussed above that require action by the caller, such as saving state or passing parameters, can be used. The reason is that the event cannot be anticipated; thus the current program cannot do these tasks. Interrupts provide no advanced notice. However, the techniques of saving processor and process state by a subroutine call can be used. To minimize the number of implemented techniques in an ISA, designers will frequently let the considerations of interrupt design drive the subroutine call/return design. The processor must perform four functions:

1. recognize interrupt events
2. terminate or hold in abeyance the executing program
3. provide for starting the interrupt service routine (a program that responds to the interrupt)
4. reinstate the interrupted program

The processor ISA and hardware must provide facilities for these four functions. The strategies and facilities are discussed in the following paragraphs. Basic to providing interrupt support in the ISA is that the program counter must be saved and restored; thus the von Neumann ISA could not support interrupts. A major issue in the design of interrupts is the storage of the return address, a similar problem to that with subroutine calls. The return address is usually the value in the program counter plus 1. This value can be stored in either a process state or a processor state location. For processors that support self-modifying programs, the return address can be stored in a memory location.

The action of an interrupt on a processor executing the serial execution model is illustrated in Figure 3.9.[23] The special problems of interrupts on pipelined processors are addressed in Chapter 6. The normal sequence of instruction is shown at the top of the figure. At the end of an instruction, i for example, an interrupt is signaled. This signal causes the sequence to be interrupted, and the interrupt handler is run as shown in the lower portion of the figure. After the completion of the interrupt handler, the normal sequence is restarted with instruction $i + 1$ being executed.

---

[23] The serial execution model requires that one instruction be completed before another instruction is started.

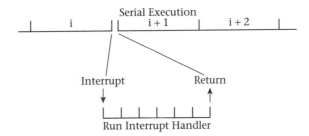

Figure 3.9 Interrupt sequence

For some interrupts, the return is not to instruction $i + 1$ but to i. For example, if the interrupt had been caused by an abnormal condition in the processor, such as an arithmetic exception in instruction i, the interrupt handler would perform whatever is required to eliminate that exception condition, and the processor would reexecute instruction i.

In addition to the four functions required of an interrupt, discussed above, there are three additional requirements:

1. a means for saving the processor and process state
2. a means of identifying the source of the interrupt and loading the proper program counter value
3. a means for restoring the processor and process state after the interrupt handler has been executed

SAVING STATE

As with subroutine calls, the program counter is the minimum processor state saved, and it is saved in either a dedicated hardware stack in the processor or a dedicated register or pushed onto a stack in memory. The use of a hardware stack is common with single-chip microcontrollers with the depth of the stack limiting the depth of interrupt nesting. A dedicated register was commonly used on early computers, but is no longer used because only one interrupt could be serviced. On the other hand, a memory stack is relatively fast, as the stack is usually cached as part of the operating system.

IDENTIFICATION OF INTERRUPT SOURCE

The source of the interrupt is identified in one of two ways. The simplest technique is to OR the interrupt signals, so any source can cause an interrupt. A common preamble to all of the interrupt handlers tests signal lines, called polling, to identify the source of the interrupt. Polling will take a number of instructions to complete. For random interrupts, the average number of polls is 1/2 the number of interrupts to be polled; however, the polling order is usually the order of the interrupt priorities. Once the source is identified, the preamble consults a table and finds the proper address to load into the program counter.

The second technique for identification of the interrupt source is called a vectored interrupt. With this technique an interrupt source sends an interrupt signal plus an identifier. This identifier is used as an index into a table that holds the program counter value for the required interrupt handler. The vectored interrupt has the shortest latency but is more complicated to implement.

RESTORING STATE

After the interrupt handler has completed its execution, a return-from-interrupt instruction is executed. This instruction finds the saved value of the interrupted program counter and places it in the program counter so that normal execution of the interrupted program can begin. Any other state that has been saved is restored either by the interrupt handler before the return or by the hardware.

OTHER CONSIDERATIONS

The timing diagram of Figure 3.9 indicates that interrupts occur at the end of an instruction execution. For external interrupts, such as I/O, this is frequently the case. Even if the interrupt signal is received during the instruction, that instruction can be allowed to complete. What about interrupts that occur during the execution of an instruction that cannot continue execution? Examples are an illegal op-code or a page fault for an instruction or data reference. For these cases, the most common solution is to abandon the execution of the interrupted instruction. After the condition that caused the interrupt is corrected by the interrupt handler, the interrupted instruction is restarted. This technique is called restart. Some processors save the state of the partially executed instructions and then continue after the problem has been corrected. This technique is called continuation.

The ISA design may also automatically save the values of registers holding the process and the processor state, or this task can be performed as a preamble and postamble to the interrupt handler. If handled by the interrupt handler, the ISA must provide the necessary move instructions for storing and restoring these state values.

Figure 3.10 shows a taxonomy of design techniques for handling interrupts that occur between and during instructions and with continuation and restart. The design choices of the IBM S360, MC68000, and the VAX-11 have been identified.

There are a number of complications with implementing interrupts. Among these is the priority given to each of the interrupt sources; some interrupts are more important than others. The issue becomes especially important under two conditions: (1) an interrupt is being handled and another interrupt occurs, and (2) two or more interrupts occur at the same time.

When a second interrupt occurs while an interrupt is being handled, the priority of the new interrupt is determined. If it has higher priority, it interrupts the current interrupt handler. If it has lower priority, it is placed in an interrupt queue for future processing. Two or more simultaneous interrupts require consulting the priority list. The highest priority interrupt is serviced, and the others are placed on the queue for future service. Note that the queue is serviced by priority, not by a first-in first-out protocol.

Most systems need to recognize and respond to interrupts from a number of sources. In addition, there are situations when the processor should not respond to the interrupt, such as when the interrupt handler is servicing an interrupt with a higher priority. There are three techniques for handling multiple interrupts: maskable,

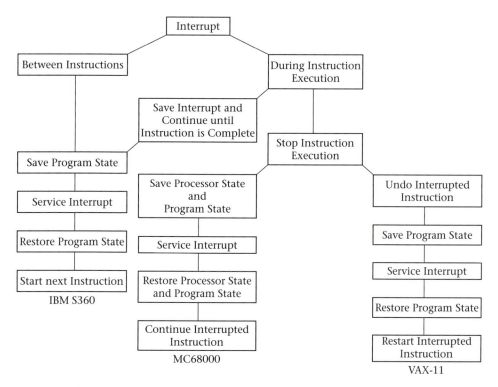

Figure 3.10 Pentium Taxonomy

nonmaskable, and priority. As its name implies, a maskable interrupt has a programmed switch that will allow the interrupt to be disabled and deferred for later service. Nonmaskable interrupts, on the other hand, must be acknowledged by the processor, and the interrupt handler will determine if an interrupt should be deferred or serviced immediately. For both of these designs, the priority is established by the operating system (assume that the interrupt service routines are components of the operating system). Priority interrupts use hardware to establish the priority and the degree of urgency for service.

For maskable interrupts, the processor must have an architected register that can be loaded with a bit pattern that turns on or off each of the interrupt lines. Thus, depending on the environment at the time, one interrupt is on and all the others are off. For example, if no I/O operation is active but a page fault is possible, the I/O interrupts are off and the page fault interrupt is on.

Polling. Some processors do not have architected interrupts. These processors respond to external events by periodically polling the devices to see if any one of them needs to interrupt the processor. If an external event needs service an event service routine is executed, the same as interrupt service routines.

The processor executes a polling loop on a periodic basis. For example, every microsecond the processor may poll all of the high-priority external event sources, but will poll something like the power line every 0.1 s for loss of power. A polling system has difficulty responding to a high-priority event when a low-priority event is being serviced. This situation requires that the event service routines contain polling loops for polling higher-priority sources.

Some supercomputers (CDC 6600, CDC 7600, and TI ASC) are multiprocessors that have a set of attached processors that perform the polling. These processors remove the polling load from the central processor. Today we find microcontrollers that use polling. An example is the keyboard control processor found in PC keyboards. These processors poll the keys to determine if one or more has been depressed.

3.2.3 DATA TYPES

Data types of the ISA handled by the processor are of two types: (1) number and logical data types and (2) program sequencing data types. Data types required for the operating system, interrupts, and managing memory are discussed in Chapter 8.

User programs need a variety of data types, primarily integers and floating point. Integers can be byte, half word, word, or double word, both signed and unsigned. Today, the IEEE floating-point data type is almost universally used for single- and double-precision data (ANSI/IEEE Standard 754-1985). Another form of integer is the decimal data type. Decimal data types are usually packed two to a byte with the range of representation 00–99. If the decimal data type requires a sign, it is assigned to a byte associated with a string of decimal data-type bytes.

Supercomputers have a vector data type that is usually a vector of single- or double-precision floating-point values. This data type requires a length value, either implicit or explicit in the instruction, to be associated with the data type.

A partial taxonomy of three descriptors (precision, name, and length) for user data types is given in Table 3.5 (Siewiorek, Bell, and Newell 1982). The use of these specifiers is illustrated by the following, with the key words underlined. A data type can be a vector of decimal digits packed two to a byte (fractional).

TABLE 3.5 DATA-TYPE SPECIFICATION

Length	Name	Precision
scalar	logical	fractional
vector	sign	quarter
matrix	decimal	half
array	octal	single
string	character	double
	byte	triple
	syllable	quadruple
	word	multiple
	unsigned integer	integer
	signed integer	
	fraction	
	floating	
	not normalized	
	complex	

3.2.3.1 User Data Types

There are a number of data types associated with user arithmetic programs. These data types can be classified according to the following taxonomy:

Fixed-point numbers
    Integers
    Fractions
    Mixed
Floating-point numbers
Logical values

Integers, fractions, and mixed data types can be either signed or unsigned. Floating-point data types are always signed. Arithmetic for floating-point data types is discussed in Section 3.4.

Unsigned Fixed-Point Integers, Fractions, and Mixed Data Types

Numbers can be given various representations: the radix point can be to the right of the LSB, making the data type an unsigned integer.[24] Placing the radix point to the left of the MSB makes the number an unsigned fraction. If the radix point is between these two limits, the data type is mixed, having both an integer and fractional part. For an n-bit data type, consider the following:

$$\text{unsigned integer} = 2^{n-1} + 2^{n-2} + 2^{n-3} + \cdots + 2^{n-n}.$$

The binary point is to the right:

| 2^{n-1} | 2^{n-2} | . | . | . | . | 2^1 | 2^{n-n} | . |

$$\text{unsigned fraction} = 2^{-1} + 2^{-2} + 2^{-3} + \cdots + 2^{-n}.$$

The binary point is to the left:

| . | 2^{-1} | 2^{-2} | . | . | . | . | . | 2^{-n} |

$$\text{unsigned mixed} = 2^{b-1} + \cdots + 2^{b-b} + 2^{-1} + 2^{-2} + \cdots + 2^{-(n-b)},$$

where b is the number of bits in the integer portion and $n - b$ is the number of bits in the fractional portion:

| 2^{b-1} | 2^{b-2} | . | 2^{b-b} | . | 2^{-1} | 2^{-2} | . | . | . | $2^{-(n-b)}$ |

Signed Integers and Fractions

One of the design problems with integer and fraction data types is the need to represent negative values. Three types of signed integer and signed fraction data types

---

[24] Also known as ordinals.

TABLE 3.6 INTEGER AND FRACTION DATA TYPES

	Sign and Magnitude		1's Complement		2's Complement	
Binary	Integer	Fraction	Integer	Fraction	Integer	Fraction
000	+0	+0	+0	+0	+0	+0
001	+1	+0.25	+1	+0.25	+1	+0.25
010	+2	+0.50	+2	+0.50	+2	+0.50
011	+3	+0.75	+3	+0.75	+3	+0.75
100	−0	−0	−3	−0.75	−4	−1.00
101	−1	−0.25	−2	−0.50	−3	−0.75
110	−2	−0.50	−1	−0.25	−2	−0.50
111	−3	−0.75	−0	−0	−1	−0.25
RANGE	$-(2^{n-1}-1)$ to $2^{n-1}-1$	$-[1-2^{-(n-1)}]$ to $1-2^{-(n-1)}$	$-(2^{n-1}-1)$ to $2^{n-1}-1$	$-[1-2^{-(n-1)}]$ to $1-2^{-(n-1)}$	$-2^{(n-1)}$ to $2^{n-1}-1$	-1 to $1-2^{-(n-1)}$

have been commonly used: sign and magnitude, 1's complement, also called digit complement, and 2's complement, also called radix complement. Table 3.6 shows the decimal representation of a 3-bit word of each of the six data types.

These strange data types are a result of the desire to represent an odd number of symbols, $x, x-1, \ldots, 0, \ldots, -x-1, -x$, with an even number of symbols in a binary word, 2^n. Thus there is either redundancy (sign and magnitude and 1's complement have two zeros) or a nonsymmetrical representation (as with 2's complement). Reducing the complexity of the ALU has been a driving force in the development of these representations.

Sign and Magnitude. The advantage of sign and magnitude is that it is natural. In other words, there is a sign bit, and the numbers represented can be symmetrical around zero. However, this system has the unusual characteristic in that there are two 0s: +0 and −0, which is far from natural. Thus there are special provisions made in the ALU to accommodate the redundant zeros.

1's Complement. 1's complement allocates a bit to the sign, as with sign and magnitude, but the magnitude bits are formed as follows. For positive integers, the magnitude bits are the same as the unsigned integer value ($2 = 0 \wedge 010$, for a 4-bit number).[25] Negative numbers are represented by the bitwise complement of the positive integer ($-2 = 1 \wedge 101$, for a 4-bit number).

The rules of arithmetic for 1's complement data types are rather complicated; they require an end-around carry, discussed in Section 3.4. As a result, this data type has disappeared from modern ISAs.

2's Complement. This representation eliminates the problems of two zeros and the end-around carry. However, the representation is not symmetrical. As shown in

---

[25] The symbol $\wedge$ is used to separate the sign bit.

Table 3.6, the largest value is $+3$ and the smallest value is -4. Changing a positive to a negative number, however, requires that the bits be complemented and a 1 added to the result ($+2 = 0 \wedge 010$, change to $-2 = 1 \wedge 101 + 1 = 1 \wedge 110$). The addition of 1 is an extra step needed to form negative values compared with the 1's complement that simplifies the arithmetic operations by eliminating the end-around carry. 2's complement arithmetic is discussed in Section 3.4.

Fractional Data Types. Table 3.6 also shows the fractional sign and magnitude and 1's and 2's complement data types. As with integer data types, there are either two zeros or the data type is not symmetrical. Fractional data types are used as a component of some floating-point data types and as the primary data type of some scientific computers.

Unsigned Decimal Data Types

There are many user applications that require decimal data types. For example, systems that deal with decimal money, such as dollars and cents, and various calculator applications all need decimal data types. Other applications are found in programming languages such as spread sheets and COBOL. Some early computers, such as the Mark 1 and the ENIAC, used decimal notation. On the other hand, binary notation was used by Zuse and Atanasoff and became established for scientific use with the von Neumann ISA.

Binary Code. With decimal notation, the decimal digits 0–9 are allocated to 4 binary bits that have 16 states. An allocation or selection of a subset of the 16 states results in 6 unused states or a redundancy of 6 states. In addition, the weights of the bits in the state can be selected (8, 4, 2, 1 is but one example, called BCD). Allocation and weights are chosen to simplify addition operations, particularly the handling of carries from one decimal digit to the next. White has estimated that there are approximately 7.6×10^7 possible allocations, only a few of which have been architected (White 1953).

The IBM S360, S370, and S390 uses the 8, 4, 2, 1 coding for decimal data types. An adder is implemented in the hardware to perform the addition properly.

Two-Out-of-Five Code. With this system 2 bits of a 5-bit symbol are always 1, thus providing a degree of error protection. If a 0 is changed to a 1 or a 1 to a 0 during a move operation, the error can be detected because the 2/5 relationship is violated. Double errors may not be detected. The IBM 650, an early decimal business computer, used a two-out-of-five code allocated as shown in Table 3.7.

Excess-Three Notation. This notation represents the 10 digits in their binary code plus three. The allocation is shown in Table 3.8.

This notation has interesting arithmetic properties. Consider the result when two numbers are added together: $(a + 3) + (b + 3) = a + b + 6$. To restore the result to excess three, 3 must be *subtracted* from the result, giving $a + b + 3$. If $a = 2$ and $b = 3$, the addition produces

$$0101 + 0110 = 1011 - 0011 = 1000 = 5,$$

the correct result in excess three.

TABLE 3.7 IBM 650 ALLOCATION

Decimal	B4	B3	B2	B1	B0
0	1	1	0	0	0
1	0	0	0	1	1
2	0	0	1	0	1
3	0	0	1	1	0
4	0	1	0	0	1
5	0	1	0	1	0
6	0	1	1	0	0
7	1	0	0	0	1
8	1	0	0	1	0
9	1	0	1	0	0

If there is a carry out, the carry is correct for the decimal digit, and 3 must be *added* to the result. Consider the addition of $7 + 6 = 13$:

$$1010 + 1001 = 10011 + 0011 = 1,0110 = 13$$

This is the correct sum in excess three. However, the carry must be properly handled as 0100, not as 0001.

Decimal Adjust. The x86 family of microprocessors encodes the digits 0–9 in binary codes: 0000 to 1001. Further, because the 8008 has only an 8-bit data type, two decimal digits are packed into 1 byte. The packed decimal digits are added by means of the 8-bit ALU, and adjustments are made after the addition to restore the packed decimal notation.

This process is illustrated below. Two unsigned decimal digits are packed into a single byte (D1 and D0). An addition adds 2 bytes together, producing a 1-byte result:

**TABLE 3.8
EXCESS-THREE CODE**

Decimal	Excess Three
0	0011
1	0100
2	0101
3	0110
4	0111
5	1000
6	1001
7	1010
8	1011
9	1100

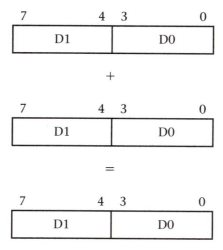

In forming the sum, there can be a carry from the least-significant digit, D0, and from the most-significant digit, D1. The values in D0 and D1 after the addition can be in the range 0000–1111. Thus a correction is needed to bring the range to 0000–1001. The decimal-correct instruction corrects the result for each digit by the following two-step rule:

Step 1.   If D0 > 9 or there has been a carry out from bit 3, add 00000110.

Step 2.   If D1 > 9 or there has been a carry out from bit 7, from the first add or from step 1, add 01100000.

The two adjustment steps will adjust the result to the proper representation and will produce a decimal carry from D1 if required. The decimal carry is used with an add-with-carry instruction for multiple precision addition.

EXAMPLE

Add the following decimal numbers by using the decimal-adjust instruction:

56 + 67, 99 + 99, 81 + 52.

Solution

56	0101 0110	99	1001 1001	81	1000 0001
+67	0110 0111	+99	1001 1001	+52	0101 0010
	1011 1101		1 0011 0010		1101 0011
	+0000 0110		+0000 0110		+0000 0000
	1100 0011		1 0011 1000		1101 0011
	+0110 0000		+0110 0000		+0110 0000
123	1 0010 0011	198	1 1001 1000	133	1 0011 0011

Signed Decimal Data Types

Most computers represent a complete decimal data type in sign and magnitude notation. A string of decimal digits is preceded or followed by a byte or half byte containing the sign. A six-digit decimal data type is shown below, allocated to three bytes. The digits may be two-out-of-five codes, excess-three, decimal adjust, or any other of the possible decimal encodings:

S	D5	D4	D3	D2	D1	D0

Because the data type itself is sign and magnitude, addition and subtraction follow the rules of arithmetic described in Section 3.4. However, the digits may be 9's or 10's complement to facilitate subtraction. The x86 architecture provides a subtract instruction with a corresponding decimal adjust for subtraction (DAS) instruction.

Floating-Point Data Types

Floating-point data types and operations were developed to remove the programming burden of scaling engineering calculations. The data type is based on commonly used scientific notation or standard notation. This notation represents the decimal value $+18.5$ as

$$+1.85 \times 10^1.$$

With this notation, the exponent value is adjusted so there is one decimal digit before the decimal point: a mixed data type. A straightforward translation of decimal scientific notation into binary suggests that $+18.5$ can be represented as

$$+1.00101000 \times 2^4.$$

For some binary base floating-point data types, the number 18.5 is normalized until there is only a fractional component:

$$+0.100101000 \times 2^5.$$

In other words, normalization continues, either left or right, until there is a 1 in the MSB of a fractional mantissa. This format, for 18.5, is then allocated to the bits in a word. Note that the exponent is shown in sign and magnitude and has a sign as well as the fraction. The technique for eliminating the exponent sign is called a biased exponent, to be discussed later:

S	Exponent	Fraction
+	+101	0.100101000

To generalize, a floating-point data type is divided into three components: sign, exponent, and mantissa. The mantissa may be a fraction, integer, or mixed data type. For most floating-point formats, the exponent is biased or excess, thus requiring no sign. The combination of these three components is the floating-point number:

$$number = sign, mantissa \times base^{exponent}.$$

With a fixed number of bits for a floating-point data type, a large exponent extends the range while reducing the accuracy. By use of floating-point, the range of a value is greater than the range of an integer with the same number of bits.

Design Decisions. Some of the design decisions faced by early designers are discussed below, along with the outcome, particularly for the IBM S360 format that is still widely used today. The IEEE floating-point format is also described in some detail. Floating-point data types are allocated to a fixed number of bits (32, 64, 80, etc.). The data-type designer must make a number of decisions for this allocation, some of which are the following.

- Radix: machine representation; 2 is common for computers, 10 for calculators
- Base: 10, 2, 16 are common[26]
- Number of bits for the exponent: 7, 8, 12 are common
- Is there a sign bit for the exponent or is the exponent biased?
- Allocation of sign bit
- Number of bits available from the word for the mantissa
- Is the mantissa an integer, a fraction, or a mixed data type?
- As floating point is an approximation, how are unusual conditions handled?

The last point is discussed in Subsection 3.5.3.1 after floating-point arithmetic is described.

Biased Exponents. Early computers with programmed floating point required that the data type and operations be provided by means of a subroutine. For these computers, it was natural to use the primary architected integer data type for the exponent as well as the mantissa. Thus, sign and magnitude, 1's complement, and 2's complement found use as both the exponent and the mantissa (leading to 2 sign bits in the format). The very early computers (Z4, Bell Labs Mark V) with architected floating point used combinations of 1's and 2's complement exponents and fractions. For example, Zuse's Z4 used 2's complement for the exponent and sign and mixed magnitude for the fraction. This choice of exponent data type then found its way into the hardware implementation of architected floating point on a number of machines such as the Atlas and the IBM Stretch, before being replaced with the biased exponent as the design of choice.

It is possible to scale data values so that the values > half scale are positive and $\leq$ half scale are negative. Half scale can be either 2^n or $2^n - 1$, depending on the details of the design. This notation, called scaled or biased, is used for the exponent in floating-point formats to eliminate an explicit sign bit for the exponent. Performing arithmetic operations, comparing, incrementing, and decrementing a 1's complement or 2's complement exponent, leads to unnecessary design complications. Therefore the

---

[26] One of the very early computers, the Bell Labs Mark V (1946), architected decimal floating point.

TABLE 3.9 BIASED EXPONENT VALUES		
Binary	Bias $= 2^{n-1} - 1$	Bias $= 2^{n-1}$
000	-3	-4
001	-2	-3
010	-1	-2
011	0	-1
100	$+1$	0
101	$+2$	$+1$
110	$+3$	$+2$
111	$+4$	$+3$

design of choice is to use a biased or excess exponent, similar to the excess-three data type discussed above.

Consider a 3-bit exponent in which the eight values are 000 to 111. Table 3.9 shows the exponent value with the two biases of $2^{n-1} - 1$ and 2^{n-1}. Keep in mind that a zero exponent is not a zero result. A zero exponent is the base to the zero power or one. Arithmetic operations on biased exponents are discussed further in Subsection 3.5.3.

The first computer known to the author that used a biased exponent is the IBM 704 (1955). Architected floating-point instructions use implemented registers and operations; thus it is not necessary that the representation of the exponent be the same as the representation of the mantissa.

In the following subsections two floating-point data types are described: the IBM S360 and the IEEE standard. Comparisons can be made between two different designs, one of base 16 and the other of base 2. These two floating-point data types are the most used in the world today.

IBM S360. The selection of the base for floating point has been hotly debated. Since the introduction of the IBM S360, the choices have been reduced to two, base 16 and base 2, even though base 8 has been popular in the past. The issue involved in the selection of the base has to do with the allocation of the bits in the word that determines whether range or accuracy is to be favored.

Sweeney (Sweeney 1965) examined the number of shifts needed for alignment before an operation and normalization needed after an operation.[27] His data, in the context of a 26-bit fraction mantissa, are tabulated in Table 3.10.

Base 16 was selected for the IBM S360 after Sweeney's extensive analysis of scientific programs and the desire for a wide range even in the single-precision format. The range of the exponent is

$$\text{range} = \text{base}^{\text{exponent}} = \text{base}^{2^{\text{number of bits}} - r}.$$

The parameter r is the number of codes in the exponent that are reserved for special

---

[27] If a result is not normalized, alignment is usually performed before it is used as an input to a following arithmetic operation.

TABLE 3.10 SHIFTS REQUIRED FOR VARIOUS FLOATING-POINT BASES

	Alignment-shift frequency					Normalization-shift frequency				
Base →	2	4	8	16	32	2	4	8	16	32
					Zero result →	1.42	1.42	1.42	1.42	1.42
Shift					Overflow →	19.65	10.67	6.52	5.50	5.69
0	32.61	38.24	45.77	47.32	52.52	59.38	72.11	79.40	82.35	83.86
1	12.11	18.54	19.77	26.02	26.37	6.78	7.96	8.75	7.29	5.99
2	8.61	12.83	11.92	10.47	5.92	3.47	3.35	1.61	1.38	0.87
3	6.72	9.87	6.26	2.24	1.82	2.35	1.49	0.38	1.01	0.88
4	7.17	3.01	1.73	1.31	2.08	1.91	0.34	0.43	1.30	0.41
5	3.88	2.05	1.10	1.70	1.87	1.06	0.14	0.71	0.32	0.88
6	4.39	1.01	0.89	1.24		0.56	0.92	0.25	0.43	
7	4.82	0.72	1.52			0.48	0.18	0.22		
8	1.29	0.63	1.00			0.16	0.13	0.28		
9	1.28	0.94				0.14	0.15			
10	1.31	0.72				0.08	0.18			
11	0.48	0.97				0.09				
12	0.58	0.74				0.32				
13	0.38	0.27				0.55				
14	0.38					0.16				
15	0.32					0.02				
16	0.33					0.04				
17	0.32					0.09				
18	0.40					0.08				
19	0.48					0.07				
20	0.36					0.12				
21	0.53					0.07				
22	0.48					0.07				
23	0.33					0.09				
24	0.36					0.11				
25	0.36					0.16				
26	0.19					0.52				
	9.50	9.43	10.04	9.07	9.42	← EXCESS SHIFT				

data representations. For the IBM floating-point format, $r = 0$, and for the IEEE floating-point format, $r = 2$.

With a 7-bit exponent, the range of an unbiased exponent is 16^0 to 16^{127}. The bias is $2^{7-1} = 64$, thus the range is approximately 16^{-65} to 16^{+63} and, in decimal, 5.4×10^{-79} to $7.2 \times 10^{+75}$. Biased exponents are discussed later in this section. The IBM S360 has two floating-point data types, single and double precision. Both of these two formats have the same range but differ in the length of the fraction:

S	7-bit exponent	24-bit fraction

S	7-bit exponent	56-bit fraction

Note that 1 bit of the byte containing the exponent, for both single and double precision, is allocated to the sign of the data type. Both the single-precision and the double-precision formats have the same exponent allocation and thus the same range.

The fraction is allocated to the bits remaining in the word after allocating the exponent and sign. The IBM S360 data type has a fraction of 24 bits for single precision and 56 bits for double precision. Because of the complications in performing arithmetic on mantissas by use of 1's and 2's complement integer data types, many floating-point data types are signed fractions or sign and magnitude.

As a historical note, the IBM S360 scientific models were introduced to compete with the very successful CDC 6600, which has only one floating-point data type allocated to a 60-bit word. The base is 2 and the exponent is 11 bits with bias. Thus the range of representation is 2^{-1024} to 2^{+1023} or approximately 10^{-300} to 10^{+300}. With a greater range and with 48 bits of fraction, the CDC 6600 commanded the respect of heavy scientific users. This format does not run out of range with long executions, and the accuracy remains satisfactory.

EXAMPLE

Determine the difference in the number of exponent bits required for equal range for base 2 and base 16. The parameter r is set to zero.

Solution

$$16^{2^{bits(16)}} = 2^{2^{bits(2)}},$$
assume bits(16) = 1,
$$16^{2^1} = 2^8 = 2^{2^{bits(2)}},$$
$$2^{bits(2)} = 8,$$
$$bits(2) = 3.$$

Thus the difference in the number of exponent bits is $3 - 1 = 2$.

Comment

Saving 2 bits in the exponent that were allocated to the fraction was a significant factor in selecting base 16 for the IBM S360 floating-point data type.

Base 16 representation requires a special approach to alignment and normalization. The fraction is divided into hexadecimal fields of 4 bits each. A normalization shift, left or right, requires that each shift be over 4 bits. Thus the 24-bit IBM S360 single-precision fraction will require, at most, 6 shifts. Each shift is accompanied by an increment or decrement of the exponent.

The fraction is normalized when the left most-significant hexadecimal field is $\neq 0$. If the 16 states of the hex field are evenly distributed, there is approximately a 3/4 wasted bit in the fraction. For worst case, 3 bits are wasted in the fraction. The designers of this data type believed that this loss of bits was a good trade-off as 2 bits are saved in the exponent (see the example above).

Table 3.10 shows the normalization-shift frequency for various bases. Note that the frequency of shifts for normalizations is less than that for alignments. For example, for input alignment with base 2, 0 shifts are required 32.61% of the time and 10 shifts are required 1.31% of the time. With base 16, 0 shifts are required 47.32% of the time. With normalization, 1.42% of all operations produce a zero result whereas 5.5% of the operations produce overflow in base 16.

EXAMPLE

For base 8, what is the weighted average number of shifts required for normalization?

Solution

Base Shifts	Frequency	Product
zero result, 0	1.42	0
overflow , 0	6.52	0
0	79.40	0
1	8.75	0.0875
2	1.61	0.0322
3	0.38	0.0114
4	0.43	0.0172
5	0.71	0.0355
6	0.25	0.0150
7	0.22	0.0154
8	0.28	0.0224
Weighted average number of base shifts		0.2366

Comment

Because 87.34% of all operations require no normalization because of a zero result, overflow, or a zero shift (result is produced in normalized form), the weighted average number of base shifts for normalization is quite small (0.2366). Note that 89.27% of all base 16 operations require no normalization.

IEEE Standard. The designers of the IEEE floating-point standard chose to use a mixed number rather than a fraction for the mantissa, calling it the significand (IEEE 1985). This representation has one bit position to the left of the radix point. Arithmetic performed in this representation is similar to the familiar scientific notation with one decimal digit to the left of the decimal point. Significand is defined in the IEEE Standard as

"The component of a binary floating point number that consists of an explicit or implicit leading bit to the left of its implied binary point and a fraction field to the right."

The IEEE floating-point data type is allocated to a binary word with a sign, an exponent that is a biased integer, and the significand:

S	Exponent	Significand

As suggested by the definition of the significand, when a number is normalized there is a 1 in the MSB position that is redundant. The leading 1 can therefore be implicit and is called a hidden bit.[28] With a hidden bit, only the fractional portion of the significand needs to be stored.

When a floating-point value is stored from the arithmetic unit, the leading 1 is dropped (hiding the hidden bit) and the fractional part is shifted one additional bit to the left, giving one additional bit of accuracy. The storage representation of the number +18.5 in the IEEE format and as a fractional mantissa are

IEEE in memory: $+0.001010 \times 2^4$
IEEE in ALU: $+1.001010 \times 2^4$
Fraction mantissa: $+0.100101 \times 2^5$

When an IEEE value is moved from storage into the ALU, the hidden bit is recovered and the representation is as shown without the hidden bit; that is a fraction mantissa. The use of a hidden bit allows the arithmetic unit to process one additional bit over the number of bits that are stored.

The IEEE standard provides for three floating-point data types:

Single precision: sign bit, 8-bit exponent, 23-bit significand
Double precision: sign bit, 11-bit exponent, 52-bit significand
Double extended precision; sign bit, $\geq$15-bit exponent, $\geq$63-bit significand

The third data type is used internally to the ALU for maintaining a high degree of accuracy and range for extended calculations. To store this format it must first be converted into either the single- or the double-precision format. An extended precision value can be reintroduced into the ALU in its extended form, thereby preserving the accuracy of long calculations.

EXAMPLE

If only 5 bits are provided for storing the fraction, what is the decimal value of numbers stored above when used in the ALU?

Solution

IEEE value: $1.00101 \times 2^4 = 1.15625 \times 16 = 18.5$.

Value with fraction mantissa: $0.10010 \times 2^5 = 0.56250 \times 32 = 18.0$.

Comment

This simple example shows that the IEEE floating point provides an additional bit of accuracy.

The exponents of the IEEE data types are biased, and the single-precision exponent is shown in Table 3.11. The single-precision data type has an 8-bit exponent with a bias of $2^{8-1} - 1$ or 127, and the double-precision bias is $2^{11-1} - 1$ or 1023. Two exponent

---

[28] A technique first used by Zuse on his Z4 in 1944–1950. The hidden bit is not explicitly defined in the IEEE specification.

**TABLE 3.11 IEEE
SINGLE-PRECISION
EXPONENTS**

Exponent	Value	Meaning
00000000	0	Reserved
00000001	1	2^{-126}
01111111	127	2^0
11111110	254	2^{+127}
11111111	255	Reserved

values, all zeros and all ones, are reserved for indicating special results, discussed in Subsection 3.5.3.1.

Summary of Floating-Point Data Types

Table 3.12 lists the parameters for a number of old and relatively new floating-point data types. The IEEE data type has become a standard. Note that the fractions or significands of all the floating-point representation included in Table 3.12 use sign and magnitude. Thus, when the fractions or significands are added, subtracted, multiplied, or divided, the operation must follow the proper rules of arithmetic discussed in Section 3.4.

EXAMPLE

Compared with base 2, how many bits are saved in the exponent and lost in the fraction for base 256? Assume no hidden bit.

Solution

Base 256 has 8-bit fields in the fraction. Thus for normalization, in the worst case, 7 bits are lost. On average, 4 bits are lost. No bits are lost with a base 2

TABLE 3.12 FLOATING-POINT DATA TYPES

Processor	Base	Radix	Exponent Representation	Fraction or Significand	Fraction or Significand Representation
Zuse Z4	2	2	2's comp. 7 bits	mixed	S-M 22 bits + sign↓
IBM 650	10	10	Bias, 2 dec. digits	fraction	S-M 8 dec. digits +
		2/5 code			sign (in a dec. digit)
IBM S360, sp	16	2	Bias, 7 bits	fraction	S-M 24 bits + sign
IBM S360, dp	16	2	Bias, 7 bits	fraction	S-M 56 bits + sign
VAX	2	2	Bias, 8 bits	fraction	S-M 23 bits + sign↓
IEEE, sp	2	2	Bias, 8 bits	mixed	S-M 23 bits + sign↓
IEEE, dp	2	2	Bias, 11 bits	mixed	S-M 52 bits + sign↓
IEEE, dex	2	2	Bias, ≥15 bits	mixed	S-M ≥ 63 bits + sign↓

Note: ↓hidden bit

system. Following the technique of the example in Subsection 3.2.3.1 we find that 3 bits are saved in the exponent for equal range.

Comment

From a bits-lost-or-saved point of view, base 256 seems to be a poor choice: lose 4 bits in the fraction, save 3 bits in the exponent.

Logical Data Types

Many computers define logical data types, also called Booleans, that are a vector of bits allocated to a byte, half-word, word, or double-word primary data type. These bit vectors are used to record binary events or states. Logical data types are used primarly for housekeeping tasks within a program and are rarely found as the input or the output of a progam.

The S360 allocates logical values to any of the data types, bytes, half words, words, and double words. The Pentium Pro can allocate a bit field of any length, as shown in Figure 3.11. One address specifies the start of the field, and a length parameter specifies the number of bits in the field.

3.2.3.2   Program Sequencing Data Types

A number of architected data types are used for controlling the sequence of the executing programs. These data types are the program counter and the indicator bits.

Program Counter

With modern computers, a program is stored in sequential memory locations and is accessed by the program counter. The program counter data type is an unsigned integer having a length equal, in many architectures, to one of the primary data types of the ISA. It is convenient to have the program counter data type the same length as a user data type, so it can be stored in memory with a context switch.[29] The Pentium Pro program counter is a 32-bit register called the extended instruction pointer (EIP) register.

The IBM S360 takes a different approach. The program counter (called the instruction address) is allocated in the 64-bit program status word (PSW), a double word that can be conveniently stored. The S360 and S370 program counters are 24 bits, whereas the S390 has a 31-bit program counter.

Branches require an EA that is loaded into the program counter when a branch is taken. There are three common forms of branch EAs that become the new program counter value. The displacement is the displacement field of the branch instruction:

Direct   PC ← (displacement)
PC relative   PC ← (PC) + (displacement)
Base relative   PC ← (base) + (displacement)

---

[29] Some single-chip microcomputers do not follow this convention. The length of the program counter is set to address the on-chip program ROM. A special hardware stack is provided to save the program counter for the return address when calling a subroutine or when responding to an interrupt.

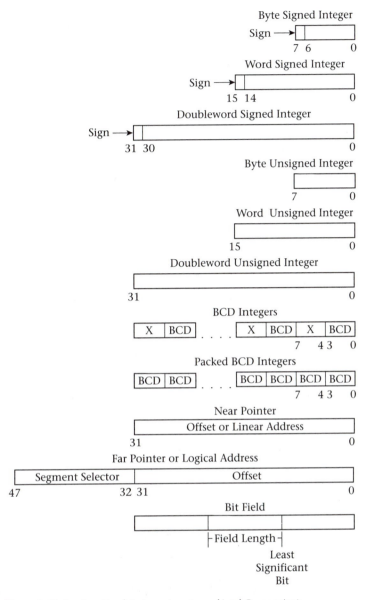

Figure 3.11 Pentium Pro data types (courtesy of Intel Corporation)

EXAMPLE

What happens when a displacement is added to the PC or a base value and there is a carry out?

Solution

There are two solutions to this design problem. First, the carry can be detected and an interrupt signaled, indicating an error. Second, the effective address wraps around and the branch is taken to a low-order address.

Comments

A designer must ensure that all such unusual situations do not result in unpredictable performance.

Indicator Bits

As data types, indicator bits are simply bits. The interesting characteristics of this data type are the methods by which they are set/reset. In Subsection 3.2.2 the use of indicator bits by branch instructions is discussed. Remember that the indicator bits permit a condition to be carried forward to a subsequent instruction that will test and branch based on the condition. Indicator bits are set/reset or recorded by two methods:

- as a side effect of an instruction
- explicitly as the primary result of an instruction

An example of side effect recording is as follows. For all arithmetic operations, the output bus of the ALU is tested for zero; if zero, the indicator is set to 1; otherwise it is reset to 0. Explicit instructions can also record a result in an indicator. For example, a Pentium Pro instruction performs the following:

> CMP – compare two operands. Compare the contents of two registers and set the status flag according to the results.

With most early computers, such as the von Neumann ISA, the branch instructions were of the test-and-branch type and did not use indicator bits to carry forward condition information.[30] The first use of indicator bits known to the author is found in the IBM 704, first installed in 1955. With the IBM 704, an input byte is checked by hardware and its parity recorded in a P bit. This bit holds the parity condition until there is another input operation that sets/resets the indicator. Thus the indicator must be used before it is changed by a following instruction. All other branches in this computer were of the test-and-branch type that tests the condition of various registers.

The use of indicator bits, as we know them today, can be traced to the IBM Stretch installed in 1961. With this machine, 64 indicator bits are grouped into an architected double word that, in addition to being tested by branch instructions, could be stored and reloaded for context switching. Seven of the bits recorded the result of an integer ALU operation as side effects: negative, zero, positive, negative sign, low, equal, and high. Ten of the bits recorded the floating-point ALU results and exceptions.

IBM S360 Condition Codes. The IBM S360 carried forward the architected indicator bits idea from the IBM Stretch in a restricted fashion. The condition code is allocated to the architected PSW along with other status information. The designers of the S360 believed that the indicators of the Stretch could be encoded, thereby

---

[30] The von Neumann ISA could branch on a previously computed value in the accumulator, ≥ 0. Likewise, the Bell Model V relay calculator could branch on the sign of a previously computed value.

TABLE 3.13 IBM S360 CONDITION CODES

Instruction	Condition Code Value			
	00	01	10	11
ADD logical	zero, no carry	not zero, no carry	zero, carry	—
SUBTRACT logical	=	not zero, no carry	zero, carry	not zero, carry
Test under mask	zero	mixed	—	ones
ADD	zero	<zero	>zero	overflow
Move long	count equal	count low	count high	dest. overlap
Compare floating point	equal	low	high	—
ADD decimal	zero	<zero	>zero	overflow
Store clock	set	not set	error	not operational

saving bits in the PSW and making room for the program counter and other control information.

Two bits are used to encode four conditions; encoded indicators are called condition codes. Further complicating the design, the conditions are recorded as side effects and are context dependent. That is, the meaning of the encoded value depends on the instruction that records the condition. A small sample of the condition coding is shown in Table 3.13.

The branch instructions have a 2-bit field that is compared with the 2-bit condition code. For example, if after performing an ADD one wants to test the result for zero, the 2 bits in the instruction would be 00. If a branch on overflow is desired, the bits would be 11.

The system of the IBM S360 opens many opportunities for programming errors. Say, for example, an ADD is performed; then the clock is stored. The information in the condition code following the add has been destroyed. A branch on 00 would now report that the clock is set, not that the result of the previous add is not zero.

Intel Architecture Family Indicator Bits. Intel literature refers to indicators as flags, the term used in this discussion. The first member of the x86 family, the i8008, has four implemented flags that are set/reset as side effects to other operations: carry, zero, positive, parity. Because the flags are implemented, their values cannot be stored and retrieved for context switching.

As the evolution of the x86 family progressed to the i8080 and the i8086, the i286 was the first member with architected flags. With the i286, 16 flags are allocated in a register that can be stored and retrieved for context switching. However, only 12 flags were assigned, leaving 4 bits for expansion.

The flags of the Intel Pentium Pro are shown in Figure 3.12. The flags are allocated to a 32-bit word. Note there are three classes of flags: status, control, and system. The auxiliary carry flag is used for performing a decimal adjust after a decimal addition. The alignment check flag is of interest because the x86 memory is byte addressable. If, for example, a word (4 bytes) is addressed and the address is not

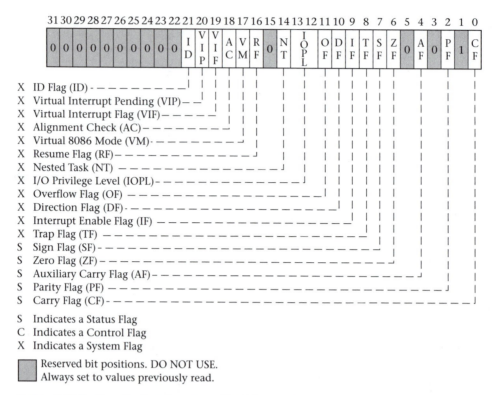

Figure 3.12 Pentium Pro flags (courtesy of Intel Corporation)

aligned on word boundaries (the two-address LSBs = 0), an interrupt is signaled and the flag is set. The interrupt handler then checks the flags to determine the cause of the interrupt.

All of the x86 status flags are set/reset as side effects of an instruction. The system flags are mixed: some are set explicitly by the operating system, such as the virtual memory flag, whereas others are set as side effects of user instructions, such as the overflow flag.

EXAMPLE

Using the Pentium Pro flags, how does one check for $(r1) \geq (r2)$?

Solution

The contents of the registers are subtracted and the flags are set as side effects. The flags are then tested by a second instruction. In this example, we are primarily interested in the side effects of the instructions.

Step 1. $(r1) - (r2) =$

    a. If the result is positive because $r1 < r2$, the sign flag is set to 1.

    b. If the result is zero, the zero flag is set to 1.

Step 2. Logical and conditional branch instructions can determine which of the four states are represented with the two flags. The first flag indicates $+$ OR $-$ and the second flag indicates $\neq$ OR $=$. After a register

TABLE 3.14 INDICATOR SUMMARY

Branch Type	Indicators	How set?	Saved with a Context Switch?
Test-and-branch	None		No
Orthogonal	Implemented	Side effect	No
Orthogonal	Implemented	Explicitly	No
Orthogonal	Architected	Side effect	Yes
Orthogonal	Architected	Explicitly	Yes

subtraction is made, the two indicator bits can be in one of the following four states:

00	Negative, not zero	$(r1) < (r2), (r2) \neq (r1)$
01	Negative, zero	$(r1) < (r2), (r2) = (r1)$
10	Positive, not zero	$(r1) > (r2), (r2) \neq (r1)$
11	Positive, zero	$(r1) > (r2), (r1) = (r2)$

If $(r1) = 5$ and $(r2) = 3$, the subtraction produces a positive and not zero result; thus the two flags are set/reset as side effect to 10. To test for $\geq$, the OR of the two indicator bits will indicate if the test is true. For this example, the OR of 10 is 1 and $5 \geq 2$.

Indicator Summary

Indicators are set/reset either as side effects or explicitly. The indicators are allocated to bits that are implemented or architected. The five variations of indicator bit design are summarized in Table 3.14. Note that many ISAs use a selection of indicator design techniques. Very few processors are consistent by using only one.

3.2.4 INSTRUCTION COMPOSITION

An instruction format is composed of the three components of an ISA: operation addresses and data type. The design and the allocation of op-codes and addresses are discussed in the following paragraphs. In general, user data types are not allocated to the instruction except for immediate integers.

There are a number of design trade-offs to be made when allocating the various fields to the instruction. For instance, the length of the instruction should be a multiple of the size of the AU. The op-code allocation should provide for a rich set of operations while keeping the number of bits to a minimum. The number of bits allocated to the register file addresses sets the size of the register file. Memory address, which, for direct addressing, can be very long, must somehow be reduced in size.

The following paragraphs provide a discussion of the techniques for allocating bits and fields to an instruction. The goal is to achieve a balance between the conflicting requirements.

Operation Codes

There are a number of ways to allocate op-codes to an instruction. The design issue is to reduce the number of bits in the instruction (small bit budget) while providing a large number of op-codes for a rich instruction set. Three design options or techniques have been used to meet these requirements.

1. A fixed-length op-code allocated to variable length instructions: IBM S360.
2. A variable-length op-code, provided by op-code expansion, allocated in a variable-length instruction: Intel x86.
3. A variable-length op-code, provided by op-code expansion, allocated in a fixed-length instruction: MIPS R2000 and IBM PowerPC.

We will look at these three techniques by examining the ISAs noted above.

IBM S360. The rationale for variable-length instruction is that the instructions that are used most frequently can be short with the infrequent instructions being long, as with Morse Code. The IBM S360 has 16-, 32-, and 48-bit instructions. However, the op-code is of the same length, 1 byte, for each of these three instruction lengths.

Within the 1-byte op-code, the four MSBs bind the instruction to the data type while the four LSBs bind the instruction to the operation. The four MSB bindings are shown in Table 3.15. For example, if the four MSBs of the op-code are 0111, the data type is short (single-precision) floating point. As this data type is 32 bits and the IBM S360 memory is byte addressed, the two LSBs of the data effective address are ignored when memory is accessed. Also, the floating-point ALU is used to execute the operation.

TABLE 3.15 IBM S360 OPERATION CODE CLASSES

Op-Code MSBs	Bindings
0000	Branching and status switching
0001	Fixed-point full word and logical
0010	Floating-point long
0011	Floating-point short
0100	Fixed-point half word and branching
0101	Fixed-point full word and logical
0110	Floating-point long
0111	Floating-point short
1000	Set system mask
1001	Fixed-point logical and I/O
1010	Not defined
1011	Not defined
1100	Not defined
1101	Logical
1110	Not defined
1111	Decimal

The four LSBs specify the operations to be performed. Note the generous provision for future expansion of data types. Designers provide for decoding of unassigned operation codes and causing a trap, so the illegal op-codes will not attempt execution.

Intel x86. The original member of the x86 architecture, the 8008, has a single 1-byte op-code. The design of the 8080 called for a richer instruction set leading to the need for an additional op-code byte. This expansion is accomplished by a technique called expanded op-codes. With expanded op-codes, reserve codes in the first op-code byte invoke fetching and decoding a second byte:

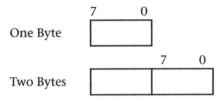

1-byte instructions can be decoded into 256 unique operations. However, with the x86, there are two reserve codes in the first byte that indicate the need to fetch and decode a second byte. These codes are 0F and 1F (in hexadecimal). The 0F code leads to a second byte of integer instructions whereas the 1F code leads to a byte of floating-point instructions. There are further expansions that are not described here, but this description gives the flavor of the technique.[31]

EXAMPLES

1. From the information given above, how many op-codes are possible with the x86 technique?

   Solution
   The number of op-codes is

   #op-codes = #one byte + #2 byte
   $$= 256 - 2 + 2 \times 256 = 254 + 512 = 766 \text{ op-codes.}$$

   Comment
   With a 2-byte op-code, the total number of op-codes is $2^{16} = 65,536$. Thus a significant number of potential op-codes are given up in order to have short op-codes for frequently used instructions.

2. 10 bits would be required for encoding the 766 instructions of the example above. What fraction of the variable-length instructions should be executed for the variable-length op-code to break even with 10 bits required for a fixed-length op-code?

   Solution
   The fraction of a 1-byte instruction length is represented by s. This problem is solved by finding s that will give the weighted average instruction length

---

[31] When the designers of the Intel 8080 were expanding the op-code set of the 8008, they ran out of time in the design schedule and left some of the op-codes unassigned. This turned out to be the key to future expansion of the Intel Architecture.

of 10:

$$10 = 8s + (1 - s)16,$$
$$-6 = -8s,$$
$$s = (6/8) = 0.75.$$

Comments

If more than 75% of the executed instructions are 1 byte and 25% are less than two bytes, the bit budget is smaller than that with a 10-bit op-code.

MIPS R2000. With a fixed instruction length of 32 bits, 6 bits were allocated to the op-code. This number of bits provides only 64 op-codes, which is insufficient for the number of desired instructions.

The solution to this design problem was to have variable-length operation codes within a fixed-length instruction that used expanded op-codes. The most frequently used operations are directly encoded in the 6-bit op-code, while a small set of the 64 possible codes are reserved as escape codes that require decoding of more bits in the instruction to obtain the full op-code. This technique does not increase the length of the instruction as with the x86.

Refer to Figure 3.13 for the following discussion. The op-code bits are 26–31 and the initial decoding of the op-code is shown at the top of the figure. For the op-code 000011, the instruction is JAL, a jump or branch instruction. If the op-code is 000000, the special instructions are invoked with bits 0–5 of the instruction. These 6 bits, found in the R format, are decoded as shown in the SPECIAL map. BCOND is expanded with bits 16–20 of the instruction while COP0 is expanded with bits 0–4. COP1, 2, and 3 are expanded with bits 16–25.

PowerPC. Another example of an expanded op-code system is found in the PowerPC ISA. This processor has a 32-bit instruction with 6 bits (bits 0–5) allocated to the op-code. Frequently used instructions such as addi (add immediate) are encoded within the 6 bits. The addi instruction has the encoding (0001110) with a 16-bit immediate operand in bit positions 16–31. The other source register, A, and destination register, D, are addressed in two 5-bit fields as this processor has a 32-word register file:

	0 5	6 10	11 15	16 30
addi	14	D	A	Immediate

Infrequently used instructions use an expanded op-code to obtain more op-code bits. The escape code is 31_{10}. Examples found in the PowerPC instruction set illustrate the use of expanding op-codes: addx, addcx, and addex:

	0 5	6 10	11 15	16 20	22 30
addx	31	D	A	B	256
addcx	31	D	A	B	10
addex	31	D	A	B	139

Each of these three instructions has the same op-code in bits 0–5, but the complete op-code requires that bits 22–30 also be decoded.

Opcode

31..29 \ 28..26	0	1	2	3	4	5	6	7
0	SPECIAL	BCOND	J	JAL	BEQ	BNE	BLEZ	BGTZ
1	ADDI	ADDIU	SLTI	SLTIU	ANDI	ORI	XORI	LUI
2	COP0	COP1	COP2	COP3	†	†	†	†
3	†	†	†	†	†	†	†	†
4	LB	LH	LWL	LW	LBU	LHU	LWR	†
5	SB	SH	SWL	SW	†	†	SWR	†
6	LWC0	LWC1	LWC2	LWC3	†	†	†	†
7	SWC0	SWC1	SWC2	SWC3	†	†	†	†

SPECIAL

5..3 \ 2..0	0	1	2	3	4	5	6	7
0	SLL	†	SRL	SRA	SLLV	†	SRLV	SRAV
1	JR	JALR	†	†	SYSCALL	BREAK	†	†
2	MFHI	MTHI	MFLO	MTLO	†	†	†	†
3	MULT	MULTU	DIV	DIVU	†	†	†	†
4	ADD	ADDU	SUB	SUBU	AND	OR	XOR	NOR
5	†	†	SLT	SLTU	†	†	†	†
6	†	†	†	†	†	†	†	†
7	†	†	†	†	†	†	†	†

BCOND

20..19 \ 18..16	0	1	2	3	4	5	6	7
0	BLTZ	BGEZ						
1								
2	BLTZAL	BGEZAL						
3								

COPz

22,21,16 \ 25..23	0	1	2	3	4	5	6	7
0,0,0	MF	MT		BCF				
0,0,1				BCT				
0,1,0								
0,1,1					CO			
1,0,0	CF	CT						
1,0,1								
1,1,0								
1,1,1								

COP0

4..3 \ 2..0	0	1	2	3	4	5	6	7
0		TLBR	TLBWI				TLBWR	
1	TLBP							
2	RFE							
3								

† Operation codes marked with a dagger cause reserved instruction exceptions and reserved for future versions of the architecture.

Figure 3.13 MIPS R2000 instruction maps (courtesy MIPS Technologies Inc.)

Register Addresses

The allocation of register addresses to the instruction format is straightforward. The questions to be resolved are the size of the register file and whether two or three addresses will be used. Register files with 32 words requiring 5 address bits are common today. Thus a three-address format uses 15 bits whereas a two-address format uses 10 bits for register addresses.

TABLE 3.16   MEMORY ADDRESSES

Processor	Bits in Instruction	Effective Address
IBM S360	12-bit displacement	Index + base + displacement
Intel Pentium	8-, 16-, 32-bit displacement	Index + base + displacement
MIPS R2000	16-bit displacement	Index + displacement
PowerPC	None	(RA) + (RB)

Memory Addresses

With the op-code and the register addresses allocated, there are usually few bits remaining to allocate to a memory address(es). For this reason, many processor designs use two design strategies to reduce the number of memory address bits. The first strategy is to use either an accumulator or a load/store architecture. These architectures, IBM S360 and x86, need only one memory address. The second strategy is to allocate only a displacement in the instruction that is used to develop a longer effective address. These strategies can be combined, as shown in Table 3.16.

Other Fields

Other fields also need to be allocated to the instruction format. Examples are shift count, masks, and mode bits. In many cases, the designer wants to use as few bits as possible and will investigate the weighted average of the design choice. For example, a computer with a 32-bit integer primary word length could use up to 5 bits as a shift count. However, investigation shows that 90% of all shifts are ≤ 4 bits. Thus a 2-bit shift count can be used; for longer shifts, multiple shift instructions will be used in the program.

3.3 CISC AND RISC ARCHITECTURAL STYLES

Section 3.1 discusses the lexical level of an ISA. In this section, we compare the specifics of the CISC and RISC architectural styles. A CISC architecture is at a higher lexical level than RISC and performs more than one operation with a single instruction. RISC architectures use simple instructions placing complexity in the software. One of the direct consequences of these two styles is that a CISC architecture needs to execute fewer instructions than a RISC architecture for the same algorithmic function. This difference is discussed, with experimental verification, in Section 3.5.

There are a number of distinguishing characteristics of CISC and RISC architectures. These differences are discussed in the context of the x86, MIPS, and R2000 processors:

1. size and function of the register file
2. accessing memory for data reads and writes
3. number of operations performed by a single instruction
4. variable or fixed instruction lengths
5. number of data types

Type of Data Movement	Source → Destination
From memory to a register	Memory location → General-purpose register Memory location → Segment register
From a register to memory	General-purpose register → Memory location Segment register → Memory location
Between registers	General-purpose register → General-purpose register General-purpose register → Segment register Segment register → General-purpose register General-purpose register → Control register Control register → General-purpose register General-purpose register → Debug register Debug register → General-purpose register
Immediate data to a register	Immediate → General-purpose register
Immediate data to memory	Immediate → Memory location

Figure 3.14 Pentium Pro move instruction (courtesy of Intel Corporation)

CISC Architecture

The Intel x86 architecture serves as a good example of a CISC architecture with a remarkable market success. The following discussion is not a complete description of this architecture; for more information, refer to Intel literature. The MMX extensions to the architecture are described in Section 8.7.

Size and Function of the Register File. The register architecture is basically a one-address accumulator, described above. The accumulator (A register: AL, AH, AX, and EAX) is supported by seven additional dedicated registers used for forming EAs and as temporary storage. A map of the general purpose registers of the Pentium Pro is shown in Figure 3.8.

The first member of the x86 architecture was the 8008, first produced in 1971.[32] This processor had only an 8-bit integer data type and four 8-bit registers (A, B, C, and D). With the i286 the registers were extended to 16 bits and four 16-bit registers were added (BP, SI, DI, and SP). The i486 further extended the word length of the registers to 32 bits named, as shown in Figure 3.8.

Accessing Memory for Data Reads and Writes. Figure 3.14 shows a number of move instructions. Note that there is no memory-to-memory move; this function is accomplished by two instructions moving the operand by means of a general-purpose register. Some of the arithmetic instructions are accumulator based and require a memory access for one of the operands. However, there are register-to-register arithmetic instructions that do not require a memory operand access. The register-to-register arithmetic instructions were provided in the 8008 to perform address arithmetic needed to compute memory effective addresses.

Number of Operations Performed by a Single Instruction. Many of the instructions perform more than one elementary function. For example, the instruction F2XM1

---

[32] The architecture of what became known as the x86 was designed by engineers at Computer Terminal Corporation, San Antonio, Texas. Intel and Texas Instruments each designed a microprocessor to the CTC instruction set specifications, with Texas Instruments delivering first.

performs the operation

$$ST \leftarrow (2^{ST} - 1),$$

where ST is the top of the floating-point evaluation stack. Some of the move instructions are conditional on a flag set by a previous instruction; Pentium Pro flags are described in Figure 3.12.

Other instructions are conditional within the instruction. For example, the CMPXCHG instruction compares two source operands (one each from the AL, AX, or EAX register, depending on the data-type size). If the operands are equal, the second operand is loaded into a destination register; otherwise the content of the destination is loaded into the AL, AX, or EAX register.

Variable or Fixed Instruction Lengths. CISC architectures use variable-length instructions to reduce the instruction bit budget and bit traffic. The reason for variable-length instruction is that simple instructions, such as a register-to-register ADD, could be encoded in one byte because no memory addresses are required. For other instructions, such as those requiring three memory addresses, the instruction is lengthened to provide the addresses. In other words, the length of the instruction will match the complexity of the instruction.

Figure 3.15 shows the Pentium Pro instruction format. Note that the smallest instruction is 1 byte. Variable-length instructions lead to a number of implementation problems, one of which is that memory modules are usually implemented with widths that are even powers of 2: for example, 4 bytes wide or 8 bytes wide. With a stream of variable-length instructions, some instructions will reside in two or more memory words and will require two or more memory accesses to fetch the instruction. Extensive hardware is used in the Pentium Pro to compensate for this problem.

EXAMPLE

A sequence of x86 instructions has the following number of bytes per instruction: #1 is 3 bytes, #2 is 2 bytes, #3 is 3 bytes, #4 is 1 byte, #5 is 7 bytes, #6 is 2 bytes, #7 is 1 byte, and # 8 is 8 bytes. The memory module and bus is 4 bytes wide. What is the weighted average number of memory cycles per instruction required for fetching this instruction stream?

Solution

A memory map of the instruction sequence is shown below, and the instruction numbers are indicated:

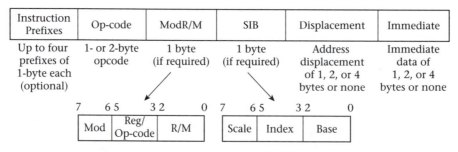

Figure 3.15 Pentium Pro instruction format (courtesy of Intel Corporation)

.Memory word, 4 bytes			
1	1	1	2
2	3	3	3
4	5	5	5
5	5	5	5
6	6	7	8
8	8	8	8
8	8	8	

The eight instructions required seven memory cycles, giving $7/8 = 0.875$ memory cycles per instruction.

Comment

For this example, the average number of bytes per instruction is $27/8 = 3.375$. However, the only paper known to the author indicates that the average Intel 8086 instruction is 2.25 bytes (Adams and Zimmerman 1989). Extensive published statistics on the IBM S360 show that this CISC architecture has approximately 4 bytes per instruction.

Another problem with variable-length instructions is that an instruction fetch page fault (for a virtual memory system, discussed in Chapter 4) can occur in the middle of the instruction fetch, since an instruction can reside in two pages. Extensive hardware support is required for overcoming this problem.

Number of Data Types. Designers of CISC architectures attempt to provide a data type for most user applications. The Pentium Pro user data types, not including floating point, are shown in Figure 3.11. Note that there are three 2's complement integers, three unsigned integers, two BCD, two-address, and 1-bit field data types. Each of these data types required specific op-codes and addresses in the instruction format – a reason for variable-length instructions.

The IEEE standard floating-point data types used with the Pentium Pro are described in Subsection 3.2.3, and the MMX data types are described in Section 8.7.

RISC Architecture

The MIPS R2000 processor is selected as an example of RISC design style. As with the x86, a complete architectural description is not given, but the five characteristics that distinguish CISC/RISC are highlighted.

Size and Function of the Register File. The register file of the MIPS R2000 architecture consists of 32, 32-bit registers, shown in Figure 3.16. These registers are used for operands, results (both integer and floating point), and index registers. One of the registers, R0, is always set to zero for use in clearing a register, providing a zero constant, and support of address arithmetic. Two 32-bit registers are provided to support

General-Purpose Registers

31   0

| 0 |
| r1 |
| r2 |
| • |
| • |
| • |
| r29 |
| r30 |
| r31 |

Multiply/Divide Registers

31   0

| HI |

31   0

| LO |

Program Counter

31   0

| PC |

Figure 3.16 MIPS R2000 registers (courtesy MIPS Technologies Inc.)

multiplication (holding the double-length product) and division (holding the quotient and the remainder). The program counter is a separately architected register.

Accessing Memory for Data Reads and Writes: The MIPS R2000 and all RISC processors are known as load/store architectures. This means that the only instructions that address memory are the load and the store instructions. All other instructions find their operands and place results in the register file.[33] The load and the store instructions require two memory accesses (instruction plus data) and operate on signed and unsigned bytes, words (2 bytes), and double words.

The MIPS R2000 instructions use the three-address register-to-register format. Other RISC processors use the two-address register-to-register architecture to save register address bits in the instruction.

Number of Operations Performed by a Single Instruction: As with most RISC architectures, the MIPS R2000 performs simple instructions. The instruction format is shown in Figure 3.17. Note that there are three types of instructions: I type, J type, and R type:

I type: These instructions perform load, store, and ALU operations with an immediate.

J type: These instructions perform branch instructions.

R type: These instructions perform ALU operations with two register sources and one register destination address.

Unlike the x86 architecture, there are no compound instructions in the MIPS R2000 ISA. However, the R-type instructions do set indicator bits as side effects that are used by following branch instructions for program flow control.

Variable or Fixed Instruction Lengths. The MIPS R2000 architecture has a fixed-length 32-bit instruction, as shown in Figure 3.17. With an op-code of 6 bits, one would assume that only 64 unique instructions could be implemented. Even for a RISC, this small number of instructions is not rich enough for practical programming. Thus the technique of expanded op-codes is used to enrich the instruction set; the specifics were discussed previously.

---

[33] The first instance of a load/store architecture known to the author was the CDC 6600, first delivered in 1964 and designed by Seymour Cray.

I-Type (Immediate)

op	rs	rt	immediate

31   26 25   21 20   16 15   0

J-Type (Jump)

op	target

31   26 25   0

R-Type (Register)

op	rs	rt	rd	shamt	funct

31   26 25   21 20   16 15   11 10   6 5   0

Figure 3.17 MIPS R2000 instruction formats (courtesy MIPS Technologies Inc.)

where:

op	is a 6-bit operation code
rs	is a 5-bit source register specifier
rt	is a 5-bit target (source/destination) register or branch condition
immediate	is a 16-bit immediate, branch displacement or address displacement
target	is a 26-bit jump target address
rd	is a 5-bit destination register specifier
shamt	is a 5-bit shift amount
funct	is a 6-bit function field

There are a number of advantages to a fixed-length instruction. Fetching across a fixed-width memory bus is quite easy. As the 32-bit word will not be split between pages, page faults will not occur during program fetches. There is little advantage in instruction decoding between the MIPS R2000 and the x86, as both require a prede-code to see if another field must be decoded.

Number of Data Types. The number of MIPS R2000 user data types is modest when compared with the data types of the x86. The data types consist of

single- and double-precision IEEE floating point
signed, 2's complement 8-, 16-, and 32-bit integers
unsigned 8-, 16-, and 32-bit integers

The MIPS R2000 memory is addressed to the byte. Thus the address for a 16-bit integer ignores the LSB of the address. The 2 LSBs of the address are ignored for 32-bit integers and single-precision floating-point data types. The three LSBs of the address are ignored for double-precision floating-point data types. Binding of the addresses to op-codes is accomplished in the instruction decoding hardware.

3.4 STATIC AND DYNAMIC INSTRUCTION STATISTICS

Reference was made earlier in this chapter to bit budget and bit traffic. Bit budget measures the number of bits, bytes, words, or instructions required for representing a program and is illustrated in the discussion above on instruction composition. With

COMMENT		INSTRUCTION
Preparation	h − 2	Load k from k_0
	h − 1	Load j_0 from j_{00}
Initial Setup	h	Load i_0 from i_{00}
New Product row procedure	h + 1	Load i from i_0 ←
New vector product procedure	h + 2	Load j from j_0 ←
Vector multiply, inner loop	h + 3	Set accumulator to zero
	h + 4	Load cumulative multiplicand from ← location specified by i
OPERATION	h + 5	Multiply-add by operand location specified by j
	h + 6	Increment j by p
Housekeeping, inner loop	h + 7	Advance i, count, refill when count reaches zero, branch to h + 4 when count does not reach zero →
End of vector multiplication procedure	h + 8	Store cumulative product at location specified by k
	h + 9	Increment k by 1
	h + 10	Advance j_0, count, refill when count reaches zero, and branch to h + 2 when count does not reach zero →
	h + 11	Increment i by n
End of product row procedure	h + 12	Reduce count of k, refill when count reaches zero, and branch to h + 1 when count does not reach zero →

Figure 3.18 Matrix multiplication program

early computers, reducing the bit budget of a program was of paramount importance because of the cost of main memory. Today, with lower-cost memory, the designer is not overly concerned with the bit budget or static instruction count. However, bit traffic, the dynamic instruction frequency of use, is of concern. Static instruction frequencies are a measure of the frequency of use of each instruction type as represented in the program. Dynamic instruction frequencies are a measure of the frequency of use of an executing program. A program with a loop that is executed 100 times will have significantly different static and dynamic statistics.

Consider the program shown in Figure 3.18 for performing matrix multiplication (Buchholz 1962). Instruction $h + 5$ performs the multiply–add operation and represents 1/15 or 6.6% of the static frequency of use. However, for a matrix dimension 32×32, the instructions $h + 4$, $h + 5$, $h + 6$, and $h + 7$ are each executed 32,768 times. The total number of instructions executed by the program is 133,271, so these four instructions have a dynamic weight of 24.6% each. The other 11 instructions collectively represent only 1.6% of the instructions executed.

A designer uses static and dynamic statistics in different ways. If there is an operation or function that is infrequently used, say square root, the designer may elect not to include it as an instruction while making sure that there are primitives that can be used to program square root. By not implementing square root, the designer can simplify the processor, an argument advanced in support of the RISC architectural style.

If a designer finds from dynamic statistics that a particular instruction represents a large fraction of all instructions executed, every effort is made to reduce the execution time of that instruction (recall Amdahl's law). A designer interested in improving the performance of the matrix multiplication program of Figure 3.18 will look first to the four instructions, $h+4$, $h+5$, $h+6$, and $h+7$.

There is an important piece of information that should be considered with instruction statistics. The availability of statistics for various computers varies from abundant to almost nonexistent. In the abundant class we find the MIPS R2000 and SPARC. Next in line is the VAX and the IBM S360. In the almost-nonexistent class is the x86 architecture. There seem to be two reasons for this. First, the x86 has not attracted the attention of academics, and second, manufacturers of this architecture gather statistics for their own engineering purposes and see no advantage in publishing their results. In other words, the availability of published statistics seems to be inversely proportional to the number of installed processors.

EXAMPLE

Compute the bit budget and the bit traffic, measured in instructions, for the vector program shown in Figure 3.18. Assume that the two source matrices and the destination matrix are 128 × 128.

Solution

The bit budget is 15 instructions. The bit traffic is determined approximately as the inner loop, $h+4$ through $h+7$, is executed 128^3 times. Thus the bit traffic for this part is $4 \times 128^3 = 8.39 \times 10^6$ instructions. The next loop is executed 128^2 times. Thus the bit traffic for this part is $5 \times 128^2 = 8.19 \times 10^4$ instructions ($h+4$ through $h+7$ counted above). The outer loop is executed 128 times. Thus the bit traffic for this part is $3 \times 128 = 3.84 \times 10^2$ instructions ($h+2$ through $h+10$ counted above). The three initialization instructions are executed once:

$$\text{bit traffic} \approx 8.39 \times 10^6 + 8.19 \times 10^4 + 3.84 \times 10^2 + 3$$
$$\approx 8.47 \times 10^6 \text{ instructions}$$

Comment

This bit traffic calculation clearly shows that significant speedup in this algorithm can come only from improvements to the inner loop. This is exactly what is done with vector computers such as the TI ASC and the CRAY-1. The CRAY-1 reduces four instructions to one by overlapping in hardware the overhead of $h+4$, $h+6$, and $h+7$ with instruction $h+5$.

High-Level Language Statistics

Remember that a program written in a high-level language is compiled into the language of the computer's ISA. Thus, it is instructive to investigate the frequency of use of the various high-level language statements before looking at the statistics of the ISA language. The information in Table 3.17 is taken from a survey of prior work directed to the development of a synthetic benchmark called Drystone (Weicker 1984). Static and dynamic statistics are reported.

TABLE 3.17 HIGH-LEVEL LANGUAGE STATIC FREQUENCY OF USE

Operation	Language		
	FORTRAN(%)	Pascal(%)	Ada(%)
Assignment	51	44.0	37.1
Call	12	31.8	26.8
Return	4	—	6.9
If	10	14.8	9.8
Loop with condition	—	3.3	1.3
Loop with "for"	9	2.8	0.9
With	—	2.1	—
Case			0.4
Exit loop	—	—	1.4
Goto	9	0.3	—
Other	5	0.1	15.4

As mentioned above, high-level languages have no explicit move statements. These statements are introduced by the compiler to match the assignment statements to the processor's memory architecture: registers, accumulator, stack, etc. Note that the assignment and the call statements constitute ~65% of all the static statements. We should expect that other high-level languages such as C and C++ will show similar static statistics even though the author knows of no published data.

Instruction Level Statistics

Like high-level language, published instruction level statistics generally report on both the static and dynamic frequencies. We look at the instruction level statistics for the three CISC processors, the IBM S360, DEC VAX, and the x86. The statistics for two RISC processors, the MIPS R2000 and SPARC, are also shown.

IBM S360. Extensive static and dynamic statistics are provided in an early study of IBM S360 programs (Alexander and Wortman 1975). A sample of these data is given in Table 3.18, showing the instructions with the most frequent occurrence. The benchmarks providing these data did not include floating-point instructions.

An interesting thing about these data is that the instructions with the highest frequency of use are those that are inserted by the compiler and are overhead to the problem, meaning they perform no useful work as specified by the high-level language program. For the dynamic statistics, 63% of the executed instructions are found before arithmetic instruction. Also, the add and the subtract instructions constitute only 9% of all executed instructions.

DEC VAX. The instruction statistics of the DEC VAX have been extensively measured by Clark and others. Some of the VAX statistics rank the instructions by frequency of use and by the time of use. This second ranking gives insight into the time burner instructions that could be the object of design improvement. A sample of these data for a multiuser workstation workload is taken from (Clark and Levy 1982) and shown in Table 3.19.

TABLE 3.18 IBM S360 INSTRUCTION WEIGHTS

	Static			Dynamic	
L	Load fixed word	29%	L	Load fixed word	27%
ST	Store	15%	BC	Branch/condition	14%
BC	Branch/condition	10%	ST	Store	10%
LA	Load address	7%	C	Compare	6%
SR	Subtract	6%	LA	Load address	6%
BAL	Branch and link	5%	SR	Subtract	5%
SLL	Shift left, single.	4%	IC	Insert char.	4%
IC	Insert char.	3%	A	Add	4%
C	Compare	3%	SLL	Shift left, single.	3%
A	Add	2%	N	And	3%

Note that 10 instructions constitute 47% of all executed instructions whereas a different set of 10 instructions constitutes 52% of execution time. Note also that one instruction, MOVC3, consumes 23% of time for the benchmarks. Because of the time consumed by this instruction, it would seem that a faster memory would be an advantage for this processor.

EXAMPLE

What will be the speedup of the VAX if the MOVC3 instruction time is cut by 50%?

Solution

The solution to this problem is a simple application of Amdahl's law:

$$\text{speedup} = \frac{77\% + 23\%}{77\% + \frac{23\%}{2}}$$

$$= \frac{100\%}{88.5\%} = 1.13.$$

TABLE 3.19 VAX INSTRUCTION STATISTICS

Instruction	Frequency of Use	Instruction	Time (%)
MOVL	0.1022	MOVC3	23.30
BEQL	0.0869	BBS	6.44
BBS	0.0525	MOVL	4.48
CMPB	0.0483	BBC	3.82
BNEQ	0.0360	CMPB	2.93
BLBC	0.0332	BEQL	2.47
INCL	0.0307	EDIV	2.43
RSB	0.0306	PROBEW	2.43
BBC	0.0261	RSB	2.03
SUBL3	0.0249	BSBW	2.00

TABLE 3.20 INTEL 8086 DYNAMIC INSTRUCTION
WEIGHTS

Rank	Instruction	Weight	Description
1	MOV	0.299	Move source to destination
2	PUSH	0.092	Push source on stack
3	CMP	0.079	Compare source with destination
4	POP	0.062	Pop TOS to destination
5	JNE	0.045	Jump if not equal
6	JE	0.036	Jump if equal
7	ADD	0.034	Add
8	CALL	0.033	Call subroutine
9	RET	0.031	Return from subroutine
10	JMP	0.023	Unconditional jump

Comment

At the time the VAX was designed, high-speed memory was very expensive. The cost of high-speed memory needed to improve MOVC3 by 50% probably exceeded 13% of the system cost, making this type of change unattractive from a cost/performance point of view.

Intel x86. One of the few sources of x86 instruction use statistics are for the 8086 executing MSDOS programs (Adams and Zimmerman 1989). The top 10 instructions executed are shown in Table 3.20. These statistics look very similar to those of the IBM S360. Note that approximately 39% of all executed instructions are either MOV or PUSH, instructions inserted by the compiler. The comparable number of the IBM S360 is 39% whereas the VAX is only 10%.

MIPS R2000 and Sun SPARC Comparison. Two modern RISC architectures are the MIPS R2000 and SPARC. These two computers are similar in most respects, save two. The MIPS R2000 uses the atomic test-and-branch instruction type whereas the SPARC uses indicators with orthogonal branch instructions. A second difference is that the MIPS R2000 uses no-op (no-operation) instructions for scheduling the execution pipeline whereas the SPARC schedules with hardware. This subject is discussed in Chapter 6.

An extensive study of instruction counts and frequencies for several of the integer and floating-point SPEC benchmarks on these two computers is available (Cmelik et al. 1991). A sample of the data is shown in Table 3.21. The authors made adjustments for low frequency of use instructions that added approximately 100 executed instructions to the SPARC data. However, the results from these benchmarks indicate that the total number of instructions executed for these two computers is approximately the same even though the distributions differ.

These two processors provide instructive examples of how architectural design decisions can affect the processor's performance. The MIPS R2000 has atomic test-and-branch instructions whereas the SPARC uses indicators. These data suggest that the two branch instruction methods result in an approximately equal number of executed

TABLE 3.21 MIPS R2000 & SUN SPARC INTEGER INSTRUCTION STATISTICS

	MIPS R2000		Sun SPARC	
	# Inst.	%	# Inst.	%
Instruction Class	Executed		Executed	
Load	220	19.83	214	18.52
Store	129	11.58	94	8.14
Control	205	18.50	234	20.26
No-op	148	13.34	12	1.02
Integer Arith.	407	36.66	580	50.20
Misc., Library	2	0.09	22	1.90
TOTAL	1111	100	1156	100

instructions. Thus there is no clear superiority of one branch technique over the other as measured by bit traffic.

The SPARC also has a larger register file than the MIPS R2000 (64 versus 32 words); thus the number of store instructions is smaller on the SPARC because of the ability to save variables in the register file. The smaller number of executed no-op instructions with the SPARC is a result of using more hardware to schedule the execution pipeline.

RISC and CISC Instructions Comparison

The instruction execution data given in the examples above give little guidance on how one can compare a RISC, such as the SPARC, with a CISC, such as the DEC VAX. As discussed in Section 3.1, the lexical level of a CISC is higher than that of a RISC. Thus it would be natural to believe that a CISC requires the execution of fewer instructions (smaller bit traffic) than does a RISC. Bhandarkar and Clark (Bhandarkar and Clark 1991) provide insight into this supposition. They have compiled and executed nine benchmarks on the VAX (CISC) and the MIPS R2000 (RISC). The instruction ratio is shown in Table 3.22. The instruction ratio is the number of instructions executed RISC/CISC. A ratio >1 means that the RISC requires a larger number of executed instructions or has a higher bit traffic.

These are rather startling numbers. From these benchmarks, we see that a RISC always executes more instructions than a CISC. Remember from Chapter 1 that the task time is the product of the number of executed instructions, the CPI, and the time/clock. One can conclude from these results that the CPI of a RISC must be approximately 1/2 that of a CISC with equal clock frequency for the performance to be equal. Chapters 5 and 6 will discuss the methods by which the CPI of a processor is determined.

3.5 ARITHMETIC

The arithmetic operations most commonly implemented in an ISA are add, subtract, multiply, and divide. The algorithms for performing these operations depend on the

TABLE 3.22 INSTRUCTION
RATIO RISC/CISC

Benchmark	Instruction Ratio
spice2g6	2.48
matrix300	2.37
nasa7	2.10
fpppp	3.88
tomcatv	2.86
doduc	2.65
expresso	1.70
eqntott	1.08
li	1.62
GEOMETRIC MEAN	2.17

specific data types of the ISA. These operations are discussed in the following paragraphs. In this section we discuss the arithmetic operation that can be performed on the data types described previously. However, before we look at how arithmetic is performed on specific data types, the basic logic of addition and subtraction is reviewed. Consider the truth table for single-digit addition. The adder has an a and a b input plus a carry in ci input. The sum s and carry out co are formed. In like fashion, the truth table of a binary subtractor is shown. The inputs are a, b, and bi (borrow) with outputs d (difference) and bo (borrow out):

	Addition					*Subtraction*			
a	$+b$	ci	s	co	a	$-b$	bi	d	bo
0	0	0	0	0	0	0	0	0	0
0	0	1	1	0	0	0	1	1	1
0	1	0	1	0	0	1	0	1	1
0	1	1	0	1	0	1	1	0	1
1	0	0	1	0	1	0	0	1	0
1	0	1	0	1	1	0	1	0	0
1	1	0	1	0	1	1	0	0	0
1	1	1	1	1	1	1	1	1	1

With addition, carries can occur at any bit position. When a carry occurs at the MSB, it is called an overflow because a value has been produced that is outside of the expressible range of the data type. A similar situation occurs with the borrow. Students may wish to answer the question of what happens if a borrow occurs at the MSB on subtraction.

A designer has the choice of implementing or not implementing the subtract operation in logic. As discussed below, subtraction can be accomplished by adding the complement of the subtrahend.

EXAMPLE

Add the unsigned values $17_{10} + 21_{10}$. Subtract the values $38_{10} - 21_{10}$ by using the rules of subtraction shown above.

Solution

Augend	17	010001	Minuend	38	100110
Addend	21	010101	Subtrahend	−21	010101
Carry		0100010	Borrow		100010
Sum = 38		100110	Difference = 17		010001

3.5.1 ADDITION/SUBTRACTION

The rules of addition and subtraction for sign and magnitude, 1's complement, and 2's complement data types are now described. Architected subtraction is frequently not architected in the ISA; the subtract function is performed by first complementing the subtrahend.

Sign and Magnitude. The rules for integer and fraction addition and subtraction (Flores 1963) are given in Table 3.23.

EXAMPLE

Assume a 6-bit sign and magnitude word; the MSB is the sign.
a. Add the following number pairs: $+13 + 11$, $-13 - 11$, $-11 + 13$, $+11 - 13$.
b. Subtract the same number pairs.

TABLE 3.23 SIGN AND MAGNITUDE ADDITION AND SUBTRACTION RULES

Addition	Augend	Addend	Rule
	+ −	+ −	Add magnitudes, append the sign of addend.
	+ −	− +	Complement addend, add to augend magnitude, if end-around carry add to result; if no end-around carry, complement the result, append sign of the augend.

Subtraction	Minuend	Subtrahend	Rule
	+ −	+ −	Complement subtrahend magnitude bits, add to minuend magnitude; if end-around carry add to result, append sign of minuend.
	+ −	− +	Add magnitudes, append sign of minuend.

Solution

a. Addition:

+13	001101	−13	101101	−11	101011	+11	001011
+11	001011	−11	101011	+13	001101	−13	101101
+24	011000	−24	111000	+2		−2	

		101011		001011
Comp	110010	Comp	110010
	11101		11101
	+0		+0
+2	000010	−2	100010

b. Subtraction:

+13	001101	−13	101101	−11	101011	+11	001011
−(+11)	001011	−(−11)	101011	−(+13)	001101	−(−13)	101101
+2		−2		+24	011000	+24	011000

	001101		001101
Comp	010100	Comp	000100
	000001		000001
	+1		+1
+2	0.00010	−2	1.00010

1's Complement. Table 3.24 lists the rules for integer and fraction addition and subtraction for 1's complement notation.

EXAMPLE

Assume a 6-bit 1's complement word:
a. Add the following number pairs: $+13 + 11$, $-13 - 11$, $-11 + 13$, $+11 - 13$.
b. Subtract the same number pairs.

TABLE 3.24   1'S COMPLEMENT ADDITION AND SUBTRACTION RULES

Addition	Augend	Addend	Rule
	+ −	+ −	Add magnitudes; if there is an end-around carry add to result, append the sign of addend
	+ −	− +	Add numbers including the sign If end-around carry, add to result, bit, append negative sign, otherwise, positive sign

Subtraction	Minuend	Subtrahend	Rule
	+ − + −	+ − − +	Complement all bits of the subtrahend, add to minuend; if end-around carry add to result, append sign of minuend

Solution

a. Addition:

```
+13    001101      −13    110010      −11    110100      +11    001011
+11   +001011      −11   +110100      +13   +00110      −13    110010
      ──────              ──────              ──────            ──────
       011000             1100110            1000001           111101
          +0                  +1                  +1               +0
         ────                ────                ────             ────
+24    011000      −24    100111      +2     00011      −2     100010
```

b. Subtraction:

```
 +13     001101       −13     110010       −11     110100       +11     001011
−(+11)   001011     −(−11)   110100     −(+13)   001101     −(−13)   110010
        ──────              ──────              ──────              ──────
 +13     001101       −13     110010       −11     110100       −11     001011
Comp   +110100      Comp   +001011      Comp   +110010      Comp   +101101
        ──────              ──────              ──────              ──────
       1000001             111101             1100110            0111000
           +1                 +0                  +1                 +0
          ────               ────                ────               ────
 +2    0.00010      −2     111101       −24    100111       +24    111000
```

2's Complement: Table 3.25 gives the rules of arithmetic for 2's complement integer and fraction data types.

EXAMPLE

Assume a 6-bit 2's complement word; one of the six bits is the sign:
a. Add the following number pairs: +13 +11, −13 −11, −11 +13, −11 −13.
b. Subtract the same number pairs.

TABLE 3.25 2'S COMPLEMENT ADDITION AND SUBTRACTION RULES

Addition	Augend	Addend	Rule
	+	+	Add magnitudes, ignore end-around carry. The sign of the result is the sign found by the result addition.
	−	−	
	+	−	
	−	+	

Subtraction	Minuend	Subtrahend	Rule
	+	+	Complement all bits of the subtrahend, add to minuend, ignore end-around carry. Add 1 to the result. The sign of the result is signfound by the addition.
	−	−	
	+	−	
	−	+	

Solution

a. Addition:

+13	001101	−13	110011	−11	110101	+11	001011
+11	+001011	−11	110101	+13	+001101	−13	110011
+24	011000	−24	101000	+2	000010	−2	111110

b. Subtraction:

+13	001101	−13	110011	−11	110101	+11	001011
−(+11)	001011	−(−11)	110101	−(+13)	001101	−(−13)	110011
+13	001101	−13	110011	−11	110101	+11	001011
Comp	+110100	Comp	+001010	Comp	+110010	Comp	+001100
	1000001		111101		1100111		010111
	+1		+1		+1		+1
+2	000010	−2	111110	−24	101000	+24	011000

3.5.2 MULTIPLICATION AND DIVISION

Multiplication and division are two instructions architected in many ISAs. Before the design specifics according to data type are discussed, the basic operations are explained. The following paragraphs discuss the algorithms of multiplication and division in the different representation but not the hardware implementation of the multiplication or division process. The rules of signs for multiplication and division are the following:

MULTIPLICATION: Like signs produce a like signed product; unlike signs produce a negative product.

DIVISION: The magnitudes are divided as nonsigned integers. Like signs produce a positive quotient and remainder; unlike signs produce a negative quotient and remainder.

Multiplication

The multiply operation is similar to that learned in grade school except the base is 2 rather than 10. The product of bit multiplication is the logical AND of the multiplier and multiplicand bits. Multiplication is performed by a three-step sequence: (1) test the LSB of the multiplier, (2) if LSB = 1, add the multiplicand to the partial product, (3) shift the multiplier one bit to the right and the partial product one bit to the left. Consider a 4-bit unsigned integer for the multiplicand and multiplier:

```
   9        1001
  ×5       ×0101
  45        1001
            0000-
            1001--
            0000---
         00101101
```

Please note the following: with 4 bits, the largest number that can be represented is $2^4 - 1 = 15$, and there is clearly an overflow with this operation as $45 > 15$. As the result is not expressible in the word length of the operands, the domain function is applied to convert the result into an expressible form. This means that the four LSBs are saved: clearly an incorrect result. Some ISAs will save both halves of a product, leaving it to the programmer to decide what to do.

If the data types are fractons, the above example becomes

$$
\begin{array}{rr}
0.5625 & 0.1001 \\
\times 0.3125 & \times 0.0101 \\
\hline
0.17578125 & 1001 \\
& 0000\text{-} \\
& 1001\text{-}\text{-} \\
& 0000\text{-}\text{-}\text{-} \\
\hline
& 0.00101101
\end{array}
$$

For fractions, the most-significant half of the result is saved as the product and the least-significant half is discarded. The result of the fraction multiply, 0.00101101, is truncated to 0.0010 or rounded up to 0.0011. Rounding is discussed further in Subsection 3.5.3.1 in the context of IEEE floating point.

Division

Division is a more difficult operation than multiplication. However, it is the inverse of multiplication: subtractions and shifts as compared with additions and shifts for multiplication. The basic idea is that the divisor (d) is subtracted from the dividend (D).

The process of division is illustrated with decimal values with the two division algorithms: restoring and nonrestoring. The restoring algorithm is described first. This algorithm consists of a number of steps listed below with the example $66 \div 12 = 5 + 6/12$, shown in Figure 3.19.

			Cycle		
		1	2	3	4
Quotient →		0	01	010	0101
		66			
d′		−96			
		−30			
d′		+96			
		66	66		
d′/2			−48		
			18	18	
d′/4				−24	
				−6	
d′/4				+24	
				18	18
d′/8					−12
					6

Figure 3.19 Restoring division, $66 \div 12$

Cycle

	1	2	3	4
Quotient →	0	01	010	0101
	66			
d'	−96			
	−30	−30		
d'/2		+48		
		18	18	
d'/4			−24	
			−6	−6
d'/8				+12
				6

Figure 3.20 Nonrestoring division, $66 \div 12$

Initialization: Multiply the divisor by a power of 2, which makes it greater than the dividend.[34] For the example, 12 is multiplied by 8, making the ratio $66 \div 96$. Call 96 the initial divisor d'.

1. Subtract d' (96) from the dividend. If the result, called partial remainder P, is negative, go to 2. If positive, go to 3.
2. Add back d'. Tally a 0 in the quotient, and go to step 4.
3. Tally a 1 in the quotient, and go to step 4.
4. Shift d' one bit to the right (divide by 2). Go to step 1.

Repeat until the number of cycles is the same as the number of bits in the operands. The remainder is the last value of the intermediate divisor: quotient $= 0101 + 0110/1100 = 5 + 6/12 = 5.5$.

The second form of division, nonrestoring division, does not require that the dividend be restored after a negative result has been obtained. The rules are given below and the operation is shown in Figure 3.20 for the same example, $66 \div 12$.

Initialization: Multiply the divisor by a power of 2, which makes it greater than the dividend. For the example used above, 12 is multiplied by 8, making the ratio $66 \div 96$.

1. Subtract the intermediate divisor (96) from the dividend. Go to step 2.
2. Tally a 0 in the quotient, shift the intermediate divisor one bit right (divide by 2) and add to the prior result. If the result is negative, go to step 2. If the result is positive, go to step 3.
3. Tally a 1 in the quotient. Then shift the intermediate divisor one bit right (divide by 2) and subtract from the dividend. If the result is negative, go to step 2. If positive, go to step 3.

Repeat until the number of cycles is equal to the number of bits in the operands. The remainder is the last value of the intermediate divisor.

With the restoring algorithm, the subtraction $D − d$ is made and if the result is negative, the subtraction is reversed. These additional steps, illustrated above, increase the time required for executing the restoring algorithm. Consider what happened with

---

[34] The CDC 6600 has an instruction that locates the leading 1 in a word to assist in this operation before division.

the first two cycles of the two algorithms. For both algorithms, the first subtraction produced a negative result:

Restoring:

Cycle 1: $D - d + d = D'$.
Cycle 2: $D' - d/2 = D''$,
$$D'' = D - d + d - d/2 = D - d/2,$$
$$D'' = 66 - 96/2 = 66 - 48 = 18.$$

Nonrestoring:

Cycle 1: $D - d = D'$.
Cycle 2: $D' + d/2 = D''$,
$$D'' = D - d + d/2 = D - d/2,$$
$$D'' = 66 - 96/2 = 66 - 48 = 18.$$

Thus we see that the two algorithms produce the same intermediate result for the two steps. With fewer steps, the nonrestoring algorithm is generally preferred.

EXAMPLE

Divide the integer 45 (101101) by 6 (0000110) by using the nonrestoring algorithm and binary arithmetic.

Solution

The solution is shown in Figure 3.21. To initialize, multiply the divisor by 8, giving $6 \times 8 = 48$. The result is $7 + 3/6$.

Data types other than sign and integer magnitude have division algorithms. Examples are 1's complement, 2's complement, 1's complement fraction, and 2's complement fraction. However, there are many complications in their algorithms that make them difficult to implement, and these data types are beyond the scope of this book. Note that because of the complications of these division algorithms, some processors that uses these data types convert the architected data type to sign and magnitude, perform division, and then convert back to the architected data type.

	Cycle	Dividend D'	Decimal	Quotient, q
		101101	45	
		−110000	−48	
	1	−000011	−3	0
		+110000	+24	
	2	0001011	21	01
		−0001100	−12	
	3	0001001	9	011
		−0000110	−6	
	4	0000011	3	0111

Figure 3.21 Restoring division, $45 \div 6$

3.5.3 FLOATING-POINT ARITHMETIC

Addition, subtraction, multiplication, and division are the operations architected in most ISAs. These operations use a combination of the techniques described in Subsections 3.5.1 and 3.5.2. We begin this discussion with floating-point addition/subtraction.

Addition/Subtraction

Recall that the IEEE floating-point data type allocates bits to a word:

S	Exponent	Significand

The sign bit is associated with the significand; in other words, this data type is sign and mixed magnitude representation. For a number of older floating-point representations, there is a fraction mantissa with the radix point to the left of the MSB. The exponent is usually biased, eliminating the need for an explicit exponent sign bit.

Addition is illustrated with decimal engineering representation: $500 + 20 = 5.2 \times 10^2$:

$$\textit{Alignment}$$

$$
\begin{array}{cc}
5.0 \times 10^2 & 5.0 \times 10^2 \\
+2.0 \times 10^1 & +0.2 \times 10^2 \\
\hline
520 & 5.2 \times 10^2
\end{array}
$$

Observe the steps needed to perform this addition:

1. The exponents are compared.
2. The mantissa with the smallest exponent is divided by 10 until the exponents are equal. Each division by 10 causes the exponent to be increased by one.
3. The adjusted mantissas are added and the exponent appended.

Addition is now illustrated with a binary base: $4 + 1.5 = 5.5$:

$$\textit{Alignment}$$

$$
\begin{array}{cc}
1.000 \times 2^2 & 1.000 \times 2^2 \\
+1.100 \times 2^0 & +0.011 \times 2^2 \\
\hline
& 1.011 \times 2^2
\end{array}
$$

Subtraction is illustrated with a binary base: $4 - 1.5 = 2.5$:

$$\textit{Alignment} \quad \textit{Normalized}$$

$$
\begin{array}{ccc}
1.000 \times 2^2 & 1.000 \times 2^2 \\
-1.100 \times 2^0 & -0.011 \times 2^2 \\
\hline
& 0.101 \times 2^2 & 1.010 \times 2^1
\end{array}
$$

The result of the subtraction (0.101×2^2) requires normalization. That is, the mantissa is shifted left until the MSB is 1 and the exponent is decremented for each shift.

EXAMPLE

What happens when there is a carry out on the addition of the significands?

Solution

After the addition, normalization shifts the result one place to the right and increments the exponent, for example, $4 + 4 = 8$:

$$
\begin{array}{r}
1.000 \times 2^2 \\
+1.000 \times 2^2 \\
\hline
10.000 \times 2^2 \\
1.000 \times 2^3
\end{array}
$$

Multiplication and Division

The IEEE floating-point data types can be multiplied and divided. In some respects, the rules are simpler than the rules of addition and subtraction. Remember that the exponent is biased and the significand is a signed mixed number.

Multiplication. The rules for floating-point multiplication are the following:

1.   Add the exponents.
2.   Multiply the signed significands.
3.   Append the exponent from rule 1 to the result.

For example, $4 \times 1.5 = 6$:

$$
\begin{array}{r}
1.00 \times 2^2 \\
\times 1.10 \times 2^0 \\
\hline
1.1000 \times 2^2
\end{array}
$$

Division. The rules for floating-point division are the following:

1.   Subtract the exponents.
2.   Divide the signed significands.
3.   Append the exponent from rule 1 to the result.

For example, $6 \div 3 = 2$:

$$
\begin{array}{r}
1.100 \times 2^2 \\
\div 1.100 \times 2^1 \\
\hline
1.000 \times 2^1
\end{array}
$$

Operations on Biased Exponents

The exponent of a floating-point data type is bound to a limited set of operations, and thus it becomes a special data type. From the examples above, we see the four operations bound to the exponent data type:

1.   Compare two exponents, select the smaller, and record the difference.
2.   Add two exponents.

3.   Subtract two exponents.
4.   Increment and decrement an exponent.

With an architected floating point (the norm today) the exponent is an implemented data type; it is not processed directly by the instructions. The exponent is
processed in the context of the complete data type by a hardwired state machine or
microprogrammed control. Thus the selection of the exponent data type is in general
purely an implementation issue, given that the designer has achieved the accuracy
and the range requirements of the floating-point data type.

What representation is desired for the exponent? Recall that 1's complement has
two zeros and the need for end-around carry. 2's complement is also messy, requiring
the complementation of the subtrahend for subtraction and the final addition of 1 to
the result. Thus, with a biased exponent, comparisons are easier to make without the
messy details of dealing with a sign. Addition and subtraction are also simpler because
of the freedom from signs.

Because a biased exponent is an excess notation (discussed previously in terms of
decimal data types), the rules for performing the operations are similar. The major
difference is the reason for using excess notation. For decimal data types, excess notation is used to provide for decimal representation and a decimal carry. For exponents,
excess notation is used for ease in implementing the required arithmetic.

EXAMPLE

Because floating-point exponents are biased (excess notation), what corrections,
if any, must be made to the result after adding or subtracting exponents? Assume
a 3-bit exponent, $n = 3$, and a bias of $2^{n-1} - 1 = 2^{3-1} - 1 = 3 = 011$: see
Table 3.9.

Solution

For a 3-bit exponent and a bias of 011, we have the following map:

Binary	Decimal
000	−3
001	−2
010	−1
011	0
100	+1
101	+2
110	+3
111	+4

For addition, $(-2) + (+1) = -1$, and in biased binary, $001 + 100 = 101$, which
is incorrect. Three must be subtracted from the result: $101 - 011 = 010$, the
correct result for −1 in biased notation.

For subtraction, $(+3) - (+1) = +2$, and in biased binary, $110 - 100 = 010$,
which is incorrect. Three must be added to the result: $010 + 011 = 101$, the
correct result for +2 in biased notation.

Comment

For addition, $(a + \text{bias}) + (b + \text{bias}) = a + b + 2\text{bias}$, requires subtracting bias. For subtraction, $(a + \text{bias}) - (b + \text{bias}) = a - b$, requires adding bias. Making the correction, either plus or minus, is greatly facilitated in the hardware if the bias is an even power of 2; 2^{n-1}. That is, instead of using the bias of 3 shown in this example, a bias of 4 could be a better choice.

3.5.3.1 Precision Treatment

Floating-point data types are approximations; thus the result of an arithmetic operation can produce results that must be interpreted and adjusted. This interpretation and adjustment are in the context of providing a result suitable as input for further operations. The following paragraphs discuss the issues involved and the procedures for handling many of the cases arising with the IEEE floating-point data types.

Operations on floating-point numbers can produce a result that is longer than the length of the source operands. The result of the operation is called the infinitely precise result (Cody et al. 1984). The additional length consists of lower-value bits of the significand. For the following discussion, these bits are called excess low-order bits (ELBs), also known as residue bits (Blaauw and Brooks 1997). There are two uses of the ELBs: support of postnormalization with guard bits and support of rounding with round and sticky bits.

Guard Bits

Normalization of IEEE floating-point data types places a 1 in the bit position to the left of the binary point of the significand. ELBs are produced from arithmetic operations and postnormalization:

S	Exponent	1. Significand	ELBs

Multiplication of two significands will produce ELBs. Consider multiplying the significands 1.125 and 1.625; a 4-bit significand is assumed:

$$
\begin{array}{ll}
1.125 & 1.001 \times 2^0 \\
\underline{\times 1.625} & \underline{\times 1.101 \times 2^0} \\
1.828125 & 1001 \\
& 1001 \\
& \underline{1001} \\
& 1.110\mathbf{101} \times 2^0 \\
& 1.75
\end{array}
$$

Three ELBs, shown as boldfaced numbers, are produced because the data type is only 4 bits whereas 7 bits were produced by the multiplication. If these bits are ignored, the result of the operation is 1.75, a poor approximation to the precise result of 1.828125. As will be discussed later in this subsection, these ELBs are saved as guard bits and will be used for rounding to improve the accuracy of the result.

When two floating-point numbers with different exponents are subtracted, there is the possibility for a substantial error in the result. Consider the following example of significand subtraction: $3 - 1.25 = 1.75$. Assume that the arithmetic unit and the significands are 3 bits. The significand denominator is aligned before the subtraction – the exponents must be equal – creating one ELB bit that is ignored by the 3-bit arithmetic unit. The computed difference is 2, and the correct difference in binary is 1.11×2^0 or 1.75; two of the result bits and the exponent are wrong:

$$
\begin{array}{ll}
1.10 \times 2^1 & 1.10 \times 2^1 \\
-1.01 \times 2^0 & -0.101 \times 2^1 \\
\hline
 & 1.00 \ \ \times 2^1
\end{array}
$$

The loss of accuracy in this example is mitigated by the use of a guard bit that extends the arithmetic unit by one digit.[35] The use of a guard bit is illustrated by the same example used above. After the addition, the guard bit provides the LSB of the normalized significand. The result, 1.75, is the correct difference:

$$
\begin{array}{ll}
1.10 \times 2^1 & 1.\mathbf{100} \times 2^1 \\
-1.01 \times 2^0 & -0.10\mathbf{1} \times 2^1 \\
\hline
 & 0.111 \times 2^1 \\
\text{Normalized} & 1.11 \times 2^0
\end{array}
$$

With addition and subtraction, one ELB is created for each difference of one in the exponents. As shown in Table 3.10, for base 2 systems, 6.78% of all normalizations will produce 1 bit and 3.47% will produce 2 bits. 59.34% require no normalization shifts. The example above is repeated with the exponent of the subtrahend changed to -1:

$$
\begin{array}{ll}
1.10 \times 2^1 & 1.1\mathbf{000} \times 2^1 \\
-1.01 \times 2^{-1} & -0.01\mathbf{01} \times 2^1 \\
\hline
 & 1.00\mathbf{11} \times 2^1 \\
\text{Truncation} & 1.00 \times 2^1
\end{array}
$$

The domain function of truncation gives a difference of 2, for which the correct difference is $3.0 - 0.625 = 2.375 = 1.0011 \times 2^1$. Truncation, also called chopping, simply drops all ELBs. With truncations the two ELBs are lost, but these bits can be saved to improve the accuracy of the result with rounding.

Another source of an ELB is found with the addition of two numbers having the same exponents, followed by normalization of the sum. The following example illustrates how ELBs can be created: $3 + 3.5 = 6.5 = 1.110 \times 2^2$. The normalized inputs are 3 bits and the ALU is 3 bits. The ELB is created because of the carry out from the addition followed by the normalization right shift:

$$
\begin{array}{ll}
 & 1.10 \times 2^1 \\
 & +1.11 \times 2^1 \\
\hline
 & 11.01 \times 2^1 \\
\text{Normalized} & 1.10\mathbf{1} \times 2^2 \\
\text{Truncation} & 1.10 \times 2^2
\end{array}
$$

---

[35] The IEEE format has a guard bit; the IBM S360 format has a guard hex digit for base 16.

If the result is truncated, the result of this addition is 6.0, not the correct 6.5. The problem here is also what to do with the **1** in the ELB. The ELB is saved as the round bit to be used for rounding the result.

Manufacturers have taken different approaches to providing guard bits. The IBM S360 uses a hex guard digit. The PowerPC, implementing the IEEE standard, uses 64-bit floating-point registers for both single- and double-precision data types. The arithmetic unit is augmented with guard, round, and sticky bits. Intel, starting with the 8087 coprocessor for the 8080, implements 80-bit floating-point registers as an evaluation stack. The 80-bit data type, called extended precision temporaries, provides ample bits to cover most guard bit requirements. Motorola, for the MC68000 series, also uses 80-bit internal floating-point registers.

Rounding

Addition, multiplication, or division of the significand can produce a result with ELBs that are outside the domain of expressible numbers and requires the application of a domain function. After postnormalization, the ELBs are saved as guard bits to participate in rounding.

We are familiar with the simple round to nearest used with decimal numbers. If the excess low-order digits (ELDs) are less than 1/2 of the result least-significant digit (LSD), round down. Otherwise round up. With this algorithm, the fractional ELDs 0.0–0.4 round to 0 whereas 0.5–0.9 round up by adding one to the LSD. Thus 84.3 rounds to 84, 84.5 rounds to 85, and 84.7 rounds to 85.

How can rounding be applied to floating-point results? There are a number of algorithms that yield varying degrees of accuracy. In some processors, rounding is determined by the designers and is wired in; for example, IBM S360 floating-point arithmetic uses truncation. With other processors, a number of choices are given with the one used selected by the user by means of the program. There are four rounding algorithms specified in the IEEE floating-point standard:

Round to nearest: This operation rounds to the value nearest to the infinitely precise value. From the two nearest representable values that are equally near, the one with a LSB of zero is selected.

Round toward 0: This operation rounds toward zero: truncation.

Round to $+\infty$: This operation, for positive numbers, rounds up closest to and no less than the infinitely precise result.

Round to $-\infty$: This operation, for negative numbers, rounds down closest to and no greater than the infinitely precise result.

Round to nearest is the IEEE default, and Table 3.26 shows the implementation rules. These rules are applied after the result of the arithmetic operation is normalized. There are three cases, and 2 bits are required for uniquely identifying them; these bits are called the round bit and the sticky bit.

The round bit is the MSB of the ELBs after normalization. If this bit is a 0, the ELBs value is $< 1/2$ of the significand LSB and the significand is not changed. If the round

TABLE 3.26 IEEE FLOATING-POINT ROUND TO NEAREST

ELBs	Rounding Action
Less than 1/2 of the significand LSB	Leave the significand unchanged.
Equal to 1/2 of the significand LSB	From the two nearest representable values that are equally near, the one with an LSB of zero is selected.
Greater than 1/2 of the significand LSB	Add 1 to the significand.

TABLE 3.27 IEEE FLOATING-POINT ROUND AND STICKY BITS

ELBs	Round Bit	Sticky Bit	Rounding Action
0xxxx	0	x	Leave the significand unchanged.
10000	1	0	Add the LSB of significand to the significand $(0 + 0 = 0, 1 + 1 = 10)$.
10010	1	1	Add 1 to the significand.

TABLE 3.28 ROUND TO NEAREST

Significand	Round and Sticky Bits		
	0x	10	11
1.1000	1.1000	1.1000	1.1001
1.0001	1.0001	1.0010	1.0010

bit is a 1, the ELBs value is $\geq 1/2$ of the significand LSB. Thus, a second bit is required for resolving the two conditions of $=$ and $>$.

The second bit, the sticky bit, is set to a 1 if there is any 1 to the right of the round bit. If the round bit is 1 and the sticky bit is 1, then the value of the ELBs is $> 1/2$ of the significand LSB. Likewise, if the round bit is 1 and the sticky bit is 0, the value of the ELBs is exactly 1/2 of the significand LSB.[36] Table 3.27 restates the information in Table 3.26 for five ELBs. An algorithm for adjusting the significand is shown for the case of the ELBs equal to 1/2 of the significand LSB.

These rules as applied to two 5-bit significands, 1.1000 and 1.0001, are shown in Table 3.28. For example, when the round and sticky bits are 10, a significand having a LSB of 1 has 1 added, if the LSB is 0 the significand is unchanged.

---

[36] The sticky bit name comes from the observation that the ELBs are sometimes formed by shifting. If a 1 is detected, a flip flop is set to 1 and it sticks in that state until the domain function is applied. The sticky bit is also the OR of all of the ELBs to the right of the round bit.

EXAMPLE

Show how the rounding action "Add the LSB of the signifi cand to the signifi - cand $(0 + 0 = 0, 0 + 1 = 10)$" meets the specifi cation for rounding when the two representable values are equally near.

Solution

Assume that the unrounded significand is 1.0001 with $R = 1$ and $S = 0$. The next lowest infinitely precise value is 1.00010 and the next highest is 1.0010. Thus the rounded significand 1.0010 is selected because its LSB is zero. The selected significand is formed by adding the significand LSB to the significand $(1.0001 + 1 = 1.0010)$:

Next lowest	1.0001|0
Significand	**1.0001|1 0**
Next highest	1.0010|0 $\checkmark$

A second case with a 0 LSB of the significand is shown below:

Next lowest	1.1000|0 $\checkmark$
Significand	**1.1000|1 0**
Next highest	1.1001|0

For this case, the rounded significand is 1.1000 and is formed by adding the LSB of the significand to the significand $(1.1000 + 0 = 1.1000)$. Thus, if $R = 1$ and $S = 0$, all that must be done is to add the LSB of the significand to the significand.

The addition of two normalized numbers, $3 + 3.5 = 6.5$, will illustrate the use of the round-to nearest algorithm. The 1 in the ELB was saved in a guard bit and becomes the round bit:

$$1.10 \times 2^1$$
$$\underline{+1.11 \times 2^1}$$
$$11.01 \times 2^1$$

Normalized	$1.10\mathbf{1} \times 2^2$
Rounded	1.10×2^2

There are no 1's to the right of the guard bit, and the sticky bit is 0. Adding 0 to the significand produces the correctly rounded result. Rounding to nearest gives the result as 6.0, another approximation to the infinitely precise result of 6.5.

The multiply case discussed previously in this subsection gives another example of the use of the round and sticky bits. The ELBs, 101, are interpreted as Round = 1, Sticky = 1. Thus the ELBs are > 1/2 the LSB of the significand and 1 is added to the significand; the rounded result is 1.875:

1.125	1.001×2^0
$\times 1.625$	$\times 1.101 \times 2^0$
1.828125	1001
	1001
	1001
	$1.110\mathbf{101} \times 2^0$
	$+1$
	1.111
	1.875

The round-to-nearest-domain function guarantees that the absolute value of the error is $\leq 1/2$ of the significand's LSB. The rounded result of this multiplication has an error of $1.828125 - 1.875 = -0.0468875$. This error is within $\pm 1/2$ the LSB of the 4-bit significand, which is $0.125/2 = 0.0625$.

EXAMPLE

What is the maximum error for the IEEE single-precision floating-point when round to nearest is used?

Solution

For the single-precision format with a 23-bit significand, the maximum error is

$$\leq \frac{2^{-23}}{2} = 2^{-24} = 5.96 \times 10^{-8}.$$

Encoding Floating-Point Data Types

Figure 3.22 displays the various data values of the IEEE floating-point standard. Shown across the top are the normal real data values that result from an arithmetic operation. There are eight regions of real numbers: $\pm \infty$, $\pm$ normalized finite, $\pm$ denormalized finite, and ± 0. Remember that this data type is sign and magnitude with two zeros.

The representation of the data types are shown to the right and the left of the figure for $+$ and $-$ values. These data types are $\pm$ zero, $\pm$ denormalized finite, $\pm$ normalized finite, $\pm \infty$, SNAN, and QNAN.

SNAN and QNAN call for explanation. NAN stands for not a number. Some arithmetic operations such as $\sqrt{-1}$ will produce a result that is not a normal real number. As such, these values are encoded as shown with 255 in the exponent. The designations S and Q mean signal and quiet, respectively. A SNAN will signal an invalid operation interrupt if the value is used on a subsequent arithmetic operation. On the other hand, a QNAN will propagate through subsequent arithmetic operations without signaling and interrupt. The exponent values 0 and 255 are reserved from the 2^8 possible exponent values along with special significand values to uniquely encode $\pm\infty$, SNAN, and QNAN.

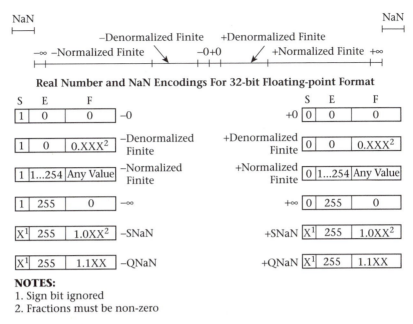

Figure 3.22 IEEE floating-point values (courtsey of Intel Corporation)

REFERENCES

Adams, T. L. and Zimmerman, R. E. (1989). "An Analysis of 8086 Instructions Set Usage in MSDOS Programs," *ASPLOS III*, pp. 152–160.

Alexander, W. G. and Wortman, D. B. (1975). "Static and Dynamic Characteristics of XPL Programs," *Computer*, **8**:11.

Bhandarkar, D. and Clark, D. W. (1991). "Performance from Architecture: Comparing a RISC and a CISC with Similar Hardware Organization," *ACM SIGARCH Computer Architecture News*, **19**:2, pp. 310–319.

Blaauw, G. A. and Brooks, F. P. Jr. (1997). *Computer Architecture, Concepts and Evolution*, Addison-Wesley Longman, Reading, MA.

Buckholz, W., ed. (1962). *Planning a Computer System*, McGraw-Hill, New York.

Clark D. W. and Levy, H. M. (1982). "Measurement and Analysis of Instruction Use in the VAX-11/780," *ACM Transactions on Computer Systems*, **1**:1.

Cmelik, R. F., Kong, S. I., Ditzel, D. R., and Kelly, E. J. (1991). "An Analysis of MIPS and SPARC Instruction Set Utilization on the SPEC Benchmarks," *ACM SIGARCH Computer Architecture News*, **19**:2, pp. 290–302.

Cody, W. J., Coone, J. T., Gay, D. M., Hanson, K., Hough, D., Kahan, W., Karpinsik, R., Palmer, J., Ris, F. N., and Stevenson, D. (1984). "A Proposed Radix-and Word-Length-Independent Standard for Floating-Point Arithmetic," *IEEE Micro*, **4**:4, pp. 86–100.

Cohen, D. (1981). "On Holy Wars and a Plea for Peace," *Computer*, **14**:10, pp. 48–54.

Eckert, J. P. (1946). *Theory and Techniques for Design of Electronic Digital Computers*, Moore School Special Course in July and August 1946. MIT Press, Cambridge , MA. Reprinted as Volume 9, The Charles Babbage Institute Reprint Series for the History of Computing, 1985.

Flores, I. (1963). *The Logic of Computer Arithmetic*, Prentice-Hall, Englewood Cliffs, N.J.

IBM. (1970). "IBM S/360 Principles of Operation," Order GA22-6821-8, IEEE, ANSI/IEEE Standard 754-1985, The Institute of Electrical and Electronics Engineers, New York, 1985.

IEEE, *ANSI/IEEE Standard 754-1985*. The Institute of Electrical and Electronics Engineers, New York, 1985.

Kirrmann, H. (1983). "Data Format and Bus Compatibility in Microprocessors," *IEEE Micro*, **3**:4, pp. 32–47.

Siewiorek, D. P., Bell, C. G., and Newell, A. (1982). *Computer Structures: Principles and Examples*, McGraw-Hill, New York.

Sweeney, D. W. (1965), "An Analysis of Floating-Point Addition," *IBM Systems Journal*, **4**, 1.

von Neumann, J. (1945). "First Draft of a Report on the EDVAC," Contract W-670-ORD-4926. Moore School of Electrical Engineering, University of Pennsylvania.

Weicker, R. P. (1984). "Dhrystone: A Synthetic Systems Programming Benchmark," *Communications of the ACM*, **27**:10.

White, G. S. (1953). "Coded Decimal Number Systems for Digital Computers," *Proc. IRE*, **41**, 10, pp. 1450–1452.

Wilkes, M. V., Wheeler, D. J., and Gill, S. (1951). *The Preparation of Programs for an Electronic Digital Computer*, Addison-Wesley, Cambridge, MA. Reprinted in the Reprint Series for the History of Computing, Vol. I, Charles Babbage Institute, Tomash Publishers, Los Angeles.

EXERCISES

3.1   Redo the example of biased exponents in Subsection 3.5.3 by using a bias of 4 rather than 3. Discuss the advantage of this change.

3.2   From Table 3.12, determine the bias for each of the floating-point formats listed. Assume that the biases are even powers of 2.

3.3   Consult Intel documentation and show how the Intel Pentium with MMX uses expanded op-codes.

3.4   What is the range, in bytes, of the length of Pentium Pro instructions? That is, how long are the shortest and the longest instructions?

3.5   Assume the following: 40% of all executed branches instructions are unconditional branches and 76% of all branches are taken. What percentage of all executed branches are taken conditional branches?

3.6   You are designing an ISA and need to allocate bits in the instruction for immediate operands. An examination of 399 immediate operands shows the following distribution:

Address Bits	Total Number	Fraction
1	41	0.103
2	89	0.223
3	47	0.118
4	90	0.226
5	46	0.115
6	57	0.143
7	18	0.045
8	4	0.010
9	5	0.012
10	2	0.005
Total	399	1.00

You have decided that you can have one of two designs:

Design a: a 4-bit short immediate and a 10-bit long immediate.
Design b: a 8-bit short immediate and a 10-bit long immediate.

Which of these two designs will give the smallest weighted average number of bits for immediate values?

3.7 Derive the rules for the x86 decimal adjust for subtraction instruction.

3.8 You are designing an excess data type that will represent 0–99 in an 8-bit byte. What is the excess value?

3.9 Show the 10 decimal digits for a 4-bit code having the weights $+6$, $+2$, -2, $+1$.

3.10 In the discussion of the IBM S360 floating-point format, the following statement is made: If the 16 states of the hex field are evenly distributed, there is approximately a 3/4 wasted bit in the fraction. For worst case, 3 bits are wasted in the fraction. Explain and justify this statement.

3.11 Using Swenney's data, Table 3.9, what is the weighted average number of shifts required for normalization with a base 2 floating-point data type?

3.12 The x86 ISA provides for a BCD data type. Is this not redundant with the decimal-adjust instruction? Explain your answer.

3.13 The Year 2000 problem is with us because the two LSD digits of the year are encoded, in BCD, into a single byte. As you should know, there are unused states in this encoding. Design a 1-byte encoding that will indicate the year within the twentieth and the twenty-first centuries. 8 bits can encode 256 states, so encoding 200 states should pose no problem.

3.14 The text states that the exponent bias of the IBM S360 floating-point format is 64. What is the binary value of the exponent and what is the value of the exponent?

3.15 The exponent bias for the IBM S360 is 2^{n-1} whereas that of the IEEE format is $2^{n-1} - 1$, where n is the number of exponent bits. Explain why these biases differ and cite the advantages and disadvantages of each.

3.16 For the IBM S360 op-codes, what are the bindings, in the four LSBs, of the floating-point and the fixed-point data types to the operations?

3.17 Explain why a hidden bit can be used only with a floating-point format of base 2.

3.18 Describe IEEE round to nearest if applied to the IBM S360 floating-point data type.

3.19 Assume that the fractional part of an IEEE floating-point significand is 4 bits and that there is a round and sticky bit. Start with 0.0100, 00 and increment the sticky bit up to 0.1011, 11. Use the rounding rules of Table 3.6; plot the rounded values of the 4-bit significand along with the infinite precise values (6 bits) for each of the infinitely precise values.

3.20   The Atanasoff Berry Computer, described in Chapter 1, uses Gaussian elimination to solve linear algebraic equations; see Figure 1.9. Show how the ABC solves for x and y by using binary data types; $3x + 2y = 12$, $4x + y = 11$.

3.21   Can the two steps of the x86 decimal-adjust operation be combined into one step? If so, describe the operation. If not, explain why not.

3.22   The text states in Section 3.3 that one advantage of a fixed-length instruction is that instructions will not cross page boundaries. Explain why this is so.

3.23   Consult Intel documentation on any member of the x86 family and explain how signed decimal arithmetic is performed.

3.24   The combinations of fixed-length/variable-length instructions and op-codes are discussed in Subsection 3.2.4. Why is the combination of fixed-length instructions and op-codes not included in the list of design options?

3.25   The program counter of the VAX is allocated to register 15 of the register file. Discuss the advantages and disadvantages of this design.

3.26   Consult the documentation for the IBM S390 and construct the equivalent of Table 3.13 IBM S360 op-code classes.

3.27   The example in Subsection 3.2.3 shows that base 16 requires 2 fewer bits than base 2 for the same range. The equality was solved by assuming one base 16 exponent bit. Show another solution of the equality that makes no such assumption and shows that the result is general.

3.28   The average length of an 8086 instruction was given as 2.25 bytes in Section 3.3. This average was found by running programs in 1989. At this time, do you think the number of bytes per Pentium Pro instructions is less than or greater than 2.25? Explain your answer and give an estimate that you would use for modeling purposes.

3.29   Provide a rationale for the round-to-nearest-domain function of the IEEE floating-point standard for the case in which $R = 1$ and $S = 0$.

3.30   Figure 3.9 shows three classes of interrupt handling methods. However, the text suggests that there are four: the combinations of between instructions or within and instruction and continuation and restart. Explain how these four methods are accomodated in Figure 3.9.

3.31   Generalize the rules for making the correction to biased exponents after an addition or subtraction.

3.32   Are the Intel integer data types one of the six data types described in Table 3.6? Explain your answer.

FOUR

MEMORY SYSTEMS

4.0 INTRODUCTION

Chapter 1 described a computer as a memory-centered system. The process state is stored in memory, then the state is modified by the processor and returned to memory. Because of the importance of memory, we first consider its architectural and implementation aspects before addressing processor design in Chapters 5 and 6. Chapter 3 discussed data types, and the point is made that data types vary in length: 1 byte, 2 bytes, etc. In this chapter the addressable unit (AU) will be the normalizing factor in discussing memory designs. For processors such as the Intel x86 and the IBM S360, the AU is a byte. For other processors, the AU may be 2 or 4 bytes.

Process State

A process is defined as a program in execution. A program is defined as a series of instructions that process data and is contained within the process state. Thus the process state consists of the program, source data, and results. Execution of the program results in the transformation of data; the memory must supply instructions and data and accept the results.

It follows then that the memory must be large enough to hold the process state, and the memory can be a limiting factor in the performance of a computer. On an instruction-by-instruction basis, the process state is modified. In some software systems, MSDOS and Windows 3.1 being examples, the instructions can be treated as data and modified by the program, called self-modifying code and discussed in Chapter 1 in the context of the von Neumann programming example. For these systems, special consideration is given to the memory system design so that the instruction portion of the process state can be modified.

Memory System Desiderata

The memory system has three desiderata:

1. Size: infinitely large, no constraints on program or data set size
2. Speed: infinitely fast, latency equal to the fastest memory technology available
3. Cost: the per bit cost should approach the lowest-cost technology available

Clearly these specifications cannot all be achieved as they are mutually exclusive. However, with the semiconductor and magnetic memory technology of today, these specifications are closely approximated.

There are two important parameters associated with a memory system (Flynn 1966).

"Latency or latent period is the total time associated with the processing (from excitation to response) of a particular data unit at a phase in the computing process."

"Bandwidth is an expression of time-rate of occurrence. In particular, computational or execution bandwidth is the number of instructions processed per second and storage bandwidth is the retrieval rate of operand and operation memory words (words/second)."

These parameters are independent and in many cases can be traded off by a designer. Some processors and memories need one or the other parameter emphasized.

An illustration of latency and bandwidth outside the computer area is found in long-distance communication. Geosynchronous satellites are ideal for computer-to-computer communications in which the long latency (approximately 250 ms) is easily absorbed in the long data transmission time. High bandwidth is paramount in this application. However, person-to-person telephonic communication is quite unpleasant with this latency. Thus, satellite telephony is being replaced with fiber-optic underwater cables that have practically zero latency. Fiber optics may eventually be replaced with low orbit satellites that will have relatively small latencies.

4.1 HIERARCHICAL MEMORY

In this section it is shown how designers implement a practical memory that approaches the performance of an ideal memory at reasonable cost. This memory system has a hierarchy of levels: The memory closest to the processor is fast and relatively small, but has a high cost per bit. This level is called the cache. The real memory, sometimes known as main memory, is slower, larger, and has a lower cost per bit than the cache. The lowest level in the hierarchy is usually a magnetic disk that has the longest latency and the lowest bandwidth; however, it can be very large and has a very low cost per bit. This hierarchy is illustrated in Figure 4.1.

Note that Figure 4.1 does not include the processor register file in the memory hierarchy. The register file is a program-managed cache and is generally not included in the memory system. Also, there can be more than one cache in the hierarchy.

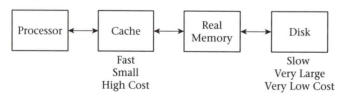

Figure 4.1 Hierarchical memory

4.2 PAGED VIRTUAL MEMORY

Paged virtual memory provides the solution to the first desideratum of a very large memory's being available to the processor. Because of the importance of this desideratum, the relationship between virtual and real memory is discussed first. With virtual memory, the processor addresses the disk, the large, slow end of the hierarchy. The memories between the processor and the disk are there to increase the effective performance (reduced latency and increased bandwidth) of the very slow disk. If every instruction and data reference were made to the disk, the processor performance would be slow indeed.

Then why is virtual memory so important? Large memory is needed for large programs and data sets. Early computers with small real memory required that the transfer of data between real memory and disk be managed explicitly by the operating system or the user. Virtual memory provides for automatic management of this portion of the memory hierarchy through a combination of hardware and software aids.

The virtual memory interface is shown in Figure 4.2. A real memory of 16M bytes and a virtual memory of 2G bytes are shown for illustration; many modern virtual-memory systems are much larger than this. Virtual-memory space is divided into equal-sized groups called pages. A page in a modern computer is 1K, 2K, or 4K bytes. Real memory is also divided into the same equal-sized groups, called page frames. When information is moved between virtual-memory space and real-memory space, a complete page is moved.

Because the real memory is smaller than the virtual memory, pages lose their virtual-address identity when they are moved to the higher level closer to the processor. Thus the processor effective address, now called the virtual address, must be translated in some way before it is presented to real memory. Note that the architecture of Figure 4.2 is similar, except for the sizes of the memories, to the ATLAS computer built in the early 1960s at The University of Manchester (Kilburn et al. 1962).

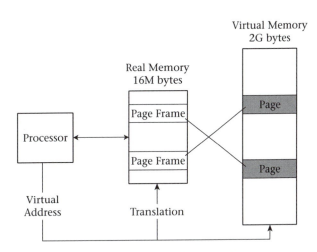

Figure 4.2 Page allocation and address translation

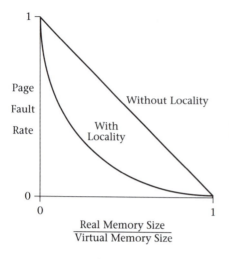

Figure 4.3 Page fault rates, without and with locality

Although the primary purpose of a virtual-memory system is to provide a transparently large address space for the processor, memory performance cannot be ignored. Figure 4.2 shows the processor accessing the real memory and the disk. If the addresses produced by the processor are randomly distributed, as shown in Figure 4.3, then the fraction of references not found in real memory, called the page fault rate,[37] will be

$$\text{Page fault rate (random distribution)} = 1 - \frac{\text{size of real memory}}{\text{size of virtual memory}}.$$

With random distribution, the example of Figure 4.2 with 16M bytes of real memory and 2G bytes of virtual memory, 0.008 of all references will be found in real memory and 0.992 found in the disk. Why provide the faster, more expensive real memory if most of the memory references will be served from the very slow disk?

The answer to the question is found in the fact that references are not randomly distributed. A processor, because of the nature of programs and data structures, produces addresses that have two forms of locality.

Spatial Locality. Portions of the address space near the current locus of reference are likely to be referenced in the near future.

Temporal Locality. Instructions and data recently referenced by a program are likely to be used again soon.

Because of locality, the page fault rate, shown in Figure 4.3, is much smaller than that expected without locality. The page fault rate[38] can now be defined as

$$\text{Page fault rate} = 1 - \frac{\text{number of references found in real memory}}{\text{total number of references}}.$$

---

[37] A page fault occurs when a reference is made to real memory and the page containing the referenced AU is not present. A page fault is similar to a cache miss, which will be discussed later.
[38] Also known as page fault ratio.

Locality significantly reduces the page fault rate with just a small (relative to virtual memory) real memory, resulting in most of the references' being served in the small fast real memory.

An instruction-address stream has spatial locality because the program counter is incrementing, and, except for branches, the next instruction is found in the next-higher address from the present instruction. For this reason, a page is larger than one instruction and a complete page is brought into real memory when only one instruction reference produces a page fault. After a page is fetched into real memory, there is a high likelihood that the next instruction will be in real memory and the latency will be real-memory latency, not disk latency. Spatial locality is sometimes called look ahead because the fetching mechanism looks ahead into the instruction or data stream.

Temporal locality is sometimes called look behind. This means that the page, once it is fetched from the disk into real memory, will be retained in anticipation of future use. Only when there is the need for a vacant page frame or a context switch will pages be returned to the disk. The data-address stream has the property of temporal locality but usually does not have spatial locality to the extent of the instruction stream. After a datum has been used, it is likely that the datum will be used again. In addition, instruction loops have temporal locality because the instructions will be executed again in the near future.

The hardware and/or software must perform a number of steps when accessing the real memory. A memory-read operation is assumed in the following discussion. The access steps are as follows:

1. Determine if the page holding the requested addressable unit (AU) is in the real memory.
2. If present, translate the page name, concatenate with the displacement, read real memory, return the AU to the processor, and continue.
3. If not present, call the page fault handler:
   a. If there is a vacant page frame, fetch the page containing the AU from the disk into real memory, return the requested AU to the processor, update the name translation table, and continue.
   b. If there is not a vacant page frame in real memory, evict a page to the disk. Return to step 3a.

Fundamental to these steps is the determination of the presence or absence of the page in real memory that holds the requested AU before accessing real memory, a process called early select. A paged memory uses congruence mapping[39] between the virtual address and the real memory. This means that the virtual address is divided into two parts, the page name and the displacement within the page, as shown in Figure 4.4. The mathematical way of looking at congruence mapping is that the virtual

---

[39] Two integers are congruent modulus m if, after division by the modulus m, both have the same remainder r.

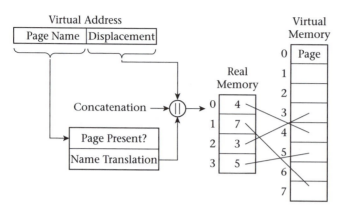

Figure 4.4 Congruence mapping (courtesy Jones and Bartlett Publishers)

address is divided by the page size; the quotient is the page name and the remainder is the displacement.

The simplified system shown in Figure 4.4 has a virtual-address space of 8 pages and a real memory of 4 page frames. Because the size of a page is an even power of 2 of the AUs, say 2K bytes, the virtual address is divided into two parts; the page name and the displacement within the page. For a 2K-byte page, the displacement is 11 bits and for this simple system, the page name is 3 bits.

The lines indicate the current allocation of the pages to real-memory page frames: page 3 is in frame 2, page 7 is in frame 1, and so on. This relationship is shown in Table 4.1. The page name is translated by a table, from 4 to 0 for example, to give the page frame address in real memory. There is no direct correspondence between the page name and the page frame address because a page can be placed in any vacant page frame. The translated page name is concatenated with the displacement to give the address of the requested AU in real memory.

There are two ways the page name can be translated into the page frame address: (1) direct translation and (2) inverted translation. Both of these methods are used in memory systems today.

TABLE 4.1 PAGE NAME TRANSLATION MAP

Page Name	Page Frame Address
4	0
7	1
3	2
5	3

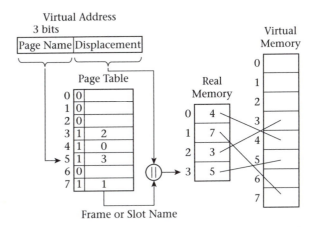

Figure 4.5 Direct name translation (courtesy Jones and Bartlett Publishers)

Direct Translation

Figure 4.4 is repeated in Figure 4.5 with a direct page table translation scheme. The page table is indexed by the page name.[40] The entries in the page table have two fields; a 1-bit field indicates if the requested page is present in real memory, whereas the other field contains the starting, or base, real-memory address of the page frame holding the page. For example, if the name of the requested page is #5, page table entry #5 is indexed, the 1 in the present bit indicates that the page is present, and its real-memory page frame starting address is 3. The value 3 is concatenated with the displacement to form the real-memory address.

If page #2 is accessed, the page table shows, by virtue of the 0 in the tag of location 2, that the page is not resident in real memory and must be fetched from virtual memory. However, real memory is full as all of the page frames are occupied. Thus one page must be selected for eviction to disk memory to make room for the requested page. There are various algorithms for making the eviction selection that are discussed later in this chapter.

A characteristic of direct name translation is that there is one table entry for each page in virtual memory. For small virtual addresses, direct name translation has proven to be quite effective. The page table is implemented in hardware and, being relatively fast, adds only a small increment of time to the latency of real memory. However, with large virtual addresses, the page table can become quite large – so large it must be stored in real memory, resulting in a significant increase in real-memory latency.

EXAMPLE

Consider a computer with a 32-bit virtual address and a 4K-byte page. How many entries are required in a direct page table? If each page table entry requires 4 bytes, what is the total size of the page table?

---

[40] The term index is used when an entry of a table is selected. The term address is used when a memory location is accessed.

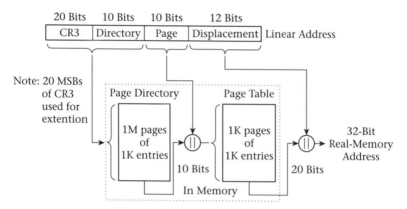

Figure 4.6 Intel 486 and Pentium Pro page name translation (courtesy Jones and Bartlett Publishers)

Solution

The number of pages in virtual memory is the number of AUs in virtual address space divided by the size of the page:

$$\text{number of pages} = (2^{32}/2^{12}) = 2^{20}.$$

As there is one page table entry for each virtual page, there are 2^{20} entries. If each entry is 4 bytes, the page table requires 2^{22} bytes or 4M bytes of memory.

Comment

For large virtual addresses, such as those found on modern processors, the size of a direct page table can be much larger than real memory.

Modern processors have even larger virtual addresses than the example above; for example, the IBM S370 has a 42-bit virtual address, and the Intel Pentium Pro and the IBM PowerPC have 52-bit virtual or linear addresses. For the Intel Pentium Pro, a multilevel direct partial page table name translation system is implemented as shown in Figure 4.6. The IBM S370 name translation system is similar and is discussed in Section 4.6.

The 32-bit offset or linear address is extended by 20 bits from control register CR3, which produces a 52-bit virtual address. The most-significant 30 bits of the linear-address index into the page directory, having 1M pages of 1K page entries each. The 10-bit output of the page directory is concatenated with the next 10 bits of the virtual address to index into the page table with 1K pages of 1K entries. The 20-bit output of the page table is concatenated with the 12-bit displacement to give the 32-bit real-memory address. As these tables are in real memory, translating a page name requires a number of memory cycles, adding to the latency of a real-memory access – a significant performance penalty. The solution to this performance problem will be discussed later in the paragraphs on special caches in this chapter.

The multilevel page table significantly reduces the size of the direct page table stored in memory. However, the complete page table is in virtual memory, and the active portion of the page table is itself paged into reserved page frames. Paging page tables introduces the problem of having page faults on the page table when the page name is translated. Thus it is possible for the system to lock up or crash because of these page faults. This problem is solved, primarily, by placing page tables in a protected region of real memory that does not have its addresses translated.

EXAMPLE

The multilevel partial page table of the Intel Pentium Pro significantly reduces the real-memory storage requirement of a direct page table. What percent of the fully populated page table is active at one time with the Pentium Pro address translation system of Figure 4.6?

Solution

The number of entries of a fully populated page table for a 52-bit virtual address and a 4K byte page is

$$\text{number of entries} = (2^{52}/2^{12}) = 2^{40}.$$

The number of entries in the partial page table for both levels is

$$\text{number of entries} = \text{page directory entries} + \text{page table entries}$$
$$= 2^{30} + 2^{20} \approx 2^{30}.$$

Thus the percent of the fully populated page table is

$$\% \text{ populated} = 100\left(\frac{2^{30}}{2^{40}}\right) = 0.097\%.$$

Comment

With a multilevel partially populated page table, the name translation page fault rate will be nonzero. However, in practice, the name translation fault rate approaches zero except after context switches. The reason for this is that, because pages have temporal locality, name translation table information has temporal locality as well. ISA support of page tables is discussed in Chapter 8.

Inverted Translation

Modern computers have virtual addresses of 52 bits. With direct name translation, the page tables will be very large or be partially populated and hierarchical, leading to page table page faults, as discussed above. A solution to these problems is found with inverted page tables used by IBM with the RS/6000 and the PowerPC, and by Hewlett-Packard with their precision architecture. In the discussion to follow, refer back to Figure 4.4, which shows a block "Page Present?, Name Translation." This block can be implemented with an inverted page table.

An inverted page table has one table entry for every page frame in real memory, resulting in a significant reduction in the size of the page table. For example, a real memory of 32M bytes and a page of 4K bytes has 8K page frames and the inverted page table needs only 8K entries with 13 index bits. This compares with a direct page table for a 52-bit virtual address of 2^{40} entries and 40 index bits. Note that the size of the virtual address does not influence the size of an inverted page table, only the size of the installed real memory.

A 52-bit virtual address with 4K bytes has a page name of 40 bits. This raises the question of how a long page name is converted into a small (13 bits for the 8K page frames) address for indexing into the page table. The solution to this problem is the use of hashing. Hashing transforms a large sparsely populated address into a small uniformly populated address. A survey of hashing can be found in Lewis and Cook (1988).

Hashing

To illustrate how hashing works, we use the following example. We want to design a system to access the records of a class of 66 students; each student has a unique social security number. A social security number has 9 decimal digits, giving approximately 10^9 unique addresses whereas there are only 66 unique addresses in the class. Thus the social security address space is sparsely populated. We would like to have a small table of 66 entries, not a large 10^9 entry table for storing student information.

To access the table we take the social security number of a student and hash it into a smaller number that will index into the small table. A simple hashing function takes the two least-significant digits of the social security number as the index into the page table. Two digits are sufficient because the class size is less than 100. The table contains pointers to each of the 66 students' records, similar to the page slot address of Figure 4.5.

To illustrate this process, the list of 66 student social security numbers is given in Table 4.2 with the first three digits suppressed. The distribution of hashed values is shown in Table 4.3. For example, the first social security number ends in 50 and one is tallied in the 50 position of Table 4.3.

Note that some of the 100 possible hash outputs have 0, 1, 2, or 4 occurrences because the output of this hash function is not uniformly distributed. What happens when there is more than one hit on a given table entry, such as 75 with 4 hits? This problem, called collision, can be resolved in a number of ways. One common solution to collisions is to link the table entries that have the same hash index into a linked list. A linked list with three items is shown in Figure 4.7. The list is accessed by the hashed page name to the first item. Item 1 has a link address to item 2 that has a link address to item 3. The last entry on the link list has a

---

TABLE 4.2 CLASS SOCIAL SECURITY NUMBERS

xxx-24-9750	xxx-06-5204	xxx-30-7338	xxx-33-5575	xxx-79-1528	xxx-24-4547
xxx-15-5434	xxx-92-3719	xxx-16-0336	xxx-07-9694	xxx-78-3559	xxx-71-3545
xxx-32-4770	xxx-79-2257	xxx-15-8675	xxx-14-2174	xxx-66-2744	xxx-49-1053
xxx-74-2329	xxx-80-3192	xxx-33-7633	xxx-65-4266	xxx-64-7567	xxx-31-9175
xxx-51-7706	xxx-23-2470	xxx-37-8075	xxx-24-7287	xxx-33-4790	xxx-25-8960
xxx-47-9713	xxx-58-9175	xxx-35-5887	xxx-67-0236	xxx-81-6899	xxx-45-5440
xxx-07-8151	xxx-19-6783	xxx-31-7123	xxx-43-5165	xxx-33-5602	xxx-92-2685
xxx-15-1499	xxx-33-7364	xxx-14-5397	xxx-15-8572	xxx-67-6292	xxx-21-2918
xxx-09-3439	xxx-94-9000	xxx-70-8804	xxx-79-1364	xxx-98-6396	xxx-27-3156
xxx-20-8363	xxx-25-7900	xxx-16-6251	xxx-54-9597	xxx-25-4877	xxx-14-2758
xxx-24-6094	xxx-03-7826	xxx-03-3545	xxx-07-7529	xxx-72-6559	xxx-72-3616

TABLE 4.3 DISTRIBUTION OF HASHED SOCIAL SECURITY NUMBERS

		U	N	I	T	S					
		0	1	2	3	4	5	6	7	8	9
	0	2		1		2		1			
T	1			1			1		1	1	
E	2			1			1		1	2	
N	3			1	1		2		1	1	
S	4	1				2	1		1		
	5	1	2		1		1	1	1	1	2
	6	1			1	2	1	2			
	7	2		1		1	4		1		
	8			1		1		2			
	9	1		2		2		1	2		2

terminator symbol T rather than a link to another item. A four-entry linked list would be required for the four social security numbers that hashed into the index 75.

The linked lists may be stored in real memory, and the items and their pointers can be in any location in the page table. For example, the collisions from hash index 75 can be stored in page table locations 75, 20, 21, and 22. Items are added to or deleted from the list by adjusting the links.

One-Level Inverted Page Table System

We now look at an inverted page table system for translating page names. A simple inverted page table system block diagram is shown in Figure 4.8. The page name is hashed into a smaller value that indexes into the page table. One of the fields of the page table entry is a tag holding the page name of the page that is resident in the addressed page frame.

The process of determining if the desired information is in the inverted page table and obtaining the page frame address is called a probe:

1. Hash the page name.
2. Index into the page table. If the tag matches the page name, go to 4; otherwise go to 3.
3. Is the link field a terminator symbol?
   Yes: page fault; call the page fault handler.
   No: use the link as an index; go to 2.
4. The page frame address is read out and concatenated with the displacement to give the real-memory address.

Figure 4.7 Linked list

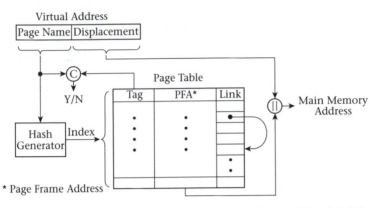

Figure 4.8 One-level inverted page tables (courtesy Jones and Bartlett Publishers)

In practice, it is desirable to make the page frame table twice the size of the number of real-memory page frames. The idea is to further spread out the hash-generated index values and reduce the number of collisions. Even so, experimental as well as theoretical evidence suggest that the weighted average number of probes for accessing an inverted page table is 1.5 with a well-designed hashing algorithm. This number of probes requires far fewer memory cycles than does a multilevel direct page table system.

EXAMPLE

Using the data from Table 4.2 and the results of using the two least-significant digit hashing shown in Table 4.3, what is the average number of probes required for accessing an item?

Solution

This is a simple weighted average problem. 48 entries can be found with 1 probe, 16 with 2 probes, 1 with 3 probes, and 1 requires 4 probes. Thus the weighted average number of probes is

$$\frac{(48 \times 1) + (16 \times 2) + (1 \times 3) + (1 \times 4)}{66} = \frac{87}{66} = 1.32 \text{ probes.}$$

Comment

An average number of 1.32 probes is very close to the 1.5 probes mentioned in the last paragraph.

Virtual-Memory Performance

Virtual memory is hierarchical, as shown in Figure 4.2. What is the effective latency of real memory with a virtual-memory system as seen by the processor? The model is a steady-state model; transients such as context switching will change the performance from that predicted by the model. The parameters of a model are

---

TABLE 4.4 VIRTUAL-MEMORY LATENCY MODEL

Event	Probability	Time	Product
Hit	$1 - P_f$	$t_t + t_{rm}$	$(1 - P_f)(t_t + t_{rm})$
Miss	P_f	$t_t + T_{drm} + t_{os}$	$P_f(t_t + T_{drm} + t_{os})$
	SUM = 1		SUM = $(1 - P_f)(t_t + t_{rm}) + P_f(t_t + T_{drm} + t_{os})$

---

t_{elrm} = effective latency of real memory
t_t = name translation time
P_f = page fault rate
t_{rm} = latency of real memory
T_{drm} = transport time to move a page to/from disk and real memory (latency + transfer time)
t_{os} = time needed by the operating system to handle a page fault

The performance model is derived with the tabular technique suggested in Chapter 2 and shown in Table 4.4. There are two events: a page fault or a page hit. There are times associated with these two events.

Collecting terms of the sum, the latency is

$$t_{elrm} = t_t + (1 - P_f)t_{rm} + P_f(T_{drm} + t_{os}).^{41}$$

The locality properties significantly improve the performance of a memory system over memory system receiving addresses that are randomly distributed over the virtual-address space. The page fault rate has been defined previously in this section and is a key parameter used in modeling performance. Although there is little published data on page fault rates, modern systems can be assumed to have a steady-state page fault rate of approximately 1×10^{-5} to 1×10^{-6}.

EXAMPLE

Consider a virtual-memory system with the following parameters. The disk-to-real-memory transport time is 20 ms, the real-memory latency is 200 ns, the weighted average number of the name translation probes is 1.5, and the page fault rate is 1×10^{-5}. The page fault handler requires 2 ms of computer time. What is the effective latency of real memory?

Solution

Use the model developed above:

$$t_{elrm} = 1.5 \times 200 \times 10^{-9} + (1 - 1 \times 10^{-5})200 \times 10^{-9}$$
$$+ 1 \times 10^{-5}(20 \times 10^{-3} + 2 \times 10^{-3})$$
$$\approx 7.2 \times 10^{-7} = 720 \text{ ns}$$

---

[41] The effective latency could have been named the weighted arithmetic mean latency.

Comment

Although 720 ns is a much longer latency than the 200-ns basic latency of the real memory, there is a speedup of 28×10^3 over the latency of the disk without real memory.

A page that is resident in real memory and has been modified by the executing program must be returned to disk before the page frame can be used to receive a new page. An additional term is introduced into the t_{earm} model: P_m is the probability that a page has been modified. Given the assumption that all the page frames in real memory are occupied, the weighted average real-memory latency model is changed to

$$t_{elrm} = t_t + (1 - P_f)t_{rm} + P_f(T_{drm} + t_{os})(1 + P_m).$$

If the memory allocation is able to have pages reserved for instructions, for these pages P_m is always zero. Some data pages may be modified and must be returned to the disk before the page frame can be used to hold a new page. A simple page fault handler may assume that all pages have been modified; in that case $P_m = 1$.

Multiprogramming

Because the ratio of T_{drm} to t_{rm} is between 1×10^5 and 1×10^6, many systems do not wait for a page fault to be serviced. Rather, a new program is placed into execution while waiting. The magnitude of the problem that leads to multiprogramming is illustrated with the following example. A 200-MIPS processor can execute 6×10^6 instructions while waiting for a 30-ms page fault to be serviced. Thus the resources of the system are more efficiently used if used with multiprogramming. However, single-user systems with no background programs resident must wait for a page fault to be serviced. The only solution to this problem is faster disks or disk caches, a topic discussed in Section 4.3.

Translation Lookaside Buffers

As discussed previously in this section both the direct and the inverted page name translation methods require several memory cycles that add to the latency of every memory access. In the example above, page name translation adds 300 ns to the latency of the real memory. Even when there is a hit on the real memory, the latency is approximately 500 ns. What can be done to eliminate or at least reduce this performance killer?

The solution to this problem is called a translation lookaside buffer (TLB). A TLB is a small fast page table implemented in registers that holds the most recently used address translations. Experiments show that if this fast memory has only a few entries, say 10 or 16, then there is a high likelihood that the translation can be successful in the TLB without having to access the page tables in memory.

A TLB that is implemented in fast registers can have a translation latency of approximately 10 ns. With this TLB, the effective memory latency for the example above will decrease from 720 ns to ~430 ns, a speedup of 1.67. The TLB is similar to a cache, discussed in Section 4.3, and a discussion of TLB design will be covered in that section.

4.3 CACHES

Section 4.2 discussed how virtual memory extends the address space of a processor. However, the latency of real memory is too long to support high-performance processors. Even with the high-speed DRAMs used today for real memory, something must be done to overcome this latency problem.

EXAMPLE

Consider a processor that requires two memory accesses per instruction and follows the serial execution model. Assume a 70-ns memory latency and cycle time. If the processor is infinitely fast, what is the MIPS rating of the system?

Solution

The time for an instruction is memory time plus processor time:

$$\text{instruction time} = 2 \times 70^{-9} + 0 = 140 \text{ ns,}$$
$$\text{MIPS} = \frac{1}{140 \times 10^{-9} \times 10^6} = 7.1$$

Comment

Modern microprocessors perform in the 100–500-MIPS range. The performance of this infinitely fast processor is limited by the memory latency.

The solution to this performance problem is to add another level to the memory hierarchy, called a cache, shown in Figure 4.1. The allocation of spaces in a three-level memory is shown in Figure 4.9. As discussed in Section 4.2, the virtual-address space is divided into equal-sized pages. These pages are placed in real-memory frames of the same size. Because a page can be placed in any vacant frame, there is no particular order to the allocation of pages to frames. With the addition of a cache, blocks of 16–32 bytes are taken from the page frames in real memory and placed into a block slot for access by the processor. For modern processors the cache usually has a latency of one processor clock, so that instructions and data may be fetched without delay except when the referenced item is not in the cache.

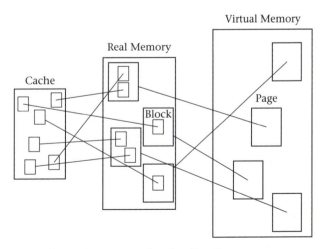

Figure 4.9 Real memory and cache allocation

TABLE 4.5 MEMORY REFERENCE STATISTICS

	SPARC Integer	SPARC Floating Point	MIPS Integer	MIPS Floating Point	IBM S360	VAX	Average
Instruction	0.79	0.80	0.76	0.77	0.50	0.65	0.71
Data Read	0.15	0.17	0.15	0.19	0.35	0.28	0.22
Data Write	0.06	0.03	0.09	0.04	0.15	0.07	0.07

Before we discuss the design of caches, it is helpful to understand the demand placed on the memory system by the processor. The memory and the memory system must support three or more reference streams from the processor:

1. Instruction fetch to processor
2. Data reads to processor
3. Data writes from the processor[42]
4. I/O

Measurements of referenced statistics for various processors, not counting I/O, are shown in Table 4.5. Approximately 71% of all memory references are instruction fetches, 22% are data reads, whereas only 7% are data writes. The inescapable conclusion from these data is that the memory system designer has the priorities of providing short latency for instruction fetches, followed by data reads and then data writes. Remember Amdahl's law: make the most frequent case fast.

Note that the load/store register file architectures (SPARC and MIPS) have fewer data memory references than do the architectures that reference memory (IBM S360 and VAX). The reason for this is that SPARC and MIPS have large register files, and instructions find many of their operands in the register file and go to memory only with load and store instructions. For the load/store register file architectures there are approximately 0.25 data accesses per instruction, whereas for the S360 the data accesses per instruction are 1.0 and, for the VAX, 0.41. These ratios suggest that a memory system designed for a VAX, say, may not be ideal for a MIPS. A memory system designer must be familiar with the dynamic statistics of a given ISA to design the memory properly.

EXAMPLE

1. Explain why the S360 has one data reference per instruction. Use the statistics from Table 4.5.

Solution
The fraction of data reads and writes is $0.35 + 0.15 = 0.5$. The fraction of instruction reads is also 0.5. Thus the number of data references per instruction is 1.0.

---

[42] If self-modifying programs are supported, modified instructions must be written into memory.

2. An instruction fetch has a latency of 100 ns and a data read of 150 ns.
   a. What is the effective memory latency time t_{el} with data writes of 200 and 250 ns? Use the averages from Table 4.5.
   b. What is the percentage of change in performance with the 250-ns data writes compared with the 200-ns data writes?

Solution

This is a simple weighted mean calculation:

a.

$$t_{el}(200 \text{ ns}) = (0.71 \times 100) + (0.22 \times 150) + (0.07 \times 200) = 118 \text{ ns},$$
$$t_{el}(250 \text{ ns}) = (0.71 \times 100) + (0.22 \times 150) + (0.07 \times 200) = 121.5 \text{ ns}.$$

b.

$$\% \text{ change in performance} = 100\left(1 - \frac{1}{S}\right) = 100\left(1 - \frac{1}{118/121.5}\right)$$
$$= 100(1 - 1.029) = -2.9\%.$$

Cache Topology

Cache topology concerns the number and the interconnection of the caches between the processor and real memory. A number of topologies are shown in Figure 4.10.

Because such a large fraction of memory references are for instructions, early computers had a one-level instruction cache; data were accessed directly from real memory. A later topology used a one-level unified cache that held both instructions and data. Two-level unified caches are a possible topology but are not known to have been used in any computer. A common topology for early microprocessors is the one-level split cache; one cache for instructions and one cache for data. With these microprocessors, the two caches are implemented on the processor chip. System designers, by using these microprocessors, could use a second-level unified cache between the on-chip split caches and the real memory. An example of a two-level split cache is the cache used with the Pentium Pro, which places the second-level unified cache within the same package as the processor with its split on-chip cache.

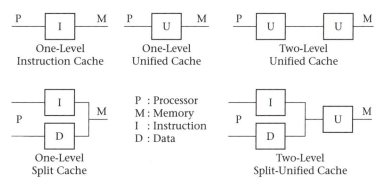

Figure 4.10 Cache topologies

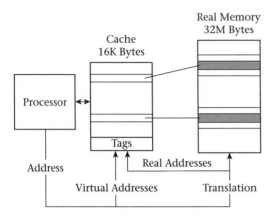

Figure 4.11 Cache allocation and addressing

Cache Allocation and Organization

We now examine the organization of caches in general followed by a discussion of the characteristics that distinguish instruction and data caches. Figure 4.11 shows the processor – cache – real-memory connections. As with the allocation of pages from disk to real memory for virtual memory, blocks in real memory are allocated to the cache when there is a cache miss. Because the size of the cache is less than the size of real memory, there is not a direct correspondence between the real-memory addresses and the cache addresses. The cache may be accessed with either untranslated virtual addresses or translated real addresses. The consequences of this design option are discussed in Section 4.5. For now, just assume that an address is presented to the cache.

There are more design options with a cache than with a virtual-memory system. Figure 4.12 shows the possible options.

- A cache is divided into $1 - S$ sets. Control bits, indicated as LRU[43] in each set, assist in selecting a block for eviction when a block must be moved into real memory.

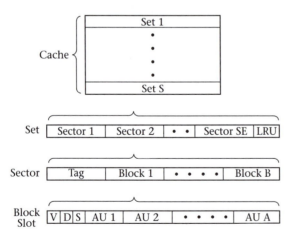

Figure 4.12 Cache partitioning (courtesy Jones and Bartlett Publishers)

---

[43] Least recently used.

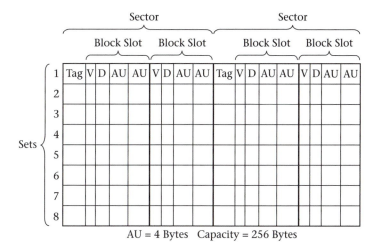

Figure 4.13 Canonical cache (courtesy Jones and Bartlett Publishers)

- A set is divided into $1 - SE$ sectors. Most modern caches have $SE = 1$. Each sector has a tag field containing the block name and the blocks of data.
- A sector is divided into $1 - B$ block slots.[44] Most modern caches have $B = 1$.
- A block and block slot are divided into $1 - A$ AUs. Each block slot may have valid, dirty, and shared bits. A valid bit indicates that the information in a block is valid, a dirty bit is used in some systems to indicate that a block has been modified by a write instruction, and a shared bit is used only in caches for multiprocessor systems.

With the partitioning options of Figure 4.12, the layout of a canonical cache is shown in Figure 4.13. This cache has eight sets, two sectors per set, two blocks per sector, and two AUs per block. Shared bits are not shown in the block.

Cache addressing, like virtual-memory page addressing, is congruence mapped. However, the address presented to a cache must be allocated to address fields for the set, the sector, the block, and the AU within the block. The canonical cache address is shown below:

Block Name	Set Index	Blk	Displacement

Set index addresses the set, blk addresses the block, and displacement addresses the AU within the block.

Most modern caches have only one block per sector and the blk field is of zero length; fully associative caches have one set, so the set index field is of zero length. With one block slot per sector, the term sector is usually not used. The following discussion of cache organization will assume one sector with one block slot and use the convention of block slot rather than sector.

---

[44] The block is the data, and the location in the cache that holds the block is a slot. This is analogous to the page and page frame of paged virtual-memory systems.

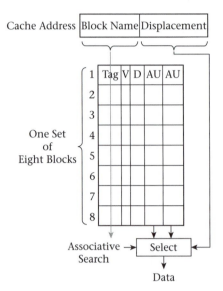

Figure 4.14 Associative cache (courtesy Jones and Bartlett Publishers)

Testing to see if a block is present is performed in a different manner with a cache than with virtual memory. Recall that virtual-memory systems looked into a page table (either direct or inverted) to see if the page of the requested AU is present before accessing real memory, a policy called early select. Caches, on the other hand, store the block name in a tag field along with the AUs, as shown in Figure 4.13. The access is made to both the blocks (sectors) and tags on the same cycle. After the access, the tags are checked to see if a valid block has been accessed. This policy is called late select.

The following discussion is couched in terms of a read operation; write operations are discussed later in this section. The organization options shown in Figures 4.12 and 4.13 are implemented in one of three organizations: associative, set associative, and direct.

Associative Cache

An associative cache has one set and is shown in Figure 4.14. This cache is shown with eight block slots with each block slot containing two AUs. The address presented to the cache is divided into a block name and a displacement. The set index and blk fields of the address are of zero length.

Each of the eight blocks consists of a tag that holds the block name of a resident block, the two AUs, a valid bit, and a dirty bit. The valid bit is required because it is possible to have a match on the tag even though the data are invalid. The valid bit is set to valid only after the block slot has been loaded with valid data after a miss. The dirty bit indicates that some portion of the block has been modified.

The block name is associatively searched against the tags and if there is a tag match *and* the valid bit is set, the AUs of the block are read out. Tag match with a set valid bit is called a cache hit, which means that the requested block is in the cache. The proper AU is selected by the displacement and passed on to the processor. A cache miss occurs if either the tag does not match or the valid bit is not set, which means

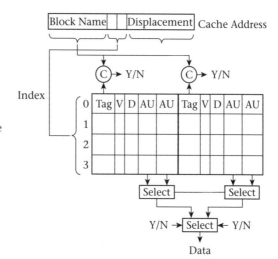

Figure 4.15 Two-way set associative cache (courtesy Jones and Bartlett Publishers)

that the requested block is not in the cache and must be fetched from real memory. The associative organization has the desirable property that a block can be placed into any block slot in the cache; there are no constraints.

Set Associative Cache

The second organization of a cache is set associative, having two or more sets. Figure 4.15 shows the organization of a two-way set associative cache of the same size as the cache shown in Figure 4.14. The two LSBs of the block name index into the cache and read its contents. The tags, holding the block names, are compared with the block name in the address. If the tag matches the block name *and* the valid bit is set, there is a hit and the AU is selected by the displacement and gated out to the processor. A miss requires a fetch from real memory.

As this cache is two-way set associative, a requested block can be placed in only one of two block slots within a set. For example, blocks that have names with LSBs = 01 can go only into the block slots with the index 01. Even if there are vacant block slots in the cache, the placement is constrained to this set. If the block slots are full and there is a request with the same set index value, there will be a set conflict miss.

Note that this organization has only two comparators, as contrasted with the eight required for the fully associative cache of Figure 4.14. One can also design a four-way set associative cache with four comparators or even a five-way with five comparators. For caches with one sector per set the number of comparators and the degree of associativity are equal to the number of block slots per set.

Direct Cache

The third organization, called a direct cache, reduces the number of comparators to one and is shown in Figure 4.16 for an eight-set cache. Three bits are taken from the block name for the set index.

The direct cache is the simplest of the organizations with only one tag comparator. However, with only one block slot per set, the direct cache is fully constrained. Blocks

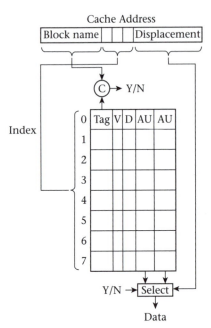

Cache Address

Figure 4.16 Direct cache (courtesy Jones and Bartlett Publishers)

with the same set index values, regardless of the block name, can be placed in only one block slot. For example, block names ending with the LSBs 010 can only be stored in set 2's block slot even if every other block slot in the cache is vacant. Thus there is a greater probability of having to evict a block from a block slot to make room for a new block, resulting in an increase in the cache miss rate (equivalent to the page fault rate discussed previously).

EXAMPLES

1. For the two-way set associative cache, which sets can hold blocks with block names ending with the LSBs 011?

    Solution
    These blocks can be stored in only the left- or the right-hand block slots of set 3.

2. For the three cache organizations illustrated in Figures 4.14– 4.16, tabulate the number of sets, the number of sectors, the number of blocks, and the number of AUs per block. Also compute the capacity of the caches in AUs and give a formula for determining the same.

    Solution
    The solution to this problem is shown in Table 4.6.

    $$\text{AUs in a cache} = \text{number of sets} \times \frac{\text{sectors}}{\text{set}} \times \frac{\text{blocks}}{\text{sector}} \times \frac{\text{AUs}}{\text{block}}.$$

    Comment
    We see that each of these three organizations is the same size. Tables 4.8, 4.9, and 4.10 show that the selection of the organization parameters can have an infl uence on the performance of the cache.

TABLE 4.6 CACHE ORGANIZATION AND CAPACITY

Organization	Sets	Sec/Set	Blks/Sector	AUs/Blk	Capacity
Associative	1	1	8	2	16 AUs
Two-way set associative	4	1	2	2	16 AUs
Direct	8	1	1	2	16 AUs

Cache Read and Write Policies

When the processor makes a read or write access of the cache, there must be a policy enforced in the hardware that governs the actions taken. We consider the read policy first. Remember, for a cache hit the tag must match the block name and the valid bit must be set.

READ HIT:

1. The referenced AU is in the cache; the AU is transferred to the processor.

READ MISS:

1. If there is a vacant block slot in which the new block can be placed, the block is fetched from real memory and placed in the block slot and the referenced AU is transferred to the processor. The tag and valid bit are updated.
2. If there is no vacant block slot in the cache that can receive the desired block (such as a full cache or a set conflict) a block must be evicted to real memory to make room. The cache control reissues the read and finds a read miss with a vacant block slot, step 1 above.

   If the cache uses a dirty bit and if the block to be evicted has not been modified, the requested block can be written into the cache without a block being evicted. There are a number of algorithms for selecting the block to evict, such as LRU or a random choice.

Write policies, needed for data caches but not needed for instruction caches, are more complicated. As with a read, there can be a hit or a miss when a store type instruction writes to the cache. The design alternatives for hit and miss are discussed below.

WRITE HIT:

1. The write is made to the cache and to real memory. This policy is called write through. Because the block in the cache and real memory are coherent,[45] when there is a subsequent read miss on the block it is not necessary to evict the block as it can be overwritten by the fetched block. A dirty bit is not required with this policy because the cache and the real memory are always coherent.

---

[45] Memory is said to be coherent if addresses point to the same value, even though there are two or more copies of the value in different storage locations.

2. The write is made to the cache only. When this write is made, the dirty bit is set to indicate that the block or a portion of the block has been modified. Because the block in the cache and real memory are now not coherent, when there is a subsequent read miss the block must be evicted to real memory before the new block is fetched. This policy is called write back.

WRITE MISS:

1. The missed block is fetched into the cache and the write is made (by either write through or write back, depending upon the write hit policy). This policy is called write allocate because the needed block is allocated to the cache before the write is performed.
2. The write is made to the real memory without writing to the cache, a policy called no-write allocate or write direct.

For most processors, the write policy is selected by the designer and wired in as a default policy. Other processors give the programmer the option of selecting a write policy. These programmer options on policy are discussed in Section 8.5.

Cache Latency Models

The weighted effective latency t_{elc} model for caches is similar to the model for the interface between real memory and the disk. The model is a steady-state model; transients such as context switching will change the performance from that predicted by the model. The parameters for this model are t_c, cache latency time; T_{rmc}, real-memory-to-cache transport time; and P_{miss}, cache miss rate:

$$P_{miss} = 1 - \frac{\text{number of references served in the cache}}{\text{total number of references to the cache}}.$$

The weighted effective latency model is derived with the tabular technique suggested in Chapter 2 and shown in Table 4.7. There are two events: a cache miss and a cache hit, and each event has its associated time:

$$\begin{aligned} t_{elc} &= (1 - P_{miss})t_c + P_{miss}(t_c + T_{rmc}) \\ &= t_c - P_{miss}t_c + P_{miss}t_c + P_{miss}T_{rmc} \\ &= t_c + P_{miss}T_{rmc}. \end{aligned}$$

TABLE 4.7   CACHE EFFECTIVE LATENCY MODEL

Event	Probability	Time	Product
Hit	$1 - P_{miss}$	t_c	$(1 - P_{miss})t_c$
Miss	P_{miss}	$(t_c + T_{rmc})$	$P_{miss}(t_c + T_{rmc})$
	SUM $= 1$		SUM $= (1 - P_{miss})t_c + P_{miss}(t_c + T_{rmc})$

The reason the time on a miss is the sum of the cache and real memory transport time is that the cache is accessed and the tag checked before the real memory is accessed. This sequence is called late select. The model can be normalized to the basic latency of the cache as this latency, for synchronous systems, is usually one processor clock. In synchronous systems, T_{rmc} is always an integer.

$$t_{elc} \text{ (in clocks)} = 1 + P_{miss} T_{rmc}$$

EXAMPLE

You are designing a cache and want to evaluate the interplay of P_{miss} and T_{rmc}. Plot the locus of cache latency for $T_{rmc} = 7$ to 14 and for $P_{miss} = 0.1$ and 0.08.

Solution

Figure 4.17 shows the plots of t_{elc} (in clocks) for these design parameters.

Comments

Note the possible design tradeoff between T_{rmc} and P_{miss}. An effective latency of 1.7 clocks can be obtained by the combination $T_{rmc} = 7$ and $P_{miss} = 0.1$, or the combination $T_{rmc} = 13$ and $P_{miss} = 0.08$.

Instruction Caches

If we consider instruction references, we can surmise that spatial locality is at work because the program counter increments from instruction to instruction. Only when a branch is taken does spatial locality fail. Spatial locality is exploited by the following strategy. When an instruction reference has a cache miss, the block containing the referenced instruction is fetched into the cache. Thus, the referenced instructions and a number of the following instructions in the sequence are placed in the cache. Then when the program counter increments for the next instruction, the desired instruction is usually found in the cache.

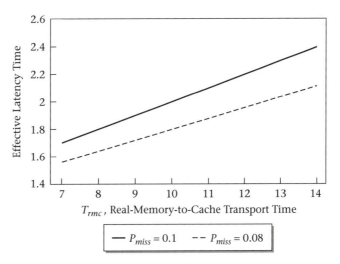

Figure 4.17 Effective latency with different T_{rmc} and P_{miss}

TABLE 4.8   INSTRUCTION CACHE P_{miss} SPEC BENCHMARKS, OVERALL

	Number of Sets						
n-Way	64	128	256	512	1K	2K	4K
1, Direct	0.051	0.039	0.031	*0.020*	0.012	0.007	0.003
2	0.034	0.024	*0.017*	0.010	0.008	0.003	0.0002
4	0.023	*0.016*	0.009	0.008	0.001	0.0002	0.0001
8	*0.016*	0.009	0.008	0.0007	0.0002	0.000	0.000

16-BYTE BLOCK, ONE BLOCK SLOT PER SET

Hit data and miss data for instruction caches can be found in a number of references (Gee et al. 1993). An abstracted set of miss data for SPEC benchmarks and a 16-byte block is shown in Table 4.8. "Overall" means the complete set of integer and floating-point benchmarks.

This table is organized so that caches of equal size are on the diagonal (lower left to upper right). For example, an 8K byte cache, shown in italics, can be organized as eight-way set associative with 64 sets. This cache can also be organized as a direct cache with 512 sets. Note that in general the organization of the cache has little influence on P_{miss}; size alone is the major determinant. For small instruction caches, there is a slight reduction in P_{miss} as the degree of associativity is increased and the number of sets decreases.

Instruction caches also support temporal locality or look behind. Particularly for scientific programs with looping, the cache should be large enough to hold a loop. After first fetching the loop, it is in the cache and will not need to be fetched again.

In the evolution of computer implementation hardware, queues have been used to perform the look ahead function while instruction buffers have been used for the look behind function (Milligan and Cragon 1995). By their design, caches perform both functions. Queues are used in conjunction with caches on a number of modern processors such as the Pentium Pro and the PowerPC.

Data Caches

Data references generally show little spatial locality,[46] but when a datum is once used it is frequently used again; this is known as temporal locality. The data cache memory saves previously referenced data items in anticipation of future use. Miss data for SPEC benchmarks are shown in Table 4.9 for a 16-byte block. Caches of equal size are shown on the diagonal.

As with instruction caches, the major determinant of P_{miss} is the size of the cache. For small caches the miss rate decreases with an increase in set associativity. However,

---

[46] Scientific programs with array data types are an exception to this statement. Spatial locality is so good that some supercomputers do not use a data cache.

TABLE 4.9 DATA CACHE P_{miss}, SPEC BENCHMARKS, OVERALL

	Number of Sets						
n-Way	64	128	256	512	1K	2K	4K
1, Direct	0.255	0.216	0.170	0.114	0.087	0.069	0.057
2		0.188	0.155	0.104	0.074	0.059	0.048	0.039
4		0.134	0.098	0.071	0.058	0.047	0.038	0.028
8		0.091	0.069	0.057	0.047	0.038	0.028	0.017

16-BYTE BLOCK, ONE BLOCK SLOT PER SET

note that a direct cache has a higher miss rate than two-, four-, or eight-way set associative caches of the same size. Direct caches have a shorter logic path, by a few gates, than the other caches. Thus it is possible, but not proven, that with a reduced clock period that is due to the shorter logic path, a cache with shorter latency can be effective even though the P_{miss} is greater. With a faster cache the processor can have a faster clock, resulting in an overall speed improvement for the computer.

Unified Caches

Unified caches store both instructions and data and are used today as a second-level cache to the on-chip instruction and data caches. As would be expected, the P_{miss} of a unified cache is between an instruction cache and a data cache. Table 4.10 shows P_{miss} data for the same SPEC benchmarks and 16-byte block.

As with instruction and data caches, the size of a unified cache is the important parameter for establishing a low P_{miss}. However, for a given size unified cache, the P_{miss} of a direct cache is approximately 20% to 25% greater than that of a two-way set associative cache. Thus second-level unified caches are generally implemented as two-way or eight-way set associative.

TABLE 4.10 UNIFIED CACHE P_{miss}, SPEC BENCHMARKS, OVERALL

	Number of Sets						
n-Way	64	128	256	512	1K	2K	4K
1, Direct	0.151	0.114	0.086	0.056	0.039	0.029	0.020
2	0.092	0.069	0.047	0.031	0.023	0.016	0.011
4	0.062	0.044	0.029	0.022	0.015	0.010	0.007
8	0.041	0.028	0.021	0.015	0.010	0.008	0.005

16-BYTE BLOCK, ONE BLOCK SLOT PER SET

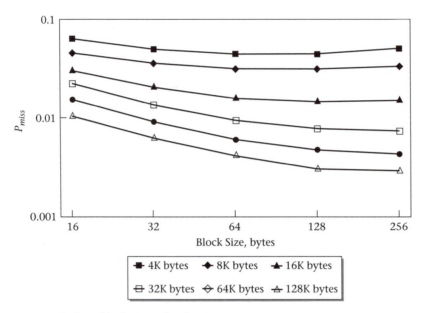

Figure 4.18 P_{miss}, block size and cache size

Block Size

The P_{miss} data presented in Tables 4.8– 4.10 are for a 16-byte block. For the designer, what determines the size of the block? There are two considerations: (1) how does block size affect P_{miss}, and (2) how does block size affect the real-memory-to-cache transport time?

For the issue of P_{miss} and block size, one can look at two extremes: a block of 1 AU at one extreme and a block the size of the cache at the other extreme. For the small block, there will be no look ahead and for the very large block there is little look behind. In both cases, the P_{miss} will be large. Figure 4.18 shows the P_{miss} for various cache sizes and block sizes for a unified cache (Gee et al. 1993). These data are for a unified cache, four-way associative organization, and combined integer and floating-point SPEC benchmarks.

Note that for small caches there is a pronounced minimum P_{miss} as the block size increases. As the cache size increases, the minimum moves out to larger block sizes. For large caches, such as the 64K-byte and the 128K-byte caches, there is a relatively constant reduction in P_{miss} with each doubling of block size – a decrease with a model that is similar to the learning curve model described in Chapter 2:

$$P_{miss}(\text{final}) = P_{miss}(\text{initial})L^{\log 2 \frac{\text{final block size}}{\text{initial block size}}}$$

The 64K-byte cache shown in Figure 4.18 has $L \approx 0.7$. In other words, as the block size doubles, the P_{miss} is approximately 0.7 the previous P_{miss}. The issue of the effect of block size on transport time is discussed in Section 4.4 in which the bus interface between the cache and the real memory is modeled.

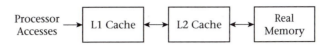

Figure 4.19 Two-level cache

Multilevel Caches

Many processors today have an instruction cache and a data cache on the processor chip with a second-level cache off-chip. A block diagram of a two-level cache is shown in Figure 4.19. The caches are commonly known as L1 and L2 caches.

For a one-level cache, the ratio of the transport time T_{rc} to the L1 cache latency can be in the range of 10–50. There are a number of reasons for this high ratio: The real memory is on a bus and there is bus synchronization time, and a block requires a number of clocks for its transfer across a bus that may be only a few bytes wide. For this reason, a second-level L2 cache is used to reduce the effect of large values of T_{rc}.

A model for the effective latency of a two-level cache t_{elc2} can be derived as follows. The L1 cache has a latency of 1 cycle, the L2 to L1 transport time is T_{c2}, and the real-memory transport time to the L2 cache is T_{rc3}. Transport times T_{c2} and T_{rc3} are in cache cycles. P_{miss1} and P_{miss2} are the miss rates of the L1 and the L2 caches, respectively. The model assumes that all references are satisfied in one of the three levels of memory.

When there is a hit on the L1 cache, the L2 cache and the real memory are "don't-care" conditions. Likewise, with a miss on the L1 cache and a hit on the L2 cache, the real memory is a don't-care condition. Table 4.11 shows the derivation of the effective latency model.

$$t_{elc2} = 1 - P_{miss1} + P_{miss1}(1 - P_{miss2})(1 + T_{c2}) + P_{miss1}P_{miss2}(1 + T_{c2} + T_{rc3})$$
$$= 1 + P_{miss1}T_{c2} + P_{miss1}P_{miss2}T_{rc3}$$

EXAMPLE

A one-level cache system has $P_{miss} = 0.1$ and $T_{rc} = 10$. Consider a two-level cache memory with $P_{miss1} = 0.1$, $P_{miss2} = 0.1$, $T_{c2} = 3$, and $T_{rc3} = 10$. What is the speedup in effective latency with the addition of the L2 cache?

Solution

The effective latency of the single-level cache system is

$$t_{elc} = 1 + 0.1 \times 10 = 2 \text{ clocks.}$$

TABLE 4.11 MULTILEVEL CACHE EFFECTIVE LATENCY

L1	L2	RM	Probability	Time	Product
Hit	x	x	$1 - P_{miss1}$	1	$1 - P_{miss1}$
Miss	Hit	x	$P_{miss1}(1 - P_{miss2})$	$1 + T_{c2}$	$P_{miss1}(1 - P_{miss2})(1 + T_{c2})$
Miss	Miss	Hit	$P_{miss1}P_{miss2}$	$1 + T_{c2} + T_{rc3}$	$P_{miss1}P_{miss2}(1 + T_{c2} + T_{rc3})$
			SUM = 1		SUM = t_{elc2}

For the two-level cache memory,

$$t_{elc2} = 1 + (0.1 \times 3) + (0.1 \times 0.1 \times 10)$$
$$= 1.4 \text{ clocks.}$$
$$\text{speedup} = 2/1.4 = 1.43.$$

Comments

By the introduction of an L2 cache that has a smaller T_c than the T_{rc} of the one-level cache, the cache latency has been significantly improved by 30%. An L2 cache will be beneficial only if t_{c2} is significantly less than the transport time between a single-level cache and real memory.

The two-level cache memory model developed above can be extended to any number of levels of cache or extended to comprehend the virtual-memory level. The P_{miss} values used in this model are called local miss probabilities; that is, the probability of a request entering a cache level and missing. Another approach to multilevel cache modeling is to use global hit probabilities. A global hit probability is the fraction of total references that are served at a given level; global hit probabilities must add to 1. The global hit probabilities for the example above are

$$P_{hit1g} = 0.9,$$
$$P_{hit2g} = 0.1 \times 0.9 = 0.09,$$
$$P_{hit3g} = 1 - 0.9 - 0.09 = 0.01.$$

EXAMPLE

Rework the example above for the two-level cache by using global hit rates.

Solution

$$t_{elc} = (0.9 \times 1) + [0.1(1 + 10)] = 2,$$
$$t_{elc2} = (0.9 \times 1) + [0.09(1 + 3)] + [0.01(1 + 3 + 10)]$$
$$= 0.9 + 0.36 + 0.14 = 1.4,$$
$$\text{speedup} = 2/1.4 = 1.43$$

A block diagram of a modern memory design is shown in Figure 4.20. This memory has two L1 caches, an instruction and data cache on the chip, with an off-chip unified L2 cache.

Because of the very close coupling between the processor and the on-chip caches, the transport time between the instruction/data caches and the unified cache can be

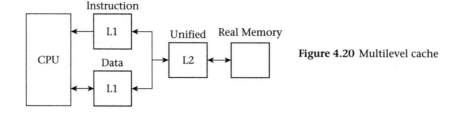

Figure 4.20 Multilevel cache

small – in the range of 2 to 4 cycles. However, the transport time between the unified cache and the real memory may be in the range of 10 to 50 cycles because of bus synchronization requirements.

EXAMPLE

The instruction and data caches of Figure 4.20 are both 8K bytes in size and two-way set associative. The unified cache is 32K bytes in size and two-way set associative. Assume a 16-byte block and a local P_{miss} of real memory of zero; that is, virtual memory is not used.

a. What fraction of instruction and data references are found in real memory?

b. If each instruction has 0.3 data references, what is the weighted average number of memory references per instruction that are satisfied in real memory?

c. Evaluate (b) under the assumption that there is no second level cache.

Solution

a. From Tables 4.8, 4.9, and 4.10 we find that the instruction cache P_{miss} is 0.017, the data cache P_{miss} is 0.104, and the unified cache P_{miss} is 0.023. The fraction of instruction references that are found in real memory is

$$0.017 \times 0.023 = 0.00039.$$

The fraction of data references that are found in real memory is

$$0.104 \times 0.023 = 0.00239.$$

b. The weighted average number of memory references per instruction that are satisfied in real memory is

$$1 \times 0.00039 + 0.3 \times 0.00239 = 0.0011.$$

c. Real-memory references per instruction without second-level cache are

$$1 \times 0.017 + 0.3 \times 0.104 = 0.048.$$

Comments

Using a second-level cache reduces the fraction of references per instruction to real memory from approximately 0.05 to approximately 0.001 per instruction. This reduces the loading on the bus and permits more concurrent I/O operations to proceed without taking too many cycles from the processor.

Special Caches

There are a number of special buffers in a processor that are cachelike in their organization and use. In general these special caches are used to take advantage of temporal locality.

A TLB is one of these special caches, mentioned briefly in Section 4.2. The TLB holds translated page names that have been translated by the page tables on a prior reference. The TLB of the Intel Pentium Pro is shown in Figure 4.21. There are two TLBs, one for instructions and one for data.

This TLB is four-way set associative and has only eight sets; a valid bit is associated with each entry. Translated addresses are stored in this cache instead of data or instructions. There is little published information on the miss rate of TLBs, but what there is

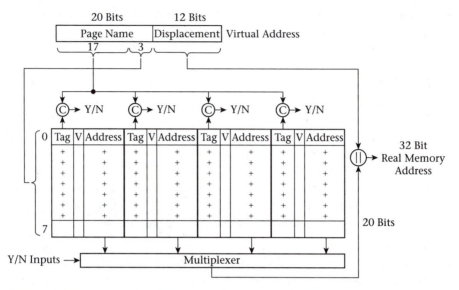

Figure 4.21 Intel Pentium Pro TLB (courtesy Jones and Bartlett Publishers)

(Saavedra and Smith 1993) suggests that $P_{miss} = 0.01 - 0.02$. However, this miss rate is not as bad as it sounds.

Instruction and data references are made to the caches, and the TLB is usually accessed in parallel with the cache access, as shown in Figure 4.22. Thus, if the cache access is a miss, the translated address is already available, assuming there is not a TLB miss. With a cache $P_{miss} = 0.1$, the number of memory references that need translation is 10%. With the TLB $P_{miss} = 0.01$, the number of references that must be translated in the page tables is $0.1 \times 0.01 = 0.001$ or 1 in 100. This ratio is even smaller when a second-level cache is used.

EXAMPLE

A cache has $P_{missC} = 0.1$, and a TLB has $P_{missTLB} = 0.01$. The latency of the cache is 1, the latency TLB is 5% of the real-memory cycle time, the table translation takes 2 memory cycles, and a memory cycle is 4 cache cycles. What is the effective real-memory latency?

Solution

The TLB is searched in parallel with the cache; its contents are used only if there is a cache miss and it is faster than the cache. Thus the TLB latency does not

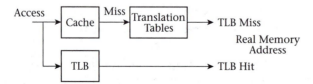

Figure 4.22 Cache and TLB access

TABLE 4.12 EFFECTIVE REAL-MEMORY LATENCY

Event	Probability	Time	Product
Hit cache	$1 - P_{missC}$	1	$1 - P_{missC}$
Miss cache, hit on TLB	$P_{missC} \times (1 - P_{miss\,TLB})$	$0.05 \times 4 + 4$	$4.2\,P_{missC} \times (1 - P_{miss\,TLB})$
Miss cache, miss on TLB	$P_{missC} \times P_{miss\,TLB}$	$1 + (2 + 1)4$	$13\,P_{missC} \times P_{miss\,TLB}$

SUM = EFFECTIVE REAL-MEMORY LATENCY

---

add to the access time on a TLB hit. Table 4.12 shows events, probabilities, and times needed to solve this example.

The effective real-memory latency is

$$1 - P_{missC} + 4.2\,P_{missC} \times (1 - P_{missTLB}) + 13\,P_{missC} \times P_{missTLB}$$

$$= (1 - 0.1) + (4.2 \times 0.1 \times 0.99) + (13 \times 0.1 \times 0.01)$$

$$= 1.33 \text{ cycles.}$$

Comments

This example shows that page table translation by a number of levels does not significantly increase the latency of real memory if a TLB is used.

Although the organization of the Intel Pentium Pro TLB is eight-way set associative, other processors use other organizations. For example, the IBM S370 uses an inverted TLB that is accessed by hashing the page name (similar to the inverted page tables discussed in Section 4.2).

A TLB has a read policy similar to that of an instruction cache. When there is a TLB miss, after the translation is performed in the page tables, the TLB is updated. As a TLB is not written by the processor, unlike a data cache, the new translation information can be overwritten into the TLB.[47] Needless to say, the TLB has no write policy. In some systems, the TLB is switched out/in on a context switch. Switching saves the time required for making page name translations when the old program is restarted.

Some TLBs have some locations hardwired to a given page frame address, usually the low address pages. The reason for this is to have an identity mapping for operating system pages. We do not want the system to have page faults when it is trying to handle a page fault.

4.4 INTERLEAVED REAL MEMORY

The real memory between the cache and the disk requires special properties. This memory is accessed only when there is a read or write miss by the cache. When such an

---

[47] A TLB is updated as a side effect of a page name translation by means of the page tables.

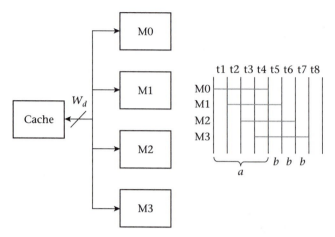

Figure 4.23 Four-way interleaved memory (courtesy Jones and Bartlett Publishers)

event occurs, it is necessary to transfer a block to/from the cache. Today, the technology used for real memory is DRAM with a latency of 10–50 cache cycles. Fortunately, a block is composed of a number of AUs; thus the bandwidth of the real memory is as important as its latency. How can we provide high bandwidth with these relatively slow memory components? The answer is found in the use of parallel memory modules called interleaving.

Figure 4.23 shows a four-way interleaved memory. Four memory modules with word-length W_d AUs are connected to a bus having width W_d AUs, and the bus is connected to the cache. The clock period of the bus is the same as the cache cycle and sets the clock period of the system. For this example, the cycle time of the memory modules is divided into four clocks. The first module, M0, is accessed, and one clock period later, M1 is accessed. This continues until all the modules have been accessed, and the process can repeat. The output (assuming a read) of M0 is available at the end of t4, of M1 at t5, and so on. The configuration is sometimes known as C access because the modules are accessed concurrently, although skewed.

The transport time T_{rc} is the time to transport a block to/from the real memory and the cache. For interleaved memories, T_{rc} in bus clocks is

$$T_{rc} = a + b\left(\frac{A}{W_d} - 1\right),$$

where a is the cycle time of the memory modules in bus clocks, the time to produce the first memory output, and the interleaving factor. The number of clocks required for producing each subsequent output is b clocks; usually equal to 1. A is the number of AUs in a block, and W_d is the width of the bus in AUs.

The transport time model is now modified to include bus synchronization time, which is discussed further in Chapter 7. Assume that the bus synchronization requires s cycles. The transport time becomes

$$T_{rc} = s + a + b\left(\frac{A}{W_d} - 1\right) \text{ clocks.}$$

EXAMPLE

Consider an interleaved memory having the following characteristics. The interleaving factor is 4, $s = 3$, $A = 32$ bytes, and $W_d = 4$ bytes. What is the block transport time?

Solution

$$T_{rc} = 3 + 4 + \left(\frac{32}{4} - 1\right) = 15 \text{ clocks.}$$

Comment

As $A \to \infty$, $T_{rc} \to A/W_d$. In other words, the time to synchronize the bus and read the first module is prorated over a large number of bytes transferred.

With this model we revisit the issue of block size. A model of the effective cache latency is derived by using the model for T_{rc} and the model for P_{miss} in the basic model for cache effective latency t_{elc}:

$$t_{elc}(\text{in clocks}) = 1 + P_{miss} T_{rc},$$

$$P_{miss}(\text{final}) = P_{miss}(\text{initial}) L^{\log 2 \frac{\text{final block size}}{\text{initial block size}}},$$

$$T_{rc} = s + a + b\left(\frac{A}{W_d} - 1\right) \text{ clocks,}$$

$$t_{elc}(\text{in clocks}) = 1 + P_{miss}(\text{initial})\, L^{\log 2 \frac{\text{final block size}}{\text{initial block size}}}\left[s + a + b\left(\frac{A}{W_d} - 1\right)\right].$$

Figure 4.24 shows, from this model, how the effective cache latency changes as the block size increases from 16 to 256 bytes. The memory parameters used in the model are $s = 4$, $a = 4$, $b = 1$, and $W_d = 8$. Cache parameters, from Figure 4.18, are for an 8K-byte unified four-way set associative cache. Initial $P_{miss} = 0.015$ for a 16-byte block and $L = 0.7$.

The significant result of Figure 4.24 is that there is an optimum block size with other memory system parameters fixed. The shallow minimum occurs, for this design, at 64 bytes. With larger block sizes, transport time overwhelms the reduction in P_{miss} and

Figure 4.24 Effective cache latency vs. block size

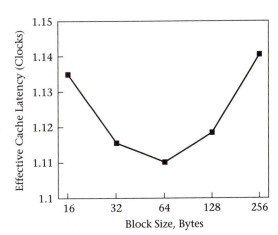

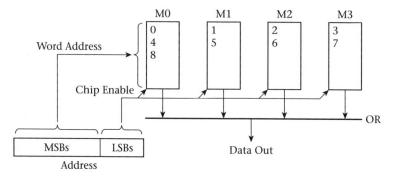

Figure 4.25 Low-order bit interleaving (courtesy Jones and Bartlett Publishers)

the effective cache latency begins to increase. Because of the shallow minimum, other design considerations may shift the block size up or down (32 or 128 bytes) from the optimum value.

This model can be used to evaluate the change in cache latency with a change in other parameters such as cache size, bus width, real-memory interleaving factor, and bus synchronization.

Interleaved Memory Addressing

A method for addressing an interleaved memory is shown in Figure 4.25 for four-way interleaving. The address is divided into two fields; the two LSBs are decoded and provide chip enable signals to each of the four modules. The MSBs are decoded and select the same row from each module. As the LSBs increment, as in reading a block of consecutive AUs, the outputs are OR'd together to provide the data out to the bus.

Note how the addresses are allocated to memory. Module M0 has addresses 0, 4, 8, etc. Module M1 has addresses 1, 5, 9, etc. As long as the address increment is 1, the data out rate will be one AU per clock. However, if the address increment is 2, the data out rate will be one AU per 2 clocks. If the increment is 4, the data out rate will be one AU per 4 clocks. In other words, the speedup of an interleaved memory system over a single memory module is

$$1 \leq \text{speedup} \leq \text{interleaving factor.}$$

EXAMPLE

A four-way interleaved memory system is accessed by an address stream with an increment of 2. What is the speedup of this interleaved memory over a single memory module?

Solution

A timing diagram, similar to Figure 4.23, can be sketched for this problem, shown in Figure 4.26. Five clocks are required for reading the first pair of AUs from M0 and M2. The next read from M0 and M2 takes four additional clocks, and so on. Thus, for this example, the number of clocks per AU is $2n+1$, where n is the number of AUs read from the memory and n is even.

Figure 4.26 Interleaving example

For one memory module, the number of clocks per AU is na clocks, where a is the interleaving factor. Thus the speedup of the interleaved memory over a single module is

$$speedup = \frac{na}{2n+1}.$$

For large n, the speedup is $(4/2) = 2$.

Wide-Word Memory

Another technique for increasing the bandwidth of a memory system is to use a wide-word memory. With this technique, a single memory cycle places a wide word consisting of a number of AUs into a buffer that is then unloaded onto the bus. Figure 4.25 is redrawn in Figure 4.27 to illustrate this technique. The address MSBs access all of the memory modules at one time. Their outputs are simultaneously placed in a buffer. The address LSBs then sequence the data from the buffer onto the data out bus.

This interleaved memory configuration is sometimes called S access because the modules are accessed simultaneously. The speedup of this configuration is identical to that of the C access configuration as shown in Figure 4.23. This configuration has the disadvantage of electrical noise problems as all of the memory module switching transients occur at the same time.

MOS DRAM Organizations

The invention of the MOS DRAM started a major revolution in computer memory design. The first DRAM organization is shown in Figure 4.28. The memory is usually a square array of one-transistor cells. The address MSBs (row address) access the rows and the address LSBs (column address) access one column. A read or write operation involves a single bit on the I/O pin.

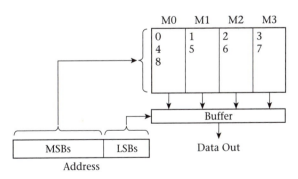

Figure 4.27 Wide-word memory (courtesy Jones and Bartlett Publishers)

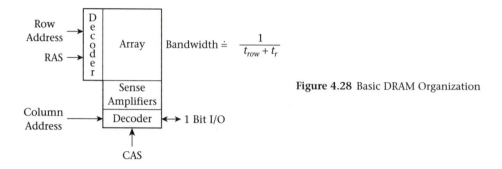

Figure 4.28 Basic DRAM Organization

An approximate and stylized timing diagram is shown in Figure 4.29 for the basic DRAM organization. The row access consisting of the row address and the row address strobe (RAS) starts a read operation. The column access starts after the row access. In general, the row access time is longer than the column access time. For $t_{row} > t_{col}$, the access time is $\approx t_{row}$. After the array is accessed, an additional time t_r is required for returning the various signals to their inactive state. Thus the cycle time is the sum $t_{row} + t_r$.[48] The bandwidth of this organization is one bit per cycle.

Cragon (Cragon 1980) pointed out that as the number of bits accessed in a row is the square root of the array bits, a significant portion of the potential bandwidth of the memory is wasted. For example, a 64K-bit array will access 256 bits in a single row access but only one bit is used. To overcome this waste in bandwidth, there have been a series of improvements to the organization to use the latent bandwidth more effectively.

The following paragraphs discuss only three of the multitude of DRAM organizations that have been produced. For every organization, the design goal has been to reduce the latency (random-access time) and to increase the bandwidth. Please note that different manufacturers use different names and terminology for describing their DRAMs.

These DRAMs operate asynchronously. That is, a controller produces various timing signals to the DRAM chips that sequence the row and column access. The output appears on the I/O pins in some guaranteed time, and it is the responsibility of the memory system designer to see that the outputs are latched into a register. This register can then be read with a system synchronous clock.

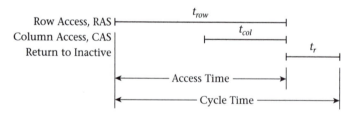

Figure 4.29 Stylized basic DRAM timing

---

[48] There are a large number of other timing parameters, but this simple model permits relative performance evaluation of the various DRAM organizations.

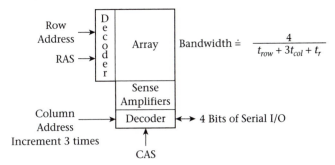

Figure 4.30 Nibble-mode DRAM

Nibble-Mode DRAM. An early variant of the basic DRAM is the nibble-mode DRAM, shown in Figure 4.30. This organization performs a read row access, then four column accesses that place a stream of 4 bits on the I/O pin. The first bit requires t_{row}. Each additional bit requires another column access cycle t_{col}; then t_r is required to complete the operation. Nibble mode provides approximately 90% increase in bandwidth over the basic DRAM organization.

Page-Mode DRAM. The number of bits in a DRAM doubled approximately every 1.5 years over the period from 1978 to 1996, an increase greater than that forecast by Moore's law. As the number of bits in the array increases, the length of the row and column lines increase, thus increasing t_{row} and t_{col} as well. The row and the column time increases are muted because of decreases in geometry. Nevertheless, the random-access cycle time is approximately that given above for the basic DRAM. Thus, DRAM designers adopted an organization similar to that of the wide-word memory discussed in the above subsection and shown in Figure 4.27.

The page-mode DRAM is shown in Figure 4.31. With this organization, B arrays (replication of the basic DRAM of Figure 4.28) are accessed simultaneously with the row address. In parallel, one bit from each bit plane is transferred to the I/O pins; the approximate bandwidth is shown in the figure. Because the arrays are stacked, each array can be smaller and the random access time is reduced over that of a single array

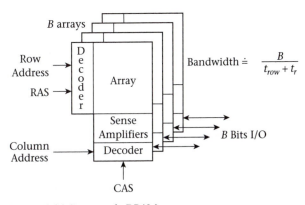

Figure 4.31 Page-mode DRAM

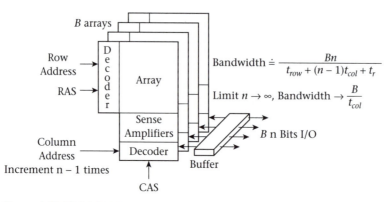

Figure 4.32 EDO DRAM

of equal capacity. If B is 4, the bandwidth of this organization is approximately twice that of the nibble-mode DRAM.

Page-mode DRAMs became practical with the maturity of VLSI and the availability of high pin packages. For example, a 1M bit $\times$ 16 requires 20 address pins and 16 I/O pins plus various control pins.

EDO DRAM. The extended data out DRAM, also know as hyperpage, adds an output buffer to the page-mode DRAM, as shown in Figure 4.32, and uses the incrementing feature of the nibble-mode DRAM. The use of this device is to perform a burst transfer of n words of B bits. The first word of B bits read from the arrays is stored in the buffer; this operation takes a full access time of t_{row}. Then the column addresses are incremented to read the next B bits while the contents of the buffer are transferred to the I/O pins. For large values of n, the streaming bandwidth approaches B/t_{col}.

When compared with that of the page-mode DRAM, the random access time ($n = 1$) has not been improved with this organization but the streaming rate is substantially improved. This improvement is important for applications such as image processing and loading caches. Clearly, the maximum value of n is the number of columns of a single array. If the addresses wrap around to another row, a new row access is required.

EXAMPLE

Assume a 4M-bit EDO DRAM with 8 I/O pins. The array has a column access rate of 33 MHz. What is the maximum streaming bandwidth of this device?

Solution

As one byte is transferred for each column cycle, the streaming bandwidth of this device is 33M bytes per second.

Synchronous-Link DRAM

A typical synchronous-link DRAM (SLDRAM) organization is similar to that of the EDO of Figure 4.32. The difference is that the system provides a clock to the DRAM and all controls are synchronized to that clock. The data input and output are also synchronous to the system clock. This organization permits a more robust memory system design as maximum and minimum access times are avoided. The SLDRAM is specified by an IEEE standards working group; the details of the SLDRAM organization are given by Gillingham and Vogley (1997).

The core of the synchronous DRAM is still the asynchronous device of Figure 4.28. The major difference is that most of the timing control is now on the DRAM chip. Multiple timing signals do not need to be generated and propagated on the memory board.

EXAMPLE

Assume the following DRAM parameters: $t_{row} = 70$ ns, $t_{col} = 25$ ns, and $t_r = 5$ ns. What is the bandwidth (BW) in bits/nanoseconds for the basic, nibble mode, page mode with four arrays, and EDO DRAMs with four arrays and $n = 8$?

Solution

$$\text{basic BW} = \frac{1}{70 + 5} = \frac{1}{75} = 0.013 \text{ bits/ns},$$

$$\text{nibble BW} = \frac{4}{70 + (3 \times 25) + 5} = \frac{4}{150} = 0.026 \text{ bits/ns},$$

$$\text{page BW} = \frac{4}{70 + 5} = \frac{4}{75} = 0.053 \text{ bits/ns},$$

$$\text{EDO BW} = \frac{4 \times 8}{70 + (7 \times 25) + 5} = \frac{32}{250} = 0.128 \text{ bits/ns}.$$

Comment

Each step upward in the complexity of organization approximately doubles the bandwidth of the DRAM. However, the page and the EDO have three additional I/O pins. Note that the burst mode bandwidth limit for the EDO is 0.16 bits/ns for very large values of n.

4.5 VIRTUAL- AND REAL-ADDRESS CACHES

Figure 4.11 shows that the address presented to the cache can be either the virtual address from the processor or the translated real address. Both of these techniques have been used with modern processors. The advantages and disadvantages of the two approaches are presented in Table 4.13. As indicated in this table, popular processors use a form of real-address cache addressing.

Real-address caches can be pipelined to overcome the performance disadvantage of this design. With this design, shown in Figure 4.33, the cache set index and displacement are provided from the virtual-address displacement, which is untranslated. While the cache and its tags are being accessed, the page name is being translated and then compared with the real tags from the cache.

TABLE 4.13 VIRTUAL- AND REAL-ADDRESS CACHES

Design	Advantages	Disadvantages
Virtual Address: Used on: Intel i860 SPUR	No added latency for address translation time. No limit on the size of the cache (can use as many bits of the virtual address as desired).	If only a portion of the virtual address is used for the cache address (to reduce the number of tag bits), different virtual addresses can point to the same cache address, called a synonym or alias.
Real Address: Used on: VAX 11/780 Pentium Pro* IBM RS/6000* IBM S370	Does not have the synonym or alias problem.	Latency added because of the need to translate the address. Latency can be small with a small dedicated TLB.

*Pipelined

Pipelining is described in detail in Chapter 6. However, it should be clear from Figure 4.33 that as long as there is a steady stream of valid addresses to this cache, there will be one cache access per clock. The stream of addresses is interrupted when there is a cache miss or some other delay.

Note that because of the limited number of virtual address displacement bits, 10–14, the size of the cache may be limited. Figure 4.33 shows a direct cache; however, n-way set associative caches can also be used to increase the size of the cache. For a pipelined real-address cache, the maximum cache size is

page size × degree of set associativity.

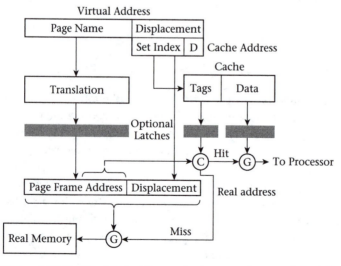

Figure 4.33 Pipelined real-address cache (courtesy Jones and Bartlett Publishers)

EXAMPLE

A byte-addressable processor has a 2K-byte page and a 16-byte block. What degree of set associativity is required for providing a cache of 8K bytes with a pipelined real address cache?

Solution

The virtual address has an 11-bit displacement field. 4 bits are taken from the virtual displacement for the cache displacement into the 16-byte block. This leaves 7 bits for the set index. The required degree of set associativity is

$$\frac{\text{desired cache size}}{\text{page size}} = \frac{2^{13}}{2^{11}} = 4.$$

Comment

This design is identical to the Intel i486 on-chip instruction and data caches. A student may wonder why the number of sets does not enter into the determination of the maximum cache size.

4.6 SEGMENTED VIRTUAL MEMORY

Most of the early thinking on virtual memory systems was based on the idea that real memory was very expensive. For example, 1M byte of core memory for an IBM S360 sold for $1.3M in 1965! Because of the cost of memory, the idea of using fixed-length pages was considered wasteful by many designers because, on average, 1/2 page of real-memory space would be wasted for each allocated working set.[49] It was posited that if the allocation unit is a single AU rather than a page, the exact amount of real memory needed could be allocated for each working set.

This line of thinking led to the concept of a segment, which is a variable-length page with granularity of one AU. Thus on a segment fault, a segment would be loaded into real memory from the virtual-memory disk. However, segmentation leads to a lot of problems. For example, if the system wants to load a segment of 3456 bytes, a vacant contiguous portion of real memory must be found or created that is equal to or larger than 3456 bytes. Unlike paged systems, in which a simple bit vector is used to indicate the use of a page frame, a segmentation system must identify the vacant portions of memory by starting address and length. This information is usually stored in a list that must be searched to find vacant contiguous locations, as the segment cannot be subdivided.

Free space (space that is not allocated to active segments) in real memory must be managed and is usually compacted into one large address space. This means that from time to time the operating system must move the allocated segments in a compact space, reclaim the deallocated space into free space, and compact the free space into contiguous locations. This overhead process has been given the quaint name of compacting garbage collection.

One of the characteristics of a segmentation system is that segments can overlap for sharing of programs and data. Two or more segments can contain the same AUs.

---

[49] Working set is the set of pages allocated to a program that ensures good performance.

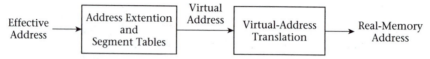

Figure 4.34 Paged segmented address translation

The benefit of sharing opens the possibility of programs that will have bugs; the responsibility to prevent these bugs is given to the software.

After a great deal of research and engineering work was expended on making pure segmentation systems work, the idea was abandoned. There was just too much hardware and software overhead, and the price of memory, the primary justification for segmentation, was going down. However, segment systems are used today in two forms: paged segmentation and virtual segmentation.

Paged Segmentation

Paged segmentation systems are used in most computer systems today for program management purposes. Instead of the allocation unit of one AU for the pure segment system, paged segmentation allocates at the page level. The management of the segments (a collection of pages) is done by the operating system, with some hardware support, and the hardware and software manage pages as described in Section 4.2.

With a paged segmented system, the effective address is extended by concatenation of an extension held in a control register or a table indexed by a portion of the effective address bits, shown in Figure 4.34. Details of the virtual-address translation tables are shown in Figures 4.6 and 4.8.

IBM S370

The complete segmentation and paging tables for the IBM S370 virtual-memory system are shown in Figure 4.35. The 24-bit logical address (effective address) is extended by 18 bits from control register 1 to give a 42-bit virtual address. The S370 24-bit logical address is divided into a segment index, page index, and byte index or displacement.

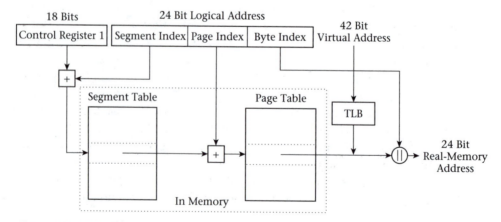

Figure 4.35 IBM S370 virtual-address translation

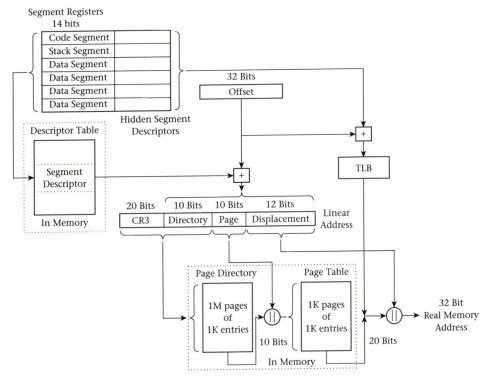

Figure 4.36 Pentium Pro segmentation

The length of the fields in the logical address vary since four configurations can be invoked. The configurations are

64K-byte segment, 4K-byte page   1M-byte segment, 4K-byte page
64K-byte segment, 2K-byte page   1M-byte segment, 2K-byte page

The control register bits are added to the segment index to index into the segment table. Bits from the segment table entry are added to the page index to index into the page table. Bits from the page table are concatenated with the byte index to give the 24-bit real-memory address. The specific allocations to control register 1, the segment table entries, and the page table entries are discussed in Section 8.2.

Because the segment and the page tables are in real memory, these tables are bypassed by the TLB holding pretranslated information.

Intel Pentium Pro

The segmentation scheme of the Intel Pentium Pro is shown in Figure 4.36. The descriptor table has the function of establishing a base address for the linear address. The length of the segment is set by an entry in the segment descriptor table.

14 bits of a 16-bit segment selector, found in a hardware register, indexes into the descriptor table that is allocated to real memory. There are six segment selector registers: one for a code segment, one for a stack segments, and four for data segments.

One of the fields of the segment descriptor provides a base address that is added to the 32-bit offset, giving the 32-bit linear address. The linear address is extended with 20 bits from CR3 and the page name is translated by a two-level table, shown in Figure 4.6.

Because the descriptor table, the page directory, and the page table are in real memory, the memory-based translation path is bypassed by a TLB and hidden segment descriptors in hardware registers. The hidden segment descriptors hold pretranslated segment descriptors, identical to those found in the descriptor table. There is a hidden segment descriptor associated with each of the six segment selectors. Thus there is a fast path for obtaining the 20-bit base address for a real-memory access.

The specific allocations to the selector, segment descriptor, page directory entry, and the page table entry are discussed in Section 8.2.

Virtual Segmentation

Virtual segmentation systems are found today in a number of highly interactive programming systems such as Lotus 1-2-3. This system is highly dynamic, with cells being allocated and deallocated frequently. The number of cells allocated and deallocated is variable, and a paged segmentation system is too inflexible. Thus a primitive pure segmentation system is implemented to automatically perform allocation, deallocation, and garbage collection. On early PCs that used i286 and i386 processors, the time overhead for these tasks was quite noticeable. MSDOS versions of this system even had a red signal that would tell the user when allocation, deallocation, and garbage collection were occurring.

4.7 DISK MEMORY

The lowest-level memory in the hierarchy is the disk. By inference we mean the hard disk in PC terminology; other forms of disks, such as floppies, are not permanently connected and can be considered to be archival. This distinction is discussed further in Chapter 7.

Disks are organized in a series of layers, as shown in Figure 4.37. A disk consists of a number of platters, and each platter has one or two surfaces. Each surface has a number of tracks that are divided into sectors consisting of an even power of 2 bytes. For some disk designs, each track has the same number of sectors. Thus the bit density decreases for the tracks near the periphery of the disk. For other designs, the bit density per track is constant and the number of sectors per track increases near

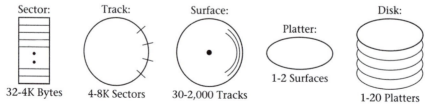

Figure 4.37 Disk organization (courtesy Jones and Bartlett Publishers)

the periphery of the disk. This technique is called a zoned disk. Usually the sector is the addressable unit of the disk; the disk sector should not be confused with the sector of a cache.

Each surface usually has one arm holding a read and a write head or a read/write head. The write heads convert the digital signal to a magnetic signal that polarizes the magnetic surface into a string of 1s and 0s. The read head, because of the rotation of the disk, senses the magnetic flux change and generates a string of ones and zeros. Note that the bit areas on the disk are not patterned (as with DRAM memory chips) but depend on the air gap in the write head to delineate the bit areas as the platter rotates.

The write or read transport time of a disk is the sum of a number of time elements. First, there is the rotational latency. Many disks have only one read/write head per surface and the disk must rotate until the desired sector is in position to be written or read. With rotation rates of 3600 to 10000 RPM, the maximum rotation latency is a full revolution time of 16.6 to 6 ms. The minimum rotation latency is zero, and the average latency is one half of a revolution or, for 5200 RPM, 5.75 ms.[50]

The second component of latency is seek latency. The head must be positioned over the addressed track adding to the latency. Positioning requires that the arm be moved, starting from an at-rest position, accelerated, and then positioned over the desired track. The minimum latency is zero if the head is already on the addressed track, but the maximum latency can be approximately 20 ms or more, depending on the number of tracks on a surface. There are various techniques for reducing seek latency for multiprogrammed computers.

There is additional latency from the operating system of approximately 1 to 2 ms, depending on the complexity of the page fault handler and the speed of the processor. The operating system or page fault handler must translate the binary virtual address into the physical addresses of the disk system: disk, platter, surface, track, and sector.

In addition to the disk latency, the data transfer time to and from the disk must be included in the transport time. The time to actually read or write the data is determined by the size of the sector, the number of contiguous sectors to be transferred, and the bit rate of the read/write process. With modern disks, the transfer rate is in the range of 5M to 15M bits/s for a single head. When multiple heads are used to transfer parallel bit streams, the total transfer rate is a multiple of the single-head rate.

The total disk transport time for a read or write has three latency components plus the transfer time:

$$\text{transport time} = \text{rotational latency} + \text{seek latency}$$
$$+ \text{operating system latency} + \text{transfer time}.$$

EXAMPLES

1. A disk rotates at 5200 RPM and the data transfer rate is 5M bytes/s when driven from 60 cycle power. The average seek time is 25 ms, and the sector is 1K bytes.

---

[50] Laptop computers that stop the disk rotation to conserve battery power will have even longer latencies because of the time (5– 20 s) required for starting the disk.

A 100-MIPS computer has a 4K-byte page and the page fault handler requires the execution of 750,000 instructions.

a. What is the transport time for a page with 60 cycle power?

b. What is the transport time for a page with 50 cycle power?

Solution

a. The latency is $[(5.75 \times 10^{-3}) + (25 \times 10^{-3}) + (7.5 \times 10^{5})]/100 \times 10^{6} \times 10^{-3} = 38.25$ ms. The transfer time is $(4 \times 1024)/(5 \times 10^{6}) = 0.819$ ms. The transport time is $(38.25 \times 10^{-3}) + (0.819 \times 10^{-3}) = 39.07$ ms.

b. At 50 cycles the average rotational latency is 6.9 milliseconds and the data transfer rate is 4.16M bytes/s. The latency is $(6.9 \times 10^{-3}) + (25.00 \times 10^{-3}) + (7.5 \times 10^{-3}) = 39.49$ ms. The transfer time is $(0.819 \times 10^{-3}) \times 60/50 = (0.819 \times 10^{-3}) \times 1.2 = 0.983$ ms. The transport time is $(39.49 \times 10^{-3}) + (0.983 \times 10^{-3}) = 40.47$ ms.

2. A disk has 128 sectors per track with 512 bytes per sector. The rotation rate is 5200 RPM. What is the transfer rate in bytes/second?

Solution

The rotation time is $60/5200 = 11.5$ ms. The transfer rate is $(128 \times 512/11.5) \times 10^{-3} = 5.7$M bytes/s.

Disk Caches

The example above for determining the transport time of a disk illustrates one of the problems with a memory hierarchy. Even though the page fault rate is very low, when a page fault does occur there is a major disruption of program execution while the page fault is being resolved. One solution to this problem is the use of a cache between the real memory and the disk, as shown in Figure 4.38.

There are two options for implementing a disk cache: (1) implement a hardware cache or (2) implement a virtual disk cache in real memory.

On the surface, the first option is straightforward: a designer need only decide on the size and select an organization. A major problem is to decide on the organization of the cache tags. The virtual address produced by the processor is a binary number but the disk address is nonbinary: disk, platter, track, and sector. If these fields are to be allocated to the cache tags, provisions must be made for disk size expansion or for replacement disks that are organized differently. The solution to this problem is to use virtual address in the tags and map the virtual address to the disk address in software when there is a disk cache miss.

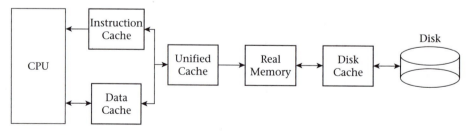

Figure 4.38 Disk cache

The second solution to the disk cache design problem allocates space in real memory for a virtual disk cache and performs all the required functions in software. Even if these functions take several hundred thousand instructions, with a 100-MIPS processor the time is small compared with the transport time of a disk-microseconds rather than milliseconds.

The MSDOS operating system provides for a virtual disk cache. Depending on the amount of memory in the system, the disk cache– a program called SMARTDrive – can be as large as 2M bytes. The page size can be selected by the user, an 8K-byte page being typical. A user also sets the size of the cache, and hit rates of 0.7 to 0.8 are achievable. SMARTDrive supports reads and writes to/from only the file system; it does not support virtual memory.

Windows95 has two virtual caches: one for the virtual-memory system consisting of a program called VCACHE, and the other for CD ROMS, called CDFS. Unlike the SMARTDrive of MSDOS, the size of both of these caches is dynamically set by the operating system. The cache sizes are set by the software to be as large as possible depending on the amount of free memory at any time. The page size of the VCACHE is fixed at 4K bytes.

EXAMPLE

A memory system with a transport time of 50 ms for a 4K-byte page is upgraded with a disk cache. The $P_{hit} = 0.75$ and the transport time for a transfer of a page from the disk cache to real memory is 50 μs. What is the speedup in the transport time given by the disk cache?

Solution

$$\text{Weighted mean transport time} = (0.75 \times 50 \times 10^{-6}) + (0.25 \times 50 \times 10^{-3})$$
$$= 12.5 \times 10^{-3} \text{ s,}$$
$$\text{speedup} = \frac{50 \times 10^{-3}}{12.5 \times 10^{-3}} = 4$$

Comment

This is a good example of Amdahl's law. Three fourths of the time was speeded up almost an infinite amount (RAM speed versus disk speed) and one fourth of the time was not speeded up. Therefore the overall speedup is simply determined as

$$\text{speedup} = \frac{1}{1 - \alpha} = \frac{1}{1 - 0.75} = \frac{1}{0.25} = 4.$$

4.8 SYSTEM OPERATION

We have looked at the components of a virtual-memory system with caches. Now we can tie all of these components together and see what happens to an address and data as they make their way through the system. For expository purposes we consider a data read operation through a system with the following components.

- L1 data cache
    Write hit: write through
    Write miss: no-write allocate
- L2 level unified cache
    Write hit: write through
    Write miss: no-write allocate
- Interleaved real memory: write through (RM)
- Translation lookaside buffer
- Inverted page table
- Disk cache (DC)
    Write hit: write back
    Write miss: no-write allocate
- Disk

A preliminary event table is shown in Table 4.14. The table is called preliminary because each one of the actions may require its own event table. Because the cache policies are write through, the caches, real memory, and the disk cache are assumed to be coherent.

Because the cache policies are write through, the caches can be overwritten when a block is moved to a higher level. With some of the events, the actions can take place in parallel reducing the time for the event. Designers search for parallel paths that can be used to reduce the time of an event.

TABLE 4.14 READ ACCESS MEMORY SYSTEM EVENTS

L1	L2	RM	DC	Disk	Action
Hit	×	×	×	×	Read datum from L1 into processor
Miss	Hit	×	×	×	Read datum from L2 into processor Overwrite block from L2 into L1
Miss	Miss	Hit	×	×	Translate address in TLB or tables Read datum from RM into processor Overwrite block from real memory into L2 Overwrite block from real memory into L1
Miss	Miss	Miss	Hit	×	Translate address into disk cache addresses Read datum from disk cache into processor Overwrite page into RM Overwrite block into L2 Overwrite block into L1 Update TLB
Miss	Miss	Miss	Miss	Hit	If page in disk cache is modified, evict to disk and read page into disk cache. If page in RM is modified, evict to disk and read page into RM. Restart the read access

For example, the case of L1 and L2 cache misses and RM hit; as soon as the datum is in the processor, the processor may proceed. Also, the transfers into the two caches can take place in parallel with the transfer to the processor. However, if there is a following cache access before the transfers are complete, that access may stall. Another example is the TLB, which can be searched in parallel with the start of the table search for address translation.

REFERENCES

Cragon, H. G. (1980). "The Elements of Single-Chip Microcomputer Architecture," *Computer*, **13**:10, pp. 27– 41.

Flynn, M. J. (1966). "Very High-Speed Computing Systems," *Proceedings of the IEEE*, **54**:12.

Gee, J. D., Hill, M. D., Pnevmatikatos, D. N., and Smith, A. J. (1993). "Cache Performance of the SPEC92 Benchmark Suit," *IEEE Micro*, **13**:4, pp. 17–27.

Gillingham, P. and Vogley, B. (1997). "SLDRAM: High-Performance, Open-Standard Memory," *IEEE Micro*, **17**:6, pp. 29– 39.

IBM (1976). "IBM System/370 Principles of Operation," Order GA22-7000-5.

Kilburn, T., Edwards, D. B. G., Lanigan, M. J., and Summer, F. H. (1962). "One-Level Storage System," *IRE Transactions on Electronic Computers*, **7**:4.

Lewis, T. G. and Cook, C. R. (1988). "Hashing for Dynamic and Static Internal Tables," *Computer*, **21**:10, pp. 45–56.

Milligan, M. K. and Cragon, H. G. (1995). "Processor Implementations Using Queues," *IEEE Micro*, **15**:4.

Saavedra, R. H. and Smith A. J. (1993). "Measuring Cache and TLB Performance and Their Effect on Benchmark Run Times," Report USCB/CSD 93/767, University of California, Berkeley.

Smith, A. J. (1987). "Line (Block) Size Choice for CPU Cache Memories," *IEEE Transactions on Computers*, **C-36**:9.

EXERCISES

4.1 There are two write hit and two write miss policies, giving four possible designs. List these four designs and discuss the feasibility of each.

4.2 An instruction cache is large enough to hold a loop. What is the instruction cache P_{miss} for a loop that is executed 50,100, and 200 times?

4.3 Derive a model for the effective cache latency of Figure 4.24. Take the first derivative, set to zero, and solve for the minimum.

4.4 Comment on the performance of an interleaved memory if the degree of interleaving is a prime number: 3, 5, 7 etc., rather than an even power of 2.

4.5 Discuss the problem of synonyms or aliases that are characteristics of virtual-address caches.

4.6 The issue of increasing the size of a pipelined real-address cache has been discussed. Using the data on the data miss rate for the SPEC benchmarks, determine the change in P_{miss} of the i486 cache for the degree of associativity: 1, 2, 4, and 8.

4.7 Refer to the discussion on zoned disks on disks in Section 4.7. Discuss the issue of transfer rates for the two techniques of assigning sectors to tracks.

4.8 Discuss the problems associated with a branch-and-link instruction that places the link in memory if the memory system has a cache.

4.9 Modify the t_{elrm} model found on model derived in Table 4.4 to comprehend a TLB.

4.10 Explain why a valid bit is needed to detect a cache hit. Why isn't a tag comparison sufficient?

4.11 The figures showing direct and inverted page tables do not show valid bits. Are valid bits needed? Explain your answer.

4.12 Figure 4.26 shows the S370 address translation path. Assume the following. Accessing the segment table and the page table in real memory takes four memory cycles each. Accessing the TLB takes 0.1 memory cycles. The TLB has a hit rate of 0.95. What is the effective address translation time for the S370?

4.13 Figure 4.33 shows that the Intel Pentium Pro TLB uses as its input the virtual or the linear address. How does this architecture overcome the delay of accessing the descriptor table?

4.14 Explain how the Intel page directory table is indexed with 30 bits if the real memory address is 32 bits.

4.15 Rework the example on the weighted average number of probes for the inverted student class file on file of Table 4.8 and Figure 4.8. Use two hashing schemes: the hash is the three least-significant digits and the hash is the one least-significant digit. Recall that, when the two least-significant digits are used, the weighted average number of probes is 1.32.

4.16 Compute and plot the effective cache latency for bus widths of 1, 2, 4, 8, 16, and 32 bytes by using the parameters of the example on page 167. Use a 64 byte block.

4.17 Table 4.8 shows P_{miss} for instruction caches and Table 4.9 shows P_{miss} for data caches. Is it possible to construct a reasonable estimate of the data in Table 4.10 by using the data from Tables 4.8 and 4.9? If so, construct the table; if not, explain why not.

4.18 The text mentions that a five-way set associative cache can be designed. Explain the advantages and the disadvantages of this design. Is a prime-number-way interleaving advantageous or disadvantageous?

4.19 Construct the event table, similar to Table 4.13, for a data write.

4.20 Assign miss rates and action times for Table 4.13 and compute a weighted average memory write time.

4.21 Redraw Figures 4.12 and 4.13 to reflect the modern cache designs that have one block slot per sector.

FIVE

PROCESSOR CONTROL DESIGN

5.0 INTRODUCTION

Recall that Figure 3.1 shows the interface between software translation and hardware interpretation of a program written in a high-level language. This chapter now describes two methods of performing the hardware translation: hardwired control and microprogramming. Today, a state diagram is routinely used to show the sequence of events required for interpreting an instruction.

A state diagram for instruction interpretation is shown in Figure 5.1 (Bell and Newell 1971). This state diagram represents a very early ISA and shows the serial execution model of the interpretation cycle; one instruction completes before another instruction begins. The three upper states are controlled by the memory, and the five lower states are controlled by the processor. Also, any state can be null to represent the interpretation of another instruction.

As a vehicle for describing hardwired and microprogrammed control, a simple load/store register file machine is used as an example. The example processor has three instruction classes: register ALU, load/store, and branch. The instruction formats for the three classes of instructions are shown below:

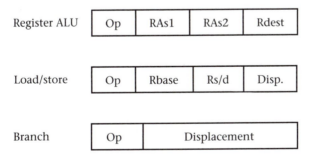

The register ALU instructions have two source and one destination operands, all in the register file. The addressing mode for the load/store instructions is base plus displacement with the base value stored in the register file. The branch instruction tests the sign bit of R1 much as the von Neumann ISA tested the contents of the accumulator. The branch target address is the program counter plus the displacement.

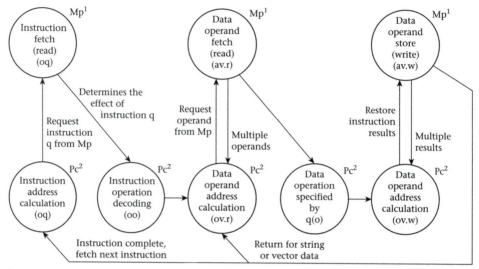

¹Mp controlled state
²Pc controlled state
  Note: Any state may be null

State name	Time in a state	Meaning
soq/oq	toq	Operation to determine the instruction q
saq/aq	taq	Access (to Mp) for the instruction q
so.o/o.o	to.o	Operation to decode the operation of q
sov.r/ov.r	tov.r	Operation to determine the variable address v
sav.r/av.r	tav.r	Access (to Mp) read the variable v
so/o	to	Operation specified in q
sov.w/ov.w	tov.w	Operation to determine the variable address v
sav.w/av.w	tav.w	Access (to Mp) to write variable v

Figure 5.1 Processor state diagram (courtesy McGraw-Hill Companies Inc.)

The type of ALU instructions and the field lengths of the instructions are ignored so that the ideas behind the design of the control unit are not obscured.

Before the details of the control are discussed, we must first look at what is controlled. For modern processor implementations the processor registers are configured into a data path. The data path to be described provides the resources to interpret the three instruction classes noted above.

Data Path

As discussed in Chapters 1 and 3, there are a number of registers within the processor. These registers are of two types: architected registers that can be accessed by the program (the register file for example) and implemented registers that are used by the control hardware as instruction side effects (the memory-address register for example). The control state machine must have the ability to load and store information in both register types.

In early computers, all of the processor registers were interconnected by point-to-point paths required by specific instructions. Modern design techniques, brought about by the desire for regular interconnections, connect these registers by means of one or more buses. A simple example of a data path is shown in Figure 5.2; this data

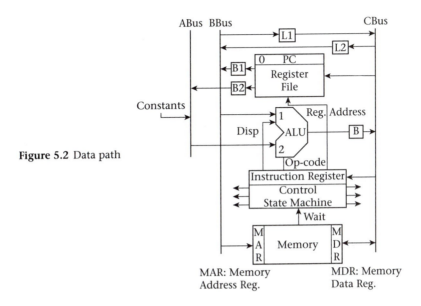

ABus BBus   CBus

Figure 5.2 Data path

MAR: Memory   MDR: Memory
Address Reg.   Data Reg.

path will be used in the following discussions of hardwired and microprogrammed control design.

The data path has three buses so that dyadic operations can be performed in one clock. In addition to the three buses, there are some dedicated transfer paths that do not map well onto a bus. These dedicated paths are associated primarily with the instruction register (the register that holds the instruction while the instruction is being executed). The various fields of the instruction are directly connected to the needed destination. For example, the op-code is connected to the control state machine and to the ALU. The address displacement is a special input to the ALU. Register addresses are input to the register file.

Because the BBus and CBus need to communicate, two links (L1 and L2) are provided. Also note that the program counter is location 0 of the register file and that there is an input to the ABus for constants such as +1, 0, −1. A buffer is placed on the output of the ALU that is loaded with the results of each ALU operation. This buffer is needed because of the long logic path of the ALU. There is also a special path from memory to signal the control state machine when a wait is required. The control state machine provides sequencing through the states and provides the logic control signals that enable the transfers to/from the bus.

Low-performance data paths can be implemented with only one bus. A two-bus data path provided additional concurrency and additional performance. These one- and two-bus data paths are valid design options for situations for which cost is more important than performances, such as some embedded microprocessors.

5.1 HARDWIRED CONTROL

We first look at hardwired control. This is a technique whereby the designers commit the control design to a state machine. The advantage of this technique is primarily speed. One can usually design a hardwired control state machine that operates at a faster clock rate and in fewer states than a microprogammed controller, to be described later in Section 5.2. A characteristic of hardwired control is that the hardware cost of the control state machine is approximately proportional to the number of instructions in the macro ISA.

The major disadvantage of hardwired control is lack of flexibility. Once the design of the control state machine is completed, a change to correct a design error or an addition to the ISA may necessitate the complete redesign of the control state machine. And, if the control state machine is implemented on a chip, the complete chip must be redesigned. Early computer designers tended to make corrections to the control state machine and data path with yellow wire. As the quantity of yellow wire increased, one had a sure indication of the difficulty of this type of design. In the sections to follow, the data path and the design technique of hardwired control state machines are described.

The basis of hardwired control is a state machine that sequences through the states of a state diagram, generating the proper control signals to the data path at each state. The state diagram is the basis for the design of a hardware state machine. This design task is accomplished by five steps.

1. Construct the state diagram.
2. Identify transfer paths on the data path.
3. Make secondary state assignments.
4. Construct a state transition truth table.
5. Write the input equations for the flip flops.

Construct State Diagram

A load/store architecture has a simple state diagram, as shown in Figure 5.3. The first step in interpretation is to fetch an instruction pointed to by the program counter. The instruction is decoded, and if the instructions require register values, the registers are accessed. The next state either computes the effective address (EA) for a memory operation or executes the function called for by the op-code. The memory state performs its read/write operations for load/store instructions. The write to register file state writes the result of an operation or the datum obtained by a load instruction. Finally, the PC

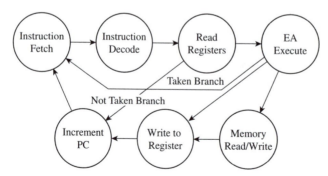

Figure 5.3 Processor state diagram

TABLE 5.1 INSTRUCTION CLASSES AND STATE USE

	Inst. Fetch	Inst. Decode	Read Registers	EA Execute	Memory R/W	Write to Register	Increment PC
ALU	X	X	X	EX		X	X
Load	X	X		EA	R	X	X
Store	X	X	X	EA	W		X
T Branch	X	X	X	EA			
NT Branch	X	X	X				X

is incremented, and the process starts over. Table 5.1 shows the states of Figure 5.3 and the instruction classes that use those states.

The state diagram of Figure 5.3 is now redrawn in Figure 5.4 to show more details of the actual flow of instruction types through the state diagram. Note that all instructions use the instruction fetch and the instruction decode states. At the decoding state, the path diverges, depending on the instruction class. Because the instruction fetch and memory read/write will access memory, there may be wait states for a slow memory to respond. If the processor has caches, a wait is required when there is a cache miss.

Branch instructions, if taken, compute the target address and return to the instruction fetch state. If the branch is not taken, the program counter is incremented with a return to the instruction fetch state.

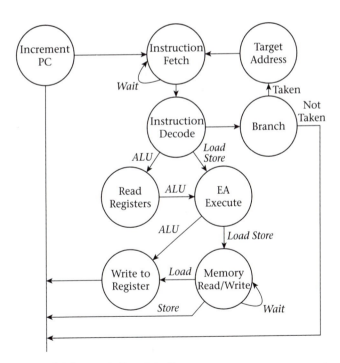

Figure 5.4 Interpretation state diagram

Identify Transfer Paths on the Data Path

The following tableau of nine drawings, Figures 5.5a–5.5i, show the flow paths that are enabled during each of the states in Figure 5.4. Transfers between registers take one clock. The memory cycle time is one clock plus any wait states. Some of the groupings of states are arbitrary; a transfer could have been placed with another function. The transfer paths are identified by shading and the number of clocks is listed for each of the nine functions.

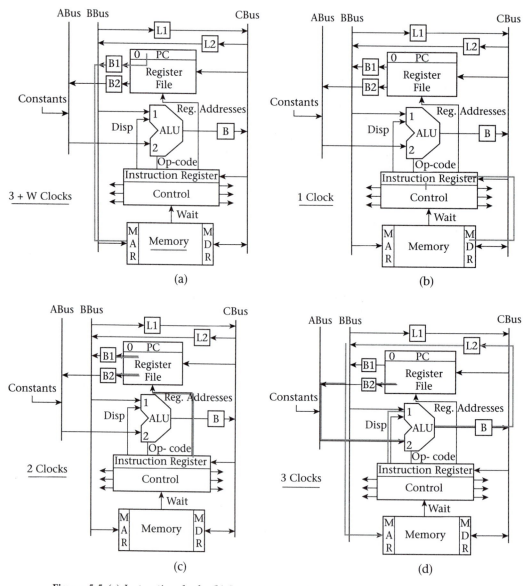

Figure 5.5 (a) Instruction fetch; (b) Instruction decode; (c) Register select; (d) Effective address; (e) Execute; (f) Memory read load; (g) Memory write store; (h) Memory increment PC; (i) Branch target address

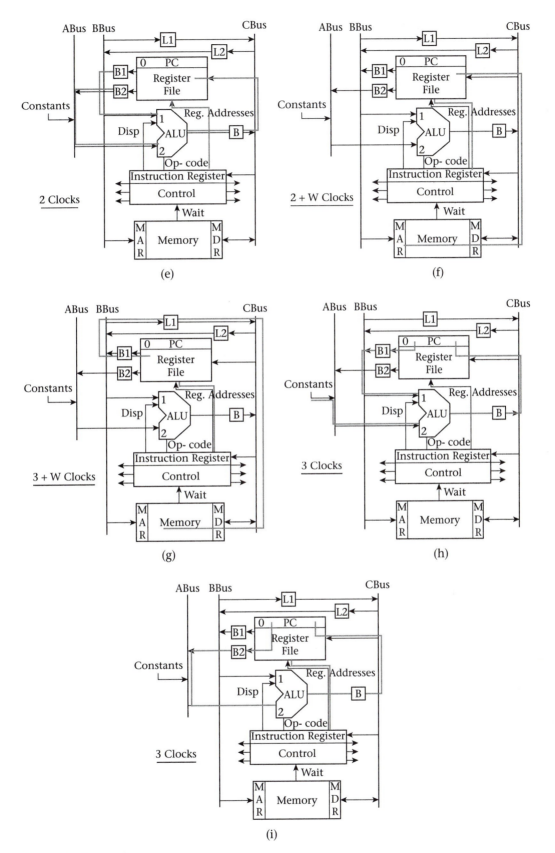

Figure 5.5 (*Continued*)

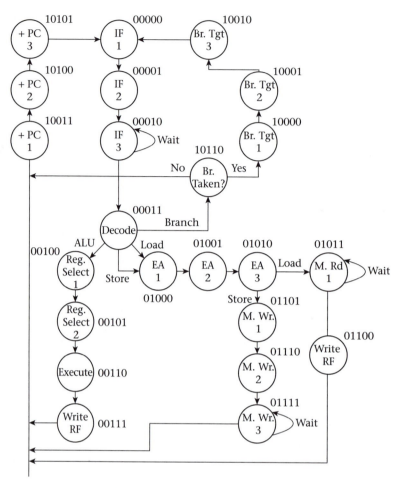

Figure 5.6 Expanded state diagram

Refine State Diagram and Make Secondary State Assignments

With the transfer paths identified in Figures 5.5a–5.5i and the required clocks per function, the state diagram of Figure 5.4 is now redrawn in Figure 5.6. Each state of the expanded state diagram is implemented to take one clock. Only when there is a wait signal from memory will a state require more than one clock.

With the state diagram of Figure 5.6, we now make the secondary state assignments. With 23 states, 5 flip flops are required for uniquely defining the states.[51] The secondary state assignments are shown adjacent to each state symbol in Figure 5.6. State machine designers will recognize that this secondary state assignment, when

---

[51] Some designers will use more than the minimum number of flip flops to be prepared for expansion in the ISA. A valid design can also be a state machine with one flip flop per state, only one of which will be a 1 at any time.

implemented, may not yield the minimum number of gates. The secondary state assignment was chosen without regard to implementation complexity.

Construct State Transition Truth Table

The state transition truth table is shown in Table 5.2. Assume that an op-code decoder generates four control signals, A, L, S, and B, for the instruction types in addition to the control signals to the ALU for selecting the operation. The memory generates the wait signal W. The ? signal is generated by the sign bit of register R1; if a branch is to be taken, ? is 1. Don't cares are indicated by x in the table.

TABLE 5.2 STATE TRANSITION TRUTH TABLE

Present State	Branch ?	Wait W	ALU A	Load L	Store S	Branch B	Next State
00000	x	x	x	x	x	x	00001
00001	x	x	x	x	x	x	00010
00010	x	1	x	x	x	x	00010
00010	x	0	x	x	x	x	00011
00011	x	x	1	x	x	x	00100
00011	x	x	x	1	x	x	01000
00011	x	x	x	x	1	x	01000
00011	x	x	x	x	x	1	10110
00100	x	x	x	x	x	x	00101
00101	x	x	1	x	x	x	00110
00011	x	x	x	x	x	x	00111
00111	x	x	x	x	x	x	10011
01000	x	x	x	x	x	x	01001
01001	x	x	x	x	x	x	01010
01010	x	x	x	1	x	x	01011
01010	x	x	x	x	1	x	01101
01011	x	1	x	x	x	x	01011
01011	x	0	x	x	1	x	01100
01100	x	x	x	x	x	x	10011
01101	x	x	x	x	x	x	01110
01110	x	x	x	x	x	x	01111
01111	x	1	x	x	x	x	01111
01111	x	0	x	x	x	x	10011
10000	x	x	x	x	x	x	10001
10001	x	x	x	x	x	x	10010
10010	x	x	x	x	x	x	00000
10011	x	x	x	x	x	x	10100
10100	x	x	x	x	x	x	10101
10101	x	x	x	x	x	x	00000
10110	1	x	x	x	x	x	10000
10110	0	x	x	x	x	x	10011

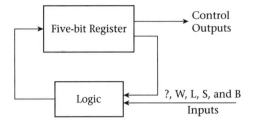

Figure 5.7 Control state machine

Write Input Equations for the Flip Flops

The control state machine, similar to that of Figure 1.1, is redrawn in Figure 5.7. The memory is a 5-bit register with inputs ?, W, A, L, S, and B along with the present state of the register bits. The control state machine transitions from state to state, generating control outputs that enable the transfer gates in the data path.

The 5-bit state register is implemented with SR flip flops named a, b, c, d, and e, reading from left to right in the secondary state assignment. The input equations for flip flop a are given below in minterm form as they would be implemented with a programmable logic array (PLA):

$$S_a = a'\,b'\,c'\,d\,e\,B + a'b'c\,d\,e + a'\,b\,c\,d'\,e' + a'\,b\,c\,d\,e\,W',$$
$$R_a = a\,b'\,c'\,d\,e' + a\,b'\,c\,d'\,e.$$

EXAMPLE

There are 23 states shown in Figure 5.6 whereas the state transition truth table has 31 entries. Why the difference?

Solution

As designed, the state transition truth table must have one entry for every outar-row of the state diagram. Count them: there are 31.

We see that this implementation of the control state machine by using a data path results in the different classes of instructions taking a different number of clocks. The number of memory wait state clocks must be added to the number of clocks required for stepping through the expanded state diagram of Figure 5.6. Note that the logic paths of the branch instructions are the same for taken and not taken.

ALU:	$11 + W$ clocks
Branch:	$8 + W$ clocks
Load:	$12 + 2W$ clocks
Store:	$13 + 2W$ clocks

EXAMPLE

Assume that the weights of the instruction classes are ALU-0.30, branch-0.30, load-0.25, and store-0.15. Assume that the processor has a cache and that there are no wait states on a cache hit but 10 wait states on a miss. The P_{miss} of the cache is 0.10. What is the CPI of the processor?

Solution

The CPI of this processor is the weighted mean of the clocks for each class of instruction. The number of wait state clocks is determined by

$$W = (1 - P_{miss}) \times 0 + P_{miss} \times 10 = 10 P_{miss}$$
$$= 10 \times 0.1 = 1 \text{clock}.$$
$$\text{CPI} = \text{ALU weight} \times \text{ALU clocks} + \text{branch weight} \times \text{branch clocks}$$
$$+ \text{load weight} \times \text{load clocks} + \text{store weight} \times \text{store clocks}$$
$$= 0.3(11 + 1) + 0.3(8 + 1) + 0.25(12 + 2) + 0.15(13 + 2)$$
$$= 3.6 + 2.7 + 3.5 + 2.25 = 12.05.$$

Comment

Computers with hardwired control and a data path similar to that of Figure 5.4 have CPIs in the range of 10 to 15. Thus this example is typical of computers of that type. Note that reducing P_{miss} by 1/2 would improve the CPI of this processor approximately 10%. Other improvements can come from eliminating clocks from the logic path. For example, one clock eliminated from the instruction fetch function will improve performance by approximately 8%.

5.2 MICROPROGRAMMED CONTROL

M. V. Wilkes first posited the idea that the best way to design a computer was to replace a hardwired control state machine with a simple control computer (Wilkes 1951). The control computer would have a very simple micro ISA and could be designed and built with few errors. The macro ISA would then be interpreted by a program, called a microprogram, running on the control computer having a micro ISA.[52] Figure 3.1 is redrawn in Figure 5.8 to show the two levels of software translation that are used with microprogrammed control.[53]

Figure 5.8 Microprogrammed lexical levels

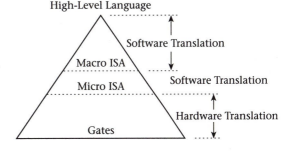

---

[52] The terms macro ISA and micro ISA are used to distinguish between the two ISAs.
[53] The software that executes on the micro ISA is sometimes called firmware because it is stored in ROM and it is between the hardware and software; thus it is firm.

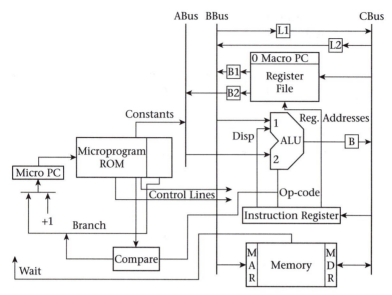

Figure 5.9 Microprogrammed control

Errors in or additions to the macro ISA could be accommodated by simple programming changes, not rewiring with yellow wire as was the current practice with hardwired control. Because of the high cost of ROM in the 1950s, microprogramming was not applied until the introduction of the IBM S360 family in the 1960s (Hellerman 1967). All members of this computer family were microprogrammed except for the highest-performance model.

Figure 5.2, showing the data path with a hardwired control state machine, is redrawn in Figure 5.9 to incorporate microprogrammed control. There are a number of important points to be noted in this figure. One can, in most cases, identify a microprogammed processor because there are two program counters: the micro PC and the macro PC. In some rare designs, a micro PC is not used and the microprogram is in the form of a linked list, a design technique mentioned in Chapter 3.

The micro PC is similar to the macro PC. Its normal sequence is to be incremented for each microinstruction executed. However, a taken microprogram branch will cause the micro PC to be loaded with a branch address from the microprogram ROM. Branches are taken when a field in the current microprogram instruction is compared with an input field with a true result. The fields may be 1 or more bits. The initial bootstrap value in the micro PC points to the instruction fetch microcode segment.

Microinstruction Set Architecture

We now discuss the technique for designing the micro ISA for the interpretation of macroinstructions. The micro-control unit interprets the macroinstructions by means of another program, called a microprogram, which is in the language of the micro ISA. As we will see, the micro ISA is unusual because the requirements for the interpretation consist mainly of transfers of bits or words from one register to another. The micro ISA has two instruction types: move and branch.

Move Microinstruction. The micro ISA has a move instruction that transfers information between the various registers, both architected and implemented, of the data path. The first step in the design of the move microinstruction is to identify the sources and destinations. To accomplish this step, we list the transfer paths from Figures 5.5a to 5.5i by using a register transfer language. The form of the move microinstruction is (source)→destination:

Instruction Fetch
>   Clock 1: (R0) → B1
>   Clock 2: (B1) → MAR
>   Clock 3+Wait: (Mem(MAR)) → MDR

Instruction Decode
>   (MDR) → IR
>   Case op-code; Add: go to Add
>   Load: go to load
>   Store: go to store
>   Branch: go to branch

Register Select, for ALU operations[54]
>   Clock 1: R(IR,RAs1) → B1
>   Clock 2: R(IR,RAs2) → B2

Effective Address [Base + Displacement]
>   Clock 1: (R(IR, Rbase)) → B2
>   Clock 2: (B2) → ALU2
>   (IR, displacement) → ALU1
>   Clock 3: (B) → CBus
>   (CBus) → BBus
>   (BBus) → MAR

Execute[55]
>   Clock 1: (B1) → ALU1
>   (B2) → ALU2
>   Clock 2: (B) → R(IR, Rdest)

Memory Read
>   Clock 1+wait: (Mem(MAR)) → MDR
>   Clock 2: (MDR) → R(IR, Rdest)

---

[54] The terminology (IR,RAs1) means the RAs1 field of the IR register.
[55] The ALU output buffer is implicitly loaded by each microinstruction that uses the ALU.

Memory Write

        Clock 1: (R(IR, RAs1)) → B1

        Clock 2: (B1) → MDR BBus

             (BBus) → CBus

             (CBus) → MDR

        Clock 3+W: (MDR) → Mem(MAR)

Increment PC

        Clock 1: (R0) → B1

        Clock 2: (B1) → ALU1

             +1 → ALU2

        Clock 3: (B) → R0

Branch Target Address (PC relative)

        Clock 1: (R0) → B2

        Clock 2: (B2) → ABus

             (ABus) → ALU2

             (IR ,Displacement) → ALU1

        Clock 3: (B) → R0

Having identified the transfer paths, we have two options for designing the move microinstruction(s):

1. We can tabulate the unique move microinstructions in the list above, (R0) → B2 for example, and have a unique op-code for each. As there are 19 such unique operations, a 5-bit op-code will suffice.
2. Use a single-bit op-code for the two microinstructions move and branch and have a source field and a destination field. This orthogonal approach will use more microinstruction bits but will provide maximum flexibility for expansion and changes.

For this example design, the second, orthogonal, approach is taken. We now list the sources and destinations required by the move microinstruction in Table 5.3. The data path design assumed that the buses do not have registers for staging; a transfer by means of a bus is accomplished by enabling the bus source and the destination ports.

For example, the contents of B1 are transferred to ALU1 by the BBus, the microinstruction Move, B1, ALU1 is used. Note that the fields of the IR are explicitly defined when a field is used as a source: for example, Move, IR, RAs2, B1 moves the RAs2 field of the macroinstruction register to B1. The macro op-code field is wired to the ALU and invoked along with the ALU when there are valid inputs to the ALU.

Branch Microinstructions. The microprogram must be able to branch. Recall from Figure 5.6 that several states have multiple outputs, an example being the decode state. Thus the micro ISA must have branch instructions, both conditional and unconditional. For this design, there are two conditional branches and one unconditional branch instruction plus the special branch when memory signals a wait:

TABLE 5.3 SOURCES AND DESTINATIONS

Sources	Destinations
R0	R0
B1	B1
B2	B2
B	MAR
R (IR, RAs1)	ALU1
R (IR, RAs2)	ALU2
R (IR, base)	R(IR, Rdest.)
Mem(MAR)	Mem(MAR)
MDR	MDR
IR, displacement	IR
Constant field	

1. The conditional branch tests the sign of register R1 and branches if positive.
2. The microinstruction also has a constant field that holds the op-codes of the macro ISA. This field is compared with the macro ISA op-codes to implement the case statement for the decode function.
3. An unconditional branch is needed to return to the beginning of a microinstruction sequence.
4. When the memory generates a wait signal, the microprogram counter is quiescent; it remains in its present state for another clock. In other words, the microprogram branches to its present location. Symbolically this branch is

$$(PC) \ W \rightarrow PC.$$

Expanded op-codes are used to uniquely define three of the branch types. The branch target address is a direct address allocated to the microinstruction. Direct addressing is chosen because of the time required for making the addition for PC relative branching and the relatively small number of branch target address bits required. The size of the branch target address depends on the expected size of the microprogram.

Microinstruction Format. What is the format of a microinstruction? Because there are only two instruction types (transfer and branch), the op-code is 1 bit. The source, destination, and constant fields have been discussed. The ALU/Mem field is two bits, which enables the ALU to perform the operation specified by the macro ISA op-code and also enables the memory for a read or write cycle:

Op	Source	Destination	Constant	ALU/Mem	Control	Branch Address

The control field specifies miscellaneous functions such as signifying that the branch microinstruction is unconditional. Codes in the control field define the three types of conditional branches and the unconditional branch instructions.

EXAMPLE

How can the three functions of the ALU/Mem field be specified with 2 bits?

Solution

There are a number of solutions to this example; one possible solution is

00 Enable ALU
11 Memory read
10 Memory write

Microprogram: The interpreter of the macro ISA can now be programmed in the language of the micro ISA. Figure 5.10 shows the program for two of the

#	Op	Source	Destination	Constant	ALU/Mem	Control	Branch Address	Comments
0	1	R0	B1					Inst. Fetch
1	1	B1	MAR					"
2	1	Mem(MAR)	MDR		M read			"
3	1	MDR	IR					"
4	0			ALU		Comp.	10	Decode
5	0			Load		Comp.	20	"
6	0			Store		Comp.	30	"
7	0			Branch		Comp.	40	"
8								
9								
10	1	R(IR, RAs1)	B1					ALU
11	1	R(IR, RAs2)	B2					"
12	1	B1	ALU1					"
13	1	B2	ALU2		ALU			"
14	1	B	R(IR, RAdest)					"
15	1	R0	B1					Increment PC
16	1	B1	ALU1					"
17			ALU2	+1				"
18	1	B	R0					"
19	0					Uncon.	0	Return to Inst. Fetch
•								
•								
40	0					test sign	46	Branch
41	1	R0	B1					Increment PC
42	1	B1	ALU1					"
43	1		ALU2	+1				"
44	1	B	R0					"
45	0					Unco.	0	Return to Inst. Fetch
46	1	R0	B1					Branch target
47	1	B1	ALU2					"
48	1	IR, RAdisp	ALU1					"
49	1	B	MAR					"
50	0					Uncon.	0	Return to Inst. Fetch
51								

Figure 5.10 ALU and branch microprograms

macroinstruction types, ALU and branch. This microprogram follows the state diagram of Figure 5.6. Recall that the first thing to do is to fetch the macroinstruction. This task is accomplished by the microinstructions in locations 0–3.

Following the macroinstruction fetch, the macro op-code is decoded by a sequence of four microbranch instructions. The branch addresses of these four instructions spread out the microinstructions for the four macroinstruction types. Once the microprogram has been debugged, it can be compacted to reduce the size of the microprogram memory.

The ALU macroinstruction type is implemented in locations 10–14, and the macroprogram counter is incremented by the microinstructions in locations 15–18. An unconditional branch returns the microprogram counter to location 0 to start the fetch of the next macroinstruction.

The macrobranch instruction begins with location 40, where the sign bit of R1 is tested. If not true, the program counter is incremented by the microinstructions in locations 41–44. The microinstruction in location 45 returns unconditionally to location 0 to start the fetch of the next macroinstruction.

From Figure 5.10 we can determine the CPI of the two implemented macroinstruction types. The ALU instruction requires $15 + W$ clocks whereas the branch instruction requires $14 + W$ clocks for both the taken and the not-taken paths. This performance is poorer than that of the hardwired implementation, which has a CPI for the ALU instructions of $11 + W$ clocks and $8 + W$ clocks for the branch instruction.

Let us examine the sources of the loss of performance. This examination will show where design changes could be made that would improve the performance of microprogrammed control.

1. The decode function is performed in one clock with the hardwired state machine. If the microinstruction ISA is implemented with a four-way branch instruction, decoding can be accomplished in one clock.

Branch	Cond 1	Dest 1	Cond 2	Dest 2	Cond 3	Dest 3	Cond 4	Dest 4

2. Two clocks (two microinstructions) are needed to load the MAR in the microinstruction fetch sequence. A transfer path directly from the register file to the MAR would eliminate this extra clock.

3. Two clocks (two microinstructions) are needed to load the register file buffers B1 and B2 for ALU macroinstructions. This task was performed in one clock with the hardwired state machine control because a dual-ported register file is assumed. To save one clock with a microprogrammed controller, a dual-ported register file is needed as well as additional source and destination fields in the microinstruction format.

4. An explicit unconditional microinstruction branch is required at the end of each sequence to return to the macroinstruction fetch sequence. This clock is not required with the hardwired state machine. A design technique that eliminates these

clocks is to give every microinstruction branching capability in addition to its primary function.[56]

The microinstruction format used above has the ability to do a few simple functions in parallel. However, increasing the amount of concurrency in the data path permits more functions to be performed in parallel, thereby increasing the speed of the processor. Additional parallelism is illustrated in the four ideas discussed above for improving performance. With increased data path concurrency, the length of the microinstruction must be increased as well. Thus it is not unusual to see microinstructions of 100 bits or more.

Microprogrammed processors with short microinstructions are called vertical microprogrammed because a sequence of microinstructions are required for performing a function. Microprogrammed processors with long microinstructions are called horizontal microprogrammed because one microinstruction can perform several functions in one clock.

EXAMPLE

The frequency of use of macroinstruction classes are ALU-0.30, branch-0.30, load-0.25, and store-0.15. What is the weighted average number of microinstructions required for performing the decode function?

Solution

From Figure 5.10 we see that the test for an ALU instruction is made followed by a test for load, store, and branch. Thus the weighted average number of microinstructions is

$$\text{Weighted average} = (0.3 \times 1) + (0.25 \times 2) + (0.15 \times 3) + (0.3 \times 4)$$
$$= 0.3 + 0.5 + 0.45 + 1.2$$
$$= 2.45 \text{ microinstructions.}$$

Comment

The use of a four-way branch microinstruction will reduce the weighted mean CPI of the processor by almost one and one half clocks or approximately 10%.

Size of the Microprogram

A few comments on the size of the microprogram are in order. For the implementation of an ISA, such as the IBM S360, a number of steps (microinstructions) are required for each of the macroinstructions. The sum of these steps is the number of microinstructions required in the ROM for a given micro ISA design. There is ample evidence that the number of bits required for implementing an ISA is a constant, not the number of steps. This means that

bits × words [horizontal] ≈ bits × words [vertical].

Table 5.4 shows the organization of the microprogram memory of four models of the IBM S370 (Case and Padegs 1978). The average size of the memory for these four

---

[56] A popular microprocessor, ARM, uses this technique at the macro ISA level.

TABLE 5.4 IBM S370 MICROPROGRAM MEMORY

Model	Words	Bits/Word	Total Bits
135	24K	16	384K
145	12K	32	384K
155	6K	69	414K
165-II	4K	105	420K
		AVERAGE	400K

models is 400K bits. The implication of this observation on microprogram memory is that a designer can trade off the complexity of the data path (more or less concurrency) for performance without significantly changing the number of bits in the microprogram. The organization of the ROM will change, but not the approximate number of bits.

EXAMPLE

We wish to evaluate the cost of microprogramming compared with that of hardwired control. Microprogramming has a fixed cost of 1000 units of chip area and a variable cost of 1 unit of chip area for the ROM to store each microinstruction. Hardwired control has a cost of 5 units of chip for each instruction. What is the break-even cost for these two design techniques?

Solution

The cost for the microprogrammed control, where n is the number of instructions implemented, is

$$\text{cost(M)} = 1000 + n.$$

The cost of the hardwired control is

$$\text{cost(H)} = 5n.$$

Equate these two costs and solve for n to find the break-even point:

$$\text{cost(M)} = \text{cost(H)},$$

$$1000 + 1n = 5n,$$

$$n = 1000/4 = 250 \text{ instructions}.$$

Comments

This model suggests that for rich CISC ISAs, microprogramming was the design of choice, as in the case of the IBM S360 family. Simple ISAs with only a few instructions are economically implemented with hardwired control.

REFERENCES

Bell, C. G. and Newell, A. (1971). *Computer Structures: Readings and Examples*, McGraw-Hill, New York.

Case, R. P. and Padegs, A. (1978). "Architecture of the IBM System/370," *Communications of the ACM,* **21**:1, pp. 73–96.

Hellerman, H. (1967). *Digital Computer System Principles,* McGraw-Hill, New York.

Wilkes, M. V. (1951). "The Best Way to Design an Automatic Calculating Machine," *Manchester University Computer Inaugural Conference,* published by Ferranti Ltd., London.

EXERCISES

5.1 For the example hardwired design, write the input equations using T and JK flip flops.

5.2 For hardwired control, assume that the increment PC states can be subsumed by the instruction fetch states and that the target address state is subsumed by the EA execute state if the clock is lengthened by 10%:

a. Draw the state transition flow-chart.

b. Derive the input equations for JK flip flops.

c. What is the speedup of this implementation over the eight state implementation?

5.3 Explain why a hardwired control unit was used with the fastest model of the IBM S360 whereas microprogrammed control was used with the lower-performance models.

5.4 An alternative way to design a hardwired state machine is to use one flip flop per state rather than encoding the states as shown in the example. Using T flip flops, write the input equations for this design technique.

5.5 Consult the library and find evidence that the number of bits of a microprogram for a given ISA is approximately equal regardless of the speed of the processor. There is available information on the IBM S360 and DEC VAX. You must look.

5.6 Write the microprogram for the macroload instruction.

5.7 Because most macroinstructions require several microinstructions for executing, what happens to the microprocessor if there is an external interrupt in the middle of the instruction execution? Are there design alternatives?

5.8 Some microprogrammed control units have the ability to call microsubroutines. What changes must be made to Figure 5.9 to provide this facility? Recall the discussion on the necessary facilities for subroutines in Chapters 1 and 3.

5.9 From the state diagram of Figure 5.1, determine the internal register organization (accumulator, register file, stack, etc.) of the processor.

5.10 Table 5.3 shows the state transition truth table for the state diagram of Figure 5.6. Instead of encoding the states with five flip flops, use one JK flip flop per state (23 flip flops). Write the J and K input equations for this control state machine.

5.11 Complete the logic equations for the b, c, d, and e flip flops for the State transition truth table of Table 5.2.

5.12   For the micro ISA, what are the operations, data types, and addresses?

5.13   Show how the microprogram of Figure 5.10 can be rewritten to use a common body of code for incrementing the program counter.

5.14   Design the state machine for the control of the von Neumann ISA described in Chapter 1.

5.15   Explain how one would design a microprogrammed processor without a macro-program counter or a microprogram counters by using linked lists.

5.16   Is the micro control unit of Figure 5.9 a Harvard or a von Neumann architecture? Explain your answer.

5.17   Can the micro control unit of Figure 5.9 execute subroutines? Explain your answer.

SIX

PIPELINED PROCESSORS

6.0 INTRODUCTION

Chapter 5 described the design of serial execution model processors that have either hardwired or microprogrammed control. In this chapter, the techniques used in pipelining are described. Pipelining, sometimes called assembly line processing, has its roots in manufacturing technology. Auto pioneer Henry Ford is generally credited with developing the assembly line for constructing the Model T automobile. There is an unverified story that Ford visited a packing plant in Chicago and saw the disassembly of beef cattle. He is said to have observed that if one can take something apart on a disassembly line then one can do the reverse. Thus the germ of an idea was planted.

A pipelined processor has functional units for each function performed in the interpretation of an instruction. In some cases, the functional units perform more than one operation. Instructions flow into the pipeline and results flow out. The transit time (latency) through the pipeline may be long, but in most cases it is the rate of flow through the pipeline that is important. This is also true of the pipeline that brings water into your home. You don't care how many miles or days it took the water to get to you from the lake; you are only concerned that the flow rate is sufficient.

Base Pipelined Processor

As discussed in Chapter 5 and shown in Figure 5.4, the steps required for interpreting an instruction of the load/store ISA are as follows:

1. Fetch instruction.
2. Decode instruction.
3. Read registers.
4. Execute.
5. Compute effective addresses for data and branch target.
6. Read or write memory.
7. Write to register.
8. Test for a branch.
9. Increment program counter.

Stage 1	Stage 2	Stage 3	Stage 4	Stage 5
Inst. Fetch Increment PC	Decode Read Registers	Eff. Address Execute Branch Test	Memory Read/Write	Write to Register

Figure 6.1 Base pipeline

These functions can be grouped into pipeline stages, as illustrated in Figure 6.1, a pipeline similar to the MIPS R2000 pipeline. This pipeline is chosen because of its simplicity; more modern pipelines such as the Intel Pentium Pro and the IBM S390 are quite complicated and do not serve as well for instructional purposes. In the discussions to follow, this pipeline will be referred to as the base pipeline.

Stage 1 performs the instruction fetch and increments the program counter for the next instruction fetch. Stage 2 also performs two functions: it decodes the instruction and fetches the source operands from the register file. Stage 3 performs one of three functions: computes the memory effective address if the instruction is a load, store, or branch; executes the integer operation; or performs the branch test. Stage 4 performs the memory read or write if the instruction is a load or store. Stage 5 writes the results of an integer operation to the register file or writes the output of a load instruction to the register file.

Note that the 9 functions map onto 5 stages. This is possible because some functions are not dependent (they can be done at the same time); for example an instruction can be fetched and the program counter incremented at the same time. In addition, some functions are not used for a particular instruction. For another example, an effective address calculation is not needed with a register add instruction, thus these functions can use the same arithmetic unit.

6.1 PERFORMANCE MODELS

As noted in the introduction, the rate of flow of instructions through the pipeline is the processing rate. The processing rate is usually measured in instructions per unit of time. Because the clock of a processor is time based, processing rate is measured in instructions per clock (IPC) or its reciprocal, clocks per instruction (CPI). IPC and CPI are equal to 1 when the work is flowing smoothly through the pipeline without delays.[57] However, there are events that cause delays or stalls in the pipeline, and CPI is defined as

$$CPI = 1 + delays.$$

The primary goal of the designer of a pipelined processor is to have delays that approach zero. Section 6.3 of this chapter describes the source of delays and the techniques for reducing them.

Pipelines present a problem in performance modeling and analysis because actions take place in a space/time relationship. This modeling and analysis problem is best

---

[57] Superscalar processors, discussed in Section 6.5, have a steady-state CPI less than 1.

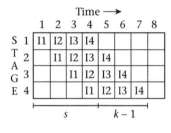

Time ⟶
	1	2	3	4	5	6	7	8
S 1	I1	I2	I3	I4				
T 2		I1	I2	I3	I4			
A 3			I1	I2	I3	I4		
G 4				I1	I2	I3	I4	
E								

Figure 6.2 Reservation table by stages (courtesy Jones and Bartlett Publishers)

Time ⟶
	1	2	3	4	5	6	7	8	9
Inst. 1	S1	S2	S3	S4					
Inst. 2		S1	S2	S3	S4				
Inst. 3			S1	S2	S3	S4			
Inst. 4				S1	S2	S3	S4		

Figure 6.3 Reservation table by instructions (courtesy Jones and Bartlett Publishers)

Time ⟶
	1	2	3	4	5	6	7	8
S 1	I1	I2	I3	I4				
T 2		I1	I2	I3	I4			
A 3			I1	I2	I3	I4		
G 4				I1	I2	I3	I4	
E								

s $k-1$

Figure 6.4 Pipeline model reservation table

solved by use of reservation tables (Davidson 1971). Two commonly used forms of reservation tables are shown in Figures 6.2 and 6.3. Figure 6.2 shows time, in clocks, moving from left to right, and the stages of the pipeline are shown in the vertical axis. One can follow an instruction down the pipeline. For example I1 starts in Stage 1 at t1 and is in the last stage, S4 at t4. At t4, four instructions, I1, I2, I3, and I4, are shown in the pipeline. A variation of this type of reservation table is used in manufacturers' literature to show the activity on memory interfaces, bus activity, and the like. Instead of stages, these drawings show various signal lines or signatures.

The other form of reservation table also uses time as the horizontal axis whereas the vertical axis displays the instructions, as shown in Figure 6.3. One follows the progress of an instruction with this reservation table by reading horizontally. Instruction I3 is in Stage 1 at t3, then Stage 2 at t4, and so on. This form of reservation table is used in manufacturers' literature to show the progress of instructions through a pipeline.

The first form of reservation table is prefered for a number of reasons. This form, being similar to what would be seen with a logic probe, seems more natural to electrical engineers. In addition, the second form has a practical problem in drafting: As the number of instructions followed increases, the chart grows in two dimensions whereas the first form grows in only one dimension.

Using reservation tables, we now derive the basic performance model of a pipeline as shown in Figure 6.4. A four-instruction sequence is broken by some event such as a taken branch or another type of delay. To generalize, the length of the sequence is k and the number of stages in the pipeline is s. Thus the number of clocks required for executing this sequence is

$$s + k - 1,$$

and

$$\text{CPI} = \frac{s + k - 1}{k} = 1 + \frac{s - 1}{k} = 1 + \frac{1}{k}(s - 1).$$

Note that this is the same form given early in this section: $\text{CPI} = 1 + \text{delays}$. By examining the limits of this model, we gain insight into the limits of pipeline performance:

As $k \to \infty$, $\text{CPI} \to 1$,
and as $k \to 1$, $\text{CPI} \to s$;
thus $1 \leq \text{CPI} \leq s$.

This means that CPI can be as bad as s (which may suggest the design of short pipelines) or as good as 1 if the sequence of unbroken instructions is long enough.

A serial execution model processor requires a number of steps for completing one instruction before another instruction can begin. A pipeline of s stages is functionally equivalent to a serial processor that requires s steps.[58] Thus the speedup of a pipelined processor compared with that of the serial execution model processor is

$$\text{speedup} = \frac{\text{number of clocks (serial)}}{\text{number of clocks (pipelined)}} = \frac{sk}{s + k - 1} = \frac{s}{1 + \frac{s-1}{k}}.$$

As $k \to \infty$, $\text{speedup} \to s$,
and as $k \to 1$, $\text{speedup} \to 1$;
thus $1 \leq \text{speedup} \leq s$.

From this speedup model we can conclude that we may want to design a pipeline with a large number of stages – the opposite conclusion from the models presented previously. What then is the proper length of a pipeline?

6.2 PIPELINE PARTITIONING

The models developed above seem ambivalent regarding the number of stages in a pipeline. To resolve this issue we will subdivide a pipeline into more and more stages, see if there is an optimum number of stages, and find an answer to this design problem.

Start with a one-stage pipeline, as shown in Figure 6.5. If there are enough logic levels between two registers, the complete interpretation of an instruction can be done in one clock. The clock period will be long, but one clock is all that is needed. Assume that the logic path can be divided into two stages. Because the length of the logic path is now $L/2$ gates, the clock period can be reduced by 1/2, and we have a two-stage pipeline with an additional register. The pipeline can then be divided into more and

---

[58] Note that the average number of states shown in Table 5.1 is 5.2. This is close to the number of stages in the basic pipeline of Figure 6.1.

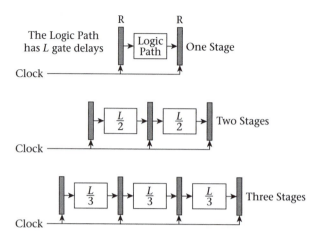

Figure 6.5 Pipeline partitioning

more stages, as shown for $L/3$. The general case is to divide the pipeline into s stages. What then is s for maximum performance of the pipeline?

The execution time of a sequence of instructions is the number of clocks × clock period = $(s + k - 1)$ clock period. What is the clock period? A first approximation is that the clock period (in gate delays) is equal to L/s because the single stage of length L has been subdivided into s stages.[59] However, there is a practical problem with this approximation.

For performance purposes, latches are used for the registers rather than memory elements such as JK flip flops. The use of latches leads to a number of problems in circuit design. First, all the logic paths in a stage must be of equal length (equal delay) so that the logic inputs arrive at all latches of the register at the same time. Second, the clock has to be distributed to all the register latches. Because of wiring problems on the chip, the clock distribution paths to the register latches will not have equal delay, resulting in clock skew (Kogge 1981).[60] Last, the latches have setup time that must be accommodated in the clock period.

Figure 6.6 shows the logic path between two latches. The clock is distributed from a common source, assumed to be placed very near to latch 1. The logic propagation delay L/s plus any output drive delays is $t(\max)$. The clock for latch 2 must be of sufficient width for the setup time of the latch; this time is w. Because of the delays in clock distribution, there can be skew time α between the clock of latch 1 and latch 2. Thus the minimum clock period is

$$T(\text{clock}, \min) = t(\max) + \alpha + w,$$
$$t(\max) = L/s.$$

---

[59] Division of L into equal parts may not always be possible; dummy logic stages must be added to the short stages to ensure error-free clocking.

[60] The first recognition known to the author of the clock skew problem was with the MARK I in 1942. The electromechanical switches were driven from a common shaft with independent gears. The subdivision of one rotation of the shaft into cycles had to accommodate the backlash in the gears and the delay in energizing clutches.

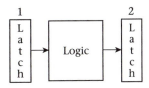

Figure 6.6 Clock period with skew and setup time

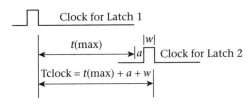

The sum of clock skew α and the latch setup time w is τ. Thus the execution time for a multistage pipeline is

$$(s + k - 1)\left(\frac{L}{s} + \tau\right).$$

To find the optimum number of pipeline stages, we take the derivative of the execution time with respect to s, set to zero, and solve for the optimum value of s.

$$s_{opt} = \sqrt{\frac{L(k - 1)}{\tau}}.$$

If the value of τ can be reduced, the optimum number of pipeline stages can be increased, thereby increasing the performance by reducing the execution time of a pipelined processor.

EXAMPLE

For a single-stage pipelined processor with $L = 128$ and an instruction sequence $k = 4$, plot the execution time for $s = 1$ to 128 for $\tau = 2$ and 4.

Solution

The solution to this problem is found by applying the parameters to the pipeline execution time equation. The base 2 logarithm of the number of stages is used in Figure 6.7.

Comments

Figure 6.7 shows that the optimum number of pipeline stages is approximately 16 for $\tau = 2$. The minimum is shallow, so finding the exact number of stages is not within the accuracy of this model. Early RISC processors had 4–5 pipeline stages; they are described as underpipelined because the number of stages is smaller than the stages for maximum performance. Most modern pipelined processors have 10–16 stages. Also shown is the reduction in processing time that can be achieved by reducing the value of τ from 4 to 2. Reducing clock skew on VLSI circuits is a major design issue today.

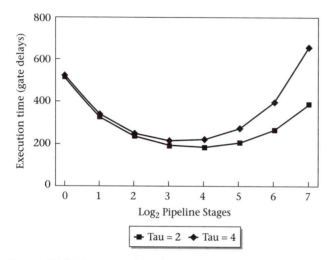

Figure 6.7 Optimum number of pipeline stages

Another design consideration regarding partitioning of a pipeline into stages is balancing the logic level in the stages. Stage 3 of the base pipeline performs two functions: decoding and reading the registers. Other pipelines, such as the Intel Pentium integer pipeline, decode in one stage and select the operand registers in the execution stage. The designer has great latitude in making pipeline partitioning. The design issue is that, to the greatest extent possible, the logic paths of all stages should be equal.

Because all the registers are clocked from a common source, the clock period is the maximum of the sum of individual stage logic delays and τ:

$$\text{clock period} = \text{MAX}[(L1 + \tau), (L2 + \tau), \ldots, (Ls + \tau)].$$

EXAMPLES

1. A processor is partitioned into a pipeline of five stages. The number of logic levels per stage is 8, 13, 10, 11, 12, and τ is 2 gate delays. What is the clock period for this processor in gate delays?

    Solution
    The clock period is

    $$\text{MAX}[(8+2), (13+2), (10+2), (11+2), (12+2)] = 15 \text{ gate delays.}$$

2. Given the pipeline from the example above, the designer can divide the second-stage logic path into two stages of 6 and 7 gate delays. Using the base pipeline model with pipeline delays of $s-1$ and a sequence of four instructions for $k = 4$, is this a wise design?

    Solution
    The new clock period is MAX(10, 8, 9, 12, 13, 14) = 14 gate delays. The execution time, in gate delays, for each of the designs is

    $$\text{execution time} = (s + k - 1) \text{ (clock period)},$$

    $$\text{execution time (first design)} = (5 + 4 - 1)15 = 120 \text{ gate delays,}$$

    $$\text{execution time (second design)} = (6 + 4 - 1)14 = 126 \text{ gate delays.}$$

Comment

This is an example of exploring design alternatives with analytic models. The first design is slightly faster and may be selected. However, recognize the limits of these models, and if there is some compelling implementation reason for using one or the other design, that design should be selected.

6.3 PIPELINE DELAYS

We now return to the problem of delays and how to reduce their effects. The models we have used to this point have had a delay of $s - 1$ at the end of each sequence of k instructions. This delay is the worst case for any processor design and will serve as a starting point for the following discussions. Delays with a pipelined processor come from the following five sources.

1. Memory delays: the latency of a memory reference is greater than one clock. Chapter 3 addressed the control of memory delays.
2. Branch delays: a change of program control to a noncontiguous instruction.
3. Structural hazard delays: the processor must stall because two or more instructions are competing for the same hardware resource.
4. Data hazard delays: an instruction stalls because of data dependencies between instructions.
5. Interrupt delays: the program is interrupted, the interrupt handler is placed in execution; when the handler completes, the program counter control is returned to the interrupted program.

As noted above, in the steady state the pipeline processes one instruction per clock. However, there are various delays that must be added to the steady-state time. There are two aspects of delays: the probability that an instruction will encounter or cause a delay, P_i, and the magnitude of the delay when it is encounted or caused, D_i. The pipeline CPI model was given as

$$\text{CPI} = 1 + \frac{1}{k}(s - 1).$$

In this form, $1/k$ is the probability that an instruction can result in a delay $(s - 1)$. To generalize,

$$\text{CPI} = 1 + \sum_{i=1}^{n} P_i D_i.$$

This simple linear combination of delays overstates the impact that delays have on a pipeline. For example, a cache delay may hide or cover a data hazard delay. Nevertheless, this model does provide insight into the effects, both singularly and in combination, of delays on pipeline performance. In general, this model gives a worst-case estimate of CPI.

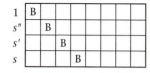

Figure 6.8 Branch strategy reservation table

6.3.1 BRANCH DELAYS

A conditional branch instruction will result in one of two outcomes: (1) the branch is not taken and the in-line instruction sequence continues, or (2) the branch is taken and a change in the value of the program counter starts another sequence. The outcome of a conditional branch will not be known until late in the pipeline. If the instruction sequence is to be changed, a number of instructions will have been partially processed and will have to be abandoned, causing a significant delay.

Two parameters are used in evaluating branching strategies. The first is the probability that an executed instruction is a branch, P_b. The second is the weighted average branch delay (WABD) for taken and not-taken branches. The CPI of the processor with branch delays is

$$\text{CPI} = 1 + P_b \, \text{WABD}.$$

The goal of branch strategy design is the reduction or elimination of WABD, thereby making CPI approach 1. The parameter P_b is determined by the executing program and cannot be influenced by the design of the branch strategy.

Figure 6.8 shows how we use reservation tables to analyze branching strategies. For this analysis, we assign the following symbols to the pipeline stages that play a role in branch strategy design:

Stage 1: the instruction fetch stage
Stage s'': the decode stage
Stage s': the stage at which the effective address of the target is known
Stage s: the stage at which the branch outcome is known.[61]

The relationship for these stages is $s'' \leq s' \leq s$ when numbering the stages from 1, the instruction fetch stage. The symbol B indicates the flow of a branch instruction down the pipeline. For example, the base pipeline of Figure 6.1 has $s'' = 2$, $s' = 3$, and $s = 3$. The branch instruction, denoted B, starts at stage 1 and progresses to stage s.

Pipeline Freeze Strategy

A study of executing branch statistics shows that approximately 60% of all branch instructions are taken and 40% are not taken – continuing in the sequence. We define P_{bt} to be the probability that a branch will be taken. Based on the statistics just cited, $P_{bt} = 0.6$, and $1 - P_{bt} = 0.4$. The parameters P_b and P_{bt} are called the workload parameters in the following paragraphs.

---

[61] It is not necessary that s'', s', and s be different stages. The Berkeley RISC I had $s'' = s' = s = 2$.

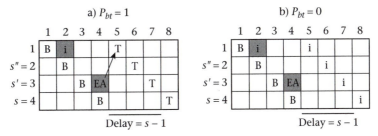

Figure 6.9 Pipeline freeze strategy

The simplest branch strategy that we can think of is to freeze the pipeline when a branch instruction is decoded in s''. Fetching of instructions is halted until the outcome of the branch is known at s. This strategy is shown in Figure 6.9.

We want to determine the WABD of this strategy so that the CPI can be determined. There are two cases to consider: case a), in which the branch is taken ($P_{bt} = 1$); and case b), in which it is not taken ($P_{bt} = 0$).

Case a) $P_{bt} = 1$ shows how the branch strategy works when the branch is taken. The branch is decoded in s'' at t2. In addition at t2, the in-line instruction i following the branch B has been fetched. Because the decoded instruction is a branch, instruction i is abandoned (indicated by shading) and no further instructions are fetched while the branch instruction works its way down the pipeline. At t3, the effective address is computed in s' and saved in a buffer (a buffer is not required if $s' = s$). At t4, the outcome of the branch is known to be taken and the target instruction T is fetched with the effective address in the buffer, which is then cleared. The delay for this case is $s - 1$ clocks.

In like fashion we look at case b), $P_{bt} = 0$, when the branch is not taken. When the not-taken outcome of the branch is know at t4, instruction i is refetched and the in-line stream starts down the pipeline. The delay for this event is $s - 1$.

For the freeze branch strategy the WABD is

$$\text{WABD(freeze)} = P_{bt}(s - 1) + (1 - P_{bt})(s - 1) = s - 1.$$

The probability that an instruction is a branch instruction has been defined as P_b. Thus the CPI of a pipeline by use of the freeze strategy is

$$\text{CPI(freeze)} = 1 + P_b\,\text{WABD} = 1 + P_b(s - 1).$$

For this strategy, the taken and the not-taken branches have the same delay, $(s - 1)$. Thus this model is the same as the basic model developed previously from Figure 6.4 in which $1/k = P_b$.

EXAMPLES

1. Consider a pipeline with $s'' = 1$, $s' = 3$, and $s = 4$. The workload characteristics are $P_b = 0.3$ and $P_{bt} = 0.65$. What is the CPI of this pipeline?

Solution

$$CPI = 1 + P_b(s - 1),$$
$$CPI = 1 + 0.3(4 - 1) = 1 + 0.9 = 1.9.$$

Comment

Because of branching, the steady-state performance of this pipeline has degenerated from CPI = 1 to CPI = 1.9, a 90% loss in performance.

2. If stage s is combined with stage s', requiring that the clock be lengthened by 20%, is performance improved?

Solution

$$CPI = 1 + 0.3(3 - 1) = 1.6,$$
$$\text{execution time} = CPI \times \text{clock period} = 1.6 \times 1.2 = 1.92.$$

There is a reduction in performance; $S = 1.9/1.92 = 0.989$.

Comment

The difference in performance is very small and the design could go either way, depending on the actual increase in the clock period.

Predict Take Strategy

The freeze strategy is a very poor strategy from the point of view of performance. Can we do better? Perhaps we can take advantage of the knowledge that approximately 60% of all branches are taken and wire this knowledge into the hardware. The reservation table for such a strategy is shown in Figure 6.10. The case for the branch being taken is shown on the left, case a). When a branch is decoded at stage s'', the fetching of the in-line instructions is terminated and the instructions already fetched are abandoned. When the effective address is known in s' at t3, the target is fetched on the next clock, t4, before the outcome of the branch is known.[62] We do this because we are predicting that the branch will be taken. When this prediction is correct, the delay is $s' - 1$.

When the branch is not taken, as shown by case b), not only are the in-line instructions abandoned but the prefetched target instruction is as well, because the prediction

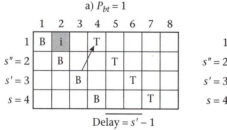
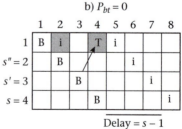

Figure 6.10 Predict take strategy

---

[62] Called speculative execution.

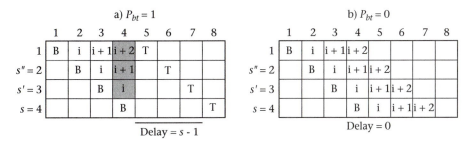

Figure 6.11 Predict not-take strategy

was wrong. The first in-line instruction must be refetched. The delay for this case is $s - 1$.

We can now derive the WABD and CPI for the predict take strategy:

$$\text{WABD(PT)} = P_{bt}(s' - 1) + (1 - P_{bt})(s - 1) = s - 1 - P_{bt}(s - s'),$$

and

$$\text{CPI(PT)} = 1 + P_b \text{ WABD} = 1 + P_b[s - 1 - P_{bt}(s - s')].$$

Predict Not-Take Strategy

Why not investigate a branch strategy that predicts that the branch will not be taken, the opposite of the predict take strategy? The reservation table for this strategy is shown in Figure 6.11.

As the hardware is predicting that the branch will not be taken, the strategy speculatively fetches as many in-line instructions as possible; $(s - 1)$ or three instructions in this example. The hardware waits until the outcome of the branch is known at stage s before fetching the target instruction. The branch target address must be saved in a buffer with this example. If the prediction is wrong and the branch is taken, as shown for case a) of Figure 6.11, the delay is $s - 1$. However, if the branch is not taken as predicted, the delay is zero, as shown with case b).

The WABD and CPI are derived as

$$\text{WABD(PNT)} = P_{bt}(s - 1) + (1 - P_{bt})0 = P_{bt}(s - 1),$$

and

$$\text{CPI(PNT)} = 1 + P_b P_{bt}(s - 1).$$

EXAMPLE

Use the pipeline and workload data from the prior example, compute the CPI for the predict take and predict not-take strategies, and compare them with the CPI for the freeze strategy.

Solution

$$CPI(PT) = 1 + 0.3[4 - 1 - 0.6(4 - 3)] = 1.72,$$
$$CPI(PNT) = 1 + 0.3 \times 0.6(4 - 1) = 1.54,$$
$$CPI(F) = 1 + 0.3 \times 3 = 1.9.$$

Comments

These results show that a significant reduction in CPI can be achieved by applying prediction strategies. The most interesting thing is that the predict not-take strategy is the best of the three, even though branches are most often taken. The reason for this is that there is a big win, zero delay, for the not-taken case that constitutes $\sim$40% of all branches. This result seems to be counter to Amdahl's law that says to speed up the most frequent case. However, if the event probabilities are approximately equal and a major reduction in the time of the smaller event probability can be achieved, then that design option should be explored; it may be the best design option.

General Prediction for Branch Target Buffers and Caches

The models developed above are based on the idea that the prediction, either taken or not taken, is a designer's choice and is wired into the processor. Is it possible to be smarter than this and have the prediction adjusted dynamically as the program executes? The answer is yes: dynamic prediction is a feasible design option and can further reduce the CPI of a processor.

When looking at the two strategies above, we see that with a dynamic prediction system there are four possible events. These events and the delays from Figures 6.10 and 6.11 are tabulated in Table 6.1.

A perfect predictor (a predictor that correctly predicts both the taken and the not-taken branches) will ensure that only the first and the fourth events will ever occur; the second and the third events will never occur. The accuracy of prediction is called A_p, and for a perfect predictor, $A_p = 1$.

The event probabilities with perfect prediction are shown in Table 6.2. Because the predictor is perfect, the probability of the first event is P_{bt} and that of the fourth event is $1 - P_{bt}$. The other two events have zero probability. This leads to the WABD model

$$WABD(A_p = 1) = P_{bt}(s' - 1) + (1 - P_{bt})0 = P_{bt}(s' - 1),$$

TABLE 6.1 GENERAL PREDICTION EVENTS AND DELAYS

Predict	Actual	Delay
Take	Taken	$s' - 1$
Take	Not taken	$s - 1$
Not take	Taken	$s - 1$
Not take	Not taken	0

TABLE 6.2 PERFECT PREDICTION

Predict	Actual	Probability	Delay
Take	Taken	P_{bt}	$s' - 1$
Take	Not taken	0	$s - 1$
Not take	Taken	0	$s - 1$
Not take	Not taken	$1 - P_{bt}$	0

and

$$\text{CPI}(A_p = 1) = 1 + P_b P_{bt}(s' - 1).$$

This result is remarkable in that, with a perfect predictor, the location of stage s' is paramount whereas the location of s, is not important. Thus the designer who wants to design a good branch strategy to reduce CPI has two tasks:

1. To devise a good predictor.
2. To place s' early in the pipeline (if $s' = 1$ and $A_p = 1$, then WABD = 0).

Remember that there can be a trade-off here. Stages can be combined to move s' forward, reducing CPI at the expense of a longer clock period. This may or may not improve performance, but the effect can be modeled. We will consider other techniques for placing s' early in the pipeline in later paragraphs.

Dynamic Branch Prediction

The first requirement for a high-performance branch strategy is a good branch predictor. In this section we discuss branch predictors that dynamically modify the prediction as the program executes. These dynamic techniques adjust the prediction on each unique branch instruction as it is executed. There are three general forms of dynamic branch prediction: (1) predict based on branch instruction characteristics, (2) predict based on target address characteristics, and (3) predict based on history. See Cragon (1991) for a more complete discussion on branch prediction.

Branch Instruction Characteristics

A straightforward branch instruction characteristic is to provide a bit in the branch instruction that can be set by the programmer/compiler. This bit will instruct the processor as to the most likely direction of the branch; the bit is not modified during execution. For example, if a loop is being programmed, the branch direction bit will be set to take the branch. If the loop is executed 100 times, the prediction will be accurate 99% of the time. A branch prediction bit is used in the PowerPC branch instruction.

The branch instruction op-codes provide insight for making branch predictions at stage s''. For example, an unconditional branch is always taken and should therefore always be predicted as taken. Statistical analysis of branch instruction op-codes shows

TABLE 6.3 BRANCH EVENTS AND DELAYS

Branch Type	Strategy	Actual	Probability	Delay
Conditional	PNT	Taken	$(1 - P_{uncb})P_{cbt}$	$s - 1$
Conditional	PNT	Not taken	$(1 - P_{uncb})(1 - P_{cbt})$	0
Unconditional	PT	Taken	P_{uncb}	$s' - 1$
Unconditional	PT	Not taken	0	0

SUM $= 1$

that the conditional branch instructions also have patterns of taken and not taken that can be used for prediction (Lee 1984).

EXAMPLE

Consider a branch strategy based on the branch instruction op-code. All unconditional branches are predicted taken and all conditional branches are predicted not taken. The fraction of all branches that are unconditional is P_{uncb}.

a. What is the WABD for this strategy?

b. Using the statistics of the previous examples and $P_{uncb} = 0.3$, find the CPI of the processor.

Solution

We can approach this problem by constructing a table of event probabilities and their delays. To solve this problem, we define P_{cbt} as the probability that a conditional branch is taken. Recall that P_{bt} is the probability that all branches are taken. In Table 6.3, the four possible states of the branch strategy are listed along with their event probabilities and delays.

From Table 6.3,

$$WABD = (1 - P_{uncb})P_{cbt}(s - 1) + P_{uncb}(s' - 1).$$

What is the value of P_{cbt}? We can find P_{cbt} by first noting that P_{bt} is the probability that all branches are taken. We then determine the weighted mean of the conditional and the unconditional branch probabilities:

$$P_{bt} = (1 - P_{uncb})P_{cbt} + P_{uncb} \times 1,$$

$$P_{cbt} = (P_{bt} - P_{uncb})/(1 - P_{uncb}).$$

From the data, $P_{cbt} = (0.6 - 0.3)/(1 - 0.3) = 0.428$. We can now compute the WABD and CPI of this strategy:

$$WABD = (1 - 0.3)0.428(4 - 1) + 0.3(3 - 1) = 1.49,$$

$$CPI = 1 + P_b WABD = 1 + (0.3 \times 1.49) = 1.44$$

Comments

By predicting on the op-code, the CPI has been reduced to 1.44 from 1.54 for the PNT strategy. The model derivation can be checked by setting P_{uncb} to 0 and 1 to see if the two models for predict taken and predict not taken are obtained.

Also by setting $P_{uncb} = 0$, meaning that all branches are conditional, $P_{cbt} = P_{bt}$, as would be expected.

Target Address Characteristic

The branch target address has two characteristics that can be used for branch prediction. The characteristics are the direction of the branch and the magnitude of the branch distance. Short branches and backward branches are characteristic of loops in a program and are usually taken. Long branches and forward branches in a program are used for major changes in program control and are usually not taken.

How are these predictions made? Consider a PC relative branch target address. Determining the direction of a branch is relatively easy as the displacement in the branch instruction is a signed integer. Thus the sign bit of the displacement can be used for prediction.

Determining the branch distance is more difficult. First a threshold value has to be determined, say 108 instructions. Then how is the comparison made between the displacement and the threshold? A subtraction would add significant time to the decode stage. A reasonable design is to set the threshold at an even power of 2 (128, not 108 as suggested above) and examine the bits in the displacement to see if the threshold is exceeded.

Branch History

Statistical studies show that if the history of the branch direction of a given branch instruction is collected in hardware, a prediction can be made the next time that branch instruction is executed. For example, if there is a bit in the branch instruction that is set or reset depending on the outcome of the current execution, that bit is a good predictor for the next execution. A branch that is taken is more likely to be followed by a taken branch than a not-taken branch the next time it is executed. A problem with this scheme is that since the bit is in the instruction, we have to deal with self-modifying code.

A more practical solution is to have a field of history bits in the instruction cache associated with each instruction. These bits are not part of the instruction but are appended in the cache. Research has shown that the more bits in the history field, the more accurate the prediction. To illustrate this, a 1-bit and a 2-bit scheme are shown in Tables 6.4 and 6.5, respectively. The data are from Lee (1984) for a test benchmark program. The first column shows the history and the prediction. The second column shows the outcome in italics. N and T are used rather than not taken and taken. For the 1-bit history, Table 6.4 shows that the pattern NN occurs with the probability 0.309 whereas the pattern NT occurs with the probability 0.071.

The hardware, looking at the history bit, will predict Not if the last occurrence was not taken and Take if the last occurrence was taken. With 1 bit, the accuracy of prediction is $A_p = 0.309 + 0.565 = 0.874$.

A history that uses 2 bits, illustrated in Table 6.5, also uses the Lee data. Read from right to left; for example NT means that the last branch was taken and the one before it was not taken. The probabilities of the correct predictions are shown in boldfaced type.

TABLE 6.4 1-BIT BRANCH HISTORY PROBABILITIES

History (Predict)	Next	Probability
N(N)	N	0.309
N(N)	T	0.071
T(T)	N	0.046
T(T)	T	0.565

TABLE 6.5 2-BIT HISTORY PROBABILITIES

History (Predict)	Next	Probability
NN(N)	N	**0.294**
NN(N)	T	0.015
NT(N)	N	**0.051**
NT(N)	T	0.019
TN(T)	N	0.017
TN(T)	T	**0.039**
TT(T)	N	0.013
TT(T)	T	**0.552**

Two takens in a row will predict taken with an accuracy of $0.552/(0.013 + 0.552) = 0.97$. Two not taken in a row will predict not taken with a prediction accuracy of $0.294/(0.294 + 0.015) = 0.95$. When the two history bits differ, the prediction is based on the historical statistics of the next execution. That is, NT will predict N because $0.051 > 0.019$. The overall accuracy of prediction when a strategy based on this benchmark data is used is $0.294 + 0.051 + 0.039 + 0.552 = 0.936$; a 10% improvement over the 1-bit history scheme.

EXAMPLE

Determine the accuracy of prediction using a 2-bit history scheme that uses the following strategy. If the two history bits are the same (NN or TT), predict N or T, respectively. If the bits differ (NT or TN), predict based on the last execution: N predict N, T predict T.

Solution

Table 6.5 is modified in Table 6.6 with the predictions changed for the cases for which the two history bits differ. The probabilities of the correct predictions are shown in boldfaced type.

The accuracy of prediction is the sum of the probabilities for which the prediction is correct; $(0.294 + 0.019 + 0.017 + 0.552) = 0.882$.

Comment

The accuracy is only slightly better than the 1-bit (0.874) scheme. The hardware

TABLE 6.6 MODIFIED 2-BIT HISTORY		
History (Predict)	Next	Probability
NN(N)	N	**0.294**
NN(N)	T	0.015
NT(T)	N	0.051
NT(T)	T	**0.019**
TN(N)	N	**0.017**
TN(N)	T	0.039
TT(T)	N	0.013
TT(T)	T	**0.552**

required for implementing this scheme is almost as complex as the 2-bit scheme and the prediction accuracy is considerably worse.

Problems exist with all predictors used with a pipelined processor. One significant problem is that the history state of a conditional branch instruction is updated after the outcome of the branch is known, at stage s. If a particular branch instruction is executed with an interval less than s, then the prediction is made with "stale" information. In other words, the last execution has not been posted. A 3-bit history may be only as good as a 2-bit history because of this delay.

Other problems with some prediction schemes, such as the 1-bit scheme of Figure 6.4, is that for pathological branching patterns, such as T, N, T, N, T, ..., the branch prediction will always be wrong. Also, when there are context switches, it takes some time to reestablish a history and the prediction accuracy may be compromised for a period of time. It is possible to save the history information as part of the processor state when making a context switch.

Reducing s'

Now that we see how to have prediction accuracy that approaches 1, how do we reduce s'? Recall that s' is the stage of the pipeline at which the effective address is known. The solution to this design problem is found in the observation that the target effective address of a branch instruction usually does not change from one execution to the next. In other words, target effective addresses have a form of temporal locality, and caches can be used to save previously computed and used effective addresses. After another execution of the branch instruction, the target effective address can be immediately available and $s' = 1$ and the WABD $= 0$. There are two forms of these effective address caches: branch target buffers (BTBs) and branch target caches (BTCs).

Branch Target Buffer

A block diagram of a BTB is shown in Figure 6.12. An entry in the BTB consists of three fields: the effective address of the branch instruction, the effective address of the branch target, and history information for prediction. The instruction addresses from the I fetch stage are routed to the instruction cache and to the BTB. The BTB is

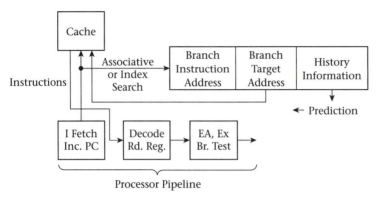

Figure 6.12 BTB

organized and accessed in any of the usual cache access schemes: direct, set associative, or full associative. If there is a hit on the BTB, meaning the branch instruction has been used previously and is still in the cache, and if the history information predicts a taken branch, then the branch target address is routed to the instruction cache and the target instruction is fetched into the decode stage.

Because the BTB access is in serial with the access of the instruction cache, the clock period of the processor may need to be increased or a second clock used, making $s' = 2$. There are a number of design questions with a BTB. What happens if there is a miss on the BTB? What happens if there is a hit on the BTB but the prediction is a not-taken branch? These questions are answered by tabulating the events and deciding on a policy with its delay.

We have to define some parameters. P_{btbh} is the BTB hit probability, P_{pbt} is the probability that the prediction is to take the branch, and A_p is the accuracy of prediction. Table 6.7 shows the events, delays, and default strategies for the behavior of the BTB. This table draws from Table 6.1 for the default delay when the prediction is wrong. When there is a BTB miss, a pipeline freeze strategy is assumed.

From Table 6.7, we can write the equation for the WABD. Note that for two events the delay is zero, and for all the other events the delay is $(s - 1)$:

$$\text{WABD} = [P_{btbh}P_{pbt}(1 - A_p) + P_{btbh}(1 - P_{pbt})(1 - A_p) + (1 - P_{btbh})](s - 1),$$
$$\text{WABD} = [1 - (P_{btbh}A_p)](s - 1).$$

TABLE 6.7   BTB EVENTS AND DELAYS

BTB	Prediction	Actual	Probability	Delay
Hit	Take	Take	$P_{btbh}P_{pbt}A_p$	0
Hit	Take	Not take	$P_{btbh}P_{pbt}(1 - A_p)$	$(s - 1)$
Hit	Not take	Not take	$P_{btbh}(1 - P_{pbt})A_p$	0
Hit	Not take	Take	$P_{btbh}(1 - P_{pbt})(1 - A_p)$	$(s - 1)$
Miss	Freeze	Don't care	$(1 - P_{btbh})$	$(s - 1)$
			SUM $= 1$	

Note that the location of stage s is now in the WABD model. However, s is important only when A_p is much less than 1. In addition, the size of the BTB can be increased, increasing its hit ratio and thereby mitigating the effects of poor branch prediction or a large s.

The BTB is accessed and the taken or not-taken path is followed based on the prediction. What happens when the prediction is wrong or there is a miss on the BTB? Remember that the outcome of the branch is not known until stage s. Thus there must be a parallel pipeline that executes a default strategy to cover these cases. In other words, this parallel pipeline operates as if the BTB did not exist. For Table 6.7, the default strategy is predict not taken with a delay of $s - 1$.

EXAMPLE

Consider the pipeline example used above with $s = 4$, $P_b = 0.3$, and $P_{bt} = 0.6$. Also assume that $P_{btbh} = 0.9$ and $A_p = 0.9$. What is the WABD and the CPI of this strategy?

Solution

$$\text{WABD} = [1 - (0.9 \times 0.9)](4 - 1) = 0.57,$$
$$\text{CPI} = 1 + (0.3 \times 0.57) = 1.17.$$

Comments

Note that the term P_{pbt} drops out of the model. With a BTB having the estimated parameters above, the CPI of the processor is now approximately 10% less than the theoretical steady state CPI of 1. This example shows the great benefit of a BTB for reducing CPI.

Branch Target Cache

Another solution to the problem of reducing s' is to use a BTC. Why store the target address that accesses the instruction cache as done with a BTC? Why not store the target instructions themselves? This is the approach taken with a BTC. A block diagram of a BTC is shown in Figure 6.13. The default pipeline is shown in this figure. Note that the BTC is similar to the BTB except that the target instruction stream

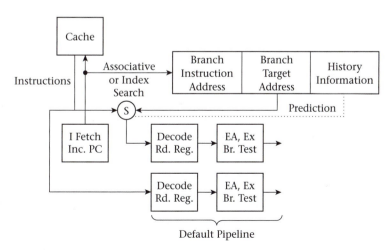

Figure 6.13 BTC

is routed into the decode stage when there is a hit and the prediction is to take the branch. This design eliminates the need to lengthen the clock or to provide a cycle delay because of the added delay in accessing the instruction cache. For this strategy $s' = 1$.

A design problem with the BTC is providing a source for the instructions following the target instruction. The solution to this problem is to have the BTC hold the target instruction and the next i target instructions; i is usually 4 or 8. For example, the AM29000 BTC holds a sequence of four target instructions.

A design problem with a BTB or BTC is finding time to update them. There are two types of updates. The first type is needed when there has been a miss (the branch has not been used before) and a complete entry must be formed. The second type of update is needed when the history field must be updated. In both cases, time must be found to update the BTB or BTC that may reduce the performance of the system. Note that not all uses of the BTB or BTC require updating. If 1 bit is used for history, when the prediction is correct, the history does not need to be updated. Saving in update time may compensate for the lower prediction accuracy.

As the BTB and BTC are caches, provisions must be made to evict an entry when the cache is full and a new entry must be created. The same strategies are applied as are applied to instruction and data caches. Also, if the BTB or BTC are set associative, there can be set conflict misses.

EXAMPLE

Assume that an update of a BTB requires one cycle and an update is required for each execution of a branch instruction; the frequency of update is P_b. What is the CPI of the processor if the update cycles are accounted for? Find the CPI by using the parameters of the preceding example.

Solution

The WABD for the BTB, derived in Table 6.7, is modified to account for the update cycle. One cycle is required for the update that is needed for each branch instruction executed:

$$\text{WABD} = (1 - P_{btbh}A_p)(s - 1) + 1,$$
$$\text{CPI} = 1 + P_b[(1 - P_{btbh}A_p)(s - 1) + 1],$$
$$\text{CPI} = 1 + 0.3(0.57 + 1) = 1.47.$$

Comment

The update cycles add 0.3 cycles ($1.47 - 1.17 = 0.3$) to the CPI and are a significant performance hit. A designer may consider having a dual-ported BTB or BTC to reduce the penalty. Another solution to this design problem may be to save the update information in a buffer and perform the update on a BTB cycle that is not a hit.

Delayed Branch

A branch strategy that has been applied successfully to short pipeline RISC processors is called delayed branch. This strategy depends on cooperation between the software and the hardware.

The compiler introduces $s - 1$ no-op instructions following each branch instruction.[63] Thus the pipeline is performing no useful work while waiting for the branch
to be resolved at stage s. The compiler then attempts to replace the no-ops with useful
instruction that can be executed in the no-op slots without destroying the logic of the
program. Several studies have shown that, on average, one no-op can be replaced with
a useful instruction.

This strategy is useful for pipelined processors with $s \leq 5$. For longer pipelines, too
many no-ops are executed, thereby increasing the number of instructions executed
for many tasks.

6.3.2 STRUCTURAL HAZARDS

Structural hazards occur when there are two or more demands on a single resource
in the same clock period. The very nature of a pipelined processor is concurrency:
designing it so that as many activities as possible are being performed at the same
time. This concurrency-directed design can lead to the simultaneous access of the same
hardware resource.

Consider the function of an ALU in a processor. With a serial execution model
processor (discussed in Chapter 5) one ALU can perform the three functions of incrementing the program counter, computing an effective address, and performing the
operation needed by the instruction. With a pipelined processor having a number of
instructions in simultaneous execution, one ALU will not support the three operations
at one time. There are three solutions to this problem that guarantee correct logical
execution of the program:

1. Use priority logic to delay all but one of the requests, resulting in delays for the
   other requesters.
2. Replicate the resource, such as three ALUs, for the example cited above.
3. Incorporate one resource that is fast enough to support all requests in one clock
   period.

Priority Selection

A number of design situations in which the priority solution is the preferred approach to structural hazards can be cited. One of these is the use of a unified cache
as a second-level cache. Recall from an example in Chapter 4 that with split first-level
caches, only a small number of memory references (instruction and data) miss and are
handled in the second-level cache. The references that miss on the first-level caches
are not likely to be correlated; that is, they do not occur at the same time. Thus there
is only a small probability that both will miss at the same time and cause a delay that
is due to two accesses to the second-level cache. Even though the probability of simultaneous access of the second-level unified cache is low, the designer must provide
priority logic to resolve this structural hazard when it does occur.

---

[63] A no-op instruction does absolutely nothing. There are no side effects except incrementing the
program counter.

A similar situation exists on the bus that connects a unified cache to real memory that is time shared with I/O. This case is influenced by the write policy of the cache. With a write through data cache, the bus is utilized approximately 50% of the time because all the read and write misses require bus transfers. This case is usually handled by giving priority to the I/O operation because these operations are at a lower frequency than cache misses. And, as discussed in Chapter 7, if some I/O devices are delayed access to the bus, a significant performance loss can occur.

Buses internal to the processor may also use priority selection. The outputs of the floating-point multiplier/divider and adder execution units of the IBM S360-91 share a single bus called the common data bus. This bus routs results to the register file and the execution unit inputs. If both execution units produce a result in the same clock, priority logic delays one result for one clock. The designers of this processor believed that the frequency of occurrence of this event would be small and the resulting delay would thus be small.

EXAMPLE

Figure 6.1 shows that two pipeline stages (stage 2 and stage 5) of the base pipeline can access the register file. Depending on the particular instructions that are flowing through the pipeline at any time, the register file may be accessed with two reads and one write in the same clock. Assume that the register file is dual ported; that is, it can perform two reads in one clock. However, if a write occurs on the same clock, it must be delayed by priority logic. Assume further that on 1/4 of the clocks there are no register file accesses, on 1/4 of the clocks there are two reads, on 1/4 of the clocks there are two reads and one write, and on 1/4 of the clocks there is a write to register file. What is the CPI of the processor, ignoring all other delays?

Solution

Only on 1/4 of the clocks when there are two reads and one write is there a stall on the register file. The structural hazard is resolved by priority logic. For this clock, the pipeline is stalled or delayed one clock:

CPI = 1 + (probability of a delay × delay),
CPI = 1 + (0.25 × 1) = 1.25.

Replicated Resources

When the probability of a conflict is such that a significant performance loss will occur by priority selection of a single resource, the resource can be replicated. There are a number of examples of this approach to solving the structural hazard problem. For example, three ALUs are used in some pipelined processors: one for incrementing the PC, another for effective address calculations, and another for the operation execution unit. Note that in these cases the ALUs can be highly specialized to the operation at hand.

EXAMPLE

The base pipeline fetches an instruction every clock and has a read or write operation on load and store instructions. Assume that 0.3 of the instructions are loads or stores. With a unified cache, the load or store instructions must be delayed one clock by priority logic. With split caches, there is no delay. Refer to Figure 4.10 for the two cache topologies. What is the speedup in CPI that results from using a split cache and ignoring cache misses? See Figure 4.10.

Solution

CPI = 1 + (probability of a delay × delay),

CPI (unified cache) = 1 + (0.3 × 1) = 1.3,

CPI (split cache) = 1 + (0.3 × 0) = 1.0,

speedup = 1.3/1.0 = 1.3.

Comment

Adding the second cache gives a significant improvement to the performance of the processor. Because of the relatively low cost of hardware, replication of resources is today a preferred solution to many structural hazard problems.

In some processors, the TLB is replicated so that name translations for instructions and data will not face structural hazards. When storage locations are replicated, care must be taken that the contents of these locations are coherent, as discussed in Chapter 4. Otherwise, the execution of the program may not be logically correct. The designer must consider whether the time lost to maintain coherency may not be greater than the delays that result from a shared resource by using priority logic.

6.3.3 DATA DEPENDENCIES

Data dependencies occur in an executing program when, because of the latency of a pipeline, the program may not execute correctly. These dependencies do not occur in a serial execution model processor. There are three classes of data dependencies:

1. Read after write (RAW), also known as a true dependency
2. Write after read (WAR), also known as an antidependency
3. Write after write (WAW), also known as an output dependency

As will be described in the following paragraphs, these three classes of dependencies are detected by the hardware, and the hardware ensures correct execution by both ad hoc and general techniques.

Read after Write Dependencies

This dependency occurs when an instruction needs an operand that will be produced by a previous instruction, but the result has not yet been produced because of the latency of the pipeline. Consider the following program fragment consisting of two instructions; instruction i is followed by instruction j. There may be zero, one, or more instructions between i and j:

i R1 = R2 + R3,

j R4 = R1 + R6.

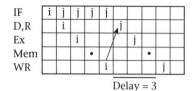

Figure 6.14 RAW dependency

Delay = 3

There is a RAW dependency on R1 as instruction j cannot be executed correctly until instruction i has posted its result to the destination register R1. Keep in mind that RAW dependencies are artifacts of the program. A smart compiler can do some rearranging of the program to reduce the frequency of occurrence of RAW dependencies, but all RAW dependencies cannot be eliminated.

The processor designer has one objective: reduce the delays when RAW dependencies do occur. These objectives can be stated in terms of CPI:

$$\text{CPI} = 1 + (\text{probability of a RAW dependency} \times \text{RAW delay})$$
$$= 1 + P_{raw}D_{raw}.$$

We now determine the value of the RAW delay. A reservation table is shown in Figure 6.14 for the two-instruction fragment executing on the five-stage pipeline of Figure 6.1.[64] Instruction i is processed down the pipeline with the result written into the register file. Because instruction j needs this result, it is delayed for three clocks until the result can be read from the register file. For many programs, a RAW dependency between adjacent instructions, defined as P_{raw}, has a probability of approximately 0.2. Thus, the CPI of this processor is

$$\text{CPI} = 1 + P_{raw}\,D_{raw},$$
$$\text{CPI} = 1 + (0.2 \times 3) = 1.6.$$

Because this is a significant reduction in performance, something must be done to overcome the loss. The technique used for reducing or eliminating this performance loss is called forwarding. The last three stages of the base pipeline and a reservation table are shown in Figure 6.15.

A logic path takes the output of the execution unit and introduces it as an input to the execution unit, bypassing the register file. Thus the execution of instruction j can start on the next clock. The result of instruction i is written into the register file normally because that result may be needed by a subsequent instruction. With forwarding and with $P_{raw} = 0.2$, CPI is

$$\text{CPI} = 1 + P_{raw}D_{raw},$$
$$\text{CPI} = 1 + (0.2 \times 0) = 1.0.$$

There is a substantial improvement in performance with forwarding. If the execution unit had been two stages instead of one, the delay for adjacent instructions with

---

[64] Note that the memory stage is bypassed even though the time slot is shown occupied. This procedure simplifies the control of the pipeline without hurting its performance.

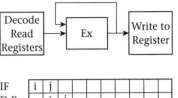

Figure 6.15 Forwarding

IF	i	j							
D,R		i	j						
Ex			i→j						
Mem				•	•				
WR					i	j			

Delay = 0

IF	i	j	j	j	j				
D,R		i				j			
Ex			i				j		
Mem				i				j	
WR					i				j

Figure 6.16 RAW control

R1	0	0	1	1	1	0	0		
R2									
R3									
R6	0	0	0	0	0	0	0		

forwarding would be one clock, and a three-stage execution unit, two clocks. For an execution unit of E stages, the RAW delay for adjacent instructions can be generalized:

RAW delay with forwarding $= E - 1$.

We have discussed the issues of performance in the presence of RAW hazards. In some situations, forwarding cannot be used to reduce delays. How then is the pipeline designed to ensure the logical correctness of the program? In other words, how are the delays inserted when needed? The solution to this problem is found in the use of control bits in the register file as shown in Figure 6.16. The program fragment is the same as that used above:

i R1 = R2 + R3,

j R4 = R1 + R6.

Each word of the register file has a control bit as shown for R1, R2, R3, and R6. When an instruction is decoded, the control bit of the destination register (R1 for instruction *i*) is set to a 1 on the next clock. A subsequent instruction, such as instruction *j*, tests the control bits for its source registers, R1 and R6 for this example. If either of the bits are 1, the instruction stalls, the bits are tested on each subsequent clock, and when both become 0, instruction *j* moves to the next stage of the pipeline. As instruction *i* writes the result into the register file, the control bit is set to zero, indicating that the RAW dependency has been satisfied. This form of control is used in the IBM S360 integer processor and a number of contemporary microprocessors.

Write after Read Dependencies

This dependency occurs when instruction execution is out of order and a later instruction writes into a source operand location before the previous instruction has read that source operand from that location. With the base pipeline of Figure 6.1, the register reads must occur before a subsequent instruction can write into the register. How then can results get out of order? With some processors, the decoder can release instructions out of order to the execution unit(s). For example, if instruction i is waiting for a RAW dependency to be resolved, the decoder can release instruction j, which has no dependencies. Consider the following three-instruction program fragment executing on a processor that can issue instructions out of order:

i R2 = R1 + R8,

j R9 = R4 × R2,

k R4 = R7 + R8.

There is a RAW dependency on R2 between instructions i and j and instruction j stalls. There are no dependencies on source operands of instruction k, which can be released to the execution unit. Instruction k may complete and write into R4 before R4 is read by instruction j, causing an incorrect result to be placed in R9.

This dependency is prevented by buffering the source operands. With instruction i in the decoder, the value in R4 is placed in buffer B1 and the value in R2 is placed in buffer B2 when it is available from instruction i:

j R9 = R4 × R2,

(R4) → B1,

(R2) → B2 when it is available from instruction i.

Instruction j becomes

j R9 = B1 × B2.

The buffering of the inputs to instruction j removes the WAR dependency because instruction k can write into R4 whenever it completes. In many designs, buffers are placed at the inputs to the ALU, and these buffers can be used to resolve WAR hazards. This use of buffers, in their general form, is called renaming.

Write after Write Dependencies

This dependency, also known as an output dependency, occurs when instruction execution is out of order and a later instruction writes into a destination location before the previous instruction has written into that location. Consider the following program fragment:

i R4 = R3 + R1,

j R4 = R7 + R8,

k R9 = R4 + R5.

Assume that there is a dependency that stalls instruction i and it completes after instruction j. The completion sequence is j, i, and k:

j R4 = R7 + R8,

i R4 = R3 + R1,

k R9 = R4 + R5.

Instruction k has an incorrect source operand in R4 and the execution is incorrect. Buffering can also be used to resolve WAW hazards. When buffering is used, the program fragment above is rewritten[65] as

i R4 = buff1 = R3 + R1,

j R4 = buff2 = R7 + R8,

k R9 = buff2 + R5.

Even if instruction i completes after instruction j, instruction k will have the correct source operands. However, there is now a RAW dependency on buff 2, which must be resolved as discussed above. With buffers, the dependency is not totally resolved because R4 is still written to the register file out of order. For this reason buffers are not a universal solution to this design problem.

Dependencies in Other Spaces

The preceding paragraphs have discussed dependencies in the general-purpose register file of a processor. Hazards and dependencies of all three types can occur in other spaces as well, including memory, caches, condition code registers, and address registers. The designer must search out and identify all potential dependencies in a design and make sure that there are hardware provisions to ensure that dependencies will not affect the logic of a program.

Buffers will not work for memory-mapped I/O (described in Chapter 7) because the sequence of writes to memory must be in order for the I/O device to operate properly. WAW dependencies can be resolved by forcing the writes to be in order. The PowerPC has an instruction *eieio* (enforce in-order execution of I/O) that forces loads and stores to be in order. This instruction is inserted as a preamble to instructions that will load or store from memory-mapped I/O. The Intel Pentium Pro, which uses memory-mapped I/O, requires that the I/O region of memory be direct and not cached. Memory has hardware that enforces in-order writes, a topic discussed further in Section 7.1.

6.4 INTERRUPTS

The general issues of interrupts, as found in serial execution model processors, are discussed in Chapter 3. A pipelined processor with a number of instructions in simultaneous execution presents a new set of problems to the designer. We like to have precise interrupts. That is, even with a number of instructions in simultaneous execution, the

---

[65] Rewriting is accomplished automatically by hardware for processors with renaming registers.

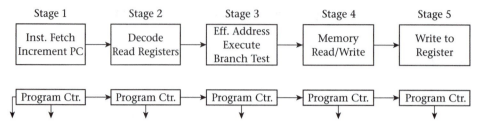

Figure 6.17 Saved program counter

processor can correctly return to the interrupted program and resume execution. If this return cannot be guaranteed, interrupts are said to be imprecise.

When an interrupt occurs, a pipeline stage may be the source of the interrupt, such as an illegal op-code detected in the decode stage. This stage is called the interrupting stage. With an external interrupt, on the other hand, the designer must identify a stage that is the interrupted stage. For the interrupted program to be restarted, the interrupted or interrupting instruction must have its program counter saved.

Any stage of the pipeline can be interrupted or interrupting, depending on the type of interrupt. It follows then that there must be a way of saving the program counter for each instruction that is being processed in the pipeline. This means that there is a program counter pipeline in parallel with the main pipeline, as shown in Figure 6.17.[66]

An important design issue with interrupts is to identify the saved program counter. To address this issue, the three types of interrupts are considered.

Asynchronous or external These interrupts can occur at any time because of events such as an I/O request. The designer selects the stage of the processor that will have its program counter saved.

Synchronous or internal These interrupts result from some event in a particular stage of the pipeline. Examples are a page fault, an illegal op-code, or an arithmetic error. The stage in which the event occurs, or the stage -1, has its program counter saved.

Software or programmed These events are explicit instructions to the processor to perform some function. Examples are a programmed context switch or a call for I/O. The saved program counter is usually the decode stage unless an effective address must be calculated to complete the operation.

---

[66] There must also be a parallel pipeline to carry control information that tells each pipeline stage what to do.

Figure 6.18 Precise interrupt design options (courtesy Jones and Bartlett Publishers)

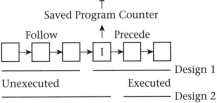

To have precise interrupts with a pipelined processor, three conditions must be satisfied (Smith and Pleszlumn 1985):

1. Instructions that precede the saved program counter must be completed and have properly modified the processor state.
2. Instructions that follow the saved program counter must be unexecuted and have not modified the processor state.
3. The instruction indicated by the saved program counter must meet either condition 1 or condition 2.

How are the three conditions for a precise interrupt satisfied? Figure 6.18 shows the two design options, design 1 and design 2. Note that different interrupts may be implemented with different designs; design uniformity is not required or achieved in most processors. For example, an illegal op-code detected at the decode stage will have its program counter value saved and it will not be executed (design 2). A breakpoint instruction, detected at the decode stage, will have its program counter value saved and will be executed (design 1).

The unexecuted instructions following the interrupted instruction can be treated in a number of ways. If there are early side effects, such as the autoincrement addressing mode of the VAX architecture, these side effects must be (1) undone and the instructions reexecuted after the interrupt is handled or (2) stored and the instructions restarted after the interrupt is handled. For processors with no early side effects, the following instructions may be abandoned and reexecuted after the interrupt handler is run. RISC design theory requires that there be no early side effects, thus permitting this simple approach to handling following instructions.

With most processors, the preceding instructions are allowed to run to completion. In other words, the preceding instructions are flushed from the pipeline. This strategy works well as long as one of the instructions being flushed does not generate an interrupt. But what happens if a flushed instruction produces an interrupt? The designer must accommodate this event; in some processors, an error signal is produced, indicating a situation that the processor cannot handle.

Other problems include making provisions for two or more simultaneous interrupts, such as an illegal op-code on the same clock as an external interrupt. Again, the designer must consider all such possibilities and provide a solution or provide an error signal to the system.

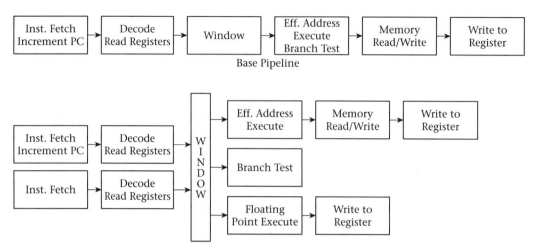

Figure 6.19 Superscalar topology

6.5 SUPERSCALAR PIPELINES

In the preceding sections, the pipelines have decoded and issued one instruction at a time to the execution unit. This results in the steady-state CPI of 1. One may ask, "Why not decode and issue more than one instruction at a time and reduce the steady-state CPI to less than 1?" This is exactly what is done in implementations called superscalar. The idea of superscalar is illustrated in Figure 6.19. The base pipeline is shown at the top of the figure with a window inserted between the decode and the execute stages. For the base pipeline, this window is simply the staging register at the output of the decode stage.

A degree 2 superscalar architecture is shown at the bottom of Figure 6.19. There are two identical pipeline stages fetching and decoding instructions; only one stage increments the PC. The number of replications before the window, also called a dispatch unit, is defined as σ, the degree of superscalar. The figure shows an integer execution unit, a branch execution unit, and a floating-point execution unit. The window releases zero, one, two, or three instructions on each clock. However, the average issue rate cannot exceed two instructions per clock. Because the pipeline stages following the window are not simply replications of the base pipeline, this design is called nonuniform superscalar. Examples of contemporary nonuniform superscalar processors are listed in Table 6.8.

We now derive a performance model for superscalar processors, as illustrated by the reservation tables shown in Figure 6.20. The pipeline illustrated has four stages: instruction fetch, decode and register read, execute, and write back, and each of these stages is duplicated.[67] For this example, $s = 4$, $\sigma = 2$, and $k = 4$.

Because instructions may not be aligned in the instruction cache, two alignment cases must be considered. For case a), the instructions are aligned and the number of clocks required for executing the program fragment is $s + (k/\sigma) - 1$. If the first

---

[67] This is a form of uniform superscalar that is not found in practice. However, it does serve as a model for performing modeling.

TABLE 6.8 EXAMPLES OF SUPERSCALAR TOPOLOGIES

Processor	σ	Execution Units
RS/6000	4	Integer, Flt. Pt. (Mpy, Add), Branch, I/O
PowerPC 601	3	Integer, Flt. Pt. (Mpy, Add, Div), Branch
Intel Pentium	2	2-Integer, Flt. Pt. Add, Flt. Pt. Mpy., Branch
Intel i860	2	Integer-Branch, Flt. Pt. Add, Flt. Pt. Mpy.
AMD-K5	4	Integer, Integer/shifter, Flt. Pt., Branch, Load/Store
MIPS-T5	4	2-Integer, Flt. Pt. Add, Flt. Pt. Mpy/Div/Sqrt, Load/Store
MC88110	2	2-Integer-Branch, Integer Mpy, Integer Div., Flt. Pt. Add, Load/Store, Bit Field, 2 Graphics

two instructions are not aligned, case b), the number of clocks is $s + (k/\sigma)$. With the probability of alignment being $1/\sigma$, the weighted average number of clocks is

$$= \frac{1}{\sigma}\left(s + \frac{k}{\sigma} - 1\right) + \left(1 - \frac{1}{\sigma}\right)\left(s + \frac{k}{\sigma}\right)$$

$$= s + \frac{k-1}{\sigma}.$$

The CPI of a degree $\sigma = 2$ superscalar processor is

$$\text{CPI} = \frac{s + \frac{k-1}{\sigma}}{k} = \frac{1}{\sigma} + \frac{1}{k}\left(s - \frac{1}{\sigma}\right).$$

	1	2	3	4	5	6	7	8
IF1	i1	i3						
If2	i2	i4						
DR1		i1	i3					
DR2		i2	i4					
EX1			i1	i3				
EX2			i2	i4				
WR1				i1	i3			
WR2				i2	i4			

$s - 1$ k/σ

Case a) Aligned
No. Base Clocks = $s + \frac{k}{\sigma} - 1$

IF1	X	i2	i4					
If2	i1	i3	X					
DR1		X	i2	i4				
DR2		i1	i3	X				
EX1			X	i2	i4			
EX2			i1	i3	X			
WR1				X	i2	i4		
WR2				i1	i3	X		

$s - 1$ $k/\sigma + 1$

Case b) Not aligned
No. Base Clocks = $s + \frac{k}{\sigma}$

Figure 6.20 Superscalar performance model

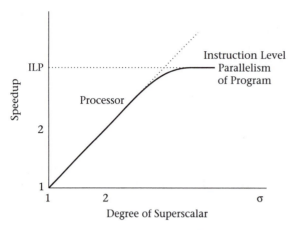

Figure 6.21 Speedup limited by σ and ILP

By setting σ to 1, we see that this is the same model developed above for a nonsuperscalar, $\sigma = 1$, processor. The speedup of a superscalar processor over a nonsuperscalar processor is

$$\text{speedup} = \frac{\text{clocks, nonsuperscalar}}{\text{clocks, superscalar}} = \frac{s + k - 1}{s + \frac{k-1}{\sigma}}$$

$$= \frac{\sigma(s + k - 1)}{\sigma s + k - 1}.$$

As $k \to \infty$, speedup $\to \sigma$.

As $\sigma \to \infty$, speedup $\to 1 + \dfrac{k - 1}{s}$.

Note that for large values of σ the speedup is limited by the delays set by k and the length of the pipeline s. In other words, the speedup of a superscalar processor is ultimately limited by the local parallelism inherent in the program. A processor cannot issue more instructions in parallel than are available from the program. This relationship is shown in Figure 6.21. As σ increases, the speedup increases linearly until the point where the instruction level parallelism (ILP) limits any further increase in speedup.

For many problems, ILP is in the range 2–4. This is the reason that most modern superscalar processors have σ in the range 2–4, as shown in Table 6.8. There is no reason to have σ too large, which costs chip area, if the anticipated programs have relatively small ILP.

EXAMPLE

The program fragment used in Chapter 3 to illustrate a load/store register file architecture, Table 3.3, is executed on the superscalar processor of Figure 6.19. What is the ILP for this program and what is the speedup of the processor over a nonsuperscalar processor? Assume that there are no cache misses.

Solution

The architecture is three-address, register to register or load/store. The program fragment required for performing the function is:

Load: R(1) ← M(B)
Load: R(2) ← M(C)
Add: R(3) ← R(1) + R(2)
Store: M(A)← R(3)

The superscalar processor uses the integer pipeline for loads and stores as well as the ALU operations – a potential structural hazard. With two-integer pipelines, two load instructions can be issued together; however, the store instruction must follow the add instruction because of the RAW dependency. We can conclude that, without stalls or delays, three clocks are required for this four-instruction fragment. The minimum CPI is $3/4 = 0.75$; however, the CPI may be degraded because of the time required for resolving the RAW dependencies and the structural conflicts in the memory system.

Comment

The RAW dependencies on R1 and R2 are called load true dependencies. These dependencies usually result in a stall delay, even with forwarding.

Note from Table 6.8 that the AMD-K5, MIPS-T5, and the MC88110 have a load/store pipeline in addition to the integer pipeline. This means that for some programs, a load or store with another instruction can be released from the window in one clock.

6.6 PIPELINED PROCESSOR MEMORY DEMAND

A pipelined processor places a significant demand on the memory system for instruction and data fetches. Because of the concurrency in the pipeline, one instruction fetch and up to one data read/write may be initiated in one clock, as shown in Figure 6.22. For superscalar processors, this maximum demand is multiplied by σ. To meet these demands on memory, modern processors have split caches, wide instruction caches for instruction fetching, and write buffers to isolate the data writes from the data reads.

In addition, for RISC-style architectures, the register files must be multiported to support concurrent reads and writes, as shown in Figure 6.23. For dyadic operations,

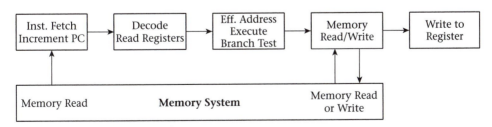

Figure 6.22 Memory demand

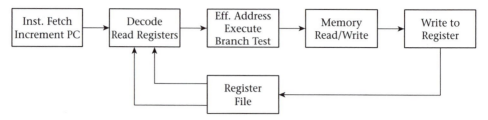

Figure 6.23 Register file accesses

there are two reads and one write per instruction. For superscalar processors the ports to the register file must, for the worst case, support $\sigma(2 \text{ reads} + 1 \text{ write})$ register cycles per clock.

EXAMPLE

Consider a superscalar processor, $\sigma = 2$, and workload. 30% of all instructions are ALU types, 30% are loads or stores, and the other 40% of instructions do not use the register file. What is the weighted average number of register file accesses per clock?

Solution

An event probability table is constructed in Table 6.9. The weighted average number of register accesses is 1.2σ and, for $\sigma = 2$, the weighted average number of register file accesses per clock is 2.4.

Comment

The value of 2.4 register file accesses per clock is a worst-case value. Because of pipelining, the accesses will not occur simultaneously as suggested by this solution. Simulations confirm this by showing that approximately 90% of all clocks will have three or fewer register file references for a $\sigma = 4$ processor (Johnson 1991).

A designer may be tempted to replicate the register file rather than make it multiported as a way of solving the structural hazard. If this is done, the design must ensure that the contents of the register files are coherent, a design problem that may cost more chip area and be slower than the multiport design because of the need to maintain coherency between the register files.

TABLE 6.9 REGISTER FILE ACCESSES PER CLOCK

Event	References	Probability	Product
ALU instruction	3σ	0.3	$0.9\,\sigma$
Load or store	σ	0.3	$0.3\,\sigma$
Other	0	0.4	0
		SUM $= 1$	1.2σ

REFERENCES

Cragon, H. G. (1991). *Branch Strategy Taxonomy and Performance Models*, IEEE Computer Society Press, Los Alamitos, CA.

Davidson, E. S. (1971). "The Design and Control of Pipelined Function Generators," presented at the IEEE Conference on Systems, Networks and Computers, Oaxtepec, Mexico, January 1971.

Johnson, M. (1991). *Superscalar Microprocessor Design*, Prentice-Hall, Englewood Cliffs, NJ.

Kogge, P. M. (1981). *The Architecture of Pipelined Computers*, Hemisphere, New York.

Lee, R. L. (1984). "Branch Prediction Strategies and Branch Target Buffer Design," *Computer*, **21**:1.

Smith, J. E. and Pleszlumn, A. R. (1985). "Implementation of Precise Interrupts in Pipelined Processors," *IEEE Transactions on Computers*, **C-34**:3, pp. 36–44.

EXERCISES

6.1 For modeling a superscalar processor, how many alignment cases must be considered for $\sigma = 3, 4$, or 5?

6.2 Show that the CPI model developed for $\sigma = 2$ from Figure 6.20 is also the general solution for any σ.

6.3 Show with reservation tables that the RAW delays with forwarding are equal to $E - 1$.

6.4 What is the RAW delay for various values of E and spacing between instructions with the dependencies? Show in table form.

6.5 Derive the WABD model for the delayed branch strategy.

6.6 Show all the steps in the derivation of the optimum number of pipeline stages.

6.7 Consider an L2 unified cache that receives misses from instruction and data L1 caches. Assume that the number of references that are correlated is the product of the two misses: P_{miss} (instruction) $\times P_{miss}$ (data). Assume an ISA that has one instruction and one data reference per instruction. If the miss rate for both L1 caches is 0.1, what is the mean access time of the unified cache?

6.8 Show by the use of reservation tables that the forwarding delay is $E - 1$ clocks for adjacent instructions.

6.9 Describe a situation in which the write to register stage of the pipeline can cause an interrupt and be the interrupting stage.

6.10 Show the derivation of the model for the number or clocks, $s + \lceil (k-1)/\sigma \rceil$, for a degree 2 superscalar processor with the probability of alignment $1/\sigma$.

6.11 What conditions or situations could result in no instructions being issued from the window of Figure 6.19?

6.12 For the superscalar processor of Figure 6.19, consider the two-instruction sequence: load floating point, add floating point

$$i\, Rx = M(Ry)$$
$$j\, Rz = Rx + Rw.$$

Show a forwarding path that will improve the performance of this program fragment. Explain how performance is improved.

6.13   Identify all forwarding paths on the superscalar processor of Figure 6.19 that will
improve performance loss that is due to RAW dependencies.

6.14   The base pipeline has $s'' = 2$, $s' = s = 3$. Compute the CPI for the three branch
strategies, freeze, predict take, and predict not take. The workload parameters are
$P_b = 0.4$ and $P_{bt} = 0.6$.

6.15   Rework the example in Subsection 6.3.2 to include cache misses. The one-level
unifi ed cache is organized direct with 8K bytes. With the split cache, the instruction and data caches are direct with 4K bytes. Use P_{miss} data from Tables 4.8–4.10.
The real memory to the unifi ed cache transport time is 10 clocks. See Figure 4.10
for the topologies of the one-level unifi ed cache and the one-level split cache.

6.16   You are redesigning the BTB of a processor and can increase the number of bits
by 50%. How would you spend these additional bits? Increase the number of
entries, thereby decreasing the miss rate? Increase the size of the history table to
improve the accuracy of prediction? Any other ideas? Justify your answer based
on the reduction in WABD.

6.17   Rework the WABD model for the BTB, Table 6.7. Change the default case when
there is a BTB miss to be predict take and predict not take.

6.18   Rework the example in the Section on BTBs by using the PT and PNT Strategies
as default. Which default strategy would you use for this design? Explain your
answer.

6.19   Examine the weighted average number of register file accesses per clock by passing the following instruction stream down the base pipeline: $\sigma = 1$. The instruction stream is load, ALU, load, other, ALU, other, other, other, ALU, store. Compute the fraction of instructions having 0, 1, 2, and 3 register file references. How
do these results compare with the result of Table 6.3 and the reported simulation?

6.20   Split caches, instruction and data, remove the structural hazard from memory
references. Discuss the requirements for maintaining coherency between these
two caches.

SEVEN

INPUT/OUTPUT

7.0 INTRODUCTION

Processors need a source of input data and a destination for output data. Processors also require storage space for large volumes of intermediate data. Thus the I/O system provides these storage facilities by connecting the processor's memory to the I/O devices. These devices vary widely in latency and bandwidth; thus, a major function of the I/O system is to match their latencies and bandwidths to that of the memory system. I/O devices consist of such diverse items as keyboards, modems, and hard disks. Each of these devices has its own latency and bandwidth requirements that must be satisfied for a properly functioning system.

Blaauw and Brooks (1997) classify I/O devices with the taxonomy shown in modified form in Figure 7.1. Store devices provide ready-access storage space. System resident and database devices are usually in the virtual-address space of the memory, providing low-latency storage space. Archive stores, on the other hand, usually require human intervention when archival information is required or needs to be stored.

Source/sink devices are used as paths to/from the computer to another device and are not generally used for storage of information. Floppy disks and Zip disks can be viewed as either archive or local media. Windows98 can use the Internet Explorer as an access method for both store devices and source/sink devices, blurring the distinction of the taxonomy.

7.1 I/O SYSTEM ARCHITECTURE

The I/O system must provide the facilities for moving information between the processor's memory and the various devices. The nature of the interface leads to major design problems. There can be a significant bandwidth difference between the memory and the device – as high as 5,000,000:1 and as low as 1:1. For example, memory may have a bandwidth of 50M bytes/s whereas a keyboard may produce input at approximately 10 bytes/s. In addition, a graphics display may accept data at 30M bytes/s. There can also be a significant latency difference – as high as 500,000:1 and as low as 1:1. The latency difference between memory (70 ns) and a disk (20 ms) is an example of these latency differences. The differences in bandwidth and latency lead to the design

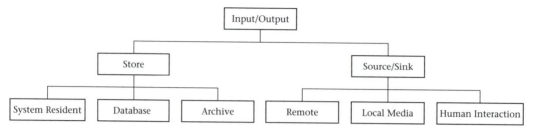

Figure 7.1 I/O device taxonomy

requirement for buffers. These buffers can be implemented in hardware or virtulized in real memory with software.

The I/O devices are usually asynchronous to the clock of the processor and memory, and also to the program executing in the processor. Asynchronism requires synchronizers at the hardware level, discussed in Section 7.5, and synchronization primitives in the processor ISA, discussed in Chapter 8.

The major tasks of the I/O system are the following:

1. to establish the connection between the memory and the I/O device
2. to synchronize and manage the control of the data transfer
3. to provide buffering when the source and sink bandwidths and latencies differ
4. to perform code conversions if required
5. to interrupt the processor when required
6. to terminate the operation when it is completed

These tasks are accomplished by hardware and software, in varying amounts of each. The more hardware oriented, the higher the performance and the higher the hardware cost. The more software oriented, the lower the performance and the lower the hardware cost. Control can be classified into two broad categories: programmed I/O and coprocessor I/O.

Programmed I/O

Programmed I/O, also known as direct I/O, is accomplished by a program executing on the processor itself to control the I/O operations and transfer the data. With programmed I/O, shown in Figure 7.2, there are several architected registers (minimally an input register and an output register) that are addressed by special move instructions.

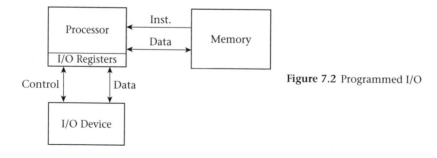

Figure 7.2 Programmed I/O

These move instructions move information from the accumulator (or general-purpose register) to/from the I/O registers. The peripherals are connected directly to the bits of these registers.

The register bits are allocated for control signals, to and from the device, and for the data path. Some implementations have a special status register to hold status and control bits so that control is not mixed with data in the same register. There may also be a counter register for counting the number of transfers so the processor will not be required to count under program control.

When the main program requires an I/O operation, the main program is suspended and an I/O subroutine is called. This subroutine performs the bit-by-bit control and data transfer between the memory and the device. After the I/O transfer is completed, control is returned from the I/O subroutine to the suspended main program. In some situations, the I/O program is inserted as an in-line code as an open subroutine.

The most significant problem with programmed I/O is that concurrency between I/O and computing is not possible. The main program is suspended while the I/O subroutine is executed, leading to performance loss.

EXAMPLE

Consider a processor with programmed I/O that executes instructions at a rate of 0.1 MIPS. An I/O subroutine for writing to a floppy disk requires 10,000 instructions and the disk has a total latency of 100 ms. A disk request is initiated every second of task time. What is the efficiency of this system?

Solution

The time that the main program is suspended is 100 ms + I/O subroutine time:

$$\text{suspend time} = 100 \times 10^{-3} + \frac{10,000}{100,000}\text{ s}$$
$$= 100 \times 10^{-3} + 100 \times 10^{-3}\text{ s}$$
$$= 200 \times 10^{-3}\text{ s,}$$

$$\text{efficiency} = 100\left(\frac{\text{task time}}{\text{total time}}\right)$$
$$= 100\left(\frac{1\text{ s}}{1\text{ s} + 200\text{ ms}}\right)$$
$$= 83\%.$$

Comment

Today, many single-chip microcomputers, or controllers, use programmed I/O. The loss of efficiency is not a concern as the major design issue is very low cost. When the I/O control subroutine is placed in very dense ROM, the total chip area is reduced from the area required by other control techniques.

Programmed I/O was used on the first computer built on the von Neumann ISA model, the EDSAC at Cambridge University built under the direction of Maurice Wilkes (Randell 1973). Recall from Chapter 3 that the EDSAC had the ability to call and return from subroutines. Punched paper tape was the input medium, and the output was a teleprinter. Input and output commands were provided in the ISA:

I, n Read the next row of holes on the input tape and place the resulting
integer, multiplied by 2^{-16}, in the storage location n.

O, n Print the character set up on the teleprinter, and set up the next character
represented by the five most-significant digits in storage location n.[68]

An early production computer that used programmed I/O is the IBM 701, which
was first delivered in 1953. The 701 had four magnetic drums for store; for source and
sink it had a card reader, card punch, printer, magnetic tape, and a graphic display
with a camera for producing hard copy.

The 701 has I/O instructions that are at a higher lexical level than the EDSAC.
Two instructions, read select RDS and write select WRS, established the path to an
addressed device and started the device operating (such as starting a tape drive). Other
instructions performed the read or write operation. All transfers were by means of the
multiplier quotient (MQ) register:

CPY Copy and skip   RDB Read backwards
WEF Write end of file   SNS Sense
REW Rewind tape   LDA Locate drum address

Simple input IN and output OUT instructions were used on the Intel 8080. These
instructions used the memory bus pins and moved a byte to/from the accumulator
and the data bus pins along with a byte address on the memory-address pins. Various
higher levels of I/O, such as buffers and channels, were implemented on special chips.
Three status bits were present on pins that were externally decoded to determine if
an I/O operation instead of a memory operation was taking place: 101 = I/O write,
110 = I/O read.

Single-chip microcontrollers such as the Intel i8048, shown in Figure 7.3, are commonly used for the control of simple devices such as microwave ovens, keyboard controllers, and handheld games. These computers use a programmed I/O that moves
either bits or bytes.

The Intel 8048 has three 8-bit I/O ports and an 8-bit bus. The ISA contains a number
of instructions that perform input and output moves between the ports and the accumulator. Outputs can be masked by use of immediate operands for bit-setting purposes.

For upward compatibility reasons, these In and Out instructions are still found on
the Pentium Pro. With this processor, the source/destination can be any of the registers AL, AX, or EAX, depending on the size of the addressed port (8, 16, or 32 bits).
Windows95 uses programmed I/O for some of its I/O functions.

Memory-Mapped I/O

Memory-mapped I/O is another form of programmed I/O that maps the device connections to bits in memory address space, as shown in Figure 7.4. An output command
is a normal store instruction that stores a pattern of bits into a designated memory location. An input command is a normal load instruction that reads a memory location.

---

[68] Note the CISC-like function of the output instruction: print one character, set up the second
character.

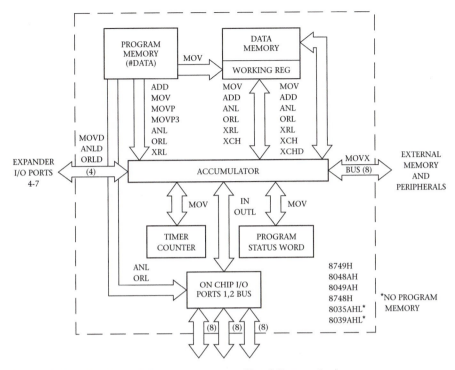

Figure 7.3 Intel 8048 block diagram (courtesy of Intel Corporation)

The major advantage of memory-mapped I/O compared with programmed I/O is that no special move instructions or special I/O registers are required. The major disadvantage is that a portion of address space must be treated specially by both the hardware and software designers. For the hardware designers, the memory-mapped bits must be real flip flops and their memory addresses blocked out of the memory-address decoder. From a software point of view, any design that interferes with a uniform memory allocation presents a design problem.

Memory-mapped I/O requires the full participation of the processor, as with programmed I/O. Thus there is a similar loss of efficiency that is due to executing the I/O control program.

The Intel Pentium Pro supports memory-mapped I/O in addition to programmed I/O. Any of the processor's instructions that reference memory can address memory-mapped I/O locations. An example of an allocation is shown in Figure 7.5. The move instruction can transfer data between any of the processor's registers and the spaces in

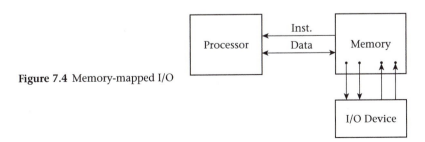

Figure 7.4 Memory-mapped I/O

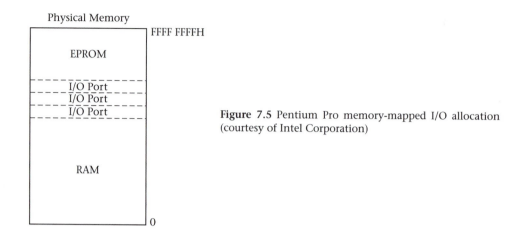

Figure 7.5 Pentium Pro memory-mapped I/O allocation (courtesy of Intel Corporation)

memory allocated for I/O. Other operations such as add, AND, OR, and test can also have one source argument in I/O space. The logical operations are useful for control of bits in the control and status registers of an I/O device that is mapped into one or more of the memory-address spaces.

Memory-mapped I/O poses a problem with caching. How are the devices connected if the I/O spaces can be cached? In general, the answer is that I/O is mapped into an uncached region of memory. This space is uncached for two reasons: cache page misses will make the time for I/O nondeterministic and fast memory reads and writes are not as important for I/O as for processor instructions and data.

In addition, the Pentium Pro does not cache a memory-mapped address so that writes are in order, a topic discussed in Subsection 6.3.3. If two instructions controlling a peripheral device by memory-mapped I/O complete out of order, the sequence of information sent to the device is incorrect and improper operation will result. For example, the command bits could be presented to the device after the data bits.

The noncached addresses are established with a set of memory-type range registers (MTRRs) that set the range limits for memory spaces. By setting limits, the MTRR registers map I/O spaces into uncached addresses.

As the IBM S360 does not use memory-mapped I/O, out-of-order writes are not an I/O problem. In-order writes are required for other purposes, and provisions are made to ensure in-order writes. The PowerPC *eieio* instruction, discussed in Subsection 6.3.3, ensures in-order writes to memory.

Interrupt I/O

In the efficiency example above, we saw that 50% of the idle time was devoted to waiting for the latency of the floppy disk. Because of this low efficiency, there are few examples of pure programmed or memory-mapped I/O in high-performance systems. Interrupts can be used to recover much of the idle time, making this time available for computing. Early mainframe computers, such as the Univac 1103 and the IBM 701, were users of this technique.

The data connection between the I/O device and the processor memory is shown in Figure 7.6 as a memory-mapped system. The processor sends a command to the

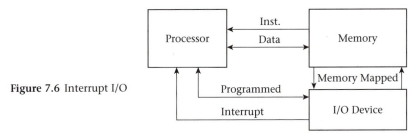

Figure 7.6 Interrupt I/O

device, usually by means of a special programmed I/O register, to start its operation. After the request is made to the device, the processor returns to the main program. When the latency is satisfied and the device is ready to transfer, the device sends an interrupt signal to the processor and the processor services the interrupt and performs the data transfer. Various status reports are sent from the device to the processor by means of the programmed I/O paths.

Interrupt I/O can be used with both programmed and memory-mapped I/O; the Intel Pentium Pro implements both techniques. The details of handling interrupts are discussed in Chapters 5 and 6.

Note that interrupt I/O will provide additional processing only if there is additional processing to be done or if the request for I/O can be made far in advance of the time it will actually be required. One or both of these conditions can be met with multi-programmed systems, discussed in Chapter 4, but not with single-user workstations without background processing.

EXAMPLE

Assume that interrupt I/O is added to the programmed I/O example. Initiating the disk transfer requires 100 instructions, and responding to the interrupt at the end of the disk latency requires another 100 instructions. What is the efficiency of the system?

Solution

The 100-ms latency can be used for useful task time work. However, the total time is increased by the time required for executing the 200 instructions associated with the subroutine call and return:

$$\text{useful time} = 1 + 0.1 \text{ s}$$
$$= 1.1 \text{ s},$$
$$\text{total time} = 1.2 + \frac{200}{100,000} \text{ s}$$
$$= 1.202 \text{ s},$$
$$\text{efficiency} = 100\left(\frac{1.1}{1.202}\right) = 91.5\%.$$

Comment

We see that the use of interrupts improves the efficiency to 91.5% from 83%. However, it is possible in some situations that the instruction time added for the interrupt can be greater than the time saved by overlapping processing with the device latency.

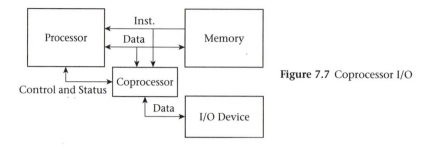

Figure 7.7 Coprocessor I/O

Coprocessor I/O

When the processor is being used to control I/O and move the data, there is a loss of processor efficiency. Thus the idea naturally arises to use a second processor or coprocessor for I/O. The autonomous coprocessor first appeared in the IBM 709 in 1959, and it performed all the I/O tasks and freed the main processor for its tasks. Figure 7.7 shows a coprocessor connecting an I/O device to the system bus. Control and status information is passed between the processor and the coprocessor by means of paths similar to those of programmed I/O. The processor sends a command to the coprocessor that autonomously performs the I/O operation.

The introduction of a coprocessor makes this configuration a multiprocessor. The problems of any multiprocessor must be addressed with coprocessor I/O. These problems include software synchronization, hardware synchronization, memory protection, and memory coherency. For students interested in these problems and their solutions, a course in multiprocessors is recommended.

There are two general types of these coprocessors: programmed I/O channel and direct memory access (DMA).

Programmed I/O Channel. A programmed I/O channel is an additional processor that is added to the system to provide I/O services by means of the programmed I/O technique. This processor, with a special-purpose ISA, is fully autonomous and can operate in parallel with the main processor.

The source of instructions for the programmed I/O channel can be either the main memory, shown in Figure 7.7, or a private memory. The main memory design is found in the IBM 360/370/390 channel. Channel control programs are placed in memory by the operating system. When the processor needs I/O service, a pointer is loaded into the channel's program counter and execution is started. The IBM channel operation is discussed further in Section 8.4.

The private memory design is found in the CDC 6600 peripheral processor. Each of the peripheral processors has its own local program memory to hold its control program. The advantage of a private memory is that main memory instruction bandwidth is not consumed during an I/O operation.

Comparing the ISAs of the IBM S360/370/390 channel with the CDC 6600 peripheral processor, one finds that the ISA of the IBM channel is high level and very CISC-like. On the other hand, the ISA of the CDC peripheral processor is low level and very RISC-like.

Direct Memory Access (DMA). DMA is a variation of programmable I/O. The DMA coprocessor receives a list of parameters from the operating system that describes the

TABLE 7.1 CONTROL METHODS

Type of I/O	Advantage	Disadvantage
Programmed	Simple, little extra hardware	Loss of processor efficiency to execute I/O subroutine. Requires special registers and move instructions
Memory mapped	Simple, little extra hardware. No special move instructions	Loss of processor efficiency to execute I/O subroutine. Requires special address logic for memory addressing
Interrupt; programmed or memory mapped	Simple, little extra hardware, improved efficiency by the processor using device latency times	Programmed: requires special registers and move commands. Memory mapped: requires special address logic for memory addressing
Coprocessor; programmed channel or DMA	Fully concurrent, no loss of processor efficiency. Transfers are direct to/from memory bypassing the processor registers	Requires significant additional hardware. May require that main memory bandwidth be increased to support extra instructions and data transfers

nature of the transfer. Examples of these parameters are type or transfer, device name, starting memory address, length of the transfer, and various control parameters. The parameter list can be transferred to the DMA by means of the system bus or a dedicated path similar to programmed I/O paths.

The DMA control is usually implemented as a hardwired state machine. The parameter list provides the inputs to the state machine; it controls and performs the transfer as specified by the parameters.

Summary of I/O Control Methods

Table 7.1 shows a summary of the I/O control methods discussed above. The advantages and disadvantages are noted.

7.2 I/O DEVICE REQUIREMENTS

The application of the processor determines the type and the quantity of the I/O devices. These requirements range from almost nothing for dedicated controllers to vast amounts for large mainframe installations. We consider two processor applications: personal computers and mainframes (commonly called servers today).

Personal Computer Devices

PCs are used in a single-user environment with limited multiprocessing activity. In general, low-latency devices are favored when the volume of data moved is small whereas high-bandwidth devices are favored where the volume of data moved is large. Operating systems such as Windows95 and Windows98 support and use virtual

TABLE 7.2 PC I/O DEVICES

Store	System resident	Hard disk	4–17G bytes 5400 RPM 8.5-9.5 ms average seek latency
	Database	CDROM	650M bytes per disk 1.8 –16M bytes per second 75–118-ms average latency
	Archive	Zip drive	100M bytes per disk 29-ms average seek time 20M bytes per second 3-s average start/stop time
Source/sink	Remote	Modem	56K baud V.90 standard
	Local media	Scanner	Flatbed Single pass Line art, halftone, gray scale, and color 75 dpi, 150 dpi, 300 dpi, 600 dpi
	Human interaction	Keyboard	104 key Data rate: typing rate
		Monitor	17-in. SVGA 0.27-mm dot pitch 1280 × 1024 noninterlaced resolution 30–70-kHz horizontal synchronization 50–100-kHz vertical synchronization

memory. Relatively large hard disk space is needed to keep a large number of large programs resident. Interconnection to various communications systems is a requirement with the widespread use of the Internet. Archival storage is needed to archive data and back up the system.

Large-screen, high-quality video is needed to support graphical programming languages and for graphics applications such as drafting, CAD, and games. High-quality audio is needed for entertainment systems and CDROM devices that support local databases.

To meet these requirements, PC manufacturers provide a wide variety of I/O devices for their customers. A small list of these devices and their characteristics are given in Table 7.2 with the taxonomy from Figure 7.1.

Mainframe or Server Devices

Mainframe and servers provide computing resources to a number of users by means of terminals and periodic processing of large batch jobs. Many mainframe installations primarily provide database facilities with only a modest requirement for computing. Typical of mainframe applications are airline reservations, credit card verification, and order entry. These applications are known as transaction processing systems; a transaction request queries a database, conducts a transaction, and updates the database to reflect the transaction. Transaction processing systems are usually real time, that is, a customer is waiting until the transaction can be completed. Thus the performance

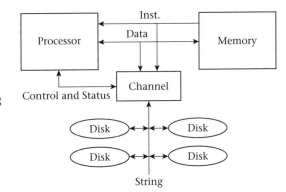

Figure 7.8 Mainframe disk string

of these systems is usually measured in transactions per second. During the Christmas season, a credit card company's server may need to respond to 50,000 transaction requests per second.

The major I/O device requirements for mainframe are usually of two types: hard disk for system resident store and network access from remote terminals. Studies by IBM have shown that the hard disk requirement is approximately 4.5G bytes per MIPS of computing capacity.[69] For a 500-MIPS mainframe, 2250G bytes of disk are needed.

EXAMPLE

A transaction processing system is considered for a PC. The PC executes instructions at 100 MIPS and has a disk with a total mean access time of 20 ms. Four-disk accesses and 100,000 instructions are needed for each transaction. How many transactions per second are possible with this system?

Solution

The total time for a transaction is the disk time plus the processor time:

$$\text{transaction time} = 4 \times 20 \times 10^{-3} + \frac{100{,}000}{100 \times 10^6}$$

$$= 80 \times 10^{-3} + 1 \times 10^{-3} = 81 \text{ ms,}$$

$$\text{transactions per second} = \frac{1}{81 \times 10^{-3}} = 12.35.$$

Comments

Even if the processing time goes to zero, the transaction rate is limited by the four-disk accesses. For PCs to be effective transaction processors, the I/O system must be improved to support many concurrent disk accesses. This is exactly what is being done by a number of PC manufacturers today.

The one-disk unit usually found with a PC does not have sufficient capacity, bandwidth, and low latency to meet the needs of transaction processing. Thus a number of disk units must be attached to an I/O channel, as shown in Figure 7.8. A channel is attached to the disks by a path called a string. The strings are usually redundant so that operation can continue in the event of a string failure. In addition, a large mainframe

---

[69] A typical PC may have 0.005G bytes per MIPS.

or server will have a number of controllers and a number of strings as several hundred disks may be attached.

The remote access requirements for mainframes are met with various dedicated and switched networking systems. In general the volume of data transferred for transaction processing is small; thus the bandwidth requirement is modest. Communication between the terminals and the mainframe is by land lines, microwave, or satellite. The latency of dedicated communications paths, even by means of geosynchronous satellites, is a small component of the total latency time because of disk accesses. Key components of the communications system are the switching computers that route information through the network. At the mainframe, the communications lines are connected to a channel controller that queues requests for mainframe service.

The World Wide Web is different from transaction processors in that both low latency and high bandwidth are required. Low latency is needed for response time and the high bandwidth is needed because of the large volume of graphics, video, and sound that is being transmitted. The WWW will be discussed further in Subsection 7.6.1.

7.3 BUSES AND CONTROLLERS

The first two I/O tasks noted in Section 7.1 concern the establishment of connections between the memory and the I/O devices and the control of data transfers over this connection. Most modern computers use a bus, or buses, for interconnecting the major components of the system. A bus serves as a pathway between components for passing addresses, instructions, and data. A simple high-level view of a bus is shown in Figure 7.9. This is the bus shown in Figure 7.6 that is used with the coprocessor I/O. This bus interconnects the processor, main memory, and I/O devices by means of their controllers. Also recall the discussion in Chapter 4 on the role played by the bus in transferring instructions and data between the processor and memory.

Buses can be classified in a number of ways: by purpose, control, and communication technique (Thurber et al. 1972). The options for bus design are as follows:

Purpose: dedicated or general purpose
Control: centralized or decentralized
Communications: synchronous or asynchronous

From the list above, we see there are eight possible design points for a bus. In the following sections, the characteristics of each of the six design parameters are discussed and correlated to bus designs used in computer systems today.

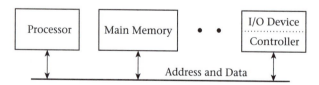

Figure 7.9 Simple bus structure

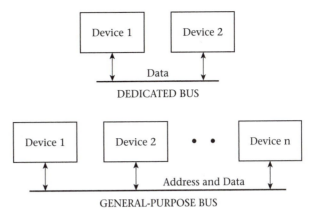

Figure 7.10 Dedicated and general-purpose buses

Dedicated or General Purpose

The major difference between dedicated and general-purpose buses is that a dedicated bus is point to point between two physical devices, whereas a general-purpose bus interconnects more than two physical devices. Figure 7.10 illustrates the two types. Dedicated buses are used in cases in which the latency and the bandwidth requirements are such that sharing the bus with another user can result in unacceptable system performance. In these cases, a special dedicated bus is provided by the designer. Note that a dedicated bus does not need address lines because the source and destination are addressed by implication. That is, device 1 always sends to device 2 or device 2 to device 1. Some dedicated buses are unidirectional with information flow in only one direction. For example, the bus that connects a memory to a graphics controller may be unidirectional.

Because dedicated buses are used internal to the processor or for special high-bandwidth applications without general-purpose capabilities, these buses are not considered further. Instead, the following paragraphs discuss the control and communications design techniques found with general-purpose buses.

General-purpose buses differ from the processor internal buses discussed in Chapter 5. A dedicated internal bus is controlled by an outside state machine or microprogrammed controller, in contrast to a general-purpose bus in which the address of the receiver is provided by the sender.

Also, with a general-purpose bus, a number of users share the same bus and simultaneous requests for the bus are resolved by one of a number of resolution techniques. Some of the devices on a general-purpose bus are both senders and receivers or only senders or only receivers. For example, a printer controller's primary function is to receive data and send some status information. A disk controller, on the other hand, sends and receives data and sends status information.

Centralized or Decentralized Control

The control of a general-purpose bus can be either centralized or decentralized. The basic requirement is to grant or not grant a device access to the bus. With centralized or decentralized control, all devices are treated equally except for their priority of access. Thus, if one of the devices is the processor, it may be given the highest priority for bus access. However, in some systems an I/O device may have the highest priority because of the loss in system performance; for example, if a disk is unable to read and misses a complete revolution, many milliseconds will be lost. A thorough discussion of priority is outside the scope of this book.

Centralized Control. A single hardware control unit will recognize a request and grant access to the bus to a requesting device. It is the responsibility of the controller to resolve simultaneous requests and assign priority to the requests. At least three designs, with modification, are used for centralized controllers: daisy chain, polling with a global counter, and polling with local counters. These designs are shown in Figure 7.11.

Convention calls the unit holding the bus controller the master whereas the control logic in the device is called a slave. Note that there are many variations on the basic designs discussed below.

DAISY CHAIN. With this design, the control lines to the devices are connected in series. When a device needs access to the bus, it sends a bus request to the bus controller. The controller then sends a bus-available query to the first device to determine its current status of activity. If the device does not want access to the bus, it passes the bus-available query on to the next device, and so on. The requesting device responds with bus-busy and is given the next access to the bus.

The advantage of daisy chain control is its simplicity, low cost, and expandability. The disadvantages are reliability; if a line breaks, all of the devices downstream are removed from the system. Also, this control favors upstream device requests leading to "hogging" of the I/O system by the upstream devices.

POLLING WITH GLOBAL COUNTER. Each device can issue a bus request to the controller. When this request is received, the controller polls the bus-request lines to identify the requester and to find which device, if any, is using the bus. The polling sequence is established by a counter in the controller that starts at 1 and increments for each poll. When the counter value equals the device number, the requesting device is identified. If the bus is idle, or when it becomes idle, the request is granted.

This system is more reliable than daisy chaining but has the same priority-favoring characteristic because the counter starts at 1 for each poll cycle. However, we can eliminate this disadvantage by assigning random addresses to the devices or by using a pseudorandom global counter. Expansion, within the limits of the controller design capacity, is relatively easy.

INDEPENDENT REQUESTS. Central control with independent requests receives bus-request signals from the various devices that can be viewed as interrupts to a processor. The status of the bus is maintained in the controller; all the grants of bus access are determined based on this status information. When the controller determines that a device can use the bus, a bus-granted signal is sent to the device.

This system is flexible because the priority can be determined by programming the bus controller with a table of priorities. Latency time is smaller than with the other two systems discussed because there is reduced communication between the controller and the devices.

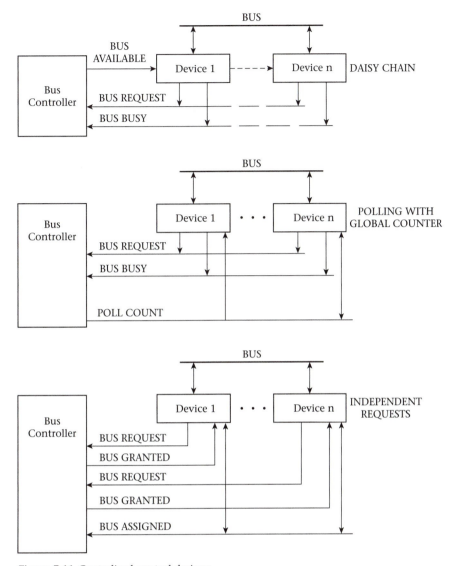

Figure 7.11 Centralized control designs

Distributed Control. Distributed control, also known as decentralized control, distributes the control function between all the devices on the bus. The major advantage of decentralized control is that the system is easily expandable by the addition of modules. As with centralized control, there are three basic designs with variations: daisy chain, polling, and independent requests. Figure 7.12 shows these designs in simplified form.

DAISY CHAIN. A device issues a bus request to the bus-request line that is attached to bus available. When a device receives the bus available, if it is not the originator of the request, it passes it on to the next devices. This continues until the requesting device receives the bus-available signal, at which time the request is granted. If the bus is being used, none of the devices can issue a bus request.

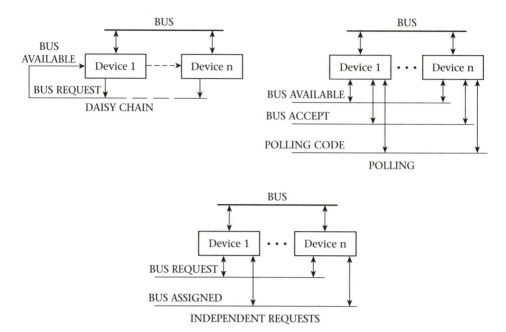

Figure 7.12 Distributed control designs

POLLING. This scheme works by giving the ability to poll to all the devices. When a device that is using the bus no longer needs the bus, it places a device-dependent code on the polling code line and signals on the bus-available line. If the code matches the code of a device desiring the bus, that device responds with a bus-accept signal. The former device that had the bus drops the polling code and bus-available lines, and the latter device starts using the bus and removes the bus-accept signal.

When the polling device does not receive a bus-accept signal, the code is changed by some allocation algorithm, and it polls again. The algorithm could be as simple as a count giving a round robin poll of the devices or the code can have priority. For example, device 3 may always ask device 7 if it wants the bus after device 3 has completed its use. On the other hand, device 4 may choose a random code for its poll.

INDEPENDENT REQUESTS. With this scheme, when any device is using the bus, it signals on the bus-assigned line. Another device desiring to use the bus places a request on the bus-request lines consisting of a code for its priority. When the current user finishes with the bus and releases it, it also removes its signal from the bus-assigned line. All devices examine all the bus requests, and the device that recognizes itself as having the highest priority takes control of the bus and signals on the bus-assigned line.

Synchronous or Asynchronous Communication

The transmission of addresses, control information, and data between two devices may be synchronous with a clock, or asynchronous without a clock and self-timed (Del Corso et al. 1986, and Di Giacomo 1990). There are advantages and disadvantages to each, as discussed in the following paragraphs.

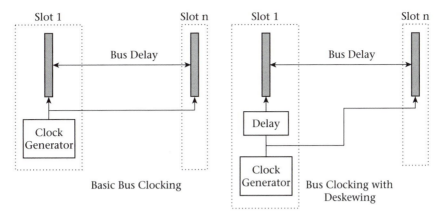

Figure 7.13 Synchronous bus clocking

Synchronous Communication. A simplified diagram of a synchronous bus (the data and clock portion) connected between two devices is shown on the left of Figure 7.13. Note that this logic diagram looks similar to that of the pipeline in Figure 6.5. Data are to be transmitted between the card in the right-hand slot to the card in the left-hand slot. The transmitter and the receiver are clocked from a common source on the left-hand card. The minimum clock period is

$$t_{\text{clk}}(\text{min}) = \text{bus delay(max)} + [\text{clock skew(max)} + \text{setup time}]$$
$$= \text{bus delay(max)} + [\text{Bus Delay(max)} + \text{setup time}]$$
$$\approx 2 \text{ bus delay(max)} + \text{setup time}.$$

The clock period of approximately 2 bus delays sets a limit on the bus bandwidth. This limit is a function of the physical length of the bus. However, the clock skew represents one half of the clock period. If that 1 bus delay can be eliminated, the bandwidth can be doubled; the clock period is approximately 1 bus delay per transfer.

To eliminate this factor from the clock period, extensive deskewing circuits are used to reduce the skew at each card slot in the bus to an acceptable level of 1–2 gate delays. Delays, shown on the right of Figure 7.13, are inserted in the clock lines to the cards; the delays are the inverse of the distance from the clock generator. Thus the clock arrives at all the cards at the same time. The use of deskewing increases the bus bandwidth by approximately a factor of 2. Even if only one additional bus slot is occupied and it is the one closest to the transmitter, the clock must be set in anticipation that at some time a distant slot will be occupied.

Asynchronous Communication. Asynchronous communication for buses was developed to overcome the worst-case clock rate limitations of synchronous systems. With asynchronous communications, data transfers occur at the fastest rate and smallest delay possible under the circumstances of the physical status of the bus. As cards are added to the bus, the timing automatically adjusts for each card. There are a number of asynchronous protocols; however, only one of the simpler ones is discussed here.

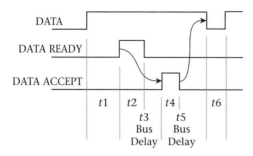

Figure 7.14 Asynchronous transfer

The timing diagram for an asynchronous exchange is shown in Figure 7.14. This figure illustrates the action when a source sends data to a destination.

The source places data on the bus, and after a time $t1$ transmits a data ready signal that has width $t2$. When the destination receives the data ready signal after time $t3$, it latches the data and may make a parity check. The receiver then informs the transmitter with a data accept signal that the data transfer has been successful. If there is a problem with the data, a data error signal (not shown) is sent to the source. The source can initiate another transfer after $t6$.

This process is rather slow because it requires a minimum of two bus delays $(t3 + t5)$ before a second transmission of data by the source. There are other protocols that reduce the number of delays and increase the bandwidth of the system, but these are outside the scope of this book.

7.3.1 BUS DESIGN EXAMPLES

There are eight design points that use the design criteria discussed above. Dedicated buses are tailored to the needs of a particular transfer path, such as the data path buses shown in Figure 5.4. However, general-purpose buses are normally standardized and are of the greatest interest to us. Table 7.3 provides examples of the four general-purpose bus types from the taxonomy: centralized and decentralized control and synchronous and asynchronous communications.

7.4 SERIAL COMMUNICATION

The buses discussed above are usually designed for parallel transfer of a number of bits, 32 for example. There are cases in which, because of the data rates or the transfer

TABLE 7.3 GENERAL-PURPOSE BUS DESIGN EXAMPLES

Control	Communications	Examples	Specification
Centralized	Synchronous	PCI	PCI SIG v2.1.
Centralized	Asynchronous	IPI	ANSI X3.129
Decentralized	Synchronous	Multibus II	ANSI/IEEE 1296
Decentralized	Asynchronous	VME	IEEE 1014
		FutureBus	IEEE 896.1

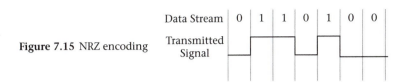

Figure 7.15 NRZ encoding

medium, serial transfer is used. Examples of this type can be found in mouse to processor, keyboard to processor, and communications by means of telephone lines. The first problem to be solved with serial communications is that the transmitter sends clocked data to the receiver and the receiver must, in some way, recover a clock from the transmitted data stream.

Clock Recovery

For most serial communication systems, data transfers are conducted over varying distances, and transmitting a clock with zero skew is impractical. For these cases, the data bit stream must be encoded in such a way as to permit a clock to be recovered by the receiver. These techniques are called implicit clock schemes.

Three techniques for clock recovery are discussed in the following paragraphs. Section 7.5 discusses the problem with synchronization between the receiver's clock and the data for which clock recovery is not possible.

Nonreturn to Zero (NRZ). The NRZ coding transmits one level for a 1 and another for a 0, as shown in Figure 7.15. The receiver's clock, which is set at the same frequency of the transmitter's, is synchronized with each transition of the incoming signal. One of the problems with this coding is that for long runs of ones or zeros, no transition occurs and the receiver's clock is without a synchronization input. For this reason, the stability of the receiver's clock oscillator and the synchronization method are important.

A new standard universal serial bus (USB) is becoming available on PCs for interfacing relatively low-bandwidth devices. This standard uses NRZ with bandwidths of 12M bits/s up to 5 m. A low-speed subchannel at 1M bits/s is supported for interfacing to devices, such as a mouse, for which cost is a consideration.

Frequency Modulation (FM). With the FM technique, a different frequency is transmitted for a 1 and a 0, as illustrated in Figure 7.16. Because there are transitions within each bit period, the clock can be recovered with greater ease.

Some modems use a type of FM that increases the bandwidth of the serial channel. For example, a four-frequency system can encode as follows:

Freq. 1   00
Freq. 2   01
Freq. 3   10
Freq. 4   11

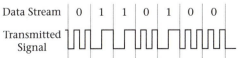

Figure 7.16 Frequency modulation

Figure 7.17 Manchester biphase-space code

The transmitter modem looks at the transmitted data stream two bits at a time and selects the frequency to transmit during a fixed period of time. The receiving modem detects the frequency and reconstitutes the data stream.[70]

Manchester Code. Another clock recovery technique is known as the Manchester code, of which there are several variations. Figure 7.17 illustrates the biphase-space version. This code ensures a transition between each bit position, which facilitates recovery of the clock. Note, however, that the code is context dependent, as illustrated by the two consecutive ones. In general, the decoder must examine two bits at a time to determine the actual data stream.

Serial Communications Protocols

Serial communication protocols can be taxonomized by the clocking method and format of the transmitted data.

Clocking

Synchronous	Clock is distributed or bits are transmitted continuously to provide clock synchronization.
Asynchronous	The line is in a quiescent state, either a 1 or 0, until a message is transmitted, at which time the receiver synchronizes its clock.

Data

Character	Encoded characters, such as ASCII.
Block	Binary message.

There are four combinations of these two characteristics. Three of these are discussed below: asynchronous character, synchronous character, and synchronous block. There is no known use of an asynchronous-block protocol.

Because these systems transmit a stream of bits, the receiver must first be able to recover the clock from the transmitted data stream, as discussed above. After the recovery of the clock, with a stream of ones and zeros, where does a character or message start and end? Thus it is necessary to provide coding that will permit character and message synchronization and recovery. Morse code provides a simple example: After each of the variable length characters is transmitted in the form of dots and dashes, the transmitter pauses before starting the next character. Word separation is identified by context.

Asynchronous-Character Protocol. With this protocol, the line is quiescent until the transmitter emits a start bit followed by the character bits, as shown in Figure 7.18. Depending on the character set, the number of character bits may be as large as 8 and

---

[70] The Touch Tone telephone is a form of FM encoding: 10 digits plus 2 control symbols are encoded.

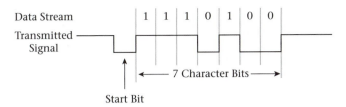

Figure 7.18 Asynchronous-character protocol

a parity or check bit may be added. The character specification must be agreed on by both the transmitter and the receiver. After the character bits are transmitted, the line is returned to the quiescent state. Some period of time must elapse before another character is transmitted.

Another asynchronous-character protocol is the RS232 standard. For this standard, the character type and the clock rate must be initialized by both the sender and the receiver. During the quiescent state the line is at zero, also known as mark, and the start of a character transmission is indicated by a 1, also known as space. During the quiescent time, the receiver samples the input line at twice the bit clock rate to detect the start bit.

Table 7.4 shows the RS232 character codes. There are three character codes: 5-bit code, 7-bit code, and 8-bit code. For the 7- and the 8-bit codes there are programmable variations.

Synchronous-Character Protocol. This protocol surrounds a text message, either fixed or variable length, with various synchronization and control information, as shown in Figure 7.19. The transmitter continuously sends a stream of SYN characters, 0010110, so that the receiver maintains bit and character synchronization. The receiver continuously looks for the bit pattern 0000001 (SOH), which indicates the beginning of a message that establishes synchronization of the message. The header provides such information as the length of the text message. Following the header is the STX character, then the body of the message begins. The message is terminated with the ETX character, which is followed by block character check information.

TABLE 7.4 RS232 CHARACTER CODES

Type	Bit Stream
5-Bit code	Start bit + 5 data bits + 1–2 mark bits
7-Bit code	Start bit + 7 data bits + 1–2 mark bits
7-Bit code	Start bit + 7 data bits + 0 + 1–2 mark bits
7-Bit code	Start bit + 7 data bits + 1 + 1–2 mark bits
7-Bit code	Start bit + 7 data bits + even parity + 1–2 mark bits
7-Bit code	Start bit + 7 data bits + odd parity + 1–2 mark bits
8-Bit code	Start bit + 8 data bits + 1–2 mark bits
8-Bit code	Start bit + 8 data bits + even parity + 1–2 mark bits
8-Bit code	Start bit + 8 data bits + odd parity + 1–2 mark bits

SYN	SYN	SOH	Header	STX	TEXT MESSAGE	ETX	BCC

SYN Establishes synchronization   0010110
SOH Heading of block msg.   0000001
STX Start of text   0000010
ETX End of text   0000011
BCC Block Character Check
Header Address and control information

Figure 7.19 Synchronous-character protocol

For this protocol the text message characters are 7-bit ASCII with odd parity. The ASCII character set reserves the control codes that are guaranteed not to appear in a text message.

Synchronous-block protocol: One of the many block oriented protocols for message synchronization is the high-level-data link control (HDLC). This protocol, shown in Figure 7.20, precedes a message with a preamble called a flag. During a quiescent period, flags are continuously transmitted to maintain clock and character synchronization. The start of a message is indicated by the address field that is constrained to exclude 01111110. The message is terminated with a frame check sum to ensure that the data has been received as transmitted (within the ability of the check sum).

The binary message can have any combination of ones and zeros; even the flag bit pattern 01111110 may exist in the message. Thus the transmitter must look for this pattern in the message and must insert a zero, called bit stuffing, to break up this pattern:

    Message   01111110
    Becomes   011111010

The receiver, having first synchronized on the address and control, removes the inserted zero.

EXAMPLE

With the HDLC protocol, if the message has five ones followed by a zero (111110), how does the receiver know that the 0 was not stuffed and is a legitimate message bit?

Solution

The pattern that is looked for by the receiver is 011111010, a 9-bit pattern. This pattern has the stuffed zero.

Flag	Address	Control	Binary Message	Frame Check	Flag

Flag   01111110
Address   8 bits
Control   8 bits
Frame Check   16 bits

Figure 7.20 HDLC synchronous-block protocol

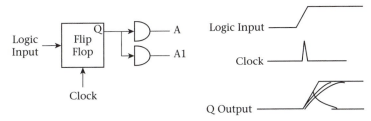

Figure 7.21 The metastability problem

7.5 CLOCK SYNCHRONIZATION

The issue of synchronization between two or more programs will be discussed in Chapter 8. In this section, we discuss the problem of synchronization between two hardware systems that communicate but have separate clocks (Kleeman and Cantoni 1987) and for which clock recovery is not a design option. For example, an I/O channel connects a disk memory (with its clock) to the real memory of the processor (with its clock).

Figure 7.21 illustrates the problem of unsynchronized clocks. A logic input signal from a system with another clock is input to a flip flop with its own clock. The two clocks are not synchronized. If an asynchronous logic input change occurs during the clock pulse or clock transition, the flip flop can be metastable for a period of time, with the final state being nondeterministic. If the output of the flip flop is used to drive two drivers with unequal thresholds, then the driver's outputs may not be logically equal for some period of time. That is, A is not equal to A1. As these signals are used as inputs to other gates, the outcome cannot be predicted and unreliable system behavior can result.

Figure 7.22 shows oscilloscope-sampled Q and Q' outputs of two cross-coupled transistor–transistor logic NAND gates (Chaney and Molnar 1973). The R and S inputs are switched simultaneously to emulate the simultaneous input logic change and the clock. Note that the time for metastability to subside is unbounded. A small fraction of switching events stay in the metastable state for a very long time; longer than 9 ns in the case of Figure 7.22.

Figure 7.22 Synchronizer metastability, 1 ns/div, 1 v/div (© 1973 IEEE)

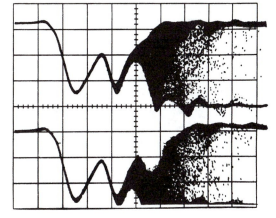

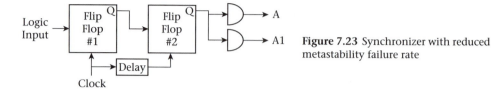

Figure 7.23 Synchronizer with reduced metastability failure rate

The problems of erroneous operation resulting from metastability occur infrequently and are very difficult to diagnose because the errors are transient.

EXAMPLE

To illustrate the magnitude of the synchronization problem assume the following. The system attempts to synchronize every 16 clocks (for a processor memory bus handshake), the clock period is 100 ns, and the synchronizer fails every 1×10^{11} attempts.

Solution

The mean time between failure (MTBF) of synchronization is

= number of clocks × clock rate × synchronizer failure rate
$$= 16 \times (100 \times 10^{-9}) \times (1 \times 10^{11})$$
$$= 1.6 \times 10^5 \text{ s}$$
$$= 1.85 \text{ days}.$$

Comment

This MTBF is small enough to make the system appear to be unreliable and long enough to make diagnosis of the problem very difficult. [71]

The preceding example suggests the two methods for reducing synchronization MTBF: reduce the frequency of synchronization and/or reduce the MTBF of the synchronizer. Remember that a failure-free synchronizer has been proven impossible to design.

The frequency of synchronization can be reduced by providing that more bits will be transferred on each synchronization. For example, synchronizing for the transfer of a 1K-byte block rather than synchronizing on every bit transferred will reduce the synchronization frequency by a factor of 8192.

After the frequency of synchronization is reduced, the MTBF of the synchronizer may be reduced. There are a number of techniques that have been used. The first step is to use very high-frequency transistors for the synchronizer. This technique reduces the period of time in which the synchronizer may be metastable.

Another technique for reducing synchronization MTBF is shown in Figure 7.23. This synchronizer works as follows. The clock is delayed for a period of time until the probability of flip flop 1 being in the metastable state is reduced to an acceptable value. Note from Figure 7.22 that the longer the wait, the lower the probability of metastability. After this delay, flip flop 2 is clocked. Because of the delay, the input to

---

[71] A rule of thumb for designers is that the MTBF of a good synchronizer system should be approximately three years.

flip flop 2 has a low probability of changing and it may not go metastable. However, because the maximum time that flip flop 1 can be metastable is unbounded, there is a small probability that the input to flip flop 2 is changing during its delayed clock and it too will go metastable. This synchronizer has a finite probability that it will exhibit metastability.

The time delay must be less than the period of the clock; otherwise the system will not function properly. The reason for this is that if another input is presented to flip flop 1 while it is metastable, it will probably remain metastable. Also, the delay must be greater than the likely maximum time of metastability. These are difficult, and contradictory, design requirements to meet for systems with very high-frequency clocks.

EXAMPLE

Take the synchronizer of Figure 7.23. Assume that 15 ns is deemed to be a sufficient clock delay to eliminate most, if not all, metastable conditions on flip flop 1. What is the minimum clock period and maximum clock rate of this system?

Solution

$$\text{minimum clock period} = 15 \text{ ns},$$
$$\text{maximum clock rate} = \frac{1}{15 \text{ ns}} = 66.6 \text{ MHz}.$$

7.6 QUEUING THEORY

When there are a number of requests for the same resource, called a structural hazard in Chapter 6, many systems establish queues to hold the requests until they can be serviced. Queuing theory was developed to permit closed-model evaluation of these systems without resorting to computer simulation. The two models discussed below are quite simple and ignore many of the complexities of some systems. Nevertheless, these models permit rapid and fairly accurate evaluation of these systems. The most important result from these models is the mean or average time required for servicing a request. The two models discussed are open systems and closed systems. A designer can usually identify the type of system being considered and apply the proper model.

7.6.1 OPEN-SYSTEM QUEUING MODEL

The open system is shown in Figure 7.24. The queue is first in first out (FIFO). Requests for service arrive, are placed in the queue, and are served when the request reaches the

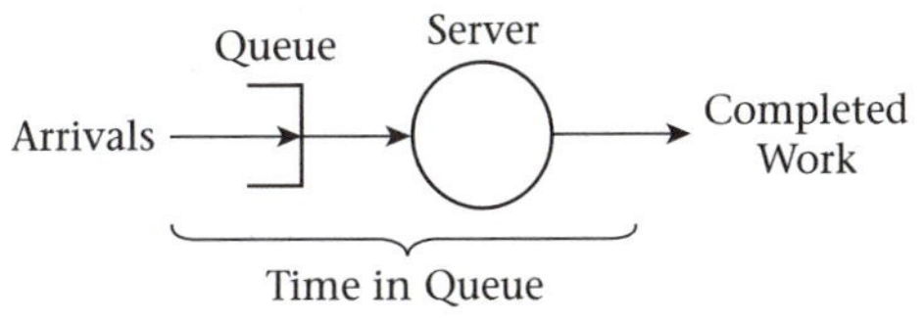

Figure 7.24 Open-system queuing model

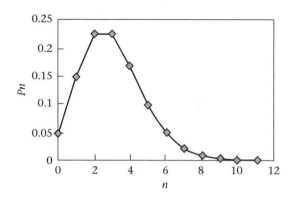

Figure 7.25 Poisson distribution, $\lambda = 3$

tail of the queue. The time in the queue is the total time in the system (queue time plus server time).

The open queuing model is applicable not only to disk I/O systems but to airport runways, grocery checkout counters, and Internet servers. The derivation of the model for the time in the queue is based on two assumptions:

1. The arrival rate and the service rate follow a Poisson distribution.
2. Requests arrive, are served, and never request service again, within the time frame of the model.

The Poisson distribution

$$P_n = \frac{\lambda^n}{n!} e^{-\lambda},$$

for $\lambda = 3$, is shown in Figure 7.25.

We now define some terms. The mean arrival rate is λ, the mean service rate is μ, and the mean time in the queue (queue time + service time) is t_q. The model for t_q, without derivation, is

$$t_q = \frac{1}{\mu - \lambda}.$$

Consider the limits of λ:

As $\lambda \to 0, t_q \to 1/\mu$,

and

as $\lambda \to \mu, t_q \to \infty$.

From experience we know that if we walk up to a bank teller, for example, and there is no one in line (in other words, $\lambda \to 0$), we will be served immediately and our mean time in the queue is $1/\mu$. On the other hand, when customers are arriving at the same mean rate that service is being provided ($\lambda \to \mu$), the mean time in the queue for some customers may be infinite.

EXAMPLE

An Internet server can perform 100 transactions per second, and requests are arriving at the rate of 80 requests per second. What is the mean time in the queue?

Solution

$$t_q = \frac{1}{\mu - \lambda} = \frac{1}{100 - 80} = \frac{1}{20} = 0.05 \text{ s.}$$

Comments

The mean time in the queue is 0.05 seconds, five times that of the unloaded system; 0.01 s.

It is not necessary to know the values of λ and μ. The model can be normalized by use of the duty cycle, also known as utilization, of the server, a parameter easier to estimate or measure in some situations. The duty cycle is defined as $\rho = (\lambda/\mu)$, and

$$t_q = \frac{1}{\mu - \lambda} = \frac{\frac{1}{\mu}}{\frac{\mu}{\mu} - \frac{\lambda}{\mu}} = \frac{1}{\mu(1 - \rho)}.$$

The normalized time in the queue is plotted in Figure 7.26 for $\mu = 1$. Note that for a duty cycle of 0.5, the time in the queue is twice the service time. For a duty cycle of 0.8, the time in the queue is five times the service time – the identical results of the previous example. The plot stops at a duty cycle of 0.9 because the asymptotic behavior of the model gives an infinite time in the queue for a duty cycle of one.

Figure 7.27 shows the system response time versus system utilization for an array of magnetic disks (Chen 1989). The value of t_q is approximately 35 ms at a duty cycle of zero. Further, at $\rho = 0.5$ the response time is approximately 70 ms, as determined by the model. The model is reasonably accurate up to a duty cycle of 0.7. The divergence is due to the operating system's turning off requests so that the response time and the queue do not increase to infinity.

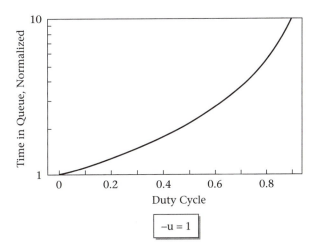

Figure 7.26 Time in queue vs. duty cycle

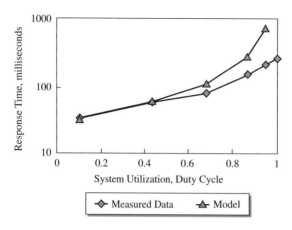

Figure 7.27 Disk system response time

EXAMPLE

An airport departure runway mean departure rate is 0.5 departures per minute or one every two minutes, not counting queue delays. At the present time, the duty cycle of the runway is 50%. There is a projection that the traffic of the airport will increase by 50% in the next year. By what percent will the takeoff delays increase?

Solution

At the present time the mean t_q, including the takeoff time itself, is

$$\frac{1}{\mu(1-\rho)} = \frac{1}{0.5(1-\rho)} = \frac{2}{1-0.5} = 4 \text{ min.}$$

With the increase in traffic, the departure rate does not change and the mean time in the takeoff queue is

$$\frac{2}{1-(0.5 \times 1.5)} = 8 \text{ min.}$$

Thus the percentage of increase in queue time is

$$\frac{100(8-4)}{4} = 100\%.$$

Comments

The model shows the exponential behavior of an open queue. From the initial conditions, a 50% increase in departures results in a 100% increase in the mean total time in the queue. The wait to takeoff increased from a mean of 2 min to a mean of 6 min, a 200% increase.

The mean number of requests in an open system (queue + server) is determined by Little's law. This law states that the number of customers in a system is equal to the arrival rate times the time in the queue:

mean number of requests in system $= \lambda t_q$.

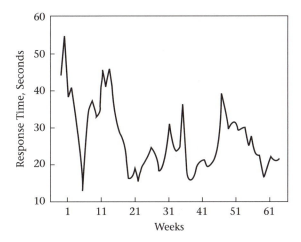

Figure 7.28 WWW response time (data courtesy Keynote Inc.)

Because there are ρ requests being served, the number of requests in the queue is the number of requests in the system minus ρ, that is: $\lambda t_q - \rho$. Thus, as t_q approaches infinity, the size of the queue approaches infinity as well. In real systems, the queue size must be finite, and when the fixed-size queue starts to fill up, requests are denied or turned off. This is what the operating system did with the disk server shown in Figure 7.27.

In the example on the first example of Subsection 7.6.1 what happens if the number of requests to the Internet server jumps to 200 per minute because of a "hot" home page?[72] The depth of the input queue and the queue time will go to ∞, an impossibility. The situation is handled by pushing the queue back to the user with a busy signal, or, in the case of an airport, not letting the planes leave the gates. The queue has not gone away, it has just been pushed back to the user.

EXAMPLES

1. Your boss shows you the following chart, Figure 7.28, of the WWW response time for a 64-week period. You are asked to explain what could have caused the substantial reduction in response time from approximately 55 s to approximately 20 s over this period. There have been periods of short response time but the level achieved at the end seems to be stable.

Solution

To obtain a reasonable answer to this problem, we must make some assumptions. Assume that the response time is for users who have been connected to their provider and does not represent a lack of modems. Also, it is reasonable to assume that the request load increased by 50% during the time in question. We assume that the capacity of the servers was increased substantially; thus the server queue delays were reduced. To find a solution, we assign the total delay

[72] During the 1998 Olympic Games at Nagano, the Internet site had 634,716,480 hits over 16 days, an average of 459 hits per second. The peak hit rate was 1840 per second.

to the servers with their queues; that is, assume no communications delay. Also assume an open-system queuing model and that the mean server service time is one request per second ($\mu = 1$) with the overall response time (t_q) of 55 s for the fifth week. What was the speedup of the servers?

We first determine the early week mean request rate:

$$t_q = \frac{1}{\mu - \lambda},$$

$$\lambda = \mu - \frac{1}{t_q} = 1 - \frac{1}{55} = 0.982 \text{ requests per second.}$$

The new servers have improved service rates (mean response time of 20 s) with the increased rate of requests for service. What is the new service rate with the assumed 50% increase in requests?

$$\mu = \frac{1}{t_q} + \lambda = \frac{1}{20} + 0.982 \times 1.5 = 1.52 \text{ services per second.}$$

The speedup of the servers is

$$S = \frac{\mu(\text{new})}{\mu(\text{old})} = \frac{1.52}{1} = 1.52.$$

Comment

It is clear that in the fifth week the servers were greatly overloaded as λ was approaching μ with a duty cycle of $0.982/1 = 0.982$. A 50% improvement in service rate yielded a speedup of $55/20 = 2.75$ in response time and a slight reduction in the server duty cycle to $(\lambda/\mu) = [(0.982 \times 1.5)/1.52] = 0.969$.

The system is still overloaded with this duty cycle.

2. How many requests are waiting in the queue of the Internet server in the fifth and the 64th weeks?

Solution

From Little's law, the mean number of requests in the queue is the total number in the system minus the probability that one request is being served. For the fifth week the mean number of requests in the queue is

$$(\lambda t_q) - \rho = (0.982 \times 55) - 0.982 = 54 - 0.982 \approx 53.$$

From Little's law, the mean number of requests in the queue in the 64th week is

$$(0.982 \times 1.5 \times 20) - 0.969 = 29.46 - 0.98 \approx 29.$$

Comment

The mean number of requests in the queue decreased from 53 to 29, a 45% reduction.

3. Restate Little's law in terms of duty cycle ρ.

Solution

Number of requests in the system $= \lambda t_q$

$$= \lambda \left[\frac{1}{\mu(1 - \rho)} \right] = \frac{\rho}{1 - \rho}.$$

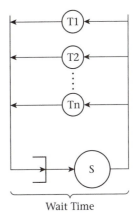

Figure 7.29 Closed-system queuing model

Comment

This statement of Little's law can be checked against the previous solution. The fifth-month duty cycle of the Internet server example is 0.982. Thus the number of requests in the system is $0.982/(1 - 0.982) = 0.982/0.018 \approx 54$, the same result obtained above.

7.6.2 CLOSED-SYSTEM QUEUING MODEL

The second model of interest is the closed-system model. This model provides the mean wait time for a closed system, such as a server with a number of terminals, as shown in Figure 7.29. For this model, there is one server, one input queue, and a number of terminals.

System users compose a request to the server and place the request on the queue. Some time later, the server returns the result of the request, and the user composes another request. Unlike the open system, requests and responses circulate through the system.

We now define some terms: t_s is the server service time, ρ is the duty cycle of the server, n is the number of terminals, t_t is the think time (the time the user takes from the response to the next request), and w is the wait time for the response. The wait time model is

$$w = \frac{nt_s}{\rho} - t_t.$$

The server duty cycle increases from 0 with no active terminals to 1 as the number of requests saturates the server, leaving no idle server time. When the server is saturated, $\rho = 1$, the wait time is

$$w = nt_s - t_t.$$

Note that this is a linear relationship without the exponential increase in service time exhibited with open systems. In addition, without a load on the server, $\rho = 0$ and w becomes very large – an absurd result from the model. There is an iterative solution

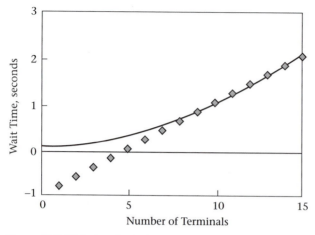

Figure 7.30 Wait time for a closed system

to this model (Denning and Buzen 1978) that removes this absurdity; however, an approximate solution is shown illustrated by assuming some values for the parameters.

Let $t_s = 0.1$ s, $t_t = 1$ s, and $\rho = 1$ (the saturated case). The plot of wait time is shown in Figure 7.30 with the wait time being negative with a small number of terminals, another absurd situation that is eliminated with the iterative solution.

What is the correct wait time plot? For one terminal, there is no other requester and the wait time is merely the service time of the server. This point is plotted at 0.1 s for the example. As the number of terminals increase, ρ increases to 1 and the system is saturated at approximately 10 terminals. As terminals are added, the wait time increases with a slope of t_s. Because many closed systems operate saturated, the saturated region is the region of general interest.

EXAMPLE

A server with 100 terminals is saturated; the measured mean wait time is 1.7 s and the measured mean think time is 2.0 s. The users are complaining about the long wait, and the facility manager wants to reduce the mean wait time to 0.5 s. What can be done?

Solution

There are two solutions to this design problem: the number of terminals can be reduced or a higher-performance server can be provided. To find the number of terminals that will give the desired mean wait time, we must first find t_s of the base system:

$$W = nt_s - t_t,$$
$$1.7 = 100t_s - 2,$$
$$t_s = \frac{1.7 + 2}{100} = 0.037 \text{ s}.$$

To reduce the wait time to 0.5 s, we find the number of terminals that will give that performance:

$$W = nt_s - t_t,$$
$$0.5 = 0.037n - 2,$$
$$n = \frac{0.5 + 2}{0.037} = 67.5 \approx 67 \text{ terminals.}$$

The alternative solution to the long wait problem is to increase the performance of the server. The needed server speedup is found by first determining the required t_s:

$$W = nt_s - t_t,$$
$$0.5 = 100t_s - 2,$$
$$t_s = \frac{0.5 + 2}{100} = 0.025 \text{ s.}$$

The required speedup is

$$\text{Speed up} = \frac{t_s(\text{old})}{t_s(\text{new})} = \frac{0.037}{0.025} = 1.48.$$

Comment

The facilities manager will need to drop 1/3 of the existing terminals to give the desired response time, not a very likely solution. The most likely solution is to upgrade the server by approximately 50%.

A word of caution is needed regarding think time. Think time is presented in the model as a fixed value. There is ample experimental evidence – and your own experience will tell you – that as the wait time decreases, think time decreases as well. We make more requests to a fast system than to a slow one. Thus the facilities manager, in the example above, should compute the required speedup by using $t_t = 1$ rather than $t_t = 2$.

REFERENCES

Blaauw, G. and Brooks, F. P. Jr. (1997). *Computer Architecture, Concepts and Evolution*, Addison-Wesley, Reading, MA.

Chaney, T. J. and Molnar, C. E. (1973). "Anomalous Behavior of Synchronizer and Arbiter Circuits," *IEEE Transactions on Computers*, **C-22**:4.

Chen, P. (1989) "An Evaluation of Redundant Arrays of Inexpensive Disks Using an Amdahl 5890," M. S. Thesis, Technical Report UCB/CSD 89/506, p. 341, Computer Science Division, University of California, Berkelay.

Del Corso, D., Kirmann, H., and Nicoud, J. D. (1986). *Microcomputer Buses and Links*, Academic, New York.

Denning, P. J. and Buzen, J. P. (1978). "The Operational Analysis of Queuing Network Models," *ACM Computing Surveys*, **10**:3.

Di Giacomo, J., ed. (1990). *Digital Bus Handbook*, McGraw-Hill, New York.

Kleeman, L. and Cantoni A. (1987). "Metastable Behavior in Digital Systems," *IEEE Design and Test*, **4**:6.

Randell, B., ed. (1973). *The Origins of Digital Computer: Selected Papers*, Springer-Verlag, New York, 1973.

Thurber, K. J., Jensen, E. D., Jack, L. A., Kenney, L. L., Patton, P. G., and Anderson, L. C. (1972). "A Systematic Approach to the Design of Digital Bussing Structures," *Fall Joint Computer Conference*, AFIPS Press, Montvale, NJ, pp. 719–736.

EXERCISES

7.1   Using the example above on WWW response time, will the result be significantly different if the estimate of 1 s for the service time is changed to 0.1 s? Work out the solution.

7.2   Write a program using the von Neumann ISA, Table 1.2, for maintaining a counter in a memory location to control a programmed I/O transfer.

7.3   Derive a model for the percentage of increase in the time in the queue that is a function of an increase in ρ from ρ_1 to ρ_2. Assume that μ does not change. Verify your solution with the example found with the airport departure runway example.

7.4   A computer's bus is 0.5 m long and the card holding the clock generator is placed in the center of the bus. What deskewing delay, in nanoseconds, is required on the clock feeding the logic on this center board? You must make an assumption as to the propagation delay down the bus for terminated lines.

7.5   For the example on terminals, in Subsection 7.6.2, recompute the server speedup needed for $t_t = 1$ rather than $t_t = 2$.

7.6   Consult the documentation for the Intel 8080 and list the complete set of codes for the three pins noted in Section 7.1.

7.7   Refer to Figure 7.13 in which deskewing delays are inserted in the clock lines. What is the magnitude of the delay for each card slot under the assumption that there can be five cards on the bus?

7.8   Why is distribution of a skew-free clock over a serial transmission path impractical? This issue is discussed in Section 7.4.

7.9   You are shown the plot of Figure 7.25. The distribution seems to be Poisson. From these data compute the value of λ.

7.10   Find the server speedup required in the last example on example in Subsection 7.6.2 if think time decreases to 1 s when the mean response time is decreased to 0.5 s.

7.11   The programmed I/O example assumed a processor with a 0.1-MIPS instruction processing rate. Rework this example with MIPS = 0.1, 1, 10, and 100. Plot your results of efficiency versus MIPS.

7.12   The example in Section 7.2 shows the system providing 12.35 transactions per second. Assume a requirement of 500 transactions per second. The processor will be unchanged but additional disks will be added. How many disks are required?

EIGHT

EXTENDED INSTRUCTION SET ARCHITECTURES

8.0 INTRODUCTION

User ISAs, discussed in Chapter 3, provide operations, addresses, and data types for many types of scientific and business applications. However, these instructions are insufficient for processors used in modern systems with operating systems, virtual memory, concurrent I/O, and in multiprocessor configurations. Thus ISAs are extended to provide support for these additional tasks. Each of these extensions to the ISA requires special data types, addresses, and operations.

The programs that provide these extended services are usually written by system software providers, not by the user. To prevent user modification or tampering with these programs, the processors operate in one of two modes: user mode or supervisor mode.

The extensions to the ISA are collectively called control instructions in the IBM S360 documentation (IBM 1970), protected mode instructions in the Intel Pentium (Intel Corporation 1993), and privileged instructions in the Pentium Pro documentation (Intel Corporation 1996). In this text we use the term privileged instructions.

Privileged instructions cannot be executed along with the user instructions when the processor is in user mode. However, when in the supervisor mode, both user and privileged instructions can be executed. If a privileged instruction is attempted when the processor is in the user mode, an interrupt is generated in the decode stage of the pipeline. The separation between the privileged instructions and the user instructions is enforced in many computers by means of a mode control switch. The instructions that switch from supervisor mode to user mode are privileged, but a user instruction can invoke privileged mode.

EXAMPLE

Give an example of transfer from user mode to supervisor mode and back to user mode.

Solution

With the IBM S360, S370, and S390, the supervisor call instruction (SVC) is a user instruction. This instruction causes an interrupt to the supervisor, and the supervisor loads a new program status word (PSW) from memory location 96 that has a control bit (bit 15) set to supervisor mode.[73] The user PSW is saved in memory location 32. After the supervisor call interrupt has been serviced, the privileged load PSW (LPSW) instruction restores the old PSW and restarts the interrupted program.

Comment

If the PR instruction is executed and the processor is not in the supervisor mode, an illegal op-code interrupt will be generated when the instruction is decoded.

The IBM S390 introduces semiprivileged instructions that can be executed in the user mode when certain authority requirements are met. Likewise, the Intel Pentium Pro has four levels of privilege. Level 0 is the operating system kernel, levels 1 and 2 are the operating system services (device drivers, etc.), and level 3 is the user or application level.

In this chapter, we discuss the privileged instructions, their operations, data types, and addresses. Two classes of extended user instructions are also discussed in Section 8.7: multiprocessor support and MMX enhancements to the Intel Pentium.

8.1 OPERATING SYSTEM KERNEL SUPPORT

A subset of privileged instructions, operating system kernel support, is discussed in this section. There are some operating system instructions that are similar to user instructions except that they use different registers. Processors may have a set of registers that are addressed only by the privileged instructions. Thus there are, in essence, other processors embedded in the user processor. However, there are common resources such as caches, ALUs, and implemented registers used by all instructions.

The processor state consists of the system data types that are collections of bits, fields of bits, and words allocated to registers that are used as semifixed indicators of some state of the process and processor. These registers hold indicator bits that define at any time the current operating mode and conditions of the processor. The processor state registers usually include the indicator bits, discussed in Chapter 3 in the context of branching. In addition to the state register data types, the memory addresses associated with these data types are described along with the operations that can be performed on the data types. The processor state registers for the IBM S370 and the Intel Pentium Pro are

IBM S370 (IBM 1976):
  PSW
  Control registers
Intel Pentium Pro (Intel 1996):
  Flag register
  Control registers
  Instruction pointer register

---

[73] IBM calls this bit *P* for problem state bit.

The PSW, flag register, and the instruction pointer register hold bits that may be changed dynamically during program execution. Control registers hold bits that are not normally modified during program execution. These bits establish the mode of operation and are swapped to/from memory because of a context switch or, with some processors, a subroutine call.

The data types described in this chapter have many bits and fields allocated to computer words. Students need not memorize these allocations, as detailed knowledge can always be obtained from the manufacturers' literature. However, students should understand why the data types exist and have a general understanding of the function and the purpose of the data types.

The operating system kernel data types exist to control the system, not produce results. Thus they never leave the system as outputs. The data types are transferred to dedicated registers in the processor, where they perform their intended function. These data types may be modified by privileged instructions during program execution or by side effects to user instructions.

IBM S360, S370, and S390

The IBM S360 family of computers was designed from the beginning to be controlled by an operating system. Thus a number of hardware and software concepts were introduced that facilitate the design and use of an operating system. We look at the data types, addresses, and operations that support the operating system kernel.

Data Types. Figure 8.1 shows the PSWs for the IBM S360 basic control (BC) mode and the S370 extended control (EC) Mode. The S370 extended the S360 with virtual memory requiring additions to the S360 PSW. Note that the program counter, called the instruction address, is found in the PSW as is the 2 bit conditing code (CC). Bits 0–7 set the control of the interrupts.

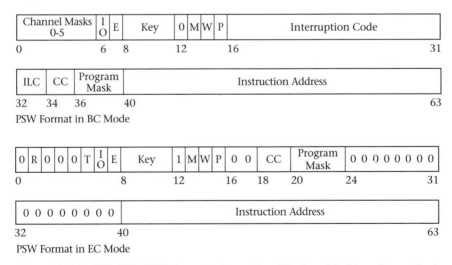

Figure 8.1 IBM S360, S370 PSWs (courtesy International Business Machines Corporation)

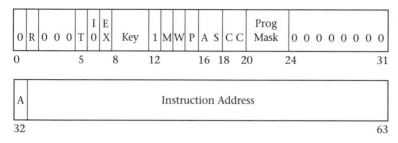

Figure 8.2 IBM S390 PSW (courtesy International Business Machines Corporation)

A 4-bit key provides protection for 2048-byte blocks in memory.[74] Each block in memory has an associated 7-bit key, called key in storage. For CPU writes, the 4-bit key in the PSW must match the corresponding 4-bit key in storage. CPU reads are permitted if the key matches or if bit 4 in the key in storage is zero. This key mechanism provides protection from unauthorized reads and writes. The key in the PSW is modified by a privileged instruction.

The 4-bit program mask augments the condition code for fixed-point overflow, decimal overflow, floating-point underflow, and floating-point significance when the result fraction of a floating-point operation is zero. An interrupt is generated when any of the mask bits are set to 1. The operating system kernel then determines the source of the interrupt by examination of the condition code, key, and/or the interrupt code.

The S390 PSW, EC mode, reallocates all the bits except the instruction address, key, and a few other bits, as shown in Figure 8.2. The major difference from the S370 is that the instruction address has been increased to 31 bits from 24. Reference should be made to an operations manual for a full description of the bits.

In addition to the PSW data type, the IBM S370 has a 16-word 32-bit control register (CR) file.[75] One or more bits in these registers is assigned to functions needing control or specification. Some of the bits are assigned to virtual-memory address translation and others to multiprocessing (for example, the time of day clock mask). Other bits control the recording of program events, such as successful branches. Finally, bits control how machine checks are handled: logout or not logout. Table 8.1 shows the general functions allocated to each of the CR words. Refer to any detailed architectural description of the IBM S370 to obtain the exact allocations.

Addresses. The contents of the PSW and the CRs are moved to/from memory by special instructions. Thus a source and a destination address are required. The PSW and CRs are addressed by implication in the instruction op-code, and memory is addressed by a computed effective address.

The S370 provides a region of real memory that is directly accessed – i.e., the addresses are not mapped by the virtual-memory system. This region of memory, 0–1FC, is used to store PSWs, CRs, and machine-check information. Space is also provided to

---

[74] A block may or may not be a virtual-memory page as the S370 can have 4096-byte pages.
[75] The S360 did not have CRs; they were added with the S370 and their use expanded with the S390.

TABLE 8.1 IBM S370 CR ALLOCATIONS

Word	Primary Use
0	Multiprocessing, dynamic address translation, timer
1	Dynamic address translation
2	Channel masks
3	Unassigned
4	Unassigned
5	Unassigned
6	Unassigned
7	Unassigned
8	Monitor
9	Program-event recording
10	Program-event recording
11	Program-event recording
12	Unassigned
13	Unassigned
14	Machine-check handling
15	Machine-check handling

---

store floating-point and general register values. The reason this region is direct mapped is to ensure that its contents are never paged out to the disk; the contents are always directly accessible by the processor.

Operations. Before the operations are described, it is instructive to examine the six instruction formats of the IBM S370 shown in Figure 8.3. The instructions can be 2, 4, or 6 bytes long. A wide variety of addressing options are provided. The formats associated with each of the instructions of interest are indicated in the text by their two-character format codes, such as RR for register to register.

The IBM S360 has 11 privileged instructions: 5 for the kernel (plus 1 nonprivileged instruction), 4 for I/O, and 2 for multiprocessing. The IBM S360 set of instructions is a smaller set than the 26 of the IBM S370 and the 55 privileged and semiprivileged instructions of the IBM S390. For instructional purposes, the simple S360 set is described.

Table 8.2 shows the instructions that are used to modify the status of the CPU by loading and storing the bits in the PSW. Note that the storage key can be loaded or stored but the system mask and the program mask can only be loaded into the PSW. The diagnose instruction invokes hardware diagnostics that are unique to the processor model.

Intel Pentium Pro

The Intel Pentium Pro evolved from the Intel 8008, which was not designed to be under the control of an operating system. Thus some of the features have the appearance of being added on to a simpler architecture. The operating system has four levels of privilege with processor state data types, addresses, and operations for the support of the operating system kernel.

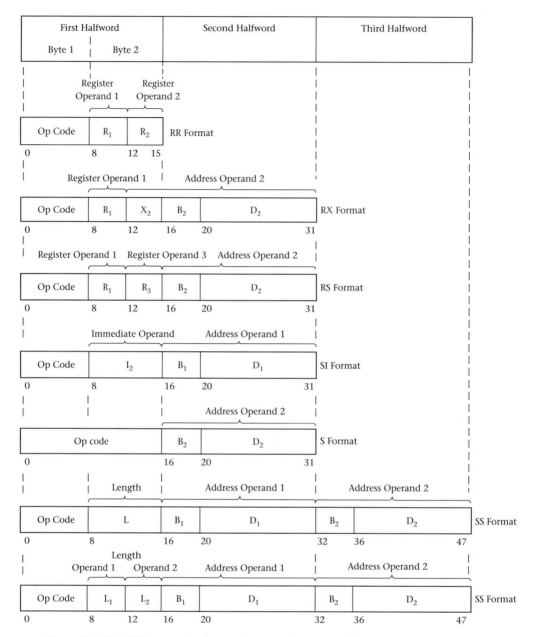

Figure 8.3 IBM S370 instruction formats (courtesy International Business Machines Corporation)

Data Types. The processor state data types of the Intel Pentium Pro consist of bits allocated to the instruction pointer (EIP) register, the flag register (EFLAG), also known as indicator bits, and four CRs.[76] These registers are in hardware and establish the

---

[76] The addition of the letter "E" to IP and FLAG register names occurred with the Intel 386 when these registers were extended to 32 bits from 16 bits of the Intel 286.

TABLE 8.2 IBM S360 STATUS MODIFICATION INSTRUCTIONS

Name	Mnemonic (Format)	Function
Insert storage key*	ISK (RR)	The storage key associated with the block in memory addressed by R_2 is placed in bits 24–28 of the register addressed by R_1.
Set storage key*	SSK (RR)	Bits 24–28 of the register addressed by R_1 are placed in the storage key associated with the block of memory addressed by R_2.
Load PSW *	LPSW (SI)	The current PSW is replaced with the double word $m(D_2 + (B_2))$. The current PSW is not retained.
Set system mask*	SSM (SI)	The addressed byte replaces the system mask of the current PSW.
Set program mask	SPM (RR)	Bits 2–7 of the register addressed by R_1 replace the condition code and program mask of the current PSW.
Diagnose*	None	The CPU performs builtin hardware diagnostic tests specific to the processor model.

* Privileged.

sequencing of instructions, the operating modes of the processor and assist in the translation of the virtual-memory address.

The EIP is a 32-bit data type that points to the first byte of an instruction. The EIP is incremented after each instruction is decoded; the size of the increment is equal to the number of bytes in the current instruction.

Figure 8.4 shows the bit allocation to the flag register. Note that bits 0–7 have been discussed in Chapter 3, Figure 3.12, in the context of indicators for branching. The details regarding the use of the flag bits can be found in an Intel Pentium Pro user's manual.

The four Pentium Pro CRs are shown in Figure 8.5. We note a few interesting aspects of these registers. The page directory base in CR3 was discussed in Chapter 4, Figure 4.6, in the context of extending the linear address to 52 bits. Also note that CR2 holds the page fault linear address that is used to reference memory for the page fault handler.

Addresses. The instruction pointer, flag register, and CRs are implemented in hardware and are loaded from and stored to memory by means of the general registers, shown in Figure 3.8. Two addresses are required, the source and the sink address. For both the flag register and the CRs, both the addresses are implicit in the instruction op-code. The instruction pointer is addressed by implication by means of the op-code when it is stored during a context switch.

Operations. The only ISA operation for the flag register and the CRs are special move instructions, shown in Table 8.3. Status flag bits are moved to/from memory by means of register AH, and CR data types are moved to/from memory by means of a general-purpose register, shown in Figure 3.8. The flag register can also be pushed

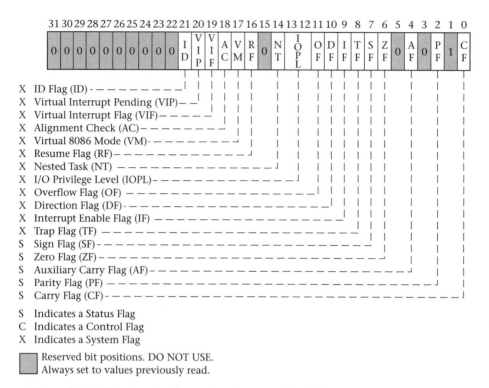

Figure 8.4 Intel Pentium Pro flag register (courtesy of Intel Corporation)

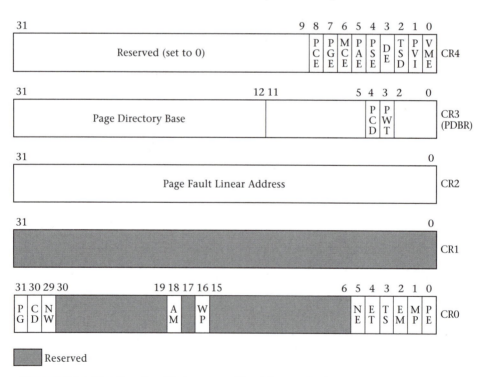

Figure 8.5 Intel Pentium Pro CRs (courtesy of Intel Corporation)

TABLE 8.3 FLAG REGISTER AND CR INSTRUCTIONS

Name	Mnemonic	Function
Load status flag into AH register	LAHF	The low bite of the EFAGS register is moved to the AH register.
Store AH into flags	SAHF	The SF, ZF, AF, PF, and CF flags are moved to the flag register. Bits 1, 3, and 5 are unchanged.
Push EFLAGS onto the procedure stack*	PUSHF	Pushes the contents of the flag register onto the procedure stack and decrements the stack pointer.
Pop the procedure stack into the flag register*	POPF	Pops the top of the procedure stack onto the flag register and increments the stack pointer.
Move to/from CRs*	MOV CRn	Moves 32-bit words between general-purpose register and one of the CRs. There are eight of these instructions.

* Privileged.

and popped to/from the procedure stack. Operations on the instruction pointer are described in the section on interrupt handling.

Note that some of the bits in the flag register are set/reset as side effects of the user instruction set. With the move instructions, the state of the flag register can be saved by move instructions executed for a context switch.

8.2 VIRTUAL-MEMORY SUPPORT

The primary task of the virtual-memory support ISA is the allocation, protection, and management of the segment tables and page tables that are used to translate virtual addresses to real-memory addresses. Chapter 4 described the overall operation of paged and segmented virtual-memory systems.

IBM S370

The primary difference between the IBM S370 and the IBM S360 was the addition of virtual memory. Because of tight hardware and software development schedules, virtual memory was not included in the S360.[77] The IBM literature refers to the virtual

---

[77] The S360 Model 67, a precursor to the S370, provided virtual memory.

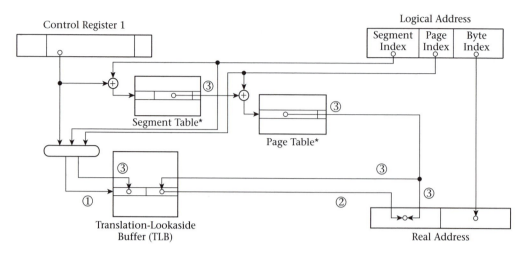

Figure 8.6 S370 Virtual-address translation (courtesy International Business Machines Corporation)

memory as dynamic address translation. The PSW in the EC mode has bit 5 (T), shown in Figure 8.1, that invokes dynamic address translation when set. If not set, all effective addresses are direct real-memory addresses. Figure 8.6, similar to Figure 4.35, shows the IBM S370 paged segmented address translation process.

Data Types. Four data types are required for address translation: the segment table address in CR 1, the page table address in the segment table, the page address in the page table, and the TLB entries, all shown in Figure 8.7. The CRs and the TLB are implemented in hardware whereas the segment table and the page table reside in real memory. Recall from Chapter 4 that the fields of the logical address vary in length depending on the size of the segment and the size of the page.

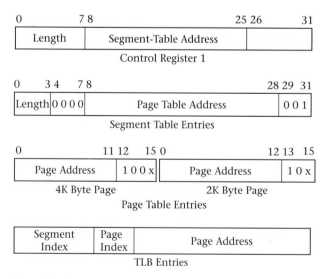

Figure 8.7 IBM S370 virtual-memory data types

In CR 1, there are two allocated fields, an 18-bit segment table address and an 8-bit segment length field; a segment can be as large as 2^8 pages. Six bits are unallocated. The index into the page table is formed by adding the segment table address, in CR 1, to the segment index, from the logical address.

The segment table entry contains the 21-bit page table address, which is added to the page index field from the logical address, producing an index into the page table. The 4-bit field holds the length of the page table in units of 1/16 of the maximum size of the table. The value is compared with the page index field of the logical address to ensure that a reference is not made to an out-of-bounds page table entry.

The IBM S370 supports two page sizes, 2K and 4K bytes, which are selected in CR 0 by bits 8 and 9. The page table data types are also shown in Figure 8.7. Each page table entry is 16 bits. Bit 12 or 13, depending on page size, is the present bit for the page. If the present bit is a 0, the translation proceeds. If the present bit is a 1, a page translation interrupt is generated. The page address is concatenated with the byte index field of the logical address to form the real-memory address.

The TLB data type entries consist of the tag – portions of the segment index and the page index – to establish the presence of the entry and the real-memory page address. The size and the organization of the TLB depend on the particular IBM S370 model.

Addresses. The virtual-memory support data types are allocated to spaces with addresses, as shown in Table 8.4. Note that untranslated real-memory addresses are used for the segment table and page table entries. The reason for this is to position these tables in memory so that page faults will not occur when they are accessed serving a page fault.

Operations. There are two privileged instructions for explicitly loading and storing CRs, as shown in Table 8.5. A nonprivileged move instruction (from the user instruction set) moves the segment table and the page table entries into their proper place in memory. The PTLB instruction purges or clears the TLB, and the SPX instruction achieves the same end as a side effect.

Intel Pentium Pro

The Pentium Pro uses a paged segmented virtual-memory system, described in Section 4.6. The virtual-address generation and address translation system for 4K-byte pages is shown in Figure 8.8. This figure is similar to Figure 4.36. Another virtual-address translation configuration is provided for 4M-byte pages; the selection between the two is made by bit 4 (PSE) in CR 4, shown in Figure 8.5.

TABLE 8.4 IBM S370 VIRTUAL-MEMORY SUPPORT DATA TYPES

Data Type	Allocation	Address
CR 1	Hardware register	Implied in op-code
Segment table entry	Real memory	Untranslated real-memory address
Page table entry	Real memory	Untranslated real-memory address
TLB	Hardware registers	Implied in instructions that handle page faults

TABLE 8.5 IBM S370 VIRTUAL-MEMORY SUPPORT INSTRUCTIONS

Name	Mnemonic (Format)	Function
Load control*	LCTI (RS)	The set of control registers beginning with (R_1) through (R_3) are loaded from $m(D_2 + (B_2))$.
Store control*	STCTL (RS)	The set of control registers beginning with (R_1) through (R_3) are stored in $m(D_2 + (B_2))$.
Move	MVC (SS)	The number of bytes L are moved from $m(D_1 + (B_1))$ to $m(D_2 + (B_2))$.
Purge TLB*	PTLB (S)	All information in the TLB is marked invalid.
Set prefix *	SPX (S)	SPX is used with multiprocessor configurations. The TLB is marked invalid as a side effect.

* Privileged.

Data Types. There are six data types for the paged segmented Pentium Pro virtual memory. These are the segment selectors in the segment registers, CR 3, the segment descriptor table entries, the page directory table entries, page table entries, and the TLB entries.

Figure 8.9 shows the segment selector data type. This data type is held in hardware registers, as described in Section 4.6, and contains the 14-bit index into the segment

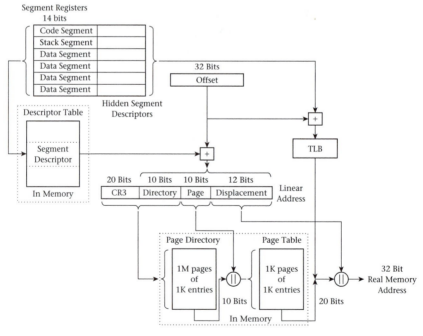

Figure 8.8 Pentium Pro segmented virtual-address system

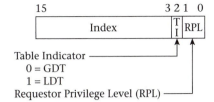

Figure 8.9 Segment selector (courtesy of Intel Corporation)

descriptor table. There are two segment descriptor tables, global and local, selected by bit 2. The two RPL bits select one of the four access privilege levels, discussed in Section 8.0.

Allocations to CRs are shown in Figure 8.5. The 20 MSBs of CR 3 extend the linear address to 52 bits. The PCD and PWT bits control caching of the page directory and page table entries in the processor's data cache.

Figure 8.10 shows the segment descriptor data type. The data type is allocated to 8 bytes, indicated by 4 and 0. The two major components of the segment descriptor are the base address of the page directory and the size limit of the segment. The 32-bit base address is formed by bits 16–31 of word 0, bits 0–7, and bits 24–31 of word 4. Likewise, the segment limit is formed from bits 0–15 of word 0 and bits 16–19 of word 4, giving a 20-bit segment limit.

Note the G-Granularity flag in the segment descriptor. If the G flag is 0, the segment size can vary between 1 byte and 1M bytes in 1-byte steps. If G is 1, the segment size can vary between 4K bytes and 4G bytes in 4K-byte (one-page) steps.

If the value of the 20 MSBs of the processor's 32-bit offset or effective address is greater than the value of the 20-bit segment limit field, an addressing error interrupt will be generated, which must be handled by the operating system.

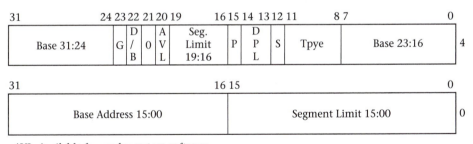

AVL–Available for use by system software
BASE–Segment base address
D/B–Default operation size (0 = 16-bit segment; 1 = 32-bit segment)
DPL–Descriptor privilege level
G–Granularity
LIMIT–Segment Limit
P–Segment present
S–Descriptor type (0 = system; 1 = application)
TYPE–Segment type

Figure 8.10 Pentium Pro segment descriptor data type (courtesy of Intel Corporation)

EXAMPLE

Show the calculation for the maximum segment size for the two cases of granularity.

Solution

The segment limit is 2^{20} of the granularity increments. Thus,

For $S = 0$ size (1-byte increment) $= 1 \times 2^{20} = 2^{20} = 1M$ byte,
For $S = 1$ size (4K-byte increment) $= 2^{12} \times 2^{20} = 2^{32} = 4G$ bytes.

Recall from Figure 8.8 that the linear address is formed by adding the 32-bit segment descriptor base address to the 32-bit offset. The 10 MSBs of the linear address are concatenated with 20 bits from CR 3 to form the index into the page directory, as also shown in Figure 4.6.

The page directory and the page table entries data types are shown in Figure 8.11. The page directory is indexed to find the page table base address. The page table base address is concatenated with 10 bits from the linear address to form the index into the page table.

Page-Directory Entry (4-KByte Page Table)

31		12 11	9 8	7	6	5	4	3	2	1	0
Page-Table Base Address		Avail	G PS	0	A	PCD	PWT	U/S	R/W	P	

Available for system programmer's use — — — — — — —
Global page (Ignored) — — — — — — — — — — — — — —
Page size (0 indicates 4 KBytes) — — — — — — — — — —
Reserved (set to 0) — — — — — — — — — — — — — — — —
Accessed —
Cache disabled — — — — — — — — — — — — — — — — —
Write-through — — — — — — — — — — — — — — — — — —
User/Supervisor — — — — — — — — — — — — — — — — —
Read/Write — — — — — — — — — — — — — — — — — — —
Present —

Page-Table Entry (4-KByte Page)

31		12 11	9 8	7	6	5	4	3	2	1	0
Page Base Address		AVAIL	G 0	D	A	PCD	PWT	U/S	R/W	P	

Available for system programmer's use — — — — — — —
Global page — — — — — — — — — — — — — — — — — —
Reserved (set to 0) — — — — — — — — — — — — — — —
Dirty —
Accessed — — — — — — — — — — — — — — — — — — —
Cache disabled — — — — — — — — — — — — — — — — —
Write-through — — — — — — — — — — — — — — — — — —
User/Supervisor — — — — — — — — — — — — — — — — —
Read/Write — — — — — — — — — — — — — — — — — — —
Present —

Figure 8.11 Pentium Pro page directory and page table entries (courtesy of Intel Corporation)

TABLE 8.6 PENTIUM PRO VIRTUAL-MEMORY SUPPORT DATA TYPES

Data Type	Allocation	Address
Segment selector	Hardware register	Implied by the memory access type: CS, SS, DS, ES, FS, and GS
CR 3	Hardware register	Automatically concatenated with the linear address. Implied in op-code or as a destination for a move
Segment descriptor	Real memory	Untranslated real memory
Page directory table	Real memory	Untranslated real memory
Page table entry	Real memory	Untranslated real memory
TLB	Hardware registers	Implied in instructions that handle page faults

---

The page directory entry and the page table entry are quite similar, providing a 20-page table base address and a 20-bit page base address. Note the P-Present bits. The P bit in the page-directory entry signifies that the entry in the page table is or is not present, whereas the P bit in the page table entry signifies whether or not the page itself is present in real memory.

The organization of the Pentium Pro TLB is shown in Figure 4.21. The data type is the pretranslated real-memory page base address; the same as found in the page table entry. A valid bit permits each entry to be invalidated by a privileged instruction.

Addresses. The six virtual-memory support data types are allocated to spaces with addresses, as shown in Table 8.6.

EXAMPLE

With the descriptor table, page directory, and page table allocated to real memory, what is the maximum percent of real-memory space that can be occupied by these tables? The total real-memory address space is 2^{32} bytes.

Solution

The descriptor table is indexed by a 14-bit pointer, and the segment descriptor is 4 bytes. Thus the maximum percent of real-memory space occupied is

$$\frac{100 \times 2^{14} \times 2^2}{2^{32}} = 0.0015\%.$$

The page directory is indexed by a 30-bit pointer, and the page directory entries are 4 bytes. Thus the maximum percent of real-memory space occupied is

$$\frac{100 \times 2^{30} \times 2^2}{2^{32}} = 100\%.$$

The page table is indexed by a 20-bit pointer, and the page table entries are 4 bytes. Thus the maximum percent of real-memory space occupied is

$$\frac{100 \times 2^{20} \times 2^2}{2^{32}} = \frac{100 \times 2^{22}}{2^{32}} = 0.09\%.$$

TABLE 8.7 INTEL PENTIUM PRO VIRTUAL-MEMORY SUPPORT INSTRUCTIONS

Name	Mnemonic	Function
Move to/from segment selector register	MOV	Moves 16-bit words between a segment register and memory
Invalidate TLB entry*	INVLPG	Invalidates the TLB entry specified by the source memory operand
Move to/from CR	MOV CR3	Invalidates all TLBs when there is a write to CR3
Return from procedure	RET	CS segment selector register is loaded as a side effect of the RET instruction.

* Privileged.

Operations. The instructions for managing the virtual-memory data types are shown in Table 8.7. Because the segment descriptor, page directory, and page table data types are stored in real memory, only nonprivileged user move instructions are required for loading and storing these data types. However, interrupts will be generated if the move instruction is used with various CR bits set and the processor is in protected mode or real-address mode. As the CR bits are set with a privileged instruction, the net effect is that these moves are indirectly privileged.

Five segment selectors, other than CS, are loaded with a MOV instruction. TLB entries are loaded only as side effects of page fault processing. However, the privileged instruction INVLPG is provided for invalidating TLB entries. The TLB is also invalidated as a side effect of some other instructions. The TLB is never stored in memory, even with a context switch.

8.3 INTERRUPT SUPPORT

The general principles of interrupts have been discussed in Chapter 3. In this section, the specifics of the instruction set extensions for the IBM S360 and the Intel Pentium Pro are described.

IBM S360

The issues of the source of interrupts and how interrupts are handled have been discussed previously. The IBM S360 – hardwired control, microprogrammed control, and pipelined – handles interrupts along the lines discussed. The IBM S370 and S390 interrupt processing is similar to that of the S360. In this section we discuss the way the PSW is treated when an interrupt occurs and when control returns to the interrupted program.

Recall, from Figure 8.1, that the instruction address is held in the PSW. The currently active PSW is shown in Figure 8.12 as Current PSW. Also shown are two sets of

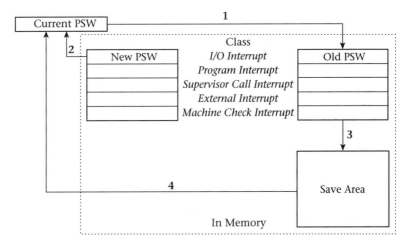

Figure 8.12 IBM S360 interrupt handling

five PSW memory locations, called Old PSW and New PSW. Each pair of PSWs is associated with the five classes of interrupts. An area in memory called Save Area is also shown.

When an interrupt occurs, its class is identified and the hardware moves the current PSW into the old PSW location, step 1, corresponding to the interrupt class. In addition, the hardware moves the corresponding new PSW, step 2, into the current PSW register. This PSW has been preconstructed by the operating system and will start the proper interrupt handler for the interrupt class. Step 3, also performed in hardware, moves the old PSW into the save area of memory, freeing up the old PSW location for another interrupt of the same class. When the interrupt handler completes its task it executes a LPSW instruction that returns the current PSW to its original state; step 2 or step 4.

Data Types. The IBM S360 interrupt data type is the PSW, shown in Figure 8.1. As noted above, the PSWs are different for the IBM S360, S370, and S390.

Addresses. The three areas shown in Figure 8.12 for the new PSW, the old PSW, and the save area are in real memory. Two addresses are needed: unmapped-memory address and an address implied in the op-code. Instructions that move PSWs as side effects also use unmapped-memory addresses.

Operations. The only explicit instruction for the support of interrupts is LPSW, which restores the state of the current PSW register, as shown in Table 8.8. Depending

TABLE 8.8 IBM S360 INTERRUPT SUPPORT INSTRUCTION

Name	Mnemonic (Format)	Function
Load PSW	LPSW (SI)	The current PSW is replaced with the double word $m(D_2 + (B_2))$. The current PSW is not retained

TABLE 8.9 INTEL PENTIUM PRO INTERRUPT DATA TYPES

Name	Description
EFLAGFS	Flag register, Figure 3.12
CS	Code segment selector*
EIP register	Instruction pointer holding the current program counter value
ESP register	Stack pointer, Figure 3.7

* The code segment registers hold the segment selectors that index into the descriptor table.

on the address, the load is either from the new PSW or save area in memory. Other nonprivileged instructions are used by the operating system to compose the various PSWs in memory.

Intel Pentium Pro

The Pentium uses a vectored interrupt. When an interrupt or exception occurs, processor state information is pushed onto a stack. The return from the interrupt pops the stack to restore the interrupted program.

Data Types. The data types, shown in Table 8.9, are associated with the processor state and are saved in response to an interrupt or exception and restored with the return.

Addresses. The registers holding these data types are addressed by implication when the interrupt or exception occurs, with the return from the interrupt or exception, or when the stack pointer is incremented or decremented as a side effect.

Operations. Some of the operations that load, store, or change the interrupt data types are listed in Table 8.10. This list is not complete; it serves only to illustrate the type of instructions provided.

TABLE 8.10 INTEL PENTIUM PRO INTERRUPT INSTRUCTIONS

Name	Mnemonic	Function
Call to interrupt procedure	INT	Calls an interrupt handler found with the destination effective address. Pushes EFAGS, CS, and EIP as side effects onto the stack
Return from procedure	RET	Pops the stack that contains the EFAGS, CS, and EIP as a side effect
Move ESP	MOV ESP	Loads the stack pointer from the effective address in real memory
Pop a value from the stack	POP	Pops the top of the stack into DS, ES, SS, FS, or GS register and increments the stack pointer

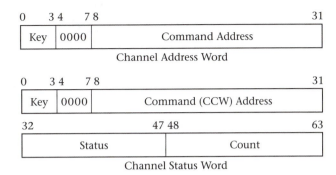

Figure 8.13 IBM S360 I/O data types

8.4 INPUT/OUTPUT SUPPORT

The general principles of I/O are described in Chapter 7. In this section the ISA support of I/O is described for two processors: the IBM S360 and the Intel Pentium Pro. The S360 is chosen because of its simplicity relative to the S370 and S390.

IBM S360

As described in Chapter 7, the IBM S360 I/O uses a coprocessor channel that executes its unique instruction set. The channels are programmable devices and can be described in typical ISA terms of data types, addresses, and operations (called channel command words). The study of the channel ISA is left to the student and is the subject of an exercise. The central processor initiates, stops, and monitors I/O activity with a small set of instructions having data types, addresses, and operations.

Data Types. Two data types are associated with I/O: the 32-bit channel address word (CAW) and the 64-bit channel status word (CSW) shown in Figure 8.13. The CAW is composed by the operating system and is stored in real memory starting at address 72. The command address in the CAW is the channel's starting program counter value. The 4-bit key is the memory protection key discussed previously in Section 8.1.

The CSW is maintained in real memory starting at address 64 and can be interrogated by the CPU to assess the status of the currently active channel. This double word contains the current channel command (CCW) address (the channel program counter value), various status bits, and a current count of I/O transfers. The 4-bit key is the memory protection key discussed previously in Section 8.1.

Addresses. The effective addresses of the I/O support instructions are the channel and the device addresses, not memory addresses. The 24-bit base plus displacement effective address is truncated to 16 bits: 8 bits address 256 channels and 8 bits address 256 devices per channel. The CAW and the CSW are addressed by implication.

Operations. There are four instructions for the IBM S360 I/O, as shown in Table 8.11. An I/O operation is initiated by the CPU by using the privileged instruction SIO. This instruction moves a program counter value from the CAW in real-memory location 72 into the program counter of the addressed channel, as shown in Figure 8.14. The channel starts executing its instructions stored in main memory. At any time, the CPU, using the privileged instruction TIO, loads status information from

TABLE 8.11   IBM S360 I/O INSTRUCTIONS

Name	Mnemonic (Format)	Function
Start I/O*	SIO(S)	Sends CAW at location 72 to the channel addressed by $(D_1 + (B_1))$ and starts the channel executing its program
Test I/O*	TIO(S)	Sets condition code in the CPU PSW for status of channel and device at address $(D_1 + (B_1))$
Test channel*	TCH(S)	Sets condition code in the CPU PSW for channel status at address $(D_1 + (B_1))$
Halt I/O*	HIO(S)	Terminates channel and device operation

* Privileged.

the channel and the device into the PSW. The TCH instruction places channel status information into the current PSW. The HIO instruction stops the current executing channel program and the device data transfer.

Intel Pentium Pro

The Pentium has two I/O facilities: I/O ports and memory-mapped I/O. The Pentium Pro I/O has evolved over many generations of processors, all the while maintaining compatibility with earlier processors and programs.

Data Types. There are no data types, as such, associated with I/O. The I/O operations transfer bits among the registers, memory locations, and the ports. These bits are allocated to the specific I/O operation required by the system.

Addresses. The I/O space is a separate address space of 64K 8-bit ports numbered 0 through FFFH. Two consecutive 8-bit ports can be used as a 16-bit port and two consecutive 16-bit ports can be used as a 32-bit port. The I/O address space is shown in Figure 7.5.

Operations. A set of instructions provides for I/O operations by means of ports. However, the ports are allocated to the processor's memory-address lines. The I/O

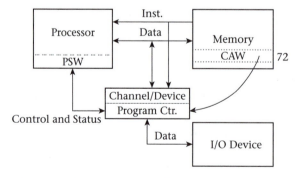

Figure 8.14 IBM S360 I/O operation

TABLE 8.12 INTEL PENTIUM PRO I/O INSTRUCTIONS

Name	Mnemonic	Function
Input from port	IN	Inputs byte, word, or double word to AL, AX, or EAX register
Output to port	OUT	Outputs byte, word, or double word from AL, AX, or EAX register
Input from port to string*	INS	Inputs byte, word, or double word to ES register
Output string to port*	OUTS	Outputs byte, word, or double word from ES

* These instructions can be preceded by the REP (repeat) instruction for moving strings.

instructions indicate that the address lines are I/O addresses, not memory addresses.[78] Data are transmitted to/from the I/O device by means of the memory data lines. The I/O instructions with partial descriptions are shown in Table 8.12. These instructions are not privileged. Memory-mapped I/O instructions have been discussed in Chapter 7. However, note that any user move instruction can be used to transfer data to/from a memory-mapped I/O location.

8.5 CACHE SUPPORT

The original idea behind caches was that a cache is transparent to the user – a cache simply reduced the memory latency. With some modern processors, this simple view no longer applies. Direct intervention by the program is often useful to provide additional capabilities and improve the performance over a transparent interface to the memory. However, the transparent cache philosophy still holds for the IBM S390. The IBM S390 Principles of Operation, p. 2-2, state the following: "The effects, except on performance, of the physical construction and use of distinct storage media are not observable by the program" (IBM 1997). Thus, the IBM S360 family cannot be used to illustrate cache support extended instruction. Instead, the PowerPC will be used along with the Intel Pentium Pro to illustrate these features.

The events that follow a cache miss are viewed as side effects to a load or store instruction. The designers of some modern processors have found that this view can be expanded and provide direct program intervention of the cache. Program intervention is found in two areas:

1. direct invocation of the side effects, that is, making the side effect the primary operation of an instruction
2. setting the policies of the cache in order to have more flexibility than that provided by a wired-in default policy

---

[78] Processors before the Pentium Pro used an output pin to signal a memory or an I/O transaction.

PowerPC

The PowerPC instruction and data cache support instructions are used as an example. Because of the functional difference between instruction and data caches, there are unique cache support instructions for both. For the details of these instructions, reference should be made to May et al. (1994).

Cache Side Effect Control. The PowerPC has six instructions that operate directly on the instruction or data caches. Two of these support instructions are provided for improving the performance of the memory system, as shown in Table 8.13. Four instructions support multiprocessor applications, discussed here rather than in Section 8.6, which discusses multiprocessor support. These instructions are used to enforce cache coherency in multiprocessor systems.

The data types are cache blocks and the addresses are translated real-memory addresses with their corresponding cache addresses.

TABLE 8.13 POWERPC CACHE SUPPORT INSTRUCTIONS

Name	Mnemonic	Function	Purpose
Data cache block touch	dcbt	Fetches a cache block associated with the virtual address ((RA) + (RB)) into the cache as would be done as a side effect for a miss on a dirty block	Prefetches a cache block before need. A subsequent load instruction using the address will have a cache hit.
Data cache block touch for store	dcbtst	Fetches a cache block associated with the virtual address ((RA) + (RB)) into the cache as would be done as a side effect for a miss on a dirty block	Prefetches a cache block before need. A subsequent store instruction using the address will have a cache hit. The block is in the cache; thus an allocate operation is not required for a store.
Data cache set to zero	dcbz	Sets all bytes in the block addressed ((RA) + (RB)) to zero.	Used to enforce cache coherency
Data cache block store	dcbst	Writes the block addressed by ((RA) + (RB)) to memory	Used to enforce cache coherency
Data cache block flush	dcbf	For the block addressed by ((RA) + (RB)); if unmodified, invalidate; if modified, copy to memory; if absent, invalidate other processors' caches	Used to enforce cache coherency
Instruction cache block invalidate	icbi	Invalidates the block addressed by ((RA) + (RB))	Used to enforce cache coherency
Instruction synchronization	isync	Waits until all previous instructions have been completed, then discards all prefetched instructions	Used to enforce context synchronization

---

TABLE 8.14 POWERPC CACHE POLICY CONTROL

Bit	Purpose
W	Write through. A write must update higher levels of the cache, real memory, or I/O. Otherwise, write back.
I	Caching inhibited. Otherwise, references are cached.
M*	Memory coherence. All memory must be coherent. Otherwise, noncoherent.

* Useful for multiprocessor applications, discussed briefly in Section 4.3.

The cache support instructions are not privileged as they are used in user programs for performance enhancement and to enforce cache coherency in multiprocessor systems. The first two instructions in the table have as their primary purpose loading the cache before need, thereby improving system performance.

Cache Policy Control. Recall from Chapter 4 that cache organizations and policies are described that conform to the expected addressing pattern. However, it is possible for the operating system to dynamically adjust some cache policy factors to favor the expected short-term addressing patterns and use.

The data type consists of the policy or mode bits that are stored in page table entry. The three policy or mode control bits, W, I, and M, are in the page table entry data type. The use of these three bits is shown in Table 8.14. The policies are applied at the page level; thus different pages can operate under different policies. The cache addresses are translated real-memory addresses.

Operations. Because the mode control bits are allocated to the 128-bit page table entry, the only instructions associated with cache mode control are the instructions that load and store page tables in real memory. As the PowerPC is a load/store architecture, page tables are moved in memory by sequences of load and store instructions.

Intel Pentium Pro

The Pentium Pro can be used in multiprocessor configurations, and program optimization is desirable. Thus this processor has instructions for direct control of its cache.

Cache Side Effect Control. The Pentium Pro has two instructions that operate directly on the L1 and L2 caches and indirectly on the L3 cache, shown in Table 8.15. These instructions are privileged.

The term invalidate is used to signify that the valid bits are changed to not valid. Some literature uses the term purge or flush to signify the same action. Flush is confusing, as this term is used in pipelined processors to signify that the work in progress is flushed from the pipeline and is completed.

Cache Policy Control. Figure 8.4 shows the Pentium Pro CRs. In CR0, bit 30 (CD, cache disable) and bit 29 (NW, not write through) set the cache policy, as shown in Table 8.16. Because the policy bits are in CR0, the policy is global in scope. This is unlike the PowerPC, in which the cache policy is set on a page basis.

TABLE 8.15 INTEL PENTIUM PRO CACHE SUPPORT INSTRUCTIONS

Name	Mnemonic	Function	Purpose
Invalidate internal caches	INVD	Invalidates the L1 and L2 caches and issues a special-function bus cycle to initiate external L3 cache invalidation. Data in the L1, L2, and L3 caches are not written back to real memory*	Permits the operating system to invalidate the cache when the system is rebooted or there is a context switch
Write back and invalidate cache	WBINVD	Writes back all modified L1 and L2 cache blocks to real memory and then invalidates the blocks. Issues a special function bus cycle to L3 caches to write back and invalidate	Permits the operating system to invalidate the cache when the system is rebooted or there is a context switch. The caches are written back to update all changes

* The L1 instruction and data caches are on the processor chip. The L2 unified cache is in the package and the L3 cache is outside the package; see Figure 4.10.

TABLE 8.16 INTEL PENTIUM PRO CACHE POLICY

CD	NW	Cache Policy
0	0	Write back
0	1	Write through
1	x	Cache disabled

Two bits in the control register control the caching policy for page tables. In CR3, bit 4 (PCD, page-level cache disable) and bit 3 (PWT, page-level writes transparent) set the policy. The policy set by these two bits is shown in Table 8.17.

8.6 MULTIPROCESSOR SUPPORT

Modern computers are a collection of cooperating autonomous processors that function asynchronously. A single processor with an autonomous coprocessor I/O channel is an example of a multiprocessor. Two or more programs executing on one processor require synchronization; however, the following discussion is in terms of two or more processors. Because these processors function asynchronously, synchronization between them is required for the programs to execute correctly. Synchronization may be required at two levels: (1) the circuit level when processors are provided with separate clocks, and (2) the program level to provide explicit synchronization by the programs.

TABLE 8.17 INTEL PENTIUM PRO PAGE TABLE CACHE POLICY

PCD	PWT	Cache Policy
0	x	Page table not cached
1	0	Page table cached, write through
1	1	Page table cached, write back

Circuit synchronization is discussed in Chapter 7. Thus this section discusses only program level synchronization. Two or more cooperating programs need to be synchronized so that variables will not be used by a processor if the variable is being modified by another processor. The most primitive means by which synchronization is established is by means of flags, called semaphores, which provide an interlock between the programs (Dijkstra 1968).

Semaphores work in the following way. Consider two processors accessing common memory by means of a bus, as shown in Figure 8.15. In the memory there is a datum that each processor will access and modify from time to time. It is imperative that if processor A has loaded the datum and is modifying it, processor B must not access the datum before processor A has written the modified datum back into memory – otherwise, processor B will obtain an incorrect value for the datum.

Two examples of applications that require synchronization are not selling the same airplane seat to two or more people if requested at the same time and not giving a busy signal to two callers who dial the same number at the same time. These are unlikely events, but must be guaranteed not to happen.

As shown in Figure 8.15, a semaphore S is allocated to each datum or to each block of data or program to be protected. If processor A can indicate to processor B, by means of the semaphore, that the datum is unavailable, the erroneous operation described above cannot happen.

The state for a binary single-bit semaphore can be defined as

$S = 1$, the datum is in use
$S = 0$, the datum is not in use.[79]

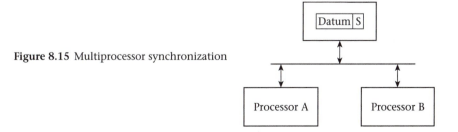

Figure 8.15 Multiprocessor synchronization

---

[79] Obviously, a system can be implemented that reverses this meaning of the semaphore.

A processor accesses the semaphore and determines if it can use the datum or if the datum is in use by another process. Reading the semaphore must be done in such a way that any other processor cannot attempt to access the semaphore while this is going on. In other words, there must be exclusive access to the semaphore in real memory. A basic design problem in achieving this end is that the instruction must be able to read–modify–write to the memory location holding the semaphore; two data memory cycles are required.

One way of ensuring exclusive access to the semaphore is by means of an atomic instruction. An atomic instruction is an instruction that performs an operation that cannot be interrupted or terminated by another processor and the semaphore cannot be accessed by another processor during the execution of the instruction.

Two distinctly different techniques are used to achieve atomic synchronization instructions with the IBM S360 and the Intel x86 architecture (before the Pentium Pro). These are discussed in the two subsequent subsections.

IBM S360

One type of synchronization instruction is test and set, first used on the IBM S360 and included in the ISA of the S370 and S390 (Falkoff et al. 1964). This instruction is not privileged, is atomic, and performs the following steps[80]:

1. As a side effect, it locks out the memory bus from other users.
2. It copies the state of S into the CC bits of the PSW.
3. It performs a write that sets S to 1. If S is already 1, its value remains 1. (Collectively, steps 1, 2, and 3 are the test and set instruction. After this instruction is executed, the lock on the memory bus is released.)
4. The processor then tests the condition code with a branch instruction to determine if access to the datum has been obtained. If $CC = 0$, access is obtained, go to step 5. If $CC = 1$, access is not obtained; the processor tries again by returning to step 1.
5. The processor uses the protected datum, which may include modifying the datum, and goes to Step 6.
6. It executes an atomic store instruction that clears S to 0, thereby releasing the datum to another user, then continues.

Data Types. There are two data types associated with synchronization. The first is the semaphore, which is a byte rather than a single bit. This approach wastes 7 bits but simplifies the design as this architecture addresses to the byte; all the bits of the byte are either 1 or 0.

The second data type is the 2-bit CC field of the PSW shown in Figures 8.1 and 8.2. These bits are set to 00 for a semaphore of 0 and 01 for a semaphore of 1.

---

[80] IBM does not use the word atomic. Instead they use the phrase "appears to be an interlocked-update reference as observed by other CPUs." An I/O channel is not considered to be a CPU and interlocks are not provided.

TABLE 8.18 IBM S360 PROCESSOR SYNCHRONIZATION INSTRUCTIONS

Name	Mnemonic (Format)	Function
Test and set	TS (SI)	The byte at address $(D_1 + (B_1))$ is copied into the condition code and 1 is written into all bits of the addressed byte
Move	MVI (SI)	Moves the immediate byte of all 0s in bits 8–15 into the byte at address $(D_1 + (B_1))$

Addresses. The effective address of the semaphore byte is base plus displacement. The other address for test and set, the CC, is implied in the op-code. The atomic store instruction uses an immediate operand of all zeros for the source. The destination address is the effective address of the semaphore byte.

Operations. Synchronization is provided by two atomic instructions, shown in Table 8.18. There are a number of complications in implementing the test and set instruction. For example, during a test and set instruction, the bus and memory are locked out from other users. As this instruction can take many clocks, the bus utilization can be adversely affected. An extreme case for the S370 and S390 would be that the first time the semaphore is accessed, it may be on the disk in virtual-address space, requiring a page fault, all the while locking out other processors from the memory system.

Other Multiprocessor Instructions. The IBM S360 provides a direct path for processors to communicate without using the system bus. Each processor has eight direct-in lines, eight direct-out lines, and eight direct-signal lines (bits 8–15 of the SI format instruction). Two instructions, shown in Table 8.19, use these lines for communication between other processors in the system.

There is a strobe signal with model-specific timing specifications that are not pertinent to the discussion of ISA.

TABLE 8.19 IBM S360 INTERPROCESSOR COMMUNICATION INSTRUCTIONS

Name	Mnemonic (Format)	Function
Read direct	RDD (SI)	Bits 8–15 of the instruction are placed on the signal-out lines. The byte on the direct-in lines is written into the byte at memory address $(D_1 + (B_1))$
Write direct	WRD (SI)	Bits 8–15 of the instruction are placed on the signal-out lines. The byte at memory address $(D_1 + (B_1))$ is placed on the direct-out lines

TABLE 8.20 INTEL PENTIUM SYNCHRONIZATION INSTRUCTION

Name	Mnemonic	Function
Lock		Turns the accompanying instruction into an atomic instruction
Bit test and set	BTS	Stores the addressed bit in the CF flag and sets the addressed bit to 1
Bit test and reset	BTR	Stores the addressed bit in CF flag and resets the addressed bit to 0

Intel Pentium

The Intel Pentium performs the test and set instruction similarly to the IBM S360, except that an explicit LOCK prefix is added to the test and set instruction to lock the bus and memory rather than the lock's being asserted by side effect.[81] The lock is good for the one instruction with the LOCK prefix, after which the lock is released. The synchronization instruction, bit test set (BTS) transfers the semaphore value into the CF flag of the processor and sets the semaphore to 1. A test is then made on the CF flag to determine whether or not a valid access was obtained.

Data Types. There are two data types: the single-bit binary semaphore and the CF flag in the flag register, shown in Figure 8.4.

Addresses. Recall that the x86 architecture can address to the bit. This is accomplished by applying a mask to an addressed byte. Thus, unlike with the IBM S370, a semaphore can be a single bit. The CF flag that stores the semaphore needs no explicit address as its address is implied in the op-code.

Operations. The first byte of the bit test and set instruction contains the LOCK prefix (see Figure 3.15). There are a number of variations of the bit test and set instruction; however, only the BTS and the BTR instructions are shown in Table 8.20.

The Pentium provides several variations of the synchronization instruction that permit the meaning of the value in the semaphore to be different from the discussion above. That is, $S = 1$ means not in use and $S = 0$ means in use. Also, the two instructions, BTS and BTR, can be used to establish and clear synchronization when preceded by the LOCK prefix.

8.7 OTHER USER ISA ENHANCEMENTS, MMX

Over the years, a number of enhancements have been made to ISAs to support specific user applications. Examples of these enhancements are found in vector supercomputers, digital signal processing (DSP) microcomputers, and LISP machines for symbolic processing.

With the explosive growth in multimedia processing, ISA enhancements for this application are also being made. An example is found in the Intel MMX enhancements

---

[81] Seventeen instructions in the ISA can use the LOCK prefix. The Pentium Pro provides for automatic locking and the LOCK prefix is not required.

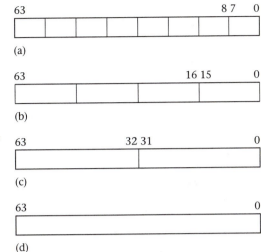

Figure 8.16 MMX data types (© 1996 IEEE)

to the Pentium Pro architecture (Intel 1997). The MMX enhancement is described with the same approach as used in the preceding subsections: data types, addresses, and operations.

Data Types. Intel designers noted that the main data types for multimedia algorithms are 8 bit pixels and 16-bit audio samples (Peleg and Weiser 1996). In addition, 32-bit and 64-bit integers are occasionally used. As the memory bus width of the Pentium is 64 bits, the memory-addressable unit is 64 bits and the other data types are allocated or packed into the AU. The MMX data types are shown in Figure 8.16. These data types are packed byte, packed word (16-bit words), packed double word, and quad word. Some of these data types are signed integers and others are ordinals.

Addresses. The designers needed to add MMX enhancements to the Pentium Pro ISA while maintaining upward compatibility with a minimum cost in additional chip area. Thus the basic memory architecture needed to be preserved. The MMX requirement led to a load/store register file architecture. In addition, with a need for a 64-bit data type, the integer registers of the Pentium Pro were inadequate. Thus the decision was made to use the eight 80-bit floating-point registers for MMX data. It was assumed that floating-point and MMX operations would not be needed at the same time.

For the type of processing envisioned for MMX, the floating-point registers presented the problem that they are organized as a push-down stack, discussed in Chapter 3, and MMX needed random access to operands. Thus the circuits of the floating-point registers were redesigned to give the registers dual-mode (random and stack) access capability. The 64-bit data types occupy the significand portion of the 80-bit internal IEEE format in the register file, as shown in Figure 8.17.

The exponent and the sign bits (bits 64–79) are set to all ones so that if, by error, a floating-point operation attempts to access the register file when occupied by MMX data, an interrupt error signal will be generated.

In addition to the register address, it is necessary to address memory for data loads and stores. These memory addresses are developed identically to all the other memory

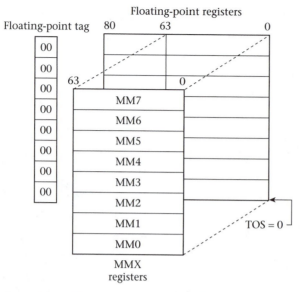

Figure 8.17 MMX register file (© 1996 IEEE)

addresses of the Pentium Pro ISA. That is, the effective address is mapped into a segmented paged virtual address. MMX data is cached in the data cache.

Operations. The MMX operations are added to the Pentium Pro ISA and consist of the basic arithmetic and logical operations applied to the packed data types. All control, such as branching, is handled normally with the Pentium Pro ISA. No indicator bits, or flags, were added. The Pentium Pro operational instructions have two addresses with the following options:

Ri ← Ri op Rj   (two-address register)
Ri ← Ri op M(EA)   (multiple accumulator)

The MMX modification provided a 64-bit ALU. The ALU can be partitioned, under the control of the instruction decoder, into two 32-bit ALUs, four 16-bit ALUs, or eight 8-bit ALUs. Because many of the multimedia data types are 8 and 16 bits, 8 or 4 integer operations can be performed by one instruction in one cycle. This subdivision of the ALU was pioneered with the ILLIAC-IV in the 1960s and was called single instruction multiple data (SIMD) by Flynn (Flynn 1966).

Note that for each of these data types, the total contents of the 64-bit AU is processed: 8 bytes, 4 words, 2 double words, or 1 quad word. As the processor is pipelined, when for example bytes are being added, the performance is 8 operations per clock while CPI = 1. The CPI measure has little relevance when measuring MMX operational performance.

EXAMPLE

If CPI is not a good measure of MMX performance, what could be?

Solution

In Chapter 2, the performance measure MFLOPS is used with supercomputers to measure the performance when executing floating-point operations. Let us suggest the following performance measure: millions of integer operations per second (MIOPS).

Comments

For a 300-MHz MMX processor executing 8-bit integer register-to-register operations, the peak MIOPS is

$$\text{MIOPS} = \frac{\text{clock frequency}}{10^6} \times \frac{64}{\text{number of operand bits}}$$

$$= \frac{300 \times 10^6}{10^6} \times \frac{64}{8} = 300 \times 8 = 2400.$$

Image and signal processing use an addition and subtraction mode called saturation arithmetic. This arithmetic provides that if the result of an addition or subtraction is greater or less than the expressible values, the domain function sets the result to the largest or the smallest representable value. The overflow or underflow indication is not saved in a flag. The MMX uses wraparound arithmetic when not using saturation arithmetic. Wraparound arithmetic truncates the result to the representable value. The examples below show addition and subtraction of the 8-bit ordinals 109 and 202.

	Addition	*Subtraction*
109	01101101	01101101
202	+11001010	−11001010
	100110111	110100011
Saturation Result	11111111	00000000
Wraparound Result	00110111	10100011

Table 8.21 shows the 47 MMX architected instructions. The MMX ISA has options for register-to-register operations and multiple accumulator operations. Note that with two exceptions, the instruction mnemonics start with the letter P for packed. Some of the data types are signed, others are ordinal (s,o); some of the arithmetic is wraparound while some is saturation (w,s).

To give a flavor of how the MMX instructions operate, three interesting instructions are now described. The first, as shown in Figure 8.18, is packed compare packed for greater than (PCMPGT) with 16-bit ordinal operands. With two 64-bit AUs in the register file, each of the words in one register is compared with the corresponding word in the other register. The words of one register are overwritten with ones if the word in the first register is greater than the word in the second register. Otherwise, the word is overwritten with zeros. The second operand can be in memory for a multiple accumulator operation. Variations of this instruction can be applied to bytes and doubles.

Figure 8.18 Packed compare instruction (© 1996 IEEE)

51	3	5	23
>	>	>	>
73	2	5	6

000 ... 0	111 ... 1	000 ... 0	111 ... 1

TABLE 8.21 MMX INSTRUCTIONS

Operation	Options	Data Type Length	Signed, Ordinal	Wraparound Saturation	Total Number
PADD, PSUB		b, w, dw	s,o	w	12
PADDS, PSUBS		b, w	s	s	2
PADDUS, PSUBUS		b, w	o	s	2
PCMPE, PCMPGT	= , >	b, w, dw	o	w	6
PMULH, PMULL	Result, either high or low	w	s	w	2
PMADDWD		w	s	w	1
PUNPCKH, PUNPCKL	High or low	b, w, dw	s	s	6
PACKSS, PACKUS		w	s,o	s	3
PAND, PANDN	AND, NOT	qw	o	w	2
PSLL, PSRL	Logical left, right shift	w, dw, qw	o	w	6
PSRA	Arithmetic right shift	w, dw	s	w	2
MOVD, MOVQ	Mem → Reg Reg → Reg Reg → Mem	d, q			2
EMMS	Clears stack	Reg. tags			1
				TOTAL	47

The packed multiply and add (PMADDWD) instruction performs the multiply and add operation so important to signal processing applications (see Figure 3.18, which shows a matrix multiplication program). This MMX instruction, shown in Figure 8.19, has as its source operands two packed 16-bit signed words. It multiplies the words together producing four 32-bit products held in a temporary implemented register. These are then added and packed into two 32-bit packed double words that replace one of the source operands. The second packed operand can be in memory for processing in a multiple accumulator architecture.

EXAMPLE

What is the peak MIOPS for the PMADDWD instruction? The latency of this instruction is three clocks but it is pipelined, and one new pair of results is produced each clock. Assume a 300-MHz clock.

Solution

The PMADDWD instruction executes four multiplies and two adds per clock or six operations. Thus,

$$\text{MIOPS} = \frac{300 \times 10^6}{10^6} \times 6 = 1800.$$

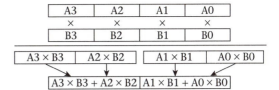

Figure 8.19 Packed multiply and add instruction (© 1996 IEEE)

The third instruction we consider is the unpack low packed data (PUNPCKLBW). This instruction can unpack bytes, words, and double words. Figure 8.20 shows the unpack bytes case. This instruction takes the four lower-order bytes of the right-hand word, stored in the register file, and interdigitates the bytes from the other source (which may be in a register or in memory). The result is stored in the first operand source register.

Packing and unpacking instructions are required for preparing data for processing in the SIMD style of the MMX instruction set architecture. These instructions are PACKSS, PACKUS, PUNPCKH, and PUNKPCKL.

8.7.1 OTHER INTEL ISA SUPPORT

The Pentium Pro provides special ISA support for software development. Each model of the Pentium family is provided with model-specific registers (MSRs) that store the support data types. This ISA support is useful for such tasks as debugging programs, system tuning, and monitoring cache miss rates.

Several dedicated registers are architected, namely, debug registers, a performance monitoring register, and a time stamp counter. Unique instructions are provided in the ISA for establishing the function of these registers and for loading and storing them. Details can be found in the Intel Pentium Pro User's Manual (Intel Corporation 1996). However, here we discuss the performance monitoring register.

The Pentium Pro has two 40-bit performance counters that can simultaneously monitor various events internal to the processor. The counters can tally the number of events or the duration of an event measured in clocks. Two 32-bit registers set up the particular function the performance counters are to monitor, and privileged instructions configure the bits in these registers.

An extensive list of 68 events can be monitored by these counters. A few of these are listed in Table 8.22. The complete list can be found in the Intel documentation. From this short list of the Pentium Pro performance monitoring capability, one can see that many of the parameters needed for performance modeling, discussed in Chapter 2, can be obtained with the processor hardware. These parameters in turn can be used to tune programs and to find improvements in the hardware implementation that may be beneficial for future models of the processor.

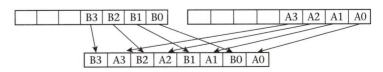

Figure 8.20 Unpack byte data (© 1996 IEEE)

TABLE 8.22 INTEL PENTIUM PRO PERFORMANCE MONITOR EVENTS

Unit Monitored	Event Description
Data cache	• All memory references
	• Weighted number of cycles while a data cache miss is outstanding
Instruction fetch unit	• Number of instruction fetches
	• Number of instruction TLB misses
	• Number of instruction fetch misses
L2 cache	• Number of L2 instruction fetches
	• Number of L2 data loads
	• Number of L2 data stores
Floating-point unit	• Number of computational floating-point operations retired
	• Number of computational floating-point operations executed

Note that these performance monitoring facilities are similar to those found with the IBM S370. Table 8.1 shows that words 9, 10, and 11 are allocated to recording program events.

REFERENCES

Dijkstra, E. W. (1968). "Co-Operating Sequential Processes," in *Programming Languages*, F. deGenuys, ed., Academic, New York.

Falkoff, J. W., Iverson, K. E., and Sussenguth, E. H. (1964). "A Formal Description of System /360," *IBM Systems Journal*, **3**:3.

Flynn, M. J. (1966). "Very High-Speed Computing Systems," *Proceedings of the IEEE*, **54**, pp. 1901–1990.

IBM (1970). "IBM S/360 Principles of Operation," order GA22-6821-8.

IBM (1976). "IBM System/370 Principles of Operation," order GA22-7000-5.

IBM (1997). "Enterprise System Architecture/390 Principles of Operation," order SA- 7201-04.

Intel Corporation (1993). "Pentium Processor User's Manual," Vol. 3, order 241-430-001.

Intel Corporation (1996). "Pentium Pro Family Developer's Manual," Vols. 1–3, order 000901-001.

Intel Corporation (1997). "Intel Architecture MMX[TM] Technology, Programmer's Reference Manual," order 243007-003.

May, C., Silha, E., Simpson, R., and Warren, H., eds. (1994). *The PowerPC Architecture*, Morgan Kaufmann, San Francisco, CA.

Peleg, A. and Weiser, U. (1996). "MMX Technology Extension to the Intel Architecture," *IEEE Micro*, **16**:4, pp. 42–50.

EXERCISES

8.1 Describe the IBM S360/370 channel ISA in terms of data types, addresses, and operations.

8.2 What instruction could be used with the IBM S360 to determine if the condition code permits access to a datum that is protected with a semaphore?

8.3   Consult the Intel Pentium Pro documentation on performance monitoring and determine how the miss rate of the instruction cache and the data cache can be determined.

8.4   The paper "PicoJava: A Direct Execution Engine for Java Bytecode" by McGhan and O'Connor, found in *Computer*, October 1998, describes a processor for executing Java programs. Write an essay describing the salient architecture and implementation features of this processor in 500 words or less.

8.5   Describe the meaning of the circled numbers 1, 2, and 3, of Figure 8.6.

8.6   Section 4.6 describes four segment/page configurations that are used with the IBM S370. For each of these configurations, list the number of bits that are added in the two adders and the bits concatenated in the real-address register of Figure 8.6. Recall that the S370 has a 24-bit effective or logical address.

8.7   What is the length of the virtual address of the Pentium Pro?

8.8   Figure 8.8 shows the Pentium Pro segmented virtual-address system for 4K-byte pages. The system can also support 1M-byte pages. Show how the linear address and tables are reconfigured for 1M-byte pages.

8.9   Explain why two adders are used for the S370 virtual-address translation, Figure 8.6, whereas only one adder is used for the Pentium Pro, Figure 8.8.

8.10 Consider the synchronization instructions discussed in Section 8.6. What happens when two or more requests to access the semaphore arrive on exactly the same clock?

8.11 Derive the model for MIOPS used in the example in Section 8.7.

8.12 What is done with the two 32-bit results computed in the multiply and add instruction shown in Figure 8.19? In other words, how can these results be used as inputs to subsequent instructions? Note that the source operands are 16 bits.

INDEX

TRADEMARKS

K5 is a trademark of Advanced Micro Devices

CDC6600 is a trademark of Control Data Corporation

LSI-11, PDP-11, and VAX are trademarks of Digital Equipment Corporation

8080, 8086, 286, Pentium, and MMX are trademarks of Intel Corporation

704, S360, S370, S390, and PowerPC are trademarks of International Business Machines

Zip is a trademark of Iomega Corporation

MS Dos, Windows95, and Windows98 are trademarks of Microsoft Corporation

MIPS R2000, and MIPS-T5 are trademarks of MIPS Computer Corporation

MC68000 and MC88110 are trademarks of Motorola, Inc.

NS 16000 is a trademark of National Semiconductor Corporation

SPARC is a trademark of Sun Microsystems

TI 9900 is a trademark of Texas Instruments Corporation

Z8000 is a trademark of Zilog Corporation

DATE DUE
